The Compassionate Rebel Revolution
Ordinary People
Changing the World

The Compassionate Rebel Revolution
Ordinary People
Changing the World

by Burt Berlowe and other contributing authors
Edited by Rebecca Janke, M.Ed

Mill City Press, Inc.

212 3ʳᵈ Avenue North, Suite 290

Minneapolis, MN 55401

612.455.2294

www.millcitypublishing.com

ISBN - 978-1-936400-08-9

LCCN - 2010914513

Cover Design & Typeset by Jenni Wheeler

Printed in the United States of America

Dedicated to the new generation of compassionate rebels.
You are the keepers of the revolution.

Table of Contents

Chapter Five: Community Builders

Chapter Six: The Care Givers

Chapter Seven: Speak Out Sisters

Chapter Eight: Generation Next: The Future Makers

Chapter Nine: The Reformers

Acknowledgements

They say that finishing a book is like having a baby, only the gestation period is a lot longer. Giving birth to this book was a five-year labor of love. There are many people who have contributed to bringing it into the world. I greatly appreciate and value the work of the extremely talented authors, photographers and editors who gave generously of their time and abilities. (See the book contributors page.) I am especially indebted to my colleague Rebecca Janke for her content editing, book fulfillment services, and constant encouragement and guidance; and to family members and friends for their technical, financial, editorial and emotional support. I also appreciate the professional assistance of Mill City Press in bringing this book to fruition.

I want to thank Friends for a Non-Violent World for making a preview launch of this book part of their recent foreign policy event, and all of the other social change organizations that have provided information used in this book and/or have helped or will help spread the word about it.

There would not have been a second compassionate rebel book without the cooperation of the people whose stories are featured on its pages. They have shown great courage in sharing the often intimate and controversial details of their lives. They are all to be commended, not just for baring their souls, but for the work they are doing to make positive change in the world. In some cases, their family members, friends, or co-workers assisted with editing their stories, finding photos, or other valuable tasks. I owe them all a debt of gratitude.

The compelling stories you are about to read are but a snapshot of a massive movement for social change. They reflect by example a much larger picture: the innumerable efforts of millions of ordinary citizens creating and spreading the compassionate rebel revolution around the planet, and, in the process, offering cause for hope in troubled times. To all of you out there, thank you for all you have done and continue to do to bring about the change we can believe in.

BOOK CONTRIBUTORS

Burt Berlowe is an award-winning author and journalist, radio show host, peace educator, and social change activist living in Minneapolis. He has published several books and articles on political and social issues, peace and justice, and grassroots activism. His books include: Nautilus award finalist *The Compassionate Rebel: Energized by Anger, Motivated by Love; The Homegrown Generation: Building Community in Central Minneapolis; Reflections in Loring Pond, A Minneapolis Neighborhood Celebrates Its First Century; Peaceful Parenting in a Violent World, The Peaceful Parenting Handbook, and The 7 Habits of Peaceful Parents.* He has been a reporter, editor and contributing writer for numerous local and national magazines and newspapers as well as the co-host of Spirit Road Radio on AM950 in Minnesota. He can be contacted at bberlowe@comcast.net or 612-722-1504.

Content editor **Rebecca Janke** is the Executive Director of Growing Communities for Peace, a non-profit organization that specializes in PreK-Adult peace education. In partnership with the Human Rights Resource Center at the University of Minnesota, she has helped develop the on-line Human Rights and Peace Book Store at www.humanrightsandpeacestore.org. She is the co-author of *Peacemakers A,B,Cs for Young Children:* a conflict resolution guide with the use of peace table, and *The Compassionate Rebel: Energized by Anger, Motivated by Love*; and the sole author of many peacemaking articles for the *Public School Montessorian*. She has served as president of the Minnesota Alliance of Peacemakers and is an active conflict resolution coach for families and couples. She can be reached at 651-214-8282 or peace@umn.edu.

Angela Andrist is an emerging writer in the Twin Cities working on her first novel.

Madeleine Baran is a freelance journalist specializing in work and poverty issues. She is former editor for *The New Standard* and *Clamor* magazine and has reported and written for Minnesota Public Radio, the *Twin Cities Daily Planet*, the *Utne Reader* and other publications.

Bill Wroblewski is a freelance writer, editor and videographer. A Midwesterner through and through, he currently lives and works in the San Francisco Bay Area.

Arletta Little, a Twin Cities writer, has recently served as interim managing director of the Givens Foundation for African-American literature.

Anne Ness is an emerging writer and book reviewer in the Twin Cities.

Heidi Rivers is a recent Twin Cities college graduate pursuing a writing career.

Jacque Blake is a freelance writer and former columnist for *Southside Pride* in Minneapolis, where she wrote about ordinary people making a difference in their communities.

Tony Simon worked for a Twin Cities publishing house and organized a Neighbors for Peace group in Minneapolis. He now lives at the Iron Knot Ranch in New Mexico where he serves Lama Shenpen.

Stacey Larsen Stafki has written for peace and justice periodicals. She recently completed graduate school at Western Washington University and now lives in Port Townsend, Washington. She runs her own business called SeedSpring and teaches in a local school.

Andrea Peterson is a freelance writer, photographer and communications specialist living in the Twin Cities.

Pat Cumbie is a Minnesota freelance writer and editor of a whole foods news-paper. Her writing has been published in many literary journals, and she was nominated for inclusion in the *Best New American Voices* anthology. She has recently published her first novel, *Where People Like Us Live*.

Jacqueline Mosio is a Minnesota writer who has lived and worked as a journalist, editor and translator in the United States and Mexico. Her work includes her latest book *Getting a Jump on Life* (with Aileen Frisch); editing *In the South Bronx of America*, photographs by Mel Rosenthal; and *Loves of the Fifth Sun and Other Stories* (fiction). Her writing and photographs have appeared in *Architecture Minnesota, Reader's Digest, Commonweal, Washington Journalism Review, The Chronicle of Higher Education, The Mexico City*

News, *La Jornada*, and *Proceso* magazine. She received her MFA in Creative Writing from Columbia University. She is currently working on the book *Marketing Hope: The Mercado Central's Impact on Immigrants and Urban Life*, which narrates the development of the Mercado Central on Lake Street in Minneapolis.

Michael Bayly, an Australian native now living in St. Paul, is a gay rights activist and freelance photographer specializing in peace and justice subjects. He is executive coordinator of the Catholic Pastoral Committee on Sexual Minorities and editor of *The Progressive Catholic Voice*. He authored the book *Creating Safe Environments for LGBT Students: A Catholic Schools Perspective*, published in 2007 by Haworth Press.

Chante Wolf, whose war veteran story is featured in this book, is a well-known peace and justice photographer in the Twin Cities and recently published a book of her photographs. She is an active member of Vets for Peace and has spoken widely about her military experiences and the treatment of combat soldiers.

Dawn Vogel is a Twin Cities photographer who specializes in illuminating people and bridging worlds.

Robert Cress works as a proofreader for the Periscope ad agency in Minneapolis.

Sid Korpi is a freelance proofreader in Minneapolis who has her own company called Proof Positive. She rescues Westies and other animals in need.

Sue Ann Martinson is a Twin Cities activist who formerly worked in publishing.

Christine Anderson is a freelance proofreader living in Lino Lakes, Minnesota.

"Perhaps then, if we listen attentively, we shall hear amid the uproar of empires and nations, a faint flutter of wings, a gentle stirring of life and hope. Some will say that hope lies in a nation; others in a person. I believe rather that it is awakened, revived, nourished by millions of solitary individuals whose deeds and works every day negate frontiers and the crudest implications of history. As a result, there shines forth fleetingly the ever-threatened truth that each and every person, on the foundation of his or her own sufferings and joys, builds for all."

Albert Camus, *The Artist and His Time*

FOREWORD
By Burt Berlowe

Change has come to America
Barack Obama

YES WE CAN! YES WE CAN!

The now-famous three-word mantra rolled rhetorically from the stage at Chicago's infamous Grant Park, reverberating through the night air, then echoing back from the multitudes gathered below. The lanky poet politician with the unusual name and brown skin that glistened and glowed in the significance of the moment had captured the attention of the world on this memorable day. As he spoke his cadence of hope and change, people cried and screamed and cheered not just for the riveting figure on the stage but for what he represented—a true coming of age for America.

Barack Obama's ascendance to the presidency on that historic November day realigned the political and cultural landscape in the United States and set the stage for a major transformation in the way we govern. It brought millions of new people—especially youth and minorities—to the polls and potentially into the government decision-making process.

As he so often said in his compelling speeches, Obama's election was about more than just himself. It was about a "movement," a grassroots uprising of ordinary people who rebelled against the status quo, who channeled their anger and frustration into positive change because they care so much about the future of the country and their fellow Americans.

Barack Obama was elected by the compassionate rebel revolution.

The compassionate rebel revolution is growing, not bit by bit, but by leaps and bounds. It is everywhere you look and anywhere you go. It is a mighty energy force that lives within all of us and surrounds us with hope in troubled times. It is moving like a bullet train across the land, picking up new, diverse passengers at stop after stop, building momentum and power as it carries democracy to the masses en route to a more peaceful and caring world. And, we might add, just in the nick of time.

Grant Park, the site of so much joy and unity on inauguration day 2008, was the focal point of a different kind of gathering forty years earlier. In 1968, it was the site of an antiwar demonstration during the nearby Democratic National Convention that led to violent confrontations between protesters and police in the park and the streets around it.

That was the year that America came apart at the seams. In the aftermath of the Summer of Love, hate and violence rocked the very foundations of our country. Assassinations claimed civil rights leader Martin Luther King Jr., then Senator Robert F. Kennedy, just a few years after his brother John had been gunned down in Dallas. Rioting and bloodshed, racism and oppression ran rampant in Deep South cities. The tumultuous demonstrations at the Democratic National Convention tore that political party and the nation as a whole into shreds and ultimately gave us Richard Nixon and a further escalation of the Vietnam War. It was like no other single year in our history.

While 1968 has its own place in history, it hardly existed in a vacuum. The rest of the century that followed was plagued by violence—a plethora of school shootings, an explosion of criminal gangs, drug-related crime, police brutality, domestic and foreign terrorism, and the first Gulf War. The 20th century as a whole was the most violent 100 years in American history.

The new century seems to be taking up where the 1900s left off. We are now nearly finished with the Decade of a Culture of Peace and Non-Violence established by the United Nations in 2000. But you wouldn't know it by looking at our world. Although there are many caring people on our planet today, we do not truly have a caring culture. There is far too much violence, hatred, intolerance and greed standing in the way. And even as America pushes democracy on other countries, our own democratic system is in danger of collapsing.

Forty years after 1968, we are once again bogged down in a seemingly endless war in a faraway land. Our traditional, top-heavy obsession with revenge, retribution and domination has once again led us down a dangerous, counterproductive path. The so-called "war on terror" has not brought us any closer to a world of peace and reconciliation. Nor has it taught us to better understand and tolerate each other's differences, to walk for awhile in someone else's shoes, to treat one another with more kindness and compassion.

But the lack of a caring culture is about more than waging war. It is seen in the continuing use and defense of genocide; torture and capital punishment; the prominence of guns in a so-called civil society; massacres in school yards, churches and places of work; the prevalence of domestic abuse; the rape and pillaging of Mother Earth; the lack of affordable health care and housing; the expanding gap between rich and poor; lingering racism and discrimination; encroachment on civil liberties and human rights; and the ruthlessness of empirical government and corporate greed and domination. As this is being written, we are in the midst of a severe economic recession that threatens the stability of American society. It often seems like our world has spun out of control into an unending, seemingly unstoppable cycle of violence and despair.

Yet we do not have to look far to find cause for hope. As the recent election demonstrated, there is a powerful people's movement stirring in the land that is bent on making change. It is newly born and reborn, a hybrid of sorts, an eclectic blend of sub-movements, individuals and causes spread far and wide with a common title that holds them together: the compassionate rebel revolution.

Compassionate rebels have always been with us. Jesus may have been the first compassionate rebel. There could have been others before him, and there have been many more since: well-known and little-known people who have turned their anger at injustice into compassionate action to make a positive difference in the world.

With all of its sound and fury, the 1960s were also the Age of Aquarius, marked by the rise of a counterculture that preached love, peace and understanding, and that brought us the civil rights, antiwar, women's rights and environmental movements, along with an emphasis on the value of public service and political and social activism. The great "peace and love" revolution promised by the hippie generation never fully materialized, but the '60s left us with a sense of hope that even amidst "shock and awe," a peaceful, caring world is possible.

The seeds of positive change planted during the 1960s have borne fruit. All around the world, people continue to work for peace and to do random acts of kindness and love every day. Often, they join with others to protest injustice or work for a just cause, changing society one act at a time.

Throughout history, these individuals and the causes and movements they have championed have been given many varied labels. But there had never been a phrase that would encompass them all.

That changed one day near the end of the 20th century. Rebecca Janke (founder of Growing Communities for Peace) and I had been planning to write a book of stories about peacemakers and were searching for a title. One day during a casual discussion, Rebecca and her business partner, Julie Penshorn, came up with the phrase "compassionate rebel." We decided to make that the title of the book and set out to find people whose stories would fit the definition: ordinary citizens who were combining compassion with rebellion to promote social change.

We subsequently interviewed fifty activists we knew or discovered who were willing to tell us their stories. We were prepared to use only those stories that fit. We ended up keeping all of them. We eventually came to believe that every person has a compassionate rebel story in them impatiently waiting to be told.

In November of 2002, Growing Communities for Peace published the book *The Compassionate Rebel: Energized by Anger, Motivated by Love*, which included those fifty never-before-told stories. In that book, we referred to a compassionate rebel revolution that was growing worldwide. As that movement grew and we realized how many more compassionate rebel stories were yet to be shared, we wrote this sequel *The Compassionate Rebel Revolution: Ordinary People Changing the World*.

We are not referring here only to the traditional meaning of the word "revolution"—overthrow of a government or social system. Rather, we imply a much broader and affirmative definition. We sometimes spell it rEvolution to indicate it is a process of transformation for individuals and the world, one where common people take varied and distinct actions that disturb the status quo in peaceful, creative and compassionate ways. While it emanates from anger and frustration, our revolution is not one of despair, but rather of hope for a better world.

* * *

"Compassionate rebel. Isn't that an oxymoron?"

I'll never forget the quizzical look on the faces of some people who posed that question after noticing the title of our first book. That kind of assumption always seemed to me to be steeped in traditionally negative views of the word "rebel" as associated with radical insurgency, violent revolution and aimless alienation from the accepted norms of society. It also presumes that people who push against the status quo can't have compassion.

Viewing rebels through that kind of narrow, refracted lens shows little appreciation of history. The fact is that without rebels, the world wouldn't be what it is today. Regardless of your religious beliefs, no one can doubt the impact of the rebellious Jesus on our current culture. Without the insurgents who fomented the American Revolution, we would all still be ruled by the British. In the arts, in science, in politics and social change, indeed in all walks of life, rebels have been pioneers, prophets and pacesetters.

The compassionate rebel revolution has placed the "rebel" concept in a new framework. For one thing, it expands the definition of rebellion. The people we have profiled in our two books rebel against the status quo, against an institution or policy or way of life, but also, in some cases, against their own past, by overcoming adversity and life's challenges en route to hope and social action.

The primary thing that compassionate rebels have in common is anger at injustice, a force that has propelled the large and small social change movements of our time. We all have experienced some injustice in our lives. We have all had times when we felt angry about something that was unfair in our personal experiences and/or in the world at large. The question is what do we do about those feelings? Anger is, above all else, a motivating force. It compels us to take action—yes, to rebel—against the injustice that is the source of our smoldering rage. Gandhi used to say that he didn't want to get rid of or suppress his anger. He would put it on the back burner and call it up when he needed it as a way to inspire him to action. Rather than just complaining or forgetting about the injustice confronting them, or reacting against it in violent, destructive or otherwise negative ways, compassionate rebels turn their anger at injustice into positive change

As powerful as this rebellion may be, it often isn't enough by itself to promote positive social change. But when combined with the giving force of compassion, it can become an amazingly effective tool for creating positive change.

The compassionate rebel revolution transcends race, age, faith, gender, geography, and political belief. It combines and propels the force and energy of millions of individual acts of caring and courage with existing sub-movements for peace, civil rights, environmental preservation, and other worthy causes into a bottom-up insurgency that is the largest and most diverse social change movement of our time. In the process, it transforms ordinary citizens from unrecognized bystanders into useful participants in society. Its goal is to spread the capacity to care and act as broadly as possible in order to bring about a culture where peace, compassion and generosity prevail over violence, hate and greed, where the power of love overcomes the love of power, and where ordinary citizens fashion true democracy for now and for future generations.

These architects of social change are everywhere. They live next door to you, down the block, in the community. They go about their daily business like everyone else—working at a regular job, attending school, raising a family, mowing their lawn and tending to their garden. But instead of merely complaining about or ignoring what they don't like, they are involved in making change in any number of creative ways—protesting a perceived injustice, laboring for the common good of humanity and sparking the fire in those around them. They are carving out new vistas, plowing new ground and redefining our cultural landscape. Everywhere you turn, ordinary people can be seen taking social problems into their own hands, wrestling with them, and molding them into life-changing solutions. They are remaking America from the ground up, as Barack Obama put it, "brick by brick, block by block, calloused hand by calloused hand."

In this second compassionate rebel anthology, we continue to tell stories of ordinary, compassionate change-makers. But unlike the first locally focused book, the everyday heroes you are about to meet come from all over the world. And their deeply personal and previously untold stories, written by a variety of authors, cover a broad range of relevant topics, including war and peace; civil and human rights; immigration; ecology and sustainability; education; community building; spirituality, health and wellness; the new youth movement; and electoral, corporate and media reform, among others.

These stories are placed in chapters that represent sub-movements that all fall under its umbrella in an historical context. In "Ground Zero Heroes" and "Peaceful Messengers" we focus on the new peace movement through stories of caring and courage during 9/11, and from Vietnam to Iraq, on the battlefield, and in the streets of communities here and abroad. "Freedom Riders/Freedom Fighters" highlights the latest version of the civil rights movement, spotlighting the struggles and triumphs of citizens of immigrant stock working to make America a better place to live.

The "Community Builders" chapter covers a variety of grassroots efforts from urban neighborhood organizing to rural co-operatives involved in wellness, sustainability and social change. In so doing, it gives examples of the ongoing neighborhood and co-op movements, and the burgeoning emphasis on preserving the health of our planet and those who inhabit it. The section of the book called "Care Givers," ranges far and wide: from a gallant mission in the wake of Katrina, and compassionate efforts to save families and children in Africa and Vietnam, to the compelling stories of people who have risen above personal setbacks to bring joy and healing to others.

"Speak Out Sisters" looks at the contemporary women's movement through the lens of several female activists struggling for personal empowerment while transforming our culture. "Generation Next" features compelling examples of a newly emerging youth movement that literally holds the future of the world in its hands.

One of the reasons why so many ordinary Americans feel hopeless and betrayed is the sense that our fundamental democracy is slipping away. The compassionate rebel revolution, in all of its previously-mentioned forms, is largely about taking back that democracy through reforming the systems that threaten it. In our closing chapter that begins with a ride on the democracy caravan, we focus on efforts to reform three of our most basic and vital forms of democracy: electoral politics, the media, and corporate capitalism. The election reform, media reform and corporate reform movements are rapidly growing as key elements of the compassionate rebel revolution.

The breadth and depth of the compassionate rebel revolution are much too big and deep to cover in any number of books. There are countless numbers of compassionate rebel stories waiting to be told; innumerable social change efforts happening too frequently and too fast to keep track of. The 100-plus stories in our two books are but a sampling of the scope of this ubiquitous movement.

There are other participants in the rEvolution that we have only touched on in this book due to space and time limitations. One is a rapidly emerging "new spirituality" movement that is seeking to appease the gnawing hunger that so many people have for inner peace and well-being. We also did not give adequate shrift to the exploding "green movement" that is taking on the threats of global warming and encouraging change in the American way of life. There are undoubtedly other compassionate rebel movements bubbling under the surface. We honor and support all of them, as well as the countless individual efforts to change the world that do not fall under a specific movement.

Despite its many highly visible and effective efforts, much of the compassionate rebel revolution remains "under the radar," essentially ignored or marginalized by mainstream media and the public at large. The sporadic news stories that do appear don't do justice to what is really happening on the streets and in the backyards and living rooms of grassroots America—from big acts of protest to everyday gestures of compassion and rebellion. The best way to bring this culture into the mainstream is through the telling of stories in books, on radio and TV, and in other venues—individual, personally compelling adventures like those in this book that tug at the emotions, intertwine with relevant political and social issues, and move people to action. Those are the stories of the compassionate rebel revolution.

Everywhere I go, I find people who feel that their voices are not being heard, that their opinions and feelings don't matter, that there is no use in bucking the system. We need to listen to these stories, promote them more widely and learn from them. It's been said that "whoever tells the stories defines the culture." If we want to change our culture, we have to change the stories that are defining it, and we have to provide venues for those stories to be told. Ultimately, the goal of telling these stories is to motivate readers to take action in their own lives that will address their concerns and positively change the world. That is the way a compassionate rebel revolution is built—one action, one story at a time.

In the closing lines of his election night speech, Barack Obama, referring to the famous words of Abraham Lincoln, talked about wanting "a government of the people, for the people and by the people." The coming months will determine whether those words turn out to be prophetic, whether the movement that put him in office will have an impact on the way he governs. That is the newest challenge of the compassionate rebel revolution.

And if we tell our stories with intensity and focus…we'll break the spells that bind us. We'll start to want that other world we say is possible with such intensity that nothing can stop us or deny us. All it takes is our willingness to act from vision, not from fear, to risk hoping, to dare to act for what we love.

Starhawk
From her book *Webs of Power: Notes from the Global Uprising*

Chapter One
Ground Zero Heroes

INTRODUCTION

No event in this young century has had the impact of the attack of September 11, 2001. It has led us to a seemingly endless war and subsequent erosions of civil and human rights, changed America's image abroad, united, then divided our country, and dramatically impacted our political, social and cultural landscape. It has also left lingering questions about what really happened on that fateful day, who is to blame, and whether we've been told the whole story.

The answers to those questions may not be far away. A grassroots movement of organizations dissatisfied with the government's version of 9/11 and intent on finding the truth, has been growing around the country, consisting of architects, attorneys, physicists, engineers, physicians, firefighters and educators, along with community activists and concerned citizens. They have produced a plethora of books, films, radio shows, websites and blogs that have raised public awareness and rallied people to action. (See resources section of this book.) The ultimate goal of this movement is to bring about a new, independent investigation into the events of September 11. Other organizations, formed by 9/11 families, have opposed our government's militant response to the attacks and continue to advocate for a more civil society.

Some magnificent examples of compassionate rebellion have emerged out of the smoldering rubble of Ground Zero. The heroes of 9/11 are many: from the first responders who saved lives at their own risk to the survivors and activists who have sought to turn the horror of that day into a quest for peace, truth and justice.

In this chapter we offer two profound stories of 9/11 valor and compassion. One is the dramatic tale of the courageous World Trade Center custodian who became a national hero, and whose explosive first-hand account raises questions about what really brought down the Twin Towers. The second story features one man's valiant effort to transform personal tragedy into a clarion call for a peaceful world.

Willie Rodriguez describes the explosions
he heard in the World Trade Center
(Photo courtesy of Willie Rodriguez)

THE LAST MAN OUT
By Burt Berlowe

William Rodriguez stops pacing the church sanctuary stage, moves away from the microphone and turns to directly face the overflow audience in front of him. His face tightens, squeezing away the engaging smile he had used to warm up the crowd. His voice gets suddenly louder, the words bursting forth like a discharge of dynamite.

"BAM! BAM!" he shouts, clapping his hands firmly twice to mimic the sensation he is describing "All of a sudden we hear an explosion so hard it pushed us upward," he exclaims, turning his palms toward the ceiling as he rocks forward on his toes. In that dramatic moment, William begins to tell the story of how he became a true American hero.

Early morning September 11, 2001, New York City. William Rodriguez is preparing to go to work as he has done for more than two decades, cleaning the stairwells, floors and gleaming offices in the north tower of the World Trade Center.

A native of Puerto Rico, William had once dreamed of becoming a famous magician/escape artist in the tradition of Houdini. For a while he worked with a magician during performances, using the stage name Roudy. He helped expose faith healers and psychics and was featured on Puerto Rico TV escaping from a chained straightjacket while hanging from a burning rope.

William immigrated to New York hoping to make it as a performer but he was a small fish in a big pond of magicians. In need of work, he took a job as a custodian at the World Trade Center in 1982. His show business aspirations ended when his responsibility for cleaning Governor Mario Cuomo's office expanded to include organizing the governor's press conferences. After Cuomo left office, William was reassigned to cleaning the staircases of the Trade Center's North Tower.

September 11, 2001 started like most other weekdays for William. He clocked in at 8 a.m. and went directly to the 106th floor to eat breakfast with Hispanic employees at the Windows on the World restaurant. He then began work in sub-basement levels (from B-1 to B-6) of the Tower.

"That was where they had all the building support companies," William explains. "Mine was ABM, American Building Maintenance. The stairwells were narrow, steep and without windows. There were ninety-seven passenger and six freight elevators in the building.

"At 8:46 a.m., I'm in the ABM office chatting with my supervisor when all of a sudden I hear

BAM! BAM!

"It came from the basement between the B2 and B3 level. I thought maybe a generator blew up. It was so loud that the floor beneath my feet vibrated and everything started shaking. The walls began cracking and the ceiling fell on us. The sprinkler system went on and everybody was screaming for help. I began to think it was a bomb. I was caught in an elevator in the 1993 World Trade Center bombing and had to break through a wall to get out so I know what a bomb sounded like.

BAM! BAM!

"A few minutes later, at about 8:54 a.m., I heard another explosion. The building creaked and oscillated and the walls broke. People thought it was an earthquake.

"Then I heard that a plane had hit the building. Two separate explosions at two different times. I turned around in the basement and couldn't see the top of the tower, only fire and smoke. I was worried about my friends in the Windows on the World restaurant.

"I found myself praying: please help me God!"
(Photo courtesy of Willie Rodriguez)

"Then out of an elevator stumbled a fellow worker, Felipe David. He had been standing in front of the freight elevator on sub level about 400 feet from our maintenance office when fire burst out of the elevator. A large fireball had shot down the elevator shaft and exploded through the doors near Felipe. He came running into our office yelling 'explosion, explosion.' When I looked at this guy, he had all his skin pulled off of his body from his armpit to his forehead and hanging from his fingertips like it was a glove. He had apparently put his hand up to cover his face. He got burned on a third of his body. He practically got vaporized."

William led Felipe out of the building and called the emergency medical unit. "I took him through the loading dock to an ambulance." Then, ignoring police orders to stay out, Willie returned to the building. "I heard a 'swooshing' sound coming from freight elevators on B2 and B3. Water from the fire sprinklers had gone into the elevator shaft. I heard people call for help. There were people encased in an elevator and in danger of drowning.

"Before that day I was agnostic. I didn't believe there was a God. But suddenly I found myself praying 'please help me God,'" Willie says, clasping his hands in a prayer position and looking upward. "There was a place near me where everything was supposed to have been cleaned away. But I found a metal pipe there that I could use to break open the elevator door. The people were stuck way up in the shaft and I needed a ladder to get up there. I prayed again. All the ladders were locked except one. I used it to extend into the shaft and was able to rescue the people.

"Everything happened so fast. Dust was flying everywhere and all of a sudden it got real hot. I threw myself on the floor and covered my face. It felt like I was burned.

"I looked skyward and cried out:
'God please help me, please give me strength.' I said that twice.

"I led some more people out of the building to an ambulance. Then I started screaming, 'I've got to go back, got to go back.' My supervisor demanded, 'Rodriguez, stay here.' 'Sir, I've got to go back and help those people,' I shouted. I ran into the building through the basement to the North Tower. There was water all over from when the sprinkler system had been activated."

William scurried from floor to floor opening doors and letting people out. There were only five master keys for the building. The port authority had four of them. William had the other one, which he used to unlock the doors and which he carries with him to this day. "This is the key of hope," he says, dangling it in front of him on the stage, "because it gave hope to a lot of people."

As William climbed the tower stairs firefighters wearily trudged with him. "They had seventy to 120 pounds of equipment on their backs plus the gear they were wearing. They bumped against people because the stairwells were not wide enough. As we went up we heard small explosions in different areas.

"BAM! BAM!

"I wondered 'what is that?' Maybe it's gas from the kitchen. But all the kitchens were electrical. Where was that coming from? I heard screams for help coming from the elevators. More people were drowning from the high water or trapped by the fire. They never had a chance. I heard that there was a man in a wheelchair on the 27th floor that needed help. I went down two floors to let the firefighters know. I had no equipment or fireproof jacket. I did that staircase every day. I was in good condition. The firefighters hadn't done that and they had all of that heavy equipment and had to get to the 27th floor. Some of them collapsed and couldn't get up. They dropped their bags to the floor. It was a shocking moment. I was afraid I would have to go up there alone.

"I called my mother from a phone in my office. She is in Puerto Rico. I let her know I was okay. She had heard about the attack. She said, 'What are you doing there? Get out now.' I lied to her and said I would. But I had to help my friends who were stuck in there. I couldn't abandon the building. My boss said to me, 'It's not your job. Get out of here.' But I continued going up by myself, letting people out along the way.

"When I got to the 33rd floor I heard loud scratching noises as if someone was moving heavy equipment and furniture around coming from the next floor up even though that floor was supposedly empty and elevators did not stop there. It was off limits due to a construction project. The new security chief had his office there. He said it was the first time he felt afraid. I continued to ascend to the 39th floor before being turned back by the firefighters who had made it that far.

"As we began our descent we heard a strong explosion. We made it to the chasm where a large metal framed front door had been blown out. The building began to collapse around us. On the main floor of the building bottoms of elevator doors were blown open with some powerful pressure from beneath. Windows, glass on the revolving doors and fluorescent lights were broken. Large ornate pieces of marble that covered walls were resting where they landed. It resembled a war zone. The smoke was so heavy it was hard to breathe and my leg was burned.

"I ran out of the building. I heard another 'BAM! BAM!' Someone yelled, 'Don't go back, the building is coming down.' I raced for the first cover I could find. I saw a parked fire truck and jumped underneath it just as the tower was collapsing."

For several minutes, William lay helpless and in pain as debris crumbled around him, his legs pinned against the bottom of the truck, his escape artist training of no use to him. "I couldn't feel my legs. I thought I had lost them. When they finally pulled me out of the black hole under the truck, I checked to make sure I still had my legs. Within a few minutes, the tires of the fire engine were blown out. I was fortunate to get out of there intact. It was a miracle." After receiving medical treatment for his injuries, William spent the rest of the day assisting in the rescue efforts and was back again at Ground Zero at dawn the next day.

William was the last person to exit the North Tower alive. Before he finally dived to safety, he had re-entered the burning structure three times, single-handedly rescuing fifteen people and evacuating hundreds more by opening doors with the master key.

Needless to say, 9/11 changed William's life forever. With no building to work in, he lost his job and his New Jersey apartment. He was homeless for a while, living in a car until a friend took him in.

At the same time, the obscure janitor and magician wannabe became a national hero. He was honored five times at the White House and by New York Mayor Rudolph Giuliani. The Republican Party wanted him to run for Congress and offered him millions of dollars in assistance. He turned it down, deciding instead to tell his story to the world and to raise questions about the strange explosions he had heard and felt that day.

During this time, a 9/11 truth movement was gradually taking hold in the U.S. It began when the victims' families pressed a reluctant Bush administration into holding hearings on the causes and impacts of the terrorist attacks. William joined the family members in pushing for an investigation, resulting in the establishment of the government-appointed 9/11 commission.

When the commission began its hearings, William offered to talk about his first-hand experiences. He wanted to find out what caused the explosions he felt that day. He was only allowed to testify behind closed doors in a private session and his questions were never addressed. His testimony is nowhere to be found in the commission's 576-page report. When the administration began to link 9/11 with the Iraq war he felt "manipulated and used."

William also contacted the FBI and the government-funded National Institute of Standards and Technology (NIST) four times to offer his testimony to help with their investigation. They never responded. The media also showed little interest in William's story. CNN spent a day interviewing him at his home but thoroughly edited the show when it went on the air to take out any areas that might cast doubt on the official government account. Some reporters warned him to keep quiet or his words could jeopardize his life, telling him, "You don't know who you are dealing with." "I tried to tell my story," he says, "but nobody wanted to listen."

Unable to get a fair hearing in the U.S., William went abroad with much different results. He did a speaking tour of Europe and Latin America. In Muslim countries, he was on the news every night. "The mindset about 9/11 changed after I visited. I met with the Venezuelan president of the national assembly who was concerned about my safety. There was an FBI agent around the hotel asking about guests. The president said they had to protect me. A documentary of my life was filmed at the palace so that they would have historical evidence if something happened. In Puerto Rico and other Latin American countries I told the story uncensored."

William returned home determined to tell America the truth about 9/11 and to use his experiences and skills to help others. His days as a magician had left him with the ability to perform in front of an audience. He had learned how to set up press conferences for Governor Cuomo. The WTC explosions lingered in his mind, leaving many unanswered questions: Were explosives planted in the building to make it easier to go down when the planes hit? How could a jetliner hit ninety floors above and burn a man's arms and face to a crisp in the basement below within seconds of impact? He had become convinced that the U.S. government was not leveling with its citizens about what really happened on that historic day. "I was a magician for thirty years. It is very easy to do misdirection, to make you look into one place while you're doing magic with the other hand. It's just a big magic trick. It's an illusion."

As William toured the U.S. the 9/11 truth movement expanded nationwide. A group called 9/11 Truth in Boston became the leading force. Academics, especially physics professors studying the collapse of the trade center towers, formed Scholars for 9/11 Truth. Citizens in communities around the country formed their own organizations and networks—all with one major purpose: to secure a new, independent investigation into the events of September 11th. "I am still searching for answers," William says. "I don't want tragedy used for political gain again. I am asking people not to be 'couch potato activists' who are concerned about a problem but don't do anything about it. We have to take action to make change."

With his powerful eyewitness story, commanding stage presence, and a passion for helping others, William Rodriguez has become a hero of the 9/11 truth movement. By blowing holes in the government version of that day, he has opened doors for others to walk through in finding the path to the truth. "It's been a mission of mine since I was pulled from the rubble to fight for victims' rights and immigrant rights, to seek the truth about 9/11 and to stand against the war in Iraq—to use the 9/11 tragedy to create a positive agenda here and abroad."

In addition to speaking engagements and media interviews, William has participated in antiwar marches and was the lead plaintiff in a RICO lawsuit against President Bush and others alleging conspiracy to commit murder and other crimes. That lawsuit was eventually dismissed but it raised the specter of possible government complicity to new levels.

As he did on that fateful September day, William is continuing to sacrifice his own needs to help others in distress. Much of the money he makes on his speaking tours goes to help 9/11 victims. He has refused the funds offered to him by the 9/11 victim's compensation fund. "I don't want to touch the September 11 money intended for others," he says. "That would seem exploitive."

William has been working at the grassroots level to help people who have been hit by all forms of disaster. He is director of the 9/11 United Services Group, a board member of the 9/11 Families Advisory Council and the lower Manhattan Development Corporation and founder of the Hispanic Victims Group. He has assisted Hispanic survivors and relatives of victims who have not been receiving adequate attention from support organizations and relief agencies because of cultural and linguistic gaps. He was a major force behind the campaign to encourage illegal immigrant survivors and relatives to come forward and talk about their fears of deportation, and in raising funds for scholarships for children of immigrant victims of the 9/11 attacks. He also has aided survivors of the Madrid bombings and worked with Spanish government officials on handling the aftermath of terrorist attacks on commuter trains.

"Besides coping with tragedy, if you're a survivor you have the difficult, frustrating job of trying to get help and answers from authorities," he says. "The September 11 families had to learn how to demand accountability from others. I am trying to take what I have learned to help others.

"Even today, every time I get on an elevator I have flashbacks to 9/11. I lost 200 friends that day. I still have survivor's guilt about that. There is a reason I survived my own tragedy, and I believe that reason is that God had this mission for me to help others who have been devastated by some misfortune." Perhaps the best description of William came from a father of a World Trade Center victim rescued by the Last Man Out: "He has saved so many people that I think the only word to properly describe him is 'angel.'"

Derrill Bodley and his daughter Deora on Fathers Day 2001 a few months before September 11 (Photo by a friend of the Bodley family)

A Song for Deora
By Burt Berlowe

Wars are poor chisels for carving out peaceful tomorrows.
—Martin Luther King Jr.

September 11th, 2001 had begun for Derrill Bodley like many other days before it, full of joy and satisfaction. He was looking forward to several more hours of doing his favorite thing: teaching music to young people, grooming the next generation of song makers, fulfilling his lifelong dream. As he drove to work in the California traffic, tunes he had taught his students that morning cruised through his mind, soothing the rush hour tension. Little did he know that the harmony he was feeling with the world was about to become the saddest and most dramatic song of his life.

Derrill could play the piano almost before he could talk. His parents were musicians: his mother a classical pianist and his father a choral conductor at the University of the Pacific near their California home. "I began playing when I was three, maybe before," he says. "My mother taught me initially, then my father taught me to play jazz, classical, just about anything. They gave me more than one record to listen to. I was an early Bartok lover. That was unusual for a small child. I had flute lessons in the fourth grade, played the saxophone in the high school band, the organ in church, and ended up at the Eastman School of Music."

Music has continued to dominate Derrill's life. He has toured with a rock band; written a variety of songs, including an infomercial used on television, and classical, jazz and pop numbers; and worked as a professor of music at University of the Pacific. One of his proudest compositions was the score for a theater production called *Compu*kids, about a group of youngsters trapped inside a computer who find a way to solve the world's problems.

The theme of *Compu*kids may have been no accident. As early as his high school years Derrill had begun to show social change tendencies. He recalls watching peace rallies on campus in the early 1960s from the sidelines and beginning to think about world issues, but being unable to fully participate. "I was sheltered in a conservatory of music," he recalls. "I became aware of what one could do to make peace. But I wasn't an activist. Musicians go through this training that makes them self-absorbed. They spend lots of time in practice rooms by themselves."

In graduate school, during the Vietnam War, Derrill enlisted in the service rather than be drafted and became a musician in a military band. "My own self-preservation led me to enlist. It guaranteed that I would not go to Vietnam." Although he never got into combat, he had friends who did and heard their stories. "It was pretty sad. Inexperienced commissioned officers from the military academy system were potentially targets of their own men. One guy threw grenades into his fellow soldiers' tent. I began to develop a position about the war. But there wasn't anything I could do about it."

After the war, Derrill went on tour as a piano player with a top forty cover band called the Executives, playing in clubs, bars and other venues throughout the Upper Midwest, and ended up making a living at it for some twenty years until he took a job as a computer software engineer in San Diego. He returned to music as a teacher in the late 1980s.

Deora came into Derrill's life in 1981, the only daughter he and his wife would have. They divorced soon after her birth but continued to share visiting rights. He later remarried and his second wife Nancy had a daughter of her own named Eva. "From the time Deora was a toddler she was living with her birth mom but would come over all the time to visit me," Derrill says. "I was an important part of her life. She liked to listen to me play music and to try to play herself. She was a normal kid who liked to read. Even when she finally went off to school at Santa Clara University to study psychology, she would visit me often in Stockton (California) some 400 miles away, and I went down there a lot. We were very close."

* * *

Derrill was teaching music on September 11th, 2001 when the news came that would so profoundly change his life. "My students started coming into class with wild stories about planes hitting the World Trade Center. At first they said it was eight planes. It started getting pretty crazy. I told them, 'We're not doing ourselves any favors by just saying this stuff; let's go find out for ourselves what's really happening.' I went to my office. Then Nancy and my brother called to tell me that Deora was almost certainly on the third plane. Nancy met me at school and we drove home together listening to the radio for news updates, waiting for some word that would confirm or end our worst fears. The confirmation came quickly.

"I was about five minutes from my house when I got a cell phone call from my ex-wife. She was hysterical, sobbing on the phone. I knew right away that Deora was on that plane.

"I began experiencing a different kind of terror from what many of the people in New York had to go through. At least, I knew right then there was no hope for survivors. There were hundreds of people who didn't know for days. I can't imagine that terror."

Derrill had steeled himself against the pain that he feared might come. "I had prepared for 'What if it's true, what am I going to do?'—for the desperate, angry, chaotic questions, 'Why did this happen? Why me? Why would anybody do this?' But anger at the terrorists never crossed my mind. I couldn't go anywhere with that. There was nothing I could do about what had already happened. I had to figure out what I could do something about."

Within hours of the Flight 93 tragedy, the stories began to come in about the probable heroism of the crew that may have prevented the flight from a possible collision with the Capitol or the White House. When the Flight 93 families were honored at a White House reception, the president's chief of staff told them, "We want to thank you for the heroism that undoubtedly saved our lives."

"The families of Flight 93 have a common belief that everyone aboard was involved in heroism," Derrill says. "We know, for example, that there was a highly spiritual man and wife who were not in a position to run down the aisle but were in a perfect position to pray, and they did. I believe those passengers were destined to be there, that they were there for a reason. I'm not an organized-religion person but I believe there is a spiritual meaning to how things happen."

Derrill has no doubt that his daughter was one of the heroes. "She was very athletic. There was lots of running and screaming on board. We believe the passengers were in control and that they defeated one of the terrorists that were guarding them, that they either disrupted the flight or took it over themselves. I believe Deora was a part of that."

Two days after 9/11, Derrill wrote a song for Deora. He had written hundreds of songs. Usually, they came gradually over days or weeks spent at the piano, laboriously matching note to note to create a finished melody. But on this particular day something different, almost magical, happened. A tune burst through him like lightning and landed on the page in seemingly an instant carrying with it something unique and special.

"It's like it came through me, not from me," he says. "I don't normally write like that. All of the notes were there the first time I played it. It was a very powerful, spiritual experience." This song actually was one of two he would use to honor his daughter. He had written a song in the 1970s after hearing the Beatles' "Imagine" and later found it to be appropriate in the aftermath of September 11. It is called "Each to Give." One verse goes like this:

The world's made up of those who do
And those to whom it's done
But peace would come to every soul
When both of these are as one.

* * *

On a frigid Valentine's Day 2002, a small group of families of 9/11 victims gathered in New York City to launch hope out of the rubble of Ground Zero. They met some distance from the tragically historic site at the UN Church Center across from the United Nations office. One by one, they spoke to a spattering of press and public with a unified message: "We believe that peaceful tomorrows begin with what we do today."

The press conference formalized the formation of September 11 Families for Peaceful Tomorrows. But the work of the new organization had already begun. There had been visits to congressional offices, fundraising at churches, and long, healing marches. And even as the U.S. was busy fighting the Taliban in Afghanistan, the families were working on ways to help the residents of that country. All of this was a far cry from the days of silent rage and prayer vigils the families had endured in previous months. Now, at last, they were ready to turn their hurt and anger into positive action.

This evolutionary process actually began a few days after the 9/11 terrorist attacks. Several affected family members became increasingly concerned about the possibility that the U.S. would respond in-kind to the terrorists' violence. While Americans in government and elsewhere were calling for revenge against Al Qaeda, the families refused to join the chorus.

For Derrill, it was a time for his thoughts on September 11 to reach fruition. "We all had the common thought that we did want Bin Laden and the other terrorists brought to justice and knew that there was a mechanism for doing that," he says. "But justice is separate from war. Justice and war are incompatible."

The day after 9/11, Derrill vowed that no more violence should be committed in his daughter's name. He borrowed the title of another like-minded organization that became the mantra for the families: Not in Our Name. "We are for a more peaceful culture," Derrill explains. "We are opposed to any method of settling conflict that includes war without end in order to preserve the peace. That makes no sense at all. We are seeking nonviolent alternatives to war."

Immediately after the press conference, Derrill and his core group began the agonizing process of networking with other September 11th families. "Some were disconnected," he says. "Some were reluctant to speak out about how they felt. It was very painful for them." Nevertheless, the organization has built its membership from fifteen founders to more than a hundred families and joined with some similar groups under the umbrella of a Family Steering Committee. They also have established collaborations with large international organizations like United for Peace and Justice, Global Exchange and International ANSWER.

Derrill also belonged to a separate ad hoc group called Families of Flight 93, whose main mission is to explore the circumstances and recorded history of the flight's hijacking and to support the families involved.

Since its formation, September 11 Families has been at the forefront of the antiwar movement. In addition to speaking at peace rallies, Derrill and others have made media appearances and appealed directly to government decision-makers in the White House and Congress. Derrill, for example, made a face-to-face entreaty to George W. Bush to use a nonviolent response to the terrorist attacks. The families have also appeared at international conferences on atom and hydrogen bomb manufacturing and testing held annually in Japan, Brazil, India, Italy and Spain.

Most significantly, the Family Steering Committee, including Peaceful Tomorrows, deserves much of the credit for the formation of the independent commission that investigated the events surrounding 9/11. It was the pressure from those families that finally convinced President Bush to establish the commission and to grudgingly agree to testify before it. September 11 Families also gave testimony before the commission, provided it with suggested questions and monitored its progress, sometimes from front row seats at the hearings.

"The pressure (to form the commission) came mainly through letter writing," Derrill recalls. "We asked for a meeting with Bush and (Secretary of State Condoleeza) Rice but never got it. We did meet with some congressional leaders and developed campaigns with other organizations like MoveOn.Org that have similar interest and overlapping activity."

Derrill has been to Afghanistan at least twice since the American invasion, accompanied by other Family members. Their mission is to help the war-torn families in that country rebuild their lives from the bottom up. Derrill was discouraged by what he found in Afghanistan, noting that the U.S. policy "has done very little to help the populace," and has resulted in war profiteering by outside corporations, while warlords run the country. He is continuing to speak out on this issue and to find funding to help the Afghan citizens. He is planning possible similar trips to Iraq and Saudi Arabia as a way to better understand and communicate with the Muslim world, "to find out why they hate us."

After the U.S. started bombing Afghanistan, Derrill saw it as "once again bringing terror from the skies" and prayed that there would be no more innocent victims like his daughter. "Bombing Afghanistan was only going to cause more problems. I went to Afghanistan to find out what was really going on there.

"In Afghanistan, we saw families that had been bombed. Each family had at least one casualty. In one case, two children who were being taken care of by neighbors stepped outside to get something. The other seven in the family were in the house when the bombs dropped. The two children were the only family members left. This happened to thousands of people in Afghanistan. It was totally shocking. The infrastructure of the country had been completely demolished by all the wars going on there for twenty-five years. Witnessing all of that was a life-transforming experience for me. When I went back a second time, I saw the same family as previously. There was only one of them left and she had no one to support her or give her money. Thousands are in the same situation."

The work of the September 11 Families has inspired other similar organizations to crop up. The most recent and most vocal have been the surviving relatives of Iraq war casualties. Several of them formed a group called Military Families Speak Out that has been using a "not in our name" strategy for Iraq, pressing for an end to U.S. involvement and for the troops to be brought home.

In every case, the decision to become involved in the public domain has been a difficult one for these families. It means continually conjuring up memories that are almost too painful to bear. For example, after months of delay and procrastination, 95 percent of eligible relatives of 9/11 victims finally applied to join the government's ambitious but much-criticized financial compensation effort. "You have to understand how hard it is for the families to go through that process," Derrill says "It brings back a lot of painful memories."

At the same time, the unwillingness to forget has been a catalyst for action. The families have published their stories in a book and recorded them on a video. And they continue to take their message to audiences everywhere. Two days after September 11th, the same day he wrote his song for Deora, Derrill voiced his feelings publicly for the first time. Speaking to a crowd of 18,000 students at the University of the Pacific, he reached for a high note: "This is not about lashing out," he cried. "This is not about vengeance. This is not about retaliation. This is about justice."

In late 2005, the Bodley family was again hit by tragedy losing Derrill in a motorcycle accident near their California home. Rather than give in to despair, the Bodleys have continued to be active in Peaceful Tomorrows' ongoing efforts for peace and justice.

On September 11, 2006, the five-year anniversary of 9/11, Peaceful Tomorrows held a groundbreaking international conference called Civilian Casualties, Civilian Solutions. The seeds planted at that conference grew into The International Network for Peace, a coalition of organizations from seventeen different countries formed by survivors of political violence to promote justice, reconciliation and genuine peace.

Peaceful Tomorrows is currently involved in a lobbying campaign opposing a military escalation in Afghanistan, is working in solidarity with a network of Iraqi activists to build a nonviolence movement in that country, and personally delivered a letter to President Obama urging the closing of Guantanamo Bay and the abolishment of torture from U.S. counter-terrorism policies.

Chapter Two
Peace Messengers

INTRODUCTION

The messengers of war are everywhere in time and space. They shout at us through the ages and miles from battlefields near and far, from political platforms and via media madness. They blast our senses with the constant noise of greed, domination and violence. And, too often, we accept their delivery, no questions asked.

The best evidence of how far we have to go to create a caring culture can be found in the universal obsession with war. Ever since mankind learned how to use clubs and bows and arrows, people everywhere have been constantly fighting with each other over one thing or another. America's first war led to the birth of our nation. It also established a precedent of using armed aggression as a means to an end. As we noted earlier, the 20th century was the most bloody, war-torn time in American history and its infant successor isn't faring much better.

We have, in fact, become addicted to war. It has become so ingrained in our culture that we cannot imagine living without it. In his insightful book *War Is a Force That Gives Us Meaning,* author Chris Hedges says: "The enduring attraction of war is this: even with its destruction and carnage, it can give us what we long for in life. It can give us purpose, meaning, a reason for living…. War makes the world understandable, a black and white tableau of them and us. It suspends thought, especially self-critical thought. All bow before the supreme effort. We are one."

Once we bow to the god (or devil) of military might, it is tempting to take the next step: becoming a war messenger ready to preach the gospel to the masses. War messengers are staunch defenders of their cause. They argue that armed conflict can be justified because it is ultimately about making the world a more peaceful place. They claim that we go to war because we care. We care about freedom, or democracy, or religion, or homeland security, or the triumph of good over evil and the survival of the fittest; and to get there we sometimes have to settle conflict and resolve differences with brute force.

But history tells us that war is never about caring. It is instead about man's inhumanity to man through greed, domination, destruction and human suffering. And it has never made the world a more peaceful place.

How do we counteract the spell that war seems to have over us and the myths it causes us to believe? How do we free ourselves from the narcotic of war that clouds our better judgment? How do we summon up the courage to turn away the messengers of war?

Fortunately, there is another kind of messenger beckoning to us on the horizon, struggling to be heard above the din of the war machine. Peace messengers call out from street corners, backyards, capitol malls and town halls; signs bobbing, fingers spread into a "V," voices hoarse from chanting, singing and speaking out. War, they tell us, has been nothing but trouble, feeding the frenzy of militarism and violence that has cost us dearly in human suffering, as well as in our pocketbooks and international image and the legacy we are leaving for our children.

Peace messengers offer us an opportunity to resist the military-industrial complex, to find better ways to resolve our differences, to promote a civil society where all people can live together and care for each other—in essence to expand the ongoing work of the compassionate rebel revolution. Chris Hedges says in his book that individual acts of charity and kindness, of basic humanity, even in the midst of war, have convinced him that the ultimate answer to war is love. That is the primary message of the peace messenger.

One of the most effective ways of delivering the message of peace is through story-telling. By placing that message within the context of lived experience and sending in into the public sphere, we can strengthen its impact on individuals and on society as a whole.

In this chapter we hear from peace messengers who have expressed their messages in a myriad of ways—from soldiers "deserting ship" to teenagers taking on military recruiters, from international conflict resolution and promoting a national Department of Peace to stopping the next war before it starts. Their lives span a chronology from Vietnam to Iraq and beyond. Some have actual combat experience. Others have been civilians in war zones or fought courageous battles at home. All have the same goals: to put an end to war and bring peace and caring to the world. Collectively and powerfully, they remind us that the messengers of peace have something important to tell us if we will just take the time to listen.

John and Cheryl Fields
(photo by Michael Bayly)

MARRIED TO THE WAR

By Burt Berlowe

Most of St. Paul's Jewish population lives in the Highland Park neighborhood, a largely prim and proper community abutting the Mississippi River that separates the capital city from neighboring Minneapolis. One of the community's main thoroughfares—St. Paul Avenue—curves into Highland from Ford Parkway on the north, carrying steady traffic between groups of cookie cutter single-family homes that squat at street level.

The St. Paul Avenue home of John and Cheryl Fields stands out from its neighbors. It is a brown, boxy, flat-topped structure elevated substantially above the street. They call it "a house with no roof."

Entering the Fields' airy upstairs living room, I am greeted by the recorded sound of Native American chanting and the smell of incense. I get the distinct feeling of being in an Indian village. It is the first hint of the unique intersection of cultures and causes that dominate John and Cheryl's life together.

John points out of a living room window facing St. Paul Avenue towards a vague image of the federal building near the site of previous Highway 55 protests over sacred Native land. He is thin as a rail with bare feet, a closely cropped gray-and-white beard, and exceptionally big blue eyes that move for emphasis when he speaks.

"Just over the Mendota Bridge a few miles is Pilot Knob at the confluence of the Mississippi and Mendota rivers," John says. "Pilot Knob is a sacred site the Native Americans have been working to save." John and Cheryl have been in the thick of that fight. They became involved when a developer indicated he wanted to build fifty condos on the hill. They have joined some 200 others in suing the suburban town of Mendota over the plan. The Pilot Knob protest is a continuation of the Highway 55 effort, with many of the same people involved. It is typical of the long-standing Field commitment to social justice.

* * *

"No Jews. No Chinks!"

Cheryl Lewis was a small child when she first saw the sign outside a Rochester, New York business in 1950. It was an early indication of the anti-Semitism prevalent in the community. Her family had previously changed their last name from Levy to the less Jewish-sounding name, Lewis. They fled Rochester for Quebec, where Cheryl spent most of her childhood, attended Hebrew School, helped at her uncle's kosher butcher shop upstairs and first learned that her grandparents were Holocaust victims. She was thirteen when the Adolf Eichmann trial was being held. "I realized early on it wasn't a perfect world," she says.

When the family moved to Beverly Hills, Cheryl gradually discovered more about the Holocaust. "The author of the book *Shindler's List* lived nearby. I met him. He actually was more Anglo than Jewish. I learned that not all gentiles are bad people. At the same time, my dad, who was a doctor, had experienced anti-Semitism while working at a Catholic hospital, supposedly a community of caring people. I was beginning to find my rebellion."

Cheryl's first personal experience with religious discrimination came when she joined a Beverly Hills neighborhood association. "Somehow, they found out I was Jewish," she says. "Maybe it was because I told them I didn't celebrate Christmas, even though I offered to celebrate with them. After that, people stopped talking to me and walked across the street to avoid me. I thought maybe I'd offended somebody. Finally, I confronted one of my neighbors. She said that three people in the neighborhood association disliked Jews. I thought we were beyond the days of wearing stars on our clothes.

"When I went to college I could not belong to certain sororities. I learned where I wasn't welcome. In a community town meeting, a German made a horrible statement about Jews. He said he had a microwave that seats three.

"Soon after that, I gave up my dream of teaching and went back to my hobby—painting—and even took a fling at the world of show business. In 1971, I was working for Diana Ross enterprises in Beverly Hills, living the Hollywood life, when I realized that I wanted to do something real, not the pretend life of the movie world. I wanted to be out there doing something for the world. During the 1960s in California, I was primarily a spectator of the protest movement. From the heliport on the roof of my apartment, I saw our own version of black America with the burnings and the demonstrations. I didn't know much about the Vietnam War until I met John. We met in a saloon in Hollywood. We've been inseparable ever since."

* * *

John Fields served as a Marine in Vietnam in 1965-66. He recalls it as "doing what our country is asking us to do. I went to Vietnam believing in God and America and came back believing none of that. I was a gung ho Marine. But as I was in rice paddies laying ammunition, I thought the world was about to end for me, and I had no say in the matter."

When John first began having medical problems, the doctors were stymied. He experienced psychosis and flashbacks. The doctors told him, "Come back if you get worse."

"When we got back from Vietnam, there was no debriefing, no recognition of what we had done. They would run us through chemical dependency treatment without even discussing our war experience. They would say, 'It's all in your head' or 'That was ten years ago, put it behind you.' But I had come to look at war as immoral. People didn't get how anyone could do such horrible things. I figured out why I did it and had a guilty conscience about it. I was just nineteen when I went to war. And then we had to shoot people. I needed alcohol to stay alive. All I could think about was 'what kind of booze can I get my hands on?' Later, I found out I had post-traumatic stress disorder (PTSD) from exposure to Agent Orange. I was beyond angry."

"I ended up marrying the war," says Cheryl. "It brought back memories of the Holocaust I thought I was rid of."

Despite John's recurring health problems, the couple went through a period Cheryl calls "the best years of our lives." They traveled to the central highlands of Mexico and started a small import business. Cheryl taught school and became dean of a college. "There was an old VFW post in the area that was not making money and was forced to close. After some major battles with the Legion, we took it over and turned it into a music club and coffee house called La Legion Americana, employing local people to help the economy. I was happy to be doing something that truly made a difference in the lives of people."

John and Cheryl also became involved with the fledgling Vietnam veteran's peace movement in southern California. "John had a burning drive to have a voice as a veteran," Cheryl explains. "When we got to Minneapolis, he started Vets for Life in 1986 with Jerry Rau, a folk singer who had served with him in Vietnam. They invited activist friends. Within a week, we had 100 people signed up.

"On the second night of Rosh Hashanah, we had an empowering event at the State Capitol where we lit candles as a protest against America's military interventionist policy. We rode a tidal wave of popularity with speaking engagements in Duluth and California. We talked about how people can make a difference in foreign policy. We didn't expect to solve all the world's problems, but we could all take on a small piece and determine what role we could play. The veteran's best role was being a messenger of peace, the antithesis of what you expect them to say. That's a powerful message. Recruiters were in the schools talking about the upside of the military. The students needed to understand the realities of what they are being asked to do—that the recruiting gets them ready to do what the government wants them to do."

Vets for Life eventually morphed into Vets for Peace and began to draw community support, including standing ovations in Minneapolis' annual May Day Parade. It organized homeless veterans and started a transitional housing project. By 1986, at least one-third of men in homeless shelters were veterans—most of whom had been in combat. "They survived the worst of situations," Cheryl continues. "But they shouldn't be in shelters. There's no dignity in that. Eventually, we started the Veterans' Incentive Project, a pilot walk-in center for vets in crisis. We were overrun with applicants in the first month. We developed a plan to convert part of Fort Snelling (a former U.S. army base) into housing for vets and had the backing of some public officials. But we couldn't make it through bureaucratic hurdles. We couldn't maintain a steady flow of funding for our group.

"John also started support groups in the 1980s to give returning vets a place to gather, talk, express their anger, cry, and heal their emotional and spiritual wounds from the war that raged inside of them. He tried to figure out a way to get other vets to come out of their foxholes and heal their broken souls. However, the VA Hospital started to move away from the rap groups and began treating vets in psych wards with medications instead. In response, John began to work with clergy to make them aware of what PTSD was and how deeply it was affecting the veterans and their families."

In 1990, John became sick again and went back in the hospital for several months. "It was a tough time for us financially," Cheryl recalls. "John wasn't getting any veteran's benefits, and I was on my first teaching job." In addition, all three of the couple's grown children had been experiencing behavioral problems they believe to be a result of John's exposure to Agent Orange. "We got by on hope, prayer, and the help of others. There were times when we came home to foreclosure notices on our door." Finally in 1992, John began collecting his military compensation. It was enough to enable Cheryl to give up full-time work.

John's health improved for a while due to Cheryl's support, professional counseling, and the fact that he was finally able to get into the Veterans Administration Hospital. But he still had relapses and a lingering rage. He was part of a successful class-action lawsuit filed by vets against the company that makes Agent Orange. The vets won a settlement of $180 million, but John ended up with only $1,200.

* * *

"This was once known as the anti-Semitic capital of the United States."

Looking out a window, Cheryl reflects on a not-so-proud chapter in the history of the Twin Cities—a time during the middle of this century when Jews were being driven from their Minneapolis homes on the city's North Side, and discrimination against them was almost a fact of life. Things are somewhat better now, at least on the surface. But for Cheryl, who has always worn her Judaism as a badge of courage and honor, there is not yet an armistice in the war against the Jews, even in the activist and academic circles she has worked in over the years.

"After the (Israel-Arab) Six-Day War, we became the victims," Cheryl says. "In 1967, a college riot chased Jews off campus for having a pro-Israel demonstration. I have lived in communities from the East to the West Coast and I've never seen anti-Semitism confronted."

Cheryl lost a job at a mental health center in Boston because of her religion. During the year and a half she worked at the Boston psychiatric facility, (before she was booted out for being Jewish), Cheryl was on the cutting edge of mental health policy. She stayed at one of the first halfway houses designed for patients who were institutionalized for their whole lives—who had no hope of being released, but who had to be re-evaluated before moving from custodial to community care.

"While working as a speech therapist, I had a teenage boy with a fissure running down the back of his head and the front of his face, and he had no speech. But he could follow verbal instructions. He was in the room on this bed, and when he saw that I was treating him like a human being, a tear rolled down his face. I was so touched by that. I realized that we have solutions to problems in our society. We're just not using them. When communities come together, like with Highway 55 and Pilot Knob, that builds common ground. Using music and arts as a common language, for example, is a step forward in making a difference in someone's life. It is very empowering to make a difference in just one life.

"My argument with the peace movement is that it only presents half of the information on the Middle East. It takes the side of the Palestinians against Israel. It's the activist community versus the Jewish community. There are so many existing prejudices that prevent a free flow of ideas.

"I've been appalled by what some people I know think of Jews. I don't have animosity towards Palestinians or Arabs. Most Palestinians want peace. But the activist movement has been excusing terrorism. There is anti-Semitism in the peace movement. I've confronted them on it. They say, 'We're just anti-Israel, not prejudiced,' but they are entrenched in their position. It seems like if you protest the war in Iraq that somehow you have to be against Israel. I went to an antiwar protest with a sign that had a Jewish symbol on it. People laughed at it. Once, I saw protestors rudely heckling some Jews who were praying. We've been to many peace organization leadership groups about that issue and they have all told us to go away. That's why John and I have quit going to peace marches. Only in recent years have I become comfortable with saying, 'I'm Jewish.'

"I wish people would understand that we all have common ancestors. We're all indigenous to somewhere. What we have in common is recognizing our connection to one another and to the planet and doing what little we can to make a better world.

"Many of our friends are from Indian reservations in Wisconsin. Being Jewish, there is a real connect. Both come from tribal traditions and Earth traditions with similar beliefs based on experience with genocide. Our histories are parallel. Their spirituality that is similar to our own. We both teach about respecting life. John and I have done much together with our Native friends — protect-the-Earth gatherings, protesting mining in Ladysmith, Wisconsin;

saving sacred land from highway construction and from development at Pilot Knob. I once asked a Native American woman, 'When do you expect this to be resolved?' She said 'Honey, we've been at this for 500 years. We're planning for the next seven generations.'

"Social justice is never over. The 1960s were a time when young people turned the social order on its head. I think we lit a fire under a lot of kids then. Educators created a lot of passion and compassion. Young people nowadays are in search of a cause. But too many of us are reluctant warriors. Working for social justice is a dirty job, but someone has to do it. We need a lot of people signing up to change the world."

*In January of 2007, John Fields became an official casualty of war when he lost his long battle with Agent Orange.

Chante Wolf
(Photo courtesy of Chante Wolf)

NOW YOU ARE CHANTE
By Burt Berlowe

Sharon Fitch recalls the prophetic, life-changing dream:

I was at this event photographing a meeting of some kind. The outside events were tearing down and the musicians were packing up when a tall dark-haired man walked up to me and touched my shoulder as he told me it was time to go inside. When I entered the building and walked into the conference room I noticed round tables with five women at each. They were from all over the world dressed in their particular culture's ceremonial dress. The conference broke for refreshments and I later found myself needing to perform some type of test to see if I was an intuitive in order to find one woman's children who she feared had gotten too close to the rushing river in back of the conference building. When I was able to perform the task required, the crowd parted and a woman in a white chiffon dress came forward and told me, 'Good, now you are Chante. Follow me.' I followed her outside and across the bridge over the river that was the concern, and into an open field. Stretched across the back side of the field were animals from all over the world. The woman pointed to them. 'Choose one,' she said. I chose the wolf. She said, 'That is good. You are the shape shifter of the wolf and protector of children.' Later, I found out that Chante means 'peace' in Sanskrit. I knew that was my mission. I changed my name to Chante Wolf...

* * *

Chante Wolf reaches out a trembling hand and picks up the loaded gun on the table nearby. With a rapid jerk, she points it at her head, pulls back the hammer and begins squeezing the trigger.

"I hate war," she mumbles through gritted teeth. "But here I am in the middle of it—a woman and a lesbian in an institution that hunts them both. I'm tired of the violence. I'm tired of being the hunted."

The war has followed Chante home, crossing miles of time and bitter memories. It is an unwelcome intruder visiting her in flashbacks, nightmares, hypersensitivity and constant rumination. She has become a prisoner of war with seemingly no way out.

How did it come to this? How is it that a promising, free-spirited young woman's journey can go so far astray? Chante has tended to view her life and the world around her from her perspective as an award-winning photographer, through a powerful telephoto lens that brings far away images into clear, immediate and dramatic focus. The camera of the mind clicks off the pictures—the memories—one by one.

* * *

Sharon Fitch grew up in a working-class home in St. Petersburg and Clearwater, Florida. "I came from a very loving family," she recalls. "My parents always taught kindness and fairness and respect for others. I had an enormous love for animals. As a child, I was always coming home with some animal following me. I had rabbits, cats, dogs, guinea pigs, hamsters, fish and birds. My first memory as a baby was of falling on my butt and our boxer Max would turn around and back up to me so I could grab onto his tail. I reached up and grabbed his tail and got up on my feet and walked behind him.

"By the time I was fifteen I wanted to be a photographer for *National*

Geographic. I just didn't know how to go about doing it. I just knew how to take pictures. I didn't care about all the technical stuff. I purchased my first camera in sixth grade, a three-dollar Brownie by mail order, and took pictures of classmates. I had my own Instamatic by high school, and later a 35-millimeter. I took pictures of everything, whatever was going on at the time. I was quite shy growing up. It was easier for me to stay behind the camera. Sometimes, I would act the class clown to cover up shyness.

"After high school, I moved with my family to Inverness in Central Florida. It was a small town with one traffic light. I missed the city. I went back to St. Petersburg and tried to go to college but I wasn't into it. I wanted to travel and take pictures. I dropped out of school and ran away to live with an uncle in North Carolina, worked at a dude ranch as a ski lift operator and won my first photo contest.

"When I finally graduated from high school in 1975, I was detached from politics. But I was for fair treatment of animals and human beings. When I was in junior high school I had picked up a New Age Bible at our county fair and started to read the messages from Jesus. I loved what he had to say and soon became known as a 'Jesus freak.'

"But the more I attended our local Baptist church, the more I saw the hypocrisy of 'do unto others.' There were no black people in our congregation and no poor people allowed. It was phony. It wasn't true spiritual connection. By coming to church, people were declaring themselves better than anyone else. It was empty. They didn't walk the talk. I became very angry and left the church. I wanted to find something I could be part of spiritually. I wanted true spirituality, true commitment to peace, kindness, generosity, and the highest possible integrity level. I fell from grace several times. So I started looking at other religions such as Buddhism, reading Wayne Dyer. That helped me come out of my shell.

"I found some kindred souls in North Carolina at a spiritual retreat in the Smoky Mountains. The wind, the colors on top of the mountain valley, the white clouds in the pink sky—that was more spirituality than I had going to church and more real. My cat Pablo and I would go up on Sundays to the top of the mountain and look out over the valley, smell the wind and the grass and just be quiet. I got more out of that than some preacher telling me how I was supposed to behave. I felt more connected to God there than anywhere. I didn't feel the need to travel worldwide anymore."

When Sharon returned home, she had a hard time finding a job because she lacked a college education. Her father, a Navy veteran, suggested the military as a way to travel and perhaps get trained as a photographer. She viewed the military as anti-women and homophobic. She had to weigh that against the potential benefits. "Our country was at peace. It was seen as a job opportunity. I would spend hours in airports watching takeoffs and landings. I always thought it would be neat to have a job in a control tower.

"In May 1980, I joined the military. Photography was closed. So I ended up in air traffic control. I was trained at Keesler Air Force Base and then stationed at McCord Air Force Base in Washington where I met and married my husband, also a traffic controller, who was half-American and half-Spanish. (My sexual orientation was still closeted.) We traveled throughout Europe taking photos. I saw things no one else in our family had and won some awards. We split up not long after that, and I ended up at Williams Air Force Base.

"The first night of basic training was very serious stuff. The training instructor and woman dorm chief confiscated anything we could use as a weapon, including fingernail files. Women joined for patriotism, economics, to escape abusive husbands, some in search of a husband. Most came from poor economic backgrounds. There were a number of them in their thirties desperately trying to find a way to support their family. Some of the black women in particular had some sad stories. It was difficult to prepare for the treatment we got as women— they tear you down and build you back up to be washed, obedient beings. They have an incredible need to have power over you.

"I soon began to change my way of thinking about the military. But I played the game. It was my saving grace. I was good at it. There were always fights, stabbings member to member. Women were being raped, being invited to entertain officers. You could hear their muffled crying when they would come home late at night—the anguish as they were sharing their experiences with trusted friends. You could hear the whispers and catch some of the stories in fleeting moments. For self-protection many women went into denial, refusing to talk about it. Most were embarrassed how they were being used as sex for visiting dignitaries, being manipulated and coerced. We were the lowest of the low. Some guys saw that as a golden opportunity for fresh meat. For my self-preservation, I watched my back. I made sure I was dating a man who was my protector.

"Once, I was in line marching to and from classes and was suddenly called out of formation and taken to an orderly room. A male staff sergeant followed me into the office of another staff sergeant, then left and closed the door behind me. My first instinct was 'Shit! Here's a four-striper, a big deal. Everybody's out of the building. I am in a very contained situation. I have to report to this guy. I have to salute him.' He puts his feet up on his chair, rearranges his crotch and proceeds to invite me to a three-day weekend with him and my commanding officer. Guess who would be the entertainment. I'm at parade rest at this point. It was all I could do to stop from jumping out of my skin. He could have raped me right there and no one would have believed me. It was my word against his. I smiled cordially, but I was shaking like a leaf. 'Thank you very much,' I said. 'It would be a lot of fun. But I have a ticket to go home to my family.' That was a lie. Before he let me go, he brushed against me and commented that no one would believe me if I said anything about the conversation."

Despite the warning, Sharon reported the incident to one of her class instructors. The staff sergeant who tried to seduce her, along with his commanding officer, were relieved of their positions. "But then I was told that 'the commanding officer is waiting for you in the hall and he's pissed.' I had no choice but to confront him. It was the only way out of the room. It was the hardest thing I could have ever done. My instructor said, 'You didn't do anything wrong. You have helped other women from having to go though this. You're brave enough for this.' I walked out into the hallway and there was the commanding officer, an older man. He got right in my face and spit all over me and called me a 'lying bitch.' I stepped back and held my finger up and said, 'Because of what you just called me is why I can't say anything to you.' I turned around and walked away from him. His mouth hit the floor. Friends cheered me on. It was really hard stuff. I was scared shitless. They could have done anything to me in retaliation. It was all I could do to just get the hell out of there.

"There was a constant realization of how dangerous it was for women to be by themselves. Our underwear disappeared off the lines. There was a gang rape of an army woman. Compounds were separated by razor wire and armed guards. We started going to showers in groups. There were too many incidences of guys watching women shower. I remember once calling my mom from the middle of war and she asked, 'Have you met anybody yet?' I said to her, 'I'm not here to get laid. I'm here to survive.'

"When I would go off the base there was nothing but whore bars and tattoo joints. I would never walk off base by myself. We would always go in groups. It was very dangerous for women. Guys in the barracks were always getting drunk. We were told to stay away from them or we could be attacked. The barracks guys hated being there. They just drank the whole time and wanted to get the hell out of there and go home. You knew that when the army guys were in town there would be horrible fights over who could beat up who better. There was wife swapping, bestiality films going around, a huge drug bust after some rats squealed to security police. They were distraught over marriage break-ups, losing money, depression and alcoholism. A lot of marriages broke up. One guy murdered his girlfriend, a phone operator. It was a violent time. The military makes you afraid. I had plenty to be afraid of. Women were constantly being hunted. We kept believing if we didn't talk about it it wouldn't happen. But it did."

Around this time, the U.S. had begun the bombing of Iraq as part of the buildup for the first Gulf War. Chante remembers how they (the administration) kept changing their story about the justification for the bombing. "First it was about oil, but that didn't pan out. Then it was about jobs. It's stupid to kill people for jobs. Then it was about Saddam, he's Hitler. I didn't know enough to question these motives and accepted that we were doing the right thing. I volunteered to go to Iraq. My marriage was over and I was the only single person in my unit. I felt obligated to volunteer. The U.S. was saying it would not send women to war. I secretly hoped they wouldn't take me up on my offer."

On the morning of January 5, 1991, Chante got a phone call from a commanding officer telling her she was going to Iraq, the only one in her squadron being shipped out. "I thought 'holy shit!' I couldn't find the cradle on the phone, I was shaking so badly. I went in the living room, knelt on my hands and knees and sobbed. I didn't want to go kicking and screaming, hanging on to furniture. But the next few days of preparation were so intense. I was so scared. My hands shook so much I couldn't eat with a fork. I had to use a spoon. To deal with it, I became the comedian of our squadron.

"I remember the night war broke out. It was midnight. We were in tents. Sirens started going off, and loudspeakers announced, 'Condition Black.' We had to get into our gear. Flashlights were bobbing around. When I went to the door of our barracks there was shouting, 'We're at war, we're at war.' I was sitting on the cot with a gas mask jiggling in my hand. There were chemicals out there and the gas mask was supposed to be first thing on. Some of the others needed help in getting theirs on. There was clamor and chaos and people were yelling 'hit the deck.' We collided at the door, rushed outside, dove into the sand and scooted up against sandbags. The electricity was off. I felt like Darth Vader in that mask. Everybody looked up to the sky not knowing what to expect. The captain said 'all clear.'

"Then thunder started as F16s took off and there was blue and orange and everything vibrated. They took off one after another—there must have been twenty of them. Everybody in Tent City was cheering and crying. It was really intense. After that, it settled to nothing again. Then we saw another wave of airplanes heading to Baghdad, maybe twenty or more. We bombed that country twenty-four hours a day for the next forty-two days. We had Scuds flying over us all the time, close enough to our barracks to kill twenty-seven of our reservists. Dangerous chemical alarms went off and people scrambled for cover. Many complained of burning sensations. The commanding officer said it was nothing. I was scared so many times of chemical exposure or of being turned into a glass parking lot.

"After the barracks was hit we were told by our commanding officers that soldiers had become complacent—that their alarms went off, but they didn't take it seriously and that was what killed them. The next morning my supervisor and one of the investigators said that the victims never knew what hit them. The alarms didn't go off. The reason the commanding officers lied was because they were losing control of us. To maintain control you have to scare people so they'll do what you tell them and don't see through the myth, the bullshit, the lies. I found out that I had courage. You get scared enough times it does something to you.

"I had some close calls, a lot of gun accidents. One of the first nights in our camp, I almost punched this guy in a hangar messing around with my gun. He was with these two young marines right out of high school. This geeky kid was taking apart my M-16. I pulled his shirt up to my face and told him, 'This is serious, we are going to war. Don't fuck with anybody's weapons.' He was oblivious to reality. But I took it very seriously. Another time, a supervisor raised his gun to the ceiling. I expected him to blow a hole in it. Fortunately, he didn't click the chamber. Others were loading M-16s, cocking and rejecting bullets with no muzzle."

Chante worked twelve-hour shifts six days a week in a room with all the ammo and guns and top secret material. But she had very little to do. To prevent boredom, she would take a comic strip and change the words to reflect the feelings she had at the time. "My drawings represented the emotional roller coaster I was on. We even paved the desert just to keep people busy.

"One day, I heard on the radio that we were going to peace talks. I just wanted to go home. They kept extending our stay to secure the area so we could always have a presence there. I had a huge guilt trip. I left before anyone else, and I had a hard time with that.

"Before leaving, I had to check for unexploded cluster bombs and loaded ordinances. I kept thinking of the insanity of it. The whole war was stupid. It trashed the environment. It wasn't a fair fight. We had 80,000 people surrender and shot thousands of them. A couple hundred had come into our camp. Rag tags bleeding, shell shocked, starving, dehydrated. The medics said it was the most pathetic thing they had ever seen."

When her tour of duty was over, Chante looked forward to going home. But she didn't realize how difficult that would be. "The first weeks at home, I didn't want to be around anybody, not even my friends. I wanted to flee to the mountains and be away from people. The only people I gave a shit about were my parents. That's when I turned a gun on myself. I had a feeling of emptiness.

I had been to hell and back. Hell is created by man and it's called war. But I had nothing to do at home, no sense of direction. So I re-enlisted."

When she finally came home for good, Chante, like many who fought beside her in the Gulf War, was greeted with a hero's welcome, showered with cheers and graffiti in a ticker tape parade. It was during that celebration of military triumph that she met representatives from Vets for Peace, a national organization of antiwar veterans. "That," she says, "is how I started my walk for peace. When I hung up from my first phone call to Vets For Peace I cried from encountering an understanding I hadn't had in so many years. I decided to dedicate the rest of my time and talents to work to dismantle our military machine. After 9/11, I jumped in with both feet. I've met veterans from World War Two who are just now talking about it, just beginning to let out the anger. There's no such thing as a good war. That's the lie people maintain so they can keep their sanity."

After finishing college with degrees in anthropology and women's studies, Chante began her emotional crusade for peace. She has been to schools, churches and community group meetings given speeches, press conferences and interviews and participated in peace rallies. She talks a lot about finding alternatives to ROTC and other military teachings. When she tells the searing story of her war experience, her anger and dismay show through her tears and dramatic gestures. Even after all of this time, the war has never left her.

"War gets to you psychologically as well as physically. I've had major flashbacks since I came home. Car alarms that are similar to sirens are a trigger. I have some symptoms of Gulf War Syndrome. I still have nightmares about war. They always have guns in them. I can't stand violence. I won't watch it. It's hard for me to keep from reacting to it. It's something that will never go away. It always comes back to haunt us."

Chante's struggle to survive the war has been aided by some powerful forces. One was her former partner Katy, who helped her finally 'come out' as a lesbian. They met at a feminist bookstore and lived together until recently.

Then there are the many friends and allies Chante has met in the peace movement, her new job doing outreach for Minnesota Vets for Peace, and her passion for photography (she has recently created a photographic book of her experiences). There is also her continuing affection for animals. On the day of our interview, her pet cat scampers around the room. At one point as the cat walks past her, she recalls the time when she pointed the gun at herself and nearly pulled the trigger.

"At that moment my cats walked in the room. I couldn't do it. I couldn't leave them. They saved my life."

Kathy Kelly
(Photo by Michael Bayly)

VOICE IN THE WILDERNESS
By Burt Berlowe

By the twenty-seventh day Kathy Kelly weighs only ninety-five pounds, ten below her normal weight. Any minute, it seems, she might just float away like a feather. Yet her bony fingers reach only for water. She has been refusing food now for almost a month, nourished by sheer willpower and the life-giving force of compassion; by memories of soup kitchen lines and starving children, for whom she has become a surrogate and symbol. It's as if she is saying, "Look at me and remember them."

Kathy has fasted many times: for ten-day stretches at the School of the Americas in Fort Benning, Georgia; fourteen days in Nicaragua; and thirty and forty days in New York City across from the United Nations building—490 days of fasts between 1999 and 2002. "After about three days you don't feel hungry," she says. "You are sustained by the energy of your commitment." She has also been part of peace teams placing themselves in harm's way of American bombs, visited the streets of Iraq's poorest neighborhoods in 100 degree heat, and been behind bars almost too many times to count.

Kathy Kelly is a different kind of war hero. She has spent much of the past twelve years embedded in the Iraq-U.S. conflict. Yet she has never carried artillery, driven a tank or worn a military uniform. Her weapons are a wealth of passion and raw courage, and an unflagging devotion to justice that has won her three Nobel Peace Prize nominations. She came gradually to this place, transformed by a series of jarring experiences that changed her view of the world.

* * *

Chicago: The Early Years

"I was born in 1952 and grew up on the south side of Chicago, a blue-collar area which Saul Bellow described as 'rows and rows of bungalows and a scrawny little park,'" Kathy recalls. "I had a secure upbringing and barely knew about problems in the outside world. Yet my neighborhood was rampant with racism, militarism and sexism. My father worried that African Americans would move into cheap houses in our community and cause white flight."

It was in high school during the turbulent 1960s that Kathy's current journey truly began. The Vietnam War was raging. Martin Luther King Jr. had stones thrown at him in a park near her neighborhood. "An energetic young teacher, a Christian brother at St. Paul-Kennedy High School, an experimental co-ed school, helped us understand King—that he was a saint and prophet of our time. We also learned that napalm, which was being used as a defoliant in trees in Vietnam, was also falling on the backs of children. The film *Night and Fog* touched me deeply. It was a film of the Holocaust camps, a graphic description that made me ask, 'Didn't they smell the burning flesh?' Average people were looking the other way, changing the subject, much like we still do in society. I didn't want to be the person to sit on the sidelines in the face of unspeakable evil."

Kathy didn't act on her feelings for some time. She went through college, got a master's degree in theology, and sat at home in an affluent university neighborhood writing papers on preferential treatment for the poor. "Then I began to realize that I had been talking the talk but not walking the walk—writing papers and teaching about love of neighbor and liberation theology, and singing pious songs about the plight of the poor. I knew there were poor people camped out underneath the tracks and that the train would pass right over them. I was preaching peace in the classroom while my own neighborhood didn't have enough of it.

"One day I found my way to a hospitality house neighborhood soup kitchen and overnight shelter clustered around a Catholic Worker house and parish on the north side of Chicago. While I was helping out there, I heard about the Catholic Worker movement. My life has never been the same since. I moved into that neighborhood and enjoyed being part of the 'do-gooders ghetto.' We felt enamored with people who had done courageous things in the civil rights movement and the movement to end the Vietnam War. Everyone routinely stayed long enough in the shelter that when they went to work at a real job they never took it for granted. The neighborhood accepted the shelter. No one would have dared drive around in a fancy car. That would insult the spirit of the community."

During her stay at the hospitality house, Kathy met and married Karl Meyer, a protégé of Dorothy Day and "one of the most intellectually honest people I have ever met, a great influence and my best friend, an advocate of simple living and nonviolent direct action. I made a choice not to have a child. That set me apart from friends who were settling down with families. I was invested with family in a different way."

In the 1980s, Central American refugees had begun moving into Kathy's neighborhood. Meanwhile, the U.S. was shoring up brutal regimes in other parts of the world and funding both sides of the Iran-Iraq war. Kathy, by now a confirmed pacifist, was unable to sit on the sidelines. She and Karl took Central American refugees into their home and joined the Pledge of Resistance and Witness for Peace in challenging the U.S. government on the funding of the contras and mercenaries in Latin America. She was later arrested for planting corn on a nuclear weapons facility in Missouri and sentenced to one year in prison. "The facility housed an intercontinental ballistic missile. We planted corn there believing that land was meant to grow corn and wheat and not to harbor weapons of mass destruction. That was our way to protest spending money for the build-up of weapons aimed at children and families. Eventually, Karl decided to organize Nashville Greenlands, a community dedicated to simple living and gardening in a blighted neighborhood in Nashville, Tennessee. I wanted to take off on a different path, continuing to organize and participate in peace teams. We went separate ways."

* * *

Battlefields Without Borders

"We called ourselves the Iraq Peace Team," Kathy says, describing one of her most prominent ventures. "We best defined ourselves as a group of people that wanted to remain alongside the Iraqis. We hoped that we could prevent bombing. We were against a war that punished twenty-three million people, forty-six percent of them children who had committed no crimes and had already been brutalized by economic sanctions.

"The Iraq Peace Team deliberately insisted that people who joined us be people we knew personally or who had worked closely with people we knew. We also insisted that people have experience in a war-zone situation of high stress. Despite the risk involved, we had hundreds of applications. We had a core group that could stay indefinitely despite having to pay their own way. We got the Iraq government to approve our movement in principle. Some in the Iraqi government didn't like us. But they didn't have enough power to kick us out."

In December of 1990, peace team volunteers set up a peace camp on the Iraq-Saudi Arabia border. Within three weeks, they had eighty-five volunteers from all over the world, with seventy-three opting to stay for the long haul. They ranged in age from twenty-two to seventy-six and included a train driver, restaurant owner, Buddhist monk, cartoonist, two economists, some priests, nuns, and others—mostly self-financed or supported by friends and peace groups at home.

From the camp, team members organized and occupied humanitarian convoys, taking food and medical supplies to Iraqi citizens under the yoke of sanctions. In time, camp members moved on to other forms of relief and protest work. The Iraq Peace Team officially disbanded in 1991 although it continued as an informal network. "During the remainder of the war and for several months afterward, we formed medical relief convoys that traveled the road between Amman and Baghdad," Kathy explains. "In accompanying the convoys we hoped that the U.S. and British forces would refrain from targeting them out of reluctance to bomb citizens of their own countries.

"We arrived in Baghdad on January 7, 1991, eleven days after the war started. We had been evacuated from an encampment near the Iraq-Saudi border. The Iraq Peace Team camp at the border numbered seventy-two people from eighteen countries. In Baghdad, we joined other international peace activists who had been at the Al Rasheed Hotel since the beginning of the war. The hotel had no running water, no electricity and very little to eat. After four days of steady bombing we were again evacuated. We traveled a very dangerous route by Iraqi bus. We were not protected, but we may have been saved by someone calling into the military and telling them not to hit that road while we were on it. We passed craters, a smoking, charred ambulance and a turned-over passenger bus. Imagining that our little bus was safe was expecting a lot. But we made it to the other side of the border where Queen Nor of Jordan had arranged for buses to transport us to Amman, Jordan.

"After the war, Iraq agreed to let us enter the country with study teams to document the combined effects of war and economic sanctions. I stayed in the region for the next six months helping to organize such teams. By 1995, we realized that although we may have begun to forget about Iraq, in fact, the war against Iraqis had never ended. The U.S./UN economic sanctions against Iraq were far more brutal and devastating than even the worst of the Desert Storm bombings.

"We decided to challenge the economic sanctions by openly defying them, bringing medicines and medical relief supplies to children and families in Iraq. We wanted a name for our group that really reflected our purpose. I called a Dominican sister we knew and asked her if she had any ideas. She said: 'You could call yourself Voices in the Wilderness. That's what you are.'"

Voices in the Wilderness was officially founded in 1996. For the next seven years, it campaigned for lifting the U.S./United Nations economic sanctions that had caused hundreds of thousands of casualties from malnutrition, disease and inadequate medical care in Iraq. It organized over seventy delegations to Iraq between 1996 and 2003 to carry donated medical supplies, toys and educational materials to hospitals, schools and families in Iraq. A website statement on Voices defines it as follows:

We are volunteer teachers, veterans, social workers, artists, health care professionals, tradespeople, and people of faith, who in the tradition of Mohandas Gandhi, practice and advocate nonviolence as a means of social change.

"The sanctions made it difficult to get access to Iraq," Kathy recalls. "The sanctions were such that not even baby milk could get through. The U.S. said, 'We had to starve you so we could stop bombing you,' and then later more or less said with the 'shock and awe' bombing: 'We have to bomb you so we can stop starving you.' What kind of logic is that? What kind of perversion?

"Through the long years of economic sanctions mothers would pull us down next to them and their sisters and brothers and would pray that what was going on there would never happen to children in our country. The same thing happened throughout the war. They would hand us their children to help rock them, to share their food and drink and to say, 'You are good man or woman.' I come back to the U.S. and people sometimes ask, "Why do they hate us so much?' I am bewildered by why they love us so much."

* * *

Consequences Without End

Kathy vividly remembers the days of "shock and awe" that marked the official beginning of the second Iraq War. "Nothing prepared me for the intensity of the bombing that went on all night. There had been this agonizing period of uncertainty when people were not sure when we would be hit. One woman said how hard it was to sit and wait for her city to be bombed. Mothers opted for C-sections because they would rather bear their babies prematurely than under bombardment. I remember mothers scooping up their children and fleeing to Syria or another nearby country, or being homeless. Even when the bombing ended there were exchanges of gunfire going on.

"People felt beleaguered and isolated after the bombing began. After the second week most people were convinced that there was no point in putting up any struggle against the U.S. Initially people thought the bombing would last only for a few days. I don't think anybody expected to be bombed morning, noon and night mercilessly so that no place was safe.

"We stayed in a small family-owned motel across from the Tigris River. The bombing caused our hotel to sway back and forth and the floors to tremble. A western journalist in the hotel across the street was hit by a tank-fired missile. There were several families living just a block away. We marveled at the ability of the adults with tiny children and teenagers to put on a poker face so as not to frighten the children, making them believe it wasn't a time for panic. In our hotel there were two delicate, engaging, darling little girls, one just a year old and the other one age three. As the days wore on, they were constantly grinding their teeth.

"Occasionally one child would play this game in which she imitated airplanes. One girl would pantomime pretending a bomb hit her and would fall backwards on the bed or on the floor. Or she would take a flashlight and pretend it was a gun and use it to shoot her mother and me. Her mother assured me that she had never played such games before. The children had to have ways to work out their anxieties. There's nothing you can tell them to make sense of war. We had a birthday party on the river bank. As we were handing out party favors for a thirteen-year-old girl named Amal, what sounded like bomb blasts went off. We hardly looked up. There was another explosion while Amal's mother was speaking to a videographer and she looked up in alarm, wanting to assure that her youngest son was safe. When we spotted him and reassured her, her expression changed to one of pure exasperation.

"So much of the area has been burned, looted and destroyed. There are many people who don't feel secure in their homes, who still don't have electricity or sanitation, not even proper garbage pickup. They don't have any guarantee that even when they work they will have regular wages. The U.S. has guarded the oil wells while turning other areas into a combat zone without protection.

"There are many people we know well in Iraq and have a kinship with. There's a civil engineer named Sattar—one of the most genuinely good people I have ever met. He speaks English perfectly and worked as a driver from Baghdad to Aman back and forth. I first met him in 1997 in Iraq. I lost track of him after the bombing had knocked out the electricity. After the bombing stopped and the occupation began I saw him. He told me he had gotten his family off to safety and come back to the city to check out a family home that houses twenty-one people. He learned that in another home three blocks away two young men were missing after it had been bombed. He went to the hospital to find them. When he went in he was horrified. There were many hundreds of people milling about looking for help. He offered to help in the emergency room cleaning wounds and applying bandages.

"The world Sattar was caught up in was so awful. There was a great deal of agony and distress. Once, in front of a food storehouse, he saw an army official shoot the lock off the door and then say to people, 'Take what you want and burn what you don't want.' Driving through Baghdad with him I shared his sense of loss and bewilderment. Other Iraqis told us they did not feel liberated and that America never wanted to save them in the first place."

* * *

Coming Home

In August of 2003, Voices in the Wilderness, along with the Palestine Right to Return Coalition, the Middle East Children's Alliance, and affiliates of the International Solidarity Movement took to the road on the Wheels of Justice Tour. Riding in a colorfully decorated school bus, the groups canvassed the United States, challenging and educating Americans on nonviolent solutions to the occupation of Palestine and Iraq, eventually ending their final leg in Canada several months later.

"There was a Mississippi Summer where the civil rights movement got oppressed people registered to vote," Kathy says. "We wanted to do an Iraq Summer to get people enlisted to prevent the next war, to educate people that war should never be a primary way to resolve conflict—not even a last resort. We needed to show our enemies that there is nothing loving about what we have done to the Iraqis while creating antagonism around the world. We held a Creative Resistance Summer Camp in New York City, bringing together artists, media activists and grassroots organizers for a month of nonviolence training."

Kathy has recently spent five weeks in Amman, Jordan amidst Iraqi families who fled their country during the war. She and three other Voices members spent the summer of 2006 in Beirut during the final days of the Israel-Hezbollah war and subsequently reported from southern Lebanon following a ceasefire.

In August of 2008, Kathy joined Witness Against War (consisting of sixteen peace organizations) on a 450-mile walk from Chicago—the site of the tumultuous 1968 Democratic convention during the Vietnam War—to St. Paul to take part in anti-Iraq war protests at the Republican National Convention. She was among several marchers arrested en route for demonstrating at Fort Hood military base.

Even with all of the horrors, setbacks and personal sacrifices Kathy has had to endure, she maintains hope that peace will come—if not with this generation, then with the next. "We need to remind ourselves that we came close to the critical mass necessary to stop the Iraq war before it started. We have the ability to tell the truth and counter the propaganda surrounding this war."

Kathy has seen the children of Iraq pained by injury and despair, playing war games, and as one little boy put it, "thinking about growing up to be a pilot so I can bomb the United States." But she has seen another side as well.

"I once watched children dance and sing and play at the Baghdad school for Music and Ballet. One little girl played the piano, another the violin. A young boy sang an Arabic translation of a song based on a melody composed by Jean Sibelius. The lyrics were written in the 1930s during the brief outbreak of peace between world wars. 'This Is My Song' expresses hope for peace among people who hold in common a deep, true love of their homeland. Remarkably, children here seem very ready to believe that Americans can be kind and just. Like children everywhere they are full of curiosity and show easy affection. In their laughter and joy rest my hopes for a peaceful world."

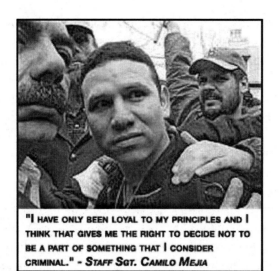

"I HAVE ONLY BEEN LOYAL TO MY PRINCIPLES AND I
THINK THAT GIVES ME THE RIGHT TO DECIDE NOT TO
BE A PART OF SOMETHING THAT I CONSIDER
CRIMINAL." - STAFF SGT. CAMILO MEJIA

Camilo Mejia with friends
(Photo from Internet)

I Won't Be Marching Anymore

By Burt Berlowe

Camilo will be remembered in the history books as the first in a long line of soldiers who rose up and helped bring an end to the occupation of Iraq. He will be remembered not as a coward, but as a hero.

—Gael Murphy, Code Pink

Once again war is marching through Camilo Mejia's mind—stark images of firefights and foxholes and faces covered with blood, sweat and dust; of skies aflame with blue smoke and screams that penetrate the sound barrier. Camilo imagines himself in the midst of the battle, trudging faithfully onward in his greenish-brown army fatigues and sand-scarred boots, acting like GI Joe, but feeling angry and scared, wanting to be somewhere else—anywhere else.

Camilo shakes himself back to reality. Home on leave from soldiering in Iraq, he is temporarily free from the horrors of combat. But he remains trapped in another, more personal kind of conflict—a war between conscience and commitment, rage and reason, good and evil, violence and peace. Summoning up all of his courage, he tells himself again and again, "I can't go back there. I can't." But guilt and shame keep pulling him back into the foxhole. What lies ahead over the hill is the most important decision of his life.

Camilo was still a teenager when the army came calling. At that time, in the mid-1990s, he was struggling to get an education in night school and adjust to American culture.

Born in Nicaragua, Camilo was raised in an atmosphere of rebellion and instability. His parents participated in the insurgency that overthrew the dictatorship in that country and then became active in the new Sandinista government. "When I was just a baby, Nicaragua was split into factions," Camilo recalls. "My mother separated from my father when I was a year old. We moved to Spanish Harlem and lived in Cuba for a while, then went back to Nicaragua where I attended a Catholic school. I had some challenges in school as part of my working class background, especially some language barriers. We were isolated from real culture. The town had one McDonald's, but hardly anybody used it. We came to the U.S. in 1994 when I was eighteen years old. I had lived in three countries in two years. I didn't have a sense of belonging in any of them."

Camilo's alienation and uncertainty about his future made him a ripe candidate for military service. He enlisted in the Army National Guard at age nineteen because it offered him a chance to make some money and have that sense of belonging and stability. "I was told I would get free tuition to finish school and would be able to leave after eight years," he explains. He soon discovered that these were empty promises. "I got a scholarship to pay half of my $26,000 tuition. But when I went to the military to ask them to cover the rest they said, 'We don't do private schools.'" In 2003, Camilo, then a staff sergeant, found out his unit was being deployed for Operation Iraqi Freedom.

During his six-month deployment in the Florida National Guard, Camilo had received commendations for his courage and commitment and was considered an exemplary and popular soldier. But the trauma of war began to change him. He watched the Iraqis turn from welcoming to hostile. "At first they were happy to see us. Then we started setting up roadblocks, raiding their homes, killing civilians, and their attitude changed. The people didn't want us there any more and we didn't want to be there.

"Right away I thought that the war didn't make sense. There were no weapons of mass destruction, no links to 9/11. We were being indoctrinated. I had signed a contract. I had signed my soul away. I had to obey orders and just keep my mouth shut. My life didn't belong to me. I pushed my principles aside and went on."

Camilo's resentment of the war continued to build, finally hitting a breaking point during battlefield action near a mosque in the Sunni Triangle. "We were scouts working with what they called 'spooks'—anonymous soldiers who had nicknames like 'Rocket' and 'Scooter.' They remained incognito and intractable. We didn't know who they were. They could have been from the CIA. They were experts in weapons and other aspects of battle. They called where we were a POW camp. It was really an orientation facility for training us in how to deal with prisoners and what we had to do to get information from them.

"First, they showed us how to use sleep deprivation. One prisoner had been up for forty-eight hours, another for seventy-one. They kept them up by constantly talking and yelling at them. 'If that doesn't work, they told us, then 'take a hammer and pound it into a wall next to them. If that doesn't work then pound on their head.' If that doesn't work, then the prisoners get placed in small isolation cells. Some of them were going crazy in those cells. One of them was spread on a blanket and hooded."

Camilo recalls one specific conversation with a "spook."

"Why is that prisoner here?" I asked.

"He had a weapon."

"What was the weapon?"

"He has wooden crates that might have explosives in them."

"But the crates are empty. He said he was going to use them for firewood."

"Yeah, but he might be planning to plant explosives in them, so we'll just call him an enemy combatant."

Another comment by a "spook" sticks in Camilo's mind. "He said that 'dealing with a prisoner is like you would treat a dog. If you yell at the dog often enough he minds. Same thing with a human being.' I had problems with that but it was difficult for me to oppose it. I had to go along with them so as not to be considered disloyal or unpatriotic.

"One time we were in a beautiful town in the Sunni Triangle near a mosque. Our soldiers would purposely start firefights. It became intense. We weren't supposed to be near a mosque. We were using it for an element of surprise. I realized that we were not there to help the Iraqi people but to be occupiers, to build bases. Our reconstruction work was cosmetic. We were actually only building military facilities. We were like a violent valet parking service.

"You've heard it said that 'We lit them up,' referring to U.S. soldiers firing on cars going through checkpoints. Once I saw this truck that had been riddled with bullets. It actually lit up with an aura around it. I saw a man inside twitching from being hit by the bullets. Instinctively, I raised my rifle and fired at the truck. I saw an American soldier behind me pointing a shotgun. I asked him what he was aiming at. He said, 'Over there—we're being attacked.' But I didn't see any evidence of that.

"I felt like a mercenary, killing because I had a contract. It was getting so every time I went to the bathroom or left the base I was afraid of getting blown up. I became a killing machine, robotic. In order to survive we would shoot at anything. One of our sergeants shot a small boy who was carrying an AK-47 rifle, then shot him again as he was crawling away. I saw a number of soldiers crying after they realized they had shot children.

"I remember one time when our squad was ambushed in Ramadi. As bullets rained down on us, we returned fire while fleeing. When we got back to base, our squad members were euphoric that no one had been hurt, but our commanding officer said that by running away we had sent the wrong message to attackers. It dawned on me that protecting our troops didn't rank very high on our leader's agenda. Medals, glory and sending the right message were all more important than the soldiers' lives.

"That's when my transformation began. When I saw what war can do to people, a real change began to take place within me. I had witnessed the suffering of a people whose country was in ruins and who were further humiliated by raids, patrols, curfews and an occupying army. I realized I had a higher purpose in life than being where I was, that I was not just against that war but against all war. My thoughts were starting to change from being just political to being personally and morally opposed to every war. But I never had much of a chance to do anything about those feelings."

In October of 2003, Camilo went home on a two-week leave to deal with some immigration issues. There he found the peace and clarity of mind to freely think about his feelings without the pressure of the battlefield. "Going home provided me with the opportunity to put my thoughts in order and to listen to what my conscience had to say. People would ask me about my war experiences and answering them took me back to all of the horrors—the firefights, the ambushes.

"The more I thought about the war and my participation in it, the more I realized it was wrong. I began to think about not going back. It was the most difficult decision I have ever made. It was a conflict between my antiwar feelings and the guilt of abandoning friends in the military and a commitment I had made. A part of me said, 'I have to go back' A part of me said, 'No, I don't.'" Finally, when the time came to leave, Camilo made the agonizing choice. The plane to Iraq left without him.

Once Camilo had decided to go AWOL, he went "underground" where he was embraced by the peace movement. After five months in hiding, he surfaced in Boston, along with about 100 supporters, where he decided to go public and turn himself in to the military as a conscientious objector.

Camilo announced his decision in a most unexpected place: the Peace Abbey, a tree-shrouded retreat center created by a Vietnam conscientious objector. Flanked by his mother, father, brother, grandmother and aunt, Camilo stood at a microphone in the middle of the abbey and addressed the media and curious onlookers. He explained his reasons for deserting the army:

I am not a criminal and I have not committed a crime. I am not turning my back on my comrades. I am doing it for them. I am saying 'no' to war. I went to Iraq and was an instrument of violence. Now I have decided to become an instrument of peace. By putting my weapon down, I choose to reassert myself as a human being. If necessary, I will sit behind bars a free man, knowing that I did the right thing. I have no regrets.

After the press conference, Camilo rode a bus with supporters to Hanscom Air Force Base to surrender to military police. Wearing a large St. Francis of Assisi medal and carrying a backpack filled with clothes and a Bible, he walked through rows of media towards the base as peace activists shouted "I love you brother" and chanted his name.

Camilo's supporters would also follow him into the courtroom when he was put on trial by the army. He had the support of organizations like Code Pink and other anti-war groups. One of the Code Pink women was thrown out of court for taking a Camilo sticker from under her skirt. The jury deliberated for only about twenty minutes before finding Camilo guilty of desertion.

In May of 2004, a U.S. military court sentenced Camilo to the maximum penalty of one year in prison, along with loss of rank, forfeiture of pay and a bad conduct discharge. The following month, the Army reviewed, then denied his CO status.

At the age of twenty-eight, two months before his service in Iraq was to be over, Camilo became the first U.S. soldier to go to prison for refusing to return to Iraq. He was incarcerated in Fort Sill, Oklahoma, 1,000 miles away from family members in Florida and California. The sentence was later reduced to nine months to be spent in solitary confinement. While he was in prison his celebrity grew among war opponents. Amnesty International declared him a prisoner of conscience. A group called Citizen Soldier adopted him as their cause and published his prison writings on the Internet—powerful letters about his life behind bars and his continuing dissatisfaction with the Iraq War.

Following his release from prison, Camilo went on a national speaking tour that took him to various antiwar rallies, as well as to churches, organizations and schools, where he told his personal story, criticized the war and urged young people to resist the pressure of military recruiters. He is once again living in Miami spending a lot of time with his daughter, while planning to become a U.S. citizen and return to college to finish his education.

One of the places Camilo visited on the tour was the Resource Center of the Americas in Minneapolis. Watching him speak that day, I noticed how different he looked than in his pictures. In those photos, taken during his military days, he has a round, clean-shaven face jutting out of his soldier's garb, giving him a look of maturity and style. In person, in casual street clothes, he looks more like his twenty-eight years, young and slim with an angular face framed by a small black beard, glasses and closely cropped black hair.

Facing a packed coffee hour crowd, Camilo began by saying, "I'm especially happy to be here. When I was in prison, you were one of the groups that helped keep me in touch with reality. I feel like this is pay back."

Camilo went on to tell his personal story and to assure everyone that he had no regrets about his decision to become a conscientious objector. He has written his own book about his war experiences and become a leader of Iraq Veterans Against the War, organizing and speaking at the IVAW-sponsored Winter Soldier hearings held on the fifth anniversary of the Iraq War. Of all of the places he has been on his tour, he said, he has most enjoyed speaking to high school kids, encouraging them to resist the temptation of recruiters and to organize to keep the military out of the schools. He calls that his "truth in recruiting campaign." Since Camilo became the first combat soldier to refuse to fight in Iraq, some 10,000 others have followed. He refers to his rebellion as a moral and spiritually driven position against a subculture of fear. "War is dehumanizing," he says. "It leaves psychological scars that are dehumanizing a whole new generation in this country."

At the end of his Resource Center presentation, Camilo urged everyone to have the courage to stand up against war. "People don't realize the power they have within them to make change," he said. "Many people have called me a coward. Others have called me a hero. I was a coward, not for leaving the war, but for being part of it in the first place. To those who have called me a hero, I say, I don't believe in heroes. But I do believe that ordinary people can do extraordinary things."

Sami Rasouli with child in Iraq
(Photo courtesy of Sami Rasouli)

GOING HOME
By Burt Berlowe

On the ground in Iraq, the once-proud city of Falujah looks very much like a ghost town. Where rows of houses, businesses and mosques once stood as friendly neighbors, there are now empty shells, piles of rubble and vacant, smoldering land. The buzzing, chattering clamor of daily life has been largely vaporized by American gunfire and smoke. Hundreds of thousands of Iraqi citizens who walked and shopped and prayed here have scrambled out of town onto dusty roads that lead to somewhere and nowhere.

Falujah has been a city under siege. The U.S. military, in a concerted effort to root out so-called insurgents, has inflicted extensive damage to the city's infrastructure, caused a massive exodus of residents, and left behind a residue of dangerous chemicals that linger invisibly in the air.

In the midst of all of this, Sami Rasouli is trying to restore Falujah one trash bag at a time. He leads a small but growing group of Iraqis up and down the city's streets picking up scattered bits and layers of garbage that have accumulated for months. In a time and place where guns, bombs and occupying soldiers prevail, the garbage bags have become small but potent weapons of peace.

After some three decades, Sami has come home. It is a bittersweet homecoming plagued by the ravages of war and memories of what used to be, balanced by opportunity and hope for better times. In reality, Sami has two homes clashing with each other in the world at large and in his own personal universe.

* * *

On the day I interview Sami in Minneapolis, he is in between visits to Iraq where he is risking his life to help return his native land to the way it was when he grew up there decades ago. His years of Americanization have not diminished his Middle Eastern accent nor his fondness for the Iraqi culture.

"When I was growing up in Iraq, life was much better than it is right now," Sami recalls wistfully. "I remember when two to four million people would come each year on religious occasions to visit the shrines that formed the nerve of the economy in Najaf and Karbala. There was prosperous housing, some of which had been converted to motels to accommodate tourists. Saddam (Hussein) was the second man in government and he was young. There were conflicts with Israel, but there was no oppression. The real trouble began with a divorce between many residents and the Saddam government, followed by the war between Iran and Iraq.

"I was twenty-four when I left Iraq. I wanted to come to the U.S. because I was inspired by western democracy and thought that America was the crown jewel of the hemisphere—a land of freedom and opportunity."

But when Sami got to the U.S., opportunity didn't exactly break down his door. He couldn't get a teaching job in Minneapolis because of his lack of formal education. About the only job available was taxi driving. "I had to take a test to be hired by Yellow Taxi. I would have failed it on my own but they needed drivers so they helped me to pass. I was new in town and would get lost occasionally. Passengers would complain about that and take advantage of it by not tipping or paying the full amount of their fare. Eventually, I learned my way around."

One day in 1989, Sami received a phone call from a fellow member of the Islam community asking for his help in mediating a dispute between two owners of a local grocery business. In order to resolve the conflict, Sami had to buy the store—not a bad outcome since he was looking for a business opportunity for himself. The following year, he took over the store. Within months, urban renewal came to his block and forced him to move, first across the street, then to a more permanent home in south Minneapolis. In 1993, the new store and restaurant opened as Sinbad's. It quickly became not only a successful business but a community gathering place.

"I wanted Sinbad's to be an embassy for Arab Muslim culture, just like a passport to Arabia for customers, with the music and aroma of the Middle East," Sami explains. "We had books and other literature on Islam and Arab culture as well as on cooking, history and political issues in Arab countries. Each customer was special to me. I would shake hands with every one of them as they would come in and leave."

As Sinbad's caught on, Sami emerged as a leader in the Muslim-Arab community, participating in the Islamic Center of Minnesota and the Arab-America anti-discrimination committee. "I am outspoken and not afraid to speak and be truthful about what's going on. Every time there was a problem in an Arab country, the media came to me."

Sami's penchant for speaking truth to power almost shattered his American dream. On August 2, 1990, as the U.S. launched an invasion of Kuwait, Sami began speaking out and participating in antiwar demonstrations. "I received lots of threats. People would call my home and business saying, 'Go back home, go back to your country.'"

In the wee hours of a Minneapolis morning, Sami's worst nightmare came true. Standing in front of his store, he wiped the sleep and tears from his eyes and blinked in disbelief, focusing on the shattered front window—one big hole made by a bullet, another, it appeared, by a large rock. Amidst the shards of scattered glass, FBI bomb squad agents scoured the premises. They found no bomb, no clues, only the remnants of a broken dream.

Then, Sami's cell phone rang. "Who in the world could be calling now?" Sami thought, slowly lifting the phone to his ear. On the other end, a woman began swearing at him. The FBI agents got on the phone and asked her to stop. But in ensuing days, even as Sami was trying to rebuild his store and his life, more hate calls flooded his phone line. He recalls how much this hurt his business. "My Muslim customers were scared to come to the store when I was having threats. They didn't want to be associated with me. They didn't want to be identified with us as being against the war in Iraq."

On September 11, 2001, Sami was driving from Minneapolis to Rochester, Minnesota when he heard the radio report of the terrorist attack in New York City. "I was shocked. When I learned that Muslim Arabs had participated in the attacks, I knew that a lot of Muslims would be targeted and wondered what their reaction would be.

"I was in my store the day after 9/11. To my surprise, people were friendly to me. There were no threats. There was never any animosity, never any negative reaction. People seemed to have an understanding of what was going on.

"I'll never forget the time that two Jewish ladies came into the store. They were crying. They hugged me and said, 'Sami, we want to let you know you shouldn't be harmed or subjected to violence because you're a Muslim. You are one of us. You serve the community. We feel towards you love and respect. If you are threatened, we offer you refuge. You can come to our home and be like one of us as long as you want.' I got that offer from other Jews as well as Christians. I was impressed by that."

At the same time, Sami became increasingly incensed by the U.S. government's response to the 9/ll attacks. "The government sat there for about a month and didn't do anything. At first, I thought, 'They are wise and are going to take peaceful measures to probe the event.' Then we attacked Afghanistan. I was against that. The fact that we had to get revenge militarily was a tragedy of policy and illustrated how much we are primitive in our thinking, that we are not solving problems by negotiation. Revenge only fuels and precipitates more violence." Once again, Sami joined antiwar demonstrations across the Twin Cities.

In November, 2003 seven months after the U.S. invasion of Iraq, Sami was faced with a life-changing decision. He had seen enough of the war from afar. He wanted to return to his native land for the first time in twenty-seven years to visit his family and examine the effects of the conflict and U.S. occupation.

But he knew that returning to Iraq for a longer stay would involve substantial sacrifice. He would have to sell Sinbad's, leaving him with no source of income and an uncertain future. He also would leave behind family and friends for a journey to a dangerous place. He knew that anyone traveling in Iraq, and especially a Muslim, would be constantly in harm's way. In the end, the desire to go to Iraq was too strong to resist. He went back to his homeland.

* * *

Sami was shocked by what he found in Iraq. "I saw how much war and sanctions had affected my people. I saw an Iraqi state of mind that was damaged beyond repair. The people had been deprived of basic needs because of the first Gulf war, the sanctions and now the beginning of the second war. When I returned to Minneapolis I couldn't function. I knew I had to go back.

"My second visit to Iraq came in November of '04, a year after the previous one. This time, I intended to stay for five years, returning on occasion to visit my kids in New York and Minneapolis, and to share my experiences with the community—to tell the truth about Iraq."

Visiting family in Muslim society can be a big deal. Actual families are often very large and sometimes include a broader community outside of immediate relatives. The Rasouli family is a good example. "I have three brothers and four sisters, thirty-eight kids by my brothers and sisters, and many cousins, I don't even know how many. My cousins invited me to a dinner in my honor including the whole family. I couldn't say 'hello' to everybody. There were just too many. I don't know how they got food for all those people during the sanctions. When it comes to hospitality and generosity they're the top. My brother in Hawaii sent money to help our sisters. Otherwise, they would have to prostitute or beg on the streets. Iraqis need jobs. Unemployment is up to sixty percent. The most vulnerable are the women. Women have two choices. They can become a police officer or a prostitute.

"Sami is an Iraqi name that means 'higher.' Rasouli means 'messenger.' Thus I am the higher messenger. I go to Iraq to build bridges between my two countries. When a local church administrator heard my name and what it means, he said, 'No wonder why you're doing this.' My name gives a sense of what I'm doing in Iraq. I always wanted to be an ambassador, to be a bridge, a teacher, closing the gap between cultures.

"The U.S. supported sanctions (against Iraq) destroyed its infrastructure. The government couldn't maintain the conditions of its own buildings, schools, and water treatment and electricity production facilities. Half a million children became victims and the survivors couldn't go to school because they had to support their families. Now we have a generation of young people in Iraq who are illiterate, who don't read, who never went to school, who never learned anything. Some are joining the insurgents and organizing criminal organizations. This is a big problem for Iraq. And now in Najaf where I was born and grew up, there is lack of security and lots of fear. People can't drive or walk around safely.

"One day I was stopped at the Syria-Iraq border with three of my sisters. A group of young Iraqi men begged me to travel with them to cross the border. They came to visit their families and couldn't get back to Iraq. American troops and their fellow Iraqis guarding the border wouldn't allow them to cross because they considered them to be terrorists. I was ready to help them, but I was cautioned that we would be considered accomplices.

"Then one of the young men drove his car to the checkpoint and said to a soldier, 'This is my country. I want to get in and be with my family.' The soldier replied, 'This is not your country anymore. This is my country.' Then he yelled, 'Get back,' took out his gun and used it to break the car's windshield.

We were angry and very sad about what happened. The action of that soldier was wrong. The whole occupation was wrong."

In Falujah, the U.S. attacks continued for a month and destroyed 5,000 homes, damaged 30,000 more and tore apart at least fifty mosques and other government buildings. About 300,000 people were displaced as refugees. Sami asserts that "Faluja was slaughtered twice: once by war, and then by the media that pictured it like it was nurturing terrorism. Residents were crying, 'How can we get our city back?' Occupation of the city made it a foreign country. One Falujan's house was taken over and used as a headquarters for U.S. forces. We went in there and found the holy Koran sitting on a table. I said, 'Thank God the Koran is untouched,' but when we opened it to read some verses there was human waste inside. It was put there to insult the owner of the house and whoever else lives in the country."

On the near and far outskirts of Falujah are the refugee camps that became safe havens for the waves of people who had to flee the city. Sami visited those camps four times. He was shocked by what he saw: large families cramped together in tiny quarters, lack of clean water for drinking and bathing, insufficient medical care. Sami worked with humanitarian organizations to deliver food and medicine to the refugees. He claims that humanitarian and human rights groups didn't help the refugees with their basic needs. "They just took their pictures, got their stories and left."

When Sami visited the camps, he listened to the residents' stories. He would then stay awhile, becoming a friend and confidant. It was much the same way in the cities. He recalls an incident where he was meeting with a sheik at a local mosque. "A woman sat in front of the door—that is taboo in that society. She said, 'I want mister Sami.' She proceeded to tell me her story.

"It's now more than 128,000 Iraqi casualties from this war, fifty-five percent of them women and children under twelve. That doesn't include those kidnapped, detained or assassinated, or where there is no information available. That number could be much more. Many Iraqis feel they were better off with Saddam than to endure this heinous crime of the war and the American killing machine in towns and cities across Iraq.

"Operation Spear and Sword replaced Iraqi Freedom. Iraqis don't see freedom and reject the occupation. Saddam Hussein took freedom and democracy away from the Iraqis. Dictatorship was imposed on them for thirty-five years. But they were a secure country. Now they are a lawless country with robbers, organized crime, kidnapping of innocent people, female prostitution."

Sami has felt the lawlessness personally. As he travels around Iraq, he realizes the constant danger that lurks everywhere. He has chosen to travel alone mostly without bodyguard protection, but he carefully selects the drivers of the cars he rides in to make sure he can trust them. The recent kidnapping of his nephew, who was later released, has made him even more aware of the constant risks he faces on the streets of an occupied country.

At the same time, Sami has received the support and camaraderie of the people of Iraq. Having left his American family behind, he found another one in Iraq, not only in his immediate relatives but among the public at-large who generally welcomed him with open arms.

At first, he stayed in hotels, but then friends he knew told him, "This is your second home," and gave him three free houses to stay in whenever he was there. "I felt like a king," he says. "No one had those privileges except Saddam when he had his castles. I feel privileged being the oppressor and the oppressed. But I don't feel comfortable with that status. I would like to be the bridge between both."

Little by little, Sami became that bridge builder. Using the model of the successful Christian peacemaking teams around the world, he established the Muslim Peacemakers Team in Iraq, a group of fifteen individuals. "We provided training, consulting and deep support," he explains. "The main thing we did was the action in Fallujah, where the U.S military drove millions of people out as refugees, spreading democracy by force."

Through the peacemaker teams, Sami has been creating an interfaith dialogue between Muslims and Jews. "Our aim is to teach all kids that we can live together. We have illustrated that Iraqis are one. We've been told that our team has removed many barriers of misunderstanding and confusion about who is with the leaders and who is against the occupation. We are working towards an environment of unity rather than divide and conquer. Iraqis have been divided by occupation and by factions—Shiites, Muslims, Kurds and Sunnis. They have political differences but not on sectarian issues."

On May 6, 2005, Sami told a prominent sheik in Falujah about his plans to lead a group of fifteen Shia from Karbala and three Christians from the U.S. and Karbala on a trash cleaning campaign through the city. The Sheik begged Sami to postpone the project because of the danger involved, explaining that he had been attacked the day before and his car damaged. Sami's response was, "We are coming to do what is our mission no matter what."

The sheik wept as he said, "God bless you. We will be waiting for you at the entrance to Falujah."

Early the next morning, the team began its unique campaign to return order to Falujah. A group of eighteen people dressed in janitor's uniforms walked the city's streets stuffing 100 garbage bags with refuse as bewildered passersby stared in disbelief. "We knocked on doors asking for refuse to collect," Sami explains. "People looked at us suspiciously, saying that we didn't look like garbage collectors, and asked what we were doing there. They hadn't seen garbage collectors for months.

"We said, 'We are the same people you are. We came to have unity and solidarity with you to share the task of cleaning the city from rubble and garbage and rebuild it again.' They were surprised by our seriousness. They cried, kissed us, asked us to stop and pray with them. We were invited to a local mosque to pray. The sheik altered his sermon to speak about the unity of Iraq. When it was over, we made a line at the door of the mosque to hug and kiss the Falujans as they left. We told them how eager we were to be in solidarity. When we were done, people thought we should do it over again.

"And in fact, we will be doing that project in twenty other cities and towns across Iraq. In addition, the Muslim Peacemakers Team is educating families on such basics as dishwashing and how to use bleach and hot water to boil food as compensation for the lack of clean water available to them."

Just before he left Iraq for the second time for a visit to Minneapolis, Sami was invited to an art show in Kabala featuring the work of local artists. He ended up bringing about fifty pieces of the artwork to the U.S. where he sold them at various venues as a fundraiser.

"Iraq is planning to bring teachers and students with scholarships to the U.S. to continue their education and provide us with a better understanding of Islamic culture," Sami says. "They ask us, 'You have the best universities in the world. How come your foreign policy comes out of such narrow thinking that you have to use force instead of other alternatives?'

"We have to conquer the stereotype we have of Muslims. In Iraq, we say the phrase 'salaam' every day. It is a greeting that means 'peace,' taken from the word 'Islam.' Islam submits to the policies of peace, God and justice and asks human beings to be good to each other. Islam is inclusive. I'm often called to be Christian, Jewish and Muslim too. We are all brothers and sisters related to each other who all came from one mother.

"I was born on one side of the world and adopted the U.S. as a second home by choice because I love freedom and democracy. This war really is absolutely not about democracy. It's all about oil and control of the fate of the globe with Iraqis paying the price. We need to come together through justice and peace."

Sami has walked that talk. His peacemaking efforts have spawned the Iraqi-American Reconciliation Project (IARP) that has brought together the work and people of Sami's two homes. IARP's mission is to promote reconciliation between Americans and Iraqis by recognizing the common humanity that they share and providing opportunities for communication and mutual understanding. Their projects include showing and selling Iraqi art, sponsoring a project that has provided clean water for Iraqi schools, hospitals and clinics, and, most recently, establishing a sister city relationship between Najaf and Minneapolis.

In late September of 2009, IARP hosted a two-week visit to Minneapolis by a group of Najaf, Iraq residents and dignitaries, accompanied by Sami, who came here for a three-month sojourn. The Iraqis stayed at the homes of local peacemakers and were treated to tours of the city and meetings with public officials.

On September 14, IARP held an Arab Night celebration at St. Joan of Arc, a progressive Catholic Church in south Minneapolis. At that event, the visiting Iraqis were formally introduced by Sami to the large crowd, who feasted on Middle Eastern food and music.

As the evening was winding down, Sami and I renewed our acquaintance. His face lit up and his voice brimmed with pride and confidence as he talked about how much his peacemaking project has grown in recent years and the potential impact the sister city program could have on the larger relationship between the two countries. "This is the beginning of the healing," he said, "This is the beginning of the reconciliation."

**Mel Duncan at Nonviolent Peaceforce international assembly
(Photo courtesy of Nonviolent Peaceforce)**

A FORCE FOR PEACE
By Burt Berlowe

The huge block of antiwar protesters filled the bridge and beyond, their chants echoing across the Potomac River. Just ahead, the White House emerged into view. It was 1969, and a national day of moratorium against U.S. involvement in Vietnam. The largest of many of the day's demonstrations was in Washington, D.C, where a half million people had taken to the streets.

One of the marchers that day was nineteen-year-old Mel Duncan, brand new awestruck member of the peace movement. He had a special reason for being there—a brother serving in Vietnam, whom he worried about constantly. The two wrote to each other often and Mel could hardly wait for the opportunity to tell his brother about this day's experience.

As they continued across the bridge toward Pennsylvania Avenue, the demonstrators were each given a card with the name of a military casualty in Vietnam. Mel trembled as he took the card, not wanting to look at it. "What if my brother's name is on it?" he thought. Finally, when the marchers reached Lafayette Park, they began shouting the names on their cards. Mel slowly turned the card over and read the name of someone he didn't know. He heaved a sigh of relief, then shouted out the name.

It wasn't until later that day that Mel realized the significance of that moment. "I didn't have to worry if I was carrying the name of my brother," he mused, "because I was carrying the name of my brother, whatever name it was."

* * *

Three decades later, Mel Duncan vividly remembers that fateful day and how it changed his life. He calls it "a powerful experience that showed me the power of active protest and organizing and the hope that could be generated for peace and brotherhood."

Mel has done more than just hold onto that memory. He has turned it into one of the most significant peacemaking efforts of our time—the creation of the world's first "peace army." He is, in a sense, finishing the work of Mahatma Gandhi, who called for a nonviolent army a century ago.

As of this writing, Mel's Nonviolent Peaceforce is getting its first true test. Its small but hardy band of volunteers from five different countries has been charged with defusing conflict in violence-torn Sri Lanka. It is just the beginning of an effort that could change the way the world deals with war.

Mel has been preparing for this day for as long as he can remember—a half-century to be exact. He has always been what might be called "an early bloomer," taking on challenges at a younger age than would be expected and staying ahead of the curve. It's as if he wanted to get a head start on that long walk across the bridge.

* * *

"Would you like to buy some corn, sir?"

Five-year-old Mel Duncan stood at yet another door trying to sell the cob of corn in his hand. He was by himself on the Davenport, Iowa street going from house to house with the homegrown corncobs. During the holiday season, he would do the same thing with Christmas trees, bought at a local store. He was learning young the value of hard work and the hardships that can accompany economic class.

"My father had been a migrant worker before I was born," Mel recalls. "He worked very hard at low-paying jobs and saved money. I learned a lot about economics from him. We were able to be middle class because my mother was a second grade teacher. I liked selling door to door. I usually sold more than we had. I saw firsthand the economic disparities in our society. I came to appreciate economic class and unions in what was a union town. I also learned a lot from my mom, who always treated her classrooms like one big family."

By the time he was sixteen years old, Mel was working for civil rights. "I was a high school football player and had black friends on the team. I had started paying attention to what was happening in the country. My most dramatic high school day was when all the black kids walked out because of unfair treatment on a number of issues and marched to the school administration building. I was the only white kid to join them. A black friend of mine and I were asked to be playground directors for the park because of the violence taking place there. I ended up doing it for three years. We're all born with certain gifts and potential and this was one of mine."

Within a few years, Mel was faced with a decision that would severely test his commitment to nonviolence. He received a notice drafting him to fight in the Vietnam War. His brother had already served in Vietnam and came back a changed man. He was never an activist before he went in. But when he returned he joined Vietnam Veterans Against the War. "It meant a lot to me that my brother was drafted and went to Vietnam. He still fights the war internally. We wrote to each other more then than at any other time. He knew about the protests and draft resistance and was supportive. He kept a journal of those days and would read it aloud in the barracks. One letter I wrote to him was about my participation in the antiwar protest of 1969."

Mel's brother's experience convinced him that he didn't want to have anything to do with war. "I chose to resist. Staring at the (enlistment) paper I was supposed to sign, I said, 'Can I really do this?' I started working on a conscientious objector (CO) status. Then I wrote a letter to the draft board indicating I was resigning from the Selective Service system. They wrote back that they didn't accept that. I wrote back and said, 'You don't understand!' When the lottery came I received a high number. But they never did contact me."

Mel came to believe that if more people voted there would be a bigger block of support for stopping the war. When he was eighteen years old, he led a legislative campaign in Minnesota to lower the voting age from twenty-one to eighteen. Under the leadership of his organization—the Minnesota Coalition to Lower the Voting Age—the measure went on the ballot as a constitutional amendment in 1970 and was approved.

"We learned how to do grassroots organizing out of the trunk of a car," Mel remembers. "We had no money. We would always make the last stop of the night in a college town so we'd have a place to stay over. It was a six-to-eight-month campaign and a very close vote. I learned a lot about media and public speaking and the legislative process and fundraising. It was a pretty good classroom. We would engage the electorate to include young people as the largest block against the war.

"In 1972, we formed a coalition for (Congresswoman) Shirley Chisholm, (Senator George) McGovern and (Senator Eugene) McCarthy and tried to take over precinct caucuses. We were discouraged at the result of the presidential election, but we also knew that we needed to keep organizing."

While in college Mel found a different kind of activism opportunity—volunteering to help people with disabilities. "As I got to know them I found out that a lot of their struggles were not problems of disability but problems of civil rights. I started organizing among people with disabilities and lobbied for accessibility issues. Eventually, handicapped people learned to lobby on their own behalf. That led to the founding of Metro Mobility and the Association of Retarded Citizens (ARC) in Minnesota, and eventually to the passage of the Americans with Disability Act in 1990. Eventually, ARC and I had a parting of the ways. I was too radical for them."

Mel Duncan with Grandkids Jose and Carolina
(Photo courtesy of the Nonviolent Peaceforce)

Mel worked for twelve years as a social worker in a day program. There he met Georgia, a single foster mom of a mentally retarded child. They later married and adopted eight children, including a Guatemalan and a Native American.

Meanwhile, the larger world had begun to beckon to Mel. He traveled to India to work on a Presbyterian church program and followed that same group on a mission to protect America's interests on the Nicaragua border. He describes that experience: "We went to support the Sandinistas during the Contra war. That was my first exposure to the concept of a peaceforce. We were part of the international Brigadistas, a cotton-coffee brigade. Once we were in a tiny village in Nicaragua late at night. A Nicaraguan guy with an AK-47 gun was guarding me. I was relieved that we had an automatic weapon to protect us. Later, I began to look deeply into the idea of revolutionary violence. I decided that it really doesn't work anymore."

During the Reagan years, Mel worked for the Jobs with Peace campaign on reducing the military budget and on economic and peace conversion. He examined the connections between labor, peace and the civil rights movement and noticed that wedges were being driven between them. That led to the formation of Minnesotans for Progressive Action (MAPA), a coalition of labor unions and environmental and peace groups coming together around common interests. He worked there for ten years, promoting economic justice campaigns and tax reform, protections for gays and lesbians, and efforts to stop nuclear waste storage. For two years in a row, MAPA helped enact legislation that mandates any corporation that receives corporate welfare to pay a living wage. The bill was vetoed but it eventually led to corporate welfare reform.

* * *

The commuter bus eased its way into Plum Village, a spiritual community in southern France. Mel Duncan gazed out the window in wonderment. He couldn't believe that he had finally made it to the hometown of Thich Nhat Hanh. His thoughts flashed back to the moment when he was first introduced to the famous Buddhist philosopher.

"It was in Oakland, California at the University of Creation Spirituality where I was studying the relationships between spirituality and justice. I was taking a class on mystics, a section on Rumi, a thirteenth century Persian poet taught by a Suffi, a mystical spiritual Islamic leader. The Suffi started talking about the differences between Western and Eastern culture—how people in Western culture try to intellectually dominate while those in Eastern culture tend to illuminate what other people are saying." Sitting in class, Mel began daydreaming about the Suffi staring at him saying, 'Your job is to enter the heart of your enemy. This could change your life.' Later the Sufi started talking about 'some guy named Thich Nhat Hanh.' From that point on, I was challenged on the concept of duality. I realized that my organizing had always been based on us versus them and that I needed to move on from that to understand unity."

As the bus jolted to a stop, Mel turned his attention to the tablet on his lap to make notes about his arrival in Plum Village. Suddenly, he was visited by a new, defining thought arising out of his collective experience: "Maybe it's time for a nonviolent peace force to be formed." He immediately wrote that on a piece of paper as something to pursue when he got back home.

Later that year, when he returned to Minnesota, Mel had much on his mind. His family was financially broke and he had to take a teaching job. But the idea of the peace force would often wake him in the middle of the night.

"One day, I was reading an article mentioning a peace conference at the Hague (in the Netherlands). I thought it would be a good place to test out my idea. I went to my church and raised money for the trip. Some 9,000 people showed up at the Hague Appeal. Every venue was jammed. During a question session some guy standing by a back wall asked about the idea of a nonviolent peace force. I was stunned. I turned and pushed through the crowd, grabbed him by the arm and said, 'Let's go out in the hall and put together a plan.' The guy, David Hartsough, told me had been sitting in a jail in Serbia having been arrested for organizing Kosovo Albanian students, and had had the same vision I did. That evening at The Hague we began pulling together people from around the world discussing the idea. We found out that all kinds of people had the same thought. We began to form the base for organizing a nonviolent peace force.

"We did a number of things. We distributed proposals electronically and began meeting with human rights and peace activists, religious and spiritual leaders, and some government and military people. We needed to do research. It wasn't enough to parachute people into areas of violent conflict with good intentions and hope that peace would break out. We had to be very disciplined and strategic. We hired a research director from Germany who did a comprehensive study of nonviolence that was over 360 pages long. We also spent time in fifteen of the most violent places in the world including Guatemala, Colombia, The Philippines, Zimbabwe and Israel-Palestine.

"What we saw for the first time is civil society around the world engaging in a dialogue with each other about the legitimacy of war. We also learned that no one can make anyone else's peace for them. The most we can do is train unarmed citizens to protect human life and human rights and provide space for people to do their jobs.

"Our organizing led us to seventy-five member organizations from around the world committed to the peace force; funding by foundations, religious institutions, individuals and the U.S. Institute of Peace; and the support of Nobel Peace Prize winners, including the Dalai Lama. Even so, we'd been doing it on a wing and a prayer, often working out of our homes and scrounging for places to stay when we were on the road. We received invitations from thirteen groups in areas of violent conflict. We formed an exploratory interim steering committee that narrowed the options to three: Guatemala, Israel-Palestine and Sri Lanka, an Islam nation just south of India.

"Research teams went to each location and held a convening event in Sri Lanka. There were representatives of member organizations from forty-three countries to officially start the Nonviolent Peaceforce. We did a closing ritual at the spot where Gandhi was assassinated. We made this huge circle and spontaneously offered prayers and songs in their native languages. A grandchild of Gandhi from Africa read from her grandfather's words. We felt like we had the strength of our ancestors with us.

"A governing council chose Sri Lanka as the site for the pilot project because we could best exercise our strategies there. Ethnic groups controlled the government and had been at war with the Singhalese Buddhists, a large majority for two decades, resulting in 65,000 casualties. Children had become child soldiers. There was a shaky cease-fire and a solid grassroots movement that we could partner with and demonstrate how to build a standing force."

Mel's Peaceforce began doing nonviolent peacekeeping in Sri Lanka. That includes standing between conflicting parties, providing unarmed bodyguards to people threatened by violence, and witnessing for peace with large groups staying in a village or on a contested border to deter attacks. They have also been dealing with the prevalence of child soldiers who are trained to kill. "We go to the most violent areas. It's very dangerous work, bringing together warring parties to do mediation. We're not doing this to create martyrs and we don't minimize the risk. It's akin to a volunteer fire department. We don't need to buy tanks and AK-47s. Instead of machine guns or weapons, we'd have thousands of people around the world ready to do phone calls, faxes and e-mails if some military group is threatening civilian populations.

"We have to build incrementally. In ten years we hope to have 2,000 full-time peacemakers, 4,000 reservists and many thousands of support people finding a way to put their comfort and even their lives on the line for peace.

"It's not enough just to resist. We have to create. We can't wait for government or the military or the UN to do it. We have to confront war and build alternatives. We have an option that is more attractive than the carnage of war.

"If you ask, 'Is there empirical evidence that would weigh on the side of hope for world peace?' I would be hard-pressed. Empirically, I could cite reasons why we're doomed. But that's not an empowering place to organize from. Hope is a choice. We have to organize more on faith than on fact.

"Who knows what's going in our subconscious. Why would I end up in Plum Village with Thich Naht Hanh? I think there are powerful forces at work in the universe. As Martin Luther King Jr. said: 'The arc is long but it bends towards justice.' "

John and Marie Braun at peace bridge protest
(Photos by Michael Bayly)

A BRIDGE TO PEACE

By Burt Berlowe

A bridge is about oneness, the establishment of oneness—peace.
—Sri Chimnoy

Atop the Sri Chimnoy Bridge that joins the Twin Cities of Minneapolis and St. Paul, a lineup of rush hour traffic is crawling its way homeward. Along the narrow pedestrian paths that border the peace bridge, hand-held signs with antiwar messages pop up and down begging for attention from oncoming motorists.

John and Marie Braun stand at either end of the bridge overlooking the Mississippi River greeting new arrivals, talking about the message, waving their own placards in the gusty, chilly breeze. Marie tightly clutches a gloved hand around a handmade sign with bold black letters on a white poster board that reads:

"U.S. Out of Iraq NOW!"

For a moment, Marie's thoughts rush like the river to another time and place. She remembers herself standing in a crowd, protest sign in hand, in front of the U.S. Interest Section in the Swedish Embassy in Baghdad with eighty-three other Americans, calling for an end to the devastating sanctions on Iraq and the more recent war, which has resulted in nearly total destruction of that country. She holds her sign high, as if trying to send its message around the world.

* * *

A confluence of three distinct tributaries—union activism, rural politics and religious values—formed the path for Marie's life journey. She was a child of the Great Depression, born into a Catholic union family in South St. Paul, Minnesota. Her father worked in the sweet pickle division of Swift and Armour and was an active member of the meat packers union during those "tough times for working people." Marie's birth certificate reads "Father's occupation: Sweet Pickle."

Marie's father wanted to be a farmer and when she was a little girl the family moved to a small farm in the Minneapolis suburb of Inver Grove. "I remember gardening and going out on the highway with my dad selling apples," she says. The family moved several times during Marie's school years before her father finally bought his own little farm in Randall, Minnesota.

Marie's dad showed her more than just how to farm. "He was a feisty man, kind and good, and he taught us to respect and care about the underdog and to question and stand up to authority when necessary. He was active in the Farm Bureau during the 1950s and later the Farmers Union. His work in the union movement taught him the need to organize, not an easy task when dealing with farmers accustomed to independent thinking.

"We were pretty traditional Catholics. We prayed the family rosary every day, went to confession every Saturday night, didn't eat meat on Friday and gave up all kinds of things for Lent. It wasn't easy for Mom and Dad to raise seven children on a shoestring budget. But we felt secure in the fact that we were good Catholics and belonged to what we were told was the 'one true church.'

"My understanding of what it meant to be Catholic began to change when a friend of mine invited me to join a parish-centered Catholic youth group called the Young Christian Workers (YCW). During the 1950s, the Catholic lay movements were gaining prominence in the United States, encouraging members to turn religious values and the social teachings of the Catholic faith into work for peace and justice. One night a week my friend and I drove from New Ulm to Springfield (Minnesota) to participate in a YCW meeting. Our meetings were based on the Observe, Judge and Act technique. You see a problem, you judge it in light of the gospels and social doctrine of the church and you take an action, however small, to try to change the situation.

"Our job was to influence people on issues and the values we espoused. We never left a meeting without an action. As young Christian workers, we were focused primarily on 'transforming the world of work.' We talked about the right to a job, to form unions, to earn a living wage and to be treated with respect at work. We were also involved in issues such as race relations, international policy, the importance of family and how to best spend our leisure time to create a better world."

For Marie, the Christian Workers movement offered a special opportunity to be involved in the issues of her day. After participating in a one-month training program in Chicago, she and a friend organized several YCW groups in the New Ulm Diocese and she later became an organizer in the St. Cloud Diocese. It was there that she met John Braun, who was later to become her husband.

In 1961, two years after moving to St. Cloud, Marie was invited to join the national staff of the YCW in Chicago. She participated in her first nonviolent training program while preparing to join a group going to Selma, Alabama during the civil rights struggle. Her work took on an international dimension when she visited YCW groups in Mexico, England, Brussels and Holland, participated in a three-week youth conference in France, and was in Rome when the international president of YCW became the first layperson to speak to a Vatican Council.

Upon leaving the national staff of the YCW, Marie spent two years with the International Catholic Auxiliaries, a women's international lay group. "We lived in a large house in Evanston, Illinois, and women from all over the world passed through that house. We prayed and worked together and we shared our stories. That was where I first heard Bishop Dom Helder Camera's famous statement: 'When I give food to the poor, they call me a saint. When I ask why the poor have no food, they call me a Communist.'

"It was there that I began to see the world through the eyes of women from other countries whose people had suffered enormously at the hands of U.S. foreign policy. I came in contact with returning Peace Corps volunteers and papal volunteers, young Americans whose eyes had been opened by their experience, and who came to understand that the work for global peace and justice must begin in our own country, where many of the problems originate.

"I remember one woman in particular, in her early thirties, about my age then, who had been a child in Germany during the rise of the Hitler regime. Hildy was intelligent, artistic, capable, and had a wonderful sense of humor. But one of the main things I remember about her was the shame and guilt that she carried about the passivity of the German people during the Holocaust. 'How could the German people, her people, have let this happen?' she asked.

"Some time later, I heard a German theologian speak about the same issue. She said the children of Germany asked their parents, 'Didn't you see anything, didn't you hear anything, didn't you smell anything?' And the parents said, 'No, we did not know.' But the children knew they knew.

"It was during those years that I first began to look seriously at the issue of war from a moral perspective. I was a child during the Second World War and lived with the fear that my father would be drafted. I was taught that the bombing of Hiroshima and Nagasaki was a good thing because it ended the war. Today, it is hard for me to believe that for years I never questioned that belief and was never encouraged to do so by my church."

* * *

From the beginning of their lives, John and Marie shared much in common. Like Marie, John was born on a farm in rural Minnesota. He also was influenced by his father. He remembers him as "an exceptionally gifted person who always stood up for the underdog. Although he had only an eighth grade education, he seemed capable of doing so many different things. He was active in community affairs and served on the boards of our local bank, school and creamery. He also played several musical instruments, a skill that fostered my interest in music."

After spending his first seventeen years on the farm, John entered the seminary at St. John's University and was ordained a Catholic priest in 1958. He served in several parishes and went on to become the religious education director for the Diocese of St. Cloud, Minnesota.

John's path continued to run parallel to Marie's. He was a member of the Young Christian Students (YCS), a sister movement to the YCW, during high school and college. "In 1952, I spent two weeks at an interracial facility called Friendship Hours in South Chicago," he says. "It was a cultural shock for me having previously lived in a totally white Catholic community."

In 1967, while attending summer school in Detroit, John experienced firsthand the race riots that engulfed the inner city. "I saw fires burning for blocks on end and felt the heat on the windows of the seminary residence where I was living. I saw tanks rolling through the streets and soldiers on army trucks aiming their guns at high-rise apartment buildings. On one occasion, I saw black children defiantly pointing their sticks at the passing trucks. At times, we had to crawl across the recreation hall floor, under the windows, to avoid gunfire. Because the local police and Michigan National Guard were unable to quell the riots, President Lyndon Johnson called in 5,000 federal troops and they closed the city down. It was a traumatic experience for me and helped me realize the seriousness of the racism in our country."

John's experience in YCS made him a good fit to become the chaplain of the YCW in the St. Cloud diocese, and he played a large part in its growth. John found his years in the priesthood very fulfilling; however, in the late 1960s he became conflicted about celibacy. After much soul searching he left the priesthood at 43 years of age.

* * *

John and Marie together on the downtown Minneapolis riverfront
(Photo by Michael Bayly)

John and Marie's paths crossed many times over the eleven years between the time they met in 1959 and John's choice to leave the priesthood. Marie fondly recalls the moment when her relationship with John took on a new dimension. He had come to visit her in Chicago. "He wasn't wearing his clerical garb; I had never seen him in 'street clothes' before. He said he was leaving the priesthood because he wanted to marry. When I asked him if he had someone special in mind, he said, 'Yes, you.'"

As he began his transition to the secular life, John went on to earn a master's degree in social work. His first internship was at a tough mental health facility in south Chicago working among very poor people with serious psychiatric problems. "I also remember that the air pollution in the city was so bad on some mornings that when I turned on the windshield wipers black soot ran down the window," he says. "At that time, the steel mills were still in full operation in the city of Gary, Indiana, adjoining Chicago."

In the early 1970s the Brauns moved to Minneapolis to be closer to their families. Marie began work on a Masters of Social Work degree at the University of Minnesota, and gave birth to a daughter they named Rebecca. Two years later, John and Marie adopted their son Matthew, who was born in Korea. The Brauns will never forget the arrival date, August 6, because it was on the same day and month in 1945 that the U.S. bombed Hiroshima, and that several decades later the UN levied the devastating sanctions on Iraq.

Because their professional lives dovetailed, the Brauns were able, in 1979, to start an outpatient mental health and chemical dependency clinic—The Counseling Clinic in Brooklyn Center. They continued to own and operate this clinic until John retired in 1995. Marie left the clinic two years later.

Upon returning to Minnesota, the Brauns sought ways to demonstrate against the Vietnam War. In the early 1970s, they became involved in Clergy and Laity Concerned About the War in Vietnam, and later Women Against Military Madness (WAMM) and the Honeywell Project, where they protested the Minnesota company's manufacture of military weapons. They were both arrested several times during the 1980s and served time in separate men's and women's jails on two occasions. John remembers being in solitary confinement for two days and, another time, being locked up with six men serving time for DWIs in the former jail library, which afforded him little opportunity to sleep.

"Iraq first came to my attention in 1990 when they invaded Kuwait and our government began talking about war," says Marie. "Many of us who had lived through the Vietnam War and had experienced the futility and terrible human costs of war were appalled that it might be happening again. Large demonstrations were organized around the United States. In Minneapolis, more than 10,000 people gathered at Northrop Auditorium to urge the administration and congress to find a nonmilitary solution. But our government was determined to go to war, and for forty-three days the allied forces rained down bombs on Iraq, more than were dropped in all of World War Two.

"Within those forty-three days, Iraq went from a highly developed, technically sophisticated and self-reliant country to a damaged nation whose people had to cope with totally new circumstances of life: no electricity, no clean or running water, food and fuel shortages, transportation problems, and for many residents no work, no income and thus, no food. People had to go to the Tigris and Euphrates Rivers for their water, their refrigerators and stoves stopped working, sewage piled up in the streets, their toilets would not flush—and before long, their children, the most vulnerable among them, became casualties of the war.

"For most Americans, the Persian Gulf War ended in February of 1991. What many of us didn't learn until much later is that more than 285,000 of the 593,000 Americans who fought in the Gulf War came home with a variety of ailments that later would become known as Gulf War Syndrome. And for the Iraqi people, the war had only just begun. The new war of sanctions, which did not allow Iraq to import sufficient medicine and food or to repair the infrastructure, continued for thirteen long years. The sanctions killed an Iraqi child every ten minutes—3,000 to 5,000 every month—and resulted in disabilities for many others. According to an article in *Foreign Affairs* magazine in 1999, the sanctions resulted in more casualties than all of the weapons of mass destruction in the history of the world. Yet there was little outcry from the public because so few people really knew about the sanctions and their impact on the people of Iraq.

"Shortly after my retirement from work in late March of 1998, during a demonstration against the sanctions on Iraq, I ran into a friend of mine, Mike Miles. He told me that Ramsey Clark, former U.S. Attorney General, had put out a call for 100 Americans who were willing to carry medicine and medical supplies into Iraq. I remember turning to my husband and saying, 'John, I want to go.' Five weeks later I was in Iraq."

Marie knew the risk involved in that decision. The U.S. government had forbidden any of its citizens from bringing needed supplies into Iraq. The penalty for breaking the sanctions was a million-dollar fine and up to twelve years in jail. Yet it was a risk she felt compelled to take. Marie traveled with former U.S. Attorney General Ramsey Clark, Kathy Kelly of Voices in the Wilderness, Bishop Thomas Gumbleton, Lucius Walker of Pastors for Peace, and seventy-nine others, on an eight-day venture to carry medical supplies into Iraq. "By taking in four million dollars in medicine we were saying, 'We do not honor these sanctions. They are illegal and a scar on the reputation of the U.S. and the UN.'"

Much of Marie's time in Iraq was spent visiting hospitals and schools, including the University of Baghdad where she was happy to see that as many as half of the students were women. Members of the group also visited the city water department, the food distribution center and hospitals in Basra in southern Iraq, where depleted uranium munitions had been used extensively. Teachers in the elementary schools had none of the basic supplies, and many of the children were thin and malnourished; some had difficulty concentrating because of the lack of a proper diet. But the most profound examples of the sanctions were to be found inside Iraq's medical facilities.

* * *

As Marie walked through the rooms and corridors of Iraq hospitals she was shocked by what she saw. "The hospitals were wards of misery staffed by doctors with no medicine or medical supplies and few medical tools. I saw mothers in hospital wards who held out their children to be photographed in the desperate hope that if Americans knew what was happening they would insist the sanctions be lifted. I looked into the eyes of these mothers and their children. It is something I will never forget.

"That experience was life-changing for me. When I returned, I felt compelled to do everything I could to work to lift the economic sanctions on Iraq. I joined with others and together we lobbied our representatives, raised money to send more people to Iraq, and organized peace vigils, demonstrations, fasts, candlelight services and sit-ins. We printed and distributed thousands of handouts relative to sanctions and brought in speakers like Kathy Kelly and Dennis Halliday, the first director of the Food for Oil Program in Iraq. We helped write a statement against the sanctions that was signed by each of the six Catholic dioceses in Minnesota. On December 28, 1998, we held the first candlelight service for the children of Iraq, the day when many Christian churches remember the slaughter of the innocents as recorded in the Bible in the Book of Matthew. Before the 2003 war, we sold 12,000 lawn signs that read 'Say No to the War on Iraq. Call Your Congressperson.'

"Then came 9/11 and the talk about permanent war. It was clear to those of us who had been involved in the peace movement that Iraq would become a target. Women Against Military Madness, the Twin Cities Peace Campaign, the Anti-War Committee, Iraq Peace Action Coalition, Veterans for Peace, church and neighborhood groups and others joined together to demonstrate against the war. We had several large demonstrations—two numbering 10,000 people. An international protest on May 15, 2003, was so large that *New York Times* writer Patrick Tyler wrote on February 17th that the demonstrations 'are reminders that there may still be two superpowers on the planet: the United States and world public opinion.'"

In 1999, during the Yugoslav war, John and Marie helped organize a weekly peace vigil on the Sri Chimnoy Bridge in Minneapolis every Wednesday evening. On the 10th anniversary of the sanctions they held a three-day fast on the bridge that included local church leaders and politicians. Shortly before the start of the 2003 Iraq war, there were fifty such vigils throughout the state.

The message behind the bridge protests has continually changed to coincide with current events, but its antiwar mission remains the same. And so does the loyalty and persistence of the dissenters. They are faithfully on the bridge every Wednesday afternoon whatever the weather, whatever the news of the day. Over time, they have noted progress in the responses from passing motorists. "There used to be more nasty comments and gestures," says John. "Now, we're getting many, many honks, raised thumbs and peace signs. It's part of the gradual process of convincing people that we need a different approach to U.S. foreign policy, that war is not the answer."

That credo extends far beyond the Wednesday protests. It is an integral part of the Brauns' daily life. Now into their 70s, they continue to stand up and speak out for peace anywhere they can. They are among the regulars who picket weapons maker and Honeywell successor Alliant Tech one morning each week in Eden Prairie, Minnesota. Marie was a featured speaker at a major antiwar rally at the State Capitol just after the Iraq war began. In 2003, she was awarded the Activist of the Year award from the Minnesota Alliance for Progressive Action, and in 2006 she and John received an honorary award from the Vincent L. Hawkinson Foundation. Marie was a chief organizer of a large protest during the 2008 Republican National Convention in St. Paul, and John and Marie served on a committee that organized an alternative event during the RNC titled "Peace Island: Hope in a Time of Crisis, A Solutions Driven Conference."

For the ex-priest and former church youth worker, peacemaking is a spiritual as well as a political quest. "While most of our peace work is related to the political realm and trying to change unjust systems of oppression," John says, "we also work with groups such as Every Church a Peace Church, whose motto is, 'The church could turn the world toward peace if every church lived and taught as Jesus lived and taught.'

"We know that it is the people who have always brought about major social changes, whether on a local, national or international level," says Marie, "and we are hopefully doing our small part to make the world a better place for our children and all future generations."

* * *

Evening brings relative calm to the Sri Chimnoy Bridge. The bumper-to-bumper rush hour traffic has given way to a normal flow. The Brauns and their fellow protesters have disbanded, leaving the pedestrian walkway to hover unoccupied over the softly running river. From a distance, the lights that line the edges of the bridge give off an eerie glow that penetrates the black sky. The lights dip up and down like an amusement park roller coaster and seem to stretch endlessly onward, as if on a journey to a distant land.

The Skog family outside their home
(Photo courtesy of the Skogs)

DOING PEACE
By Burt Berlowe

As dusk settles over the Lockheed Martin defense plant in the far-ring Minneapolis suburb of Eagan, a doozy of a Minnesota blizzard is whipping in from the north. As the day shift ends, groups of employees trudge through the wind and snow to the waiting warmth of their cars. On the sidewalk nearby, four shivering solitary figures, all of one family, walk slowly back and forth, frozen fingers clutching "No to war" signs, candles and, occasionally, cups of hot chocolate. Greg and Sue Skog and their two children have been doing this vigil at the same time and place every week for more than five years—come rain, snow, heat or gloom of night—sometimes alone, periodically joined by neighbors. It is but one part of their expanding effort to bring about a more peaceful world for generations to come.

Inside the fifth grade classroom, it was once again "duck and cover" time. Greg Skog had joined his fellow students in the drill, cowering under his desk, kneeling on his knees, hands cupped over his head. It was the peak days of the Cold War and the American government was constantly warning people about the lurking dangers of atomic warfare with the Soviet Union. In response, citizen-built underground bomb shelters were cropping up in residential backyards, and schools had initiated their own exercises to prepare students for the possibility of a nuclear attack.

"What I remember most about grade school were the "duck and cover" routines where we would have to hide under the desk," Greg says many years later. "It made me think about nuclear weapons and what we were doing to destroy ourselves. Most kids in my class didn't pay any attention to it. But it instilled in me a fear of the future. I wondered why were we doing this, were we going to have a nuclear war, how were we going to take care of these weapons? It seemed crazy to me.

"Eventually, I became unhappy with the lies and deception of the Nixon administration. That was not a popular view in our conservative neighborhood. The other kids I played with came mostly from Republican families. They liked Nixon. We would have childhood debates over who was the best president. It was sort of like kids fighting over toys. It never affected friendships."

Actually, Greg's worst squabbles in school were about more personal matters. "I'd always let big kids take my candy. I would let them take advantage of me. Mom told me, 'Don't let big kids manipulate you or take your candy. Stand up for yourself.' I changed after that. I started paying more attention to who was a friend and who I could trust, and I would stand up to anyone who tried to take advantage of me."

Greg grew up on the banks of the body of water known as White Bear Lake in the northern St. Paul suburbs. He had a rather idyllic childhood, spending most days swimming or fishing with friends and family in the largely white, middle class community. He was influenced greatly by his dad, a plumber, and, says Greg, "the kindest person I've ever known. He influenced me by his attitude towards people. He would use slang in referring to minorities, and I didn't like that. But he treated everybody with respect. Everybody liked him. Sometimes if his customers couldn't pay he would charge less or nothing or would trade services."

Greg's penchant for challenging the status quo showed up in his early religious training. "I started questioning if there is a God or not given what I had seen in the world," he says. "I grew up Catholic, went through catechism and confirmation, but was extremely confused about it, especially the teaching about serpents and snakes. I didn't understand that, and it was scary. I was intrigued by all religions but had no ideology. As I went to different churches, I saw the division of people into groups instead of working together on common issues. And there was hypocrisy. They professed compassion, kindness and caring, but didn't always practice it."

In high school, Greg began dating a classmate named Sue, a relationship that eventually led to marriage. While Greg's childhood experiences had laid some groundwork for peace activism, there was nothing in Sue's early life to suggest that she would follow that path. She was born at the cusp of the 1960s on a family hobby farm in White Bear Lake where her family grew and sold sweet corn. "We had a normal white, middle class life," she recalls. "My parents liked politics but were not activists. My dad was a Republican who switched parties after Nixon. My older sister was a hippie during the 1960s. I recall a graduation picture of her sitting on a garbage can in her gown giving a peace sign. I missed all of that because I was too young."

* * *

For a moment, Greg was in his element. He was happily perched on a bleacher seat adjoining the track where he would watch the horses compete, alert to how the outcome would affect his data-based predictions. Horse racing was his favorite hobby and he would travel around the country as a spectator and sometimes as a gambler.

But on this day, another, more critical issue was racing through Greg's mind, one that could involve a huge gamble. "Perhaps the biggest turning point in my life was at age thirty," he explains. "I freaked out. I was unhappy with everything and getting depressed. Sue wanted to have children. At the time, we were not in a stable relationship. The last thing I wanted was to bring kids into it. I love kids but was afraid to have them. At the same time I wanted to make Sue happy and I somehow felt that something was missing in my life. I kept telling myself, 'Have a little courage and have a kid.' Nine months later our daughter Chelsea was born. I realized that happy things could happen to me. I snapped out of my depression. Six years later we had Eric.

"I hadn't paid much attention to the U.S. war policy before 9/11. Having kids changed that tremendously. I was worried about what the government was going to do and its effect on our kids. I went to schools and talked to teachers about it. Kids thought it was like a video game. They didn't get it. But it made me pay attention to what is happening internationally. I couldn't find any justification for the Iraq war. I began complaining a lot to everyone about what the government was doing, One day, I was driving with Chelsea in the car and complaining a lot. She said, 'Why don't you shut up and do something about it?' I realized I had been complaining and not doing anything. I decided to change that."

Greg and Sue determined that the best way they could put their concerns into action was by working for a politician who shared their views and values. Around the country, candidates for president were out and about building their 2004 campaigns. The Skogs found their man in Ohio Democratic Congressman Dennis Kucinich. Initially, they connected to him through the Internet, then actually met him in the summer of 2002 during a campaign parade. Their participation in the parade and its aftermath was a family affair. Four-year-old Eric rode on a fire truck. Ten-year-old Chelsea made campaign signs. The whole family helped at Kucinich's campaign office.

"We were involved in his campaign for a year and a half up to the election," Sue remembers. "We were at every event. We never said 'no' to anything. And we took our kids with us wherever we went. The whole point of bringing them was we wanted them to become active in the democratic process."

Greg adds: "We went door to door to hundreds of houses and campuses. We had a benefit concert. We flyered small towns during a blizzard, going house to house. At a farm house we met a woman who had been in prison for crossing the line at the School of the Americas. She had way more courage than I had at that point. She invited us to visit her and use her hot tub at the edge of a corn field. One day when it was about ten degrees outside, we put on our trunks and sat in the hot tub."

An integral part of Kucinich's platform was a proposal to establish a Department of Peace in the federal government that would promote nonviolent policies at both the international and domestic level. As Kucinich began promoting this concept around the country, the Skogs decided to form a local group to help out in Minnesota. They met and worked with a local activist named Mary Jane Lavigne to start an organization called Do Peace that promoted Kucinich's legislation. "Our purpose," says Greg, "is to change the consciousness of America."

On September 12, 2004, the Skogs held a party for Kucinich at their Eden Prairie home, attended by some 200 people. By that time, it had become evident that Senator John Kerry was going to be the Democratic party's nominee for president. At the Skogs' gathering, Kucinich asked his supporters to campaign for Kerry. The Skogs switched campaigns.

Eden Prairie, with its plethora of white upper-income residents, has traditionally been a politically conservative bastion. As liberal Democrats, the Skogs often have felt out of place. They have the only peace sign in the neighborhood on their lawn. Once some vandals uprooted the sign and threw it up on their roof. But they have refused to concede their community to the

Republicans. "Even though we felt like the only Democrats in a Republican area at one time, when we went door to door campaigning, we found out that more people than we expected had views similar to ours," says Greg. "Some of them wanted to put out peace signs, for instance, but were afraid of what their neighbors might think." Largely due to the Skogs' organizing, Senator Kerry carried their precinct in the national election.

Greg faces a dilemma in his job as the manager of an area grocery store. "Being a grocer, I believe that the customer is always right and have to be friendly to people. When I discuss political issues with people who disagree with me I try to find out what we have in common and what we don't. I'm in the grocery industry and a union member and negotiator. I walk a fine line. I talk about politics constantly. I go as far as I can go without getting into trouble. I keep waiting for the company to call me about being too political. It's important to keep the dialogue open, to talk to people who are adversaries. If they don't work with you they will likely work against you. It's about connecting the dots and bringing people together."

Soon after the '04 election, the Skogs started the vigil at Lockheed Martin. Sue notes that "Lockheed has been a lead contractor for Star Wars spyware for spy planes as well as guided missiles and nuclear missiles made at this facility."

"We don't want corporations making weapons," Greg adds. "We have no intention of closing down Lockheed. But hopefully we can raise some awareness and change people's consciousness to work on new energy options."

Sue explains that "what we do is a vigil, not a protest. Our goal is to affect Lockheed. We carry only positive peace signs. Of 700 people who came by in an hour one day, we had five negative responses. They would say things like 'Get a job,' 'Traitor,' and 'Go home.' We have fourteen or fifteen people a week join us at the vigil. It seems like a new person shows up each week. We are there in all kinds of weather. We've held vigils during snowstorms and freezing weather, ducking in and out of the nearby 7-11 with hot chocolate in our hands. Sometimes, neighbors bring us food or drink."

"As long as we stay on the sidewalk, no one bothers us," Greg says. "Early on, the police harassed us. They were bound and determined to get rid of us. They didn't like where we were standing and told us to move off the median, threatening to arrest us and put us in jail. It escalated to the point where they surrounded us with squad cars. One day, it took an hour and a half of dialogue to resolve the conflict. After a few weeks of negotiation, we convinced them to leave us alone."

When Greg and Sue were invited to have lunch with Senator Mark Dayton

(D-Minnesota), they did something very unusual. They brought their children with them. The ultimate purpose of the meeting was to ask Senator Dayton to introduce the Department of Peace bill in the U.S. Senate. But first there would need to be time to get acquainted and to present him with information on the legislation. It was cordial but serious stuff, normally not the kind of atmosphere that would lend itself to the presence of children.

But Eric and Chelsea aren't your average kids. They have been indoctrinated into politics by working with their parents on the Kucinich and Kerry campaigns. Chelsea, the button-and sign-making artist and public speaker, has spoken about school violence before an audience of military and law enforcement people. Eric walks around at events hawking Do Peace buttons displayed on a board he holds in front of him. To illustrate the impact his kids have, Greg tells of an incident at a Department of Peace conference. "A lady came up to us and wanted to buy some buttons. I said, 'I have some in my pocket.' She said she wanted to buy from the children. It was a huge advantage having them with me."

In the end, it was the children who ultimately got through to Senator Dayton. Chelsea made the case for the DOP legislation, saying that kids wanted him to stand up for peace. The senator thanked her "for standing up for the children of the world," and agreed to put himself on the line and introduce the bill, which he later did with a speech on the Senate floor. He urged Eric and Chelsea to stay involved in politics, saying at one point, "We're all just little people here except for Chelsea, she's our start."

The Skog siblings talk openly about their political activity. Eric says he likes to carry buttons and signs at the vigils "so that people honk. It's more fun than school and peace is important." Chelsea has already set her sights high. When asked about her potential political future, she says, without hesitation, "I want to be the first woman president of the United States."

Russell Dedrick
(Photo courtesy of Russell Dedrick)

A SYMPHONY OF PEACE
By Burt Berlowe

By mid-afternoon, the symphony concert has begun. Russell Dedrick finishes pounding a huge nail into a slab of wood, then sets the hammer aside and adjusts a set of headphones plugged into his ears. The cacophonous clamor of construction sounds gives way to the mellowness of lilting violins and orchestral harmony. Russell, a flute player in his spare time, listens intently to each beat of the music and plays along with it by drumming his fingers on the slab of wood he is working on, the taps seeming to become part of the symphony. As he begins to recognize the composition being played, he goes to one of his favorite exercises, running mentally through the names of conductors he knows about, trying to guess who is wielding the baton.

As the symphony builds to a closing crescendo, Russell lets his imagination take over in the form of his fondest dream. He envisions the music being heard around the world as an anthem for peace—a lyrical call to put down arms. He picks up the hammer and goes back to work—the symphony and the dream staying in his head.

* * *

To young Russell Dedrick, the world was a stage. At any moment, his Denver, Colorado house would fill with the sounds of operatic arias and his mom would swirl from room to room playing the part of a famous diva. Other times, the bouncy notes of a jazz piano would punctuate the air as his dad played out an encore performance.

It was Russell's job to make sure the show always went on. He became a stage hand—or handyman—of sorts, helping to build a stereo system, or tear down a wall for the sake of show business. "Mom thought the whole house was an opera set, a stage where we could just make a wall fall away," Russell says years later. "She suggested getting a contractor to tear down a wall. But I did that, knocked it down and hauled the plaster out. I was able to fix things at an early age. I've always had a knack for it."

Even though music was an integral part of Russell's childhood, he didn't immediately yearn to make it a career. "I was aware that it was a hard life," he says. "My mom sang in restaurants to make a living." Instead, as he grew into adolescence, he followed his handyman instincts and worked on his uncle's ranch. Later, he went to school to become an agricultural engineer.

"Then I found a flute teacher who got me in touch with my innate love of music and I changed my major to music," he says. "After a stint as a real stage hand with a theater group, I joined the Mexico State Symphony Orchestra as a flutist.

"There was something very impressive about being in a symphony orchestra. At that time, it was the most important thing in my life. I discovered that music is a very spiritual thing. I also was infatuated with a young woman flutist in the orchestra. I had two love affairs going at once.

"But I also realized that making harmony with others (in an actual as well as musical way) can be difficult. I discovered that playing in a symphony with sixty other people, you have to get along on so many different levels. That put a kibosh on my professional music career. I never had a major music job after that."

* * *

It was the spring of 1983. On the east side of New York City, an area bus station had taken on a new purpose. It had been converted into a large cavernous room where some 300 people had gathered for a session of The Landmark Forum, a nationally known program that helps people find meaning in their lives.

Twenty-two-year-old Russell Dedrick was in the audience that day, accompanied by his companion for the evening, the female flutist he had fallen for while playing in the Mexico orchestra. It was their first formal date but they were already thinking about ways to make their relationship work. "I went at her urging," Russell recalls. "We had a great thing going but we needed some help to make sure that our relationship would work in the long run."

Going into the course, Russell had some reason to fear an intimate relationship with a woman. "One day, when I was age three or four, I was in our kitchen at home, barely able to see over the tabletop watching my grandma yelling at my dad. They were both crying. I thought grandma was hurting my dad and grew up thinking that I couldn't trust women. Whenever a woman would criticize me, I just had to get out of there. I wondered if I would even be able to trust my wife when I got married.

"After the course, I called my mom and asked her what that incident with my grandma and dad had been about. She said that grandma did a one-on-one intervention with dad and, after that, he never drank again and got treatment. I realized I had been wrong in my judgment of women. Because of the course, I eventually got to be complete with my parents and that positively affected my ability to have relationships with older men and women and my ability to trust people. Now when I find a commitment I give myself completely to it."

The Landmark course had taught Russell about more than personal relationships. "Their motto was, 'If you want something done or fixed, find the person that can do something about it.' That applies to the whole world.

"What's so attractive about Landmark education is doing the quantum shift—rather than sitting around waiting for things to happen, having people get touched, moved and inspired by possibility. This is not a 'someday it will possibly happen' It is a fundamental shift in reality."

Russell married his orchestra sweetheart and they lived in New York City until 1989. These were tough years financially as Russell struggled to find a way to make a living while still playing music. "I drove a flower truck delivering exotic plants to famous clients. Some of the tropical plants were twenty-feet-tall palm trees in flower pots the size of a table."

It took a return to a familiar place to help Russell find the path to his future. He visited the family ranch for a summer, where he worked with carpenters to build an addition to the ranch house. When he returned to from the trip, he began his own construction business and between 1985 and 1989, he made a quarter of a million dollars a year.

One day, Russell and his wife were with a friend's wife and her husband. The friend's wife was a harpist who had accompanied Russell's flute playing on occasion. She and her husband had recently been to Israel rebuilding houses and had stood in front of bulldozers with an international committee against house demolitions. The husband had started new integrated communities in areas of Israel that had previously been segregated. One of those had a community center where Israelis and Palestinians play and have fun together. That kind of work was a further incentive to Russell to pursue his dream of a peaceful world.

The two couples were talking about launching a campaign advertising Russell's construction business. The friend's husband, who works in public relations, came up with an idea: Why not call Russell The Amazing Husband Handyman. The title stuck and soon became a radio commercial played regularly on Air America Minnesota. In that commercial, Russell's wife tells listeners: "*My husband is amazing. He can fix anything.*"

That slogan and the lessons he learned in Landmark has helped Russell find ways to improve his struggling handyman business. "At an earlier time I may have thrown up my hands and gone into bankruptcy court over my business. Not any more. We all have to have to show up as leaders who are looking to make a fundamental shift in the world.

"As an example," I became involved with a group called the Hunger Project. We broadcast by satellite around the world and raised a quarter of a million dollars in donations. We took out full page ads in many major newspapers that there was this tremendous problem in Africa. Later, I got into the peace movement in protests during the first Gulf War then to involvement in Minnesota Democratic politics. I decided I wanted to work in the trenches."

Whatever thoughts Russell had about wanting a more peaceful world were strengthened by the terrorist attack of 9/11 and the response of the Bush administration in invading Afghanistan and Iraq. Russell decided that if he wanted to help promote international peace he would have to go straight to the source. He took his family to visit the United Nations office in Washington, D.C.

"A friend of mine had been appointed head of military peacekeeping for the United Nations. It was valuable to be able to meet so many people from different countries. We toured incredible pieces of art that showed each country's dedication to peace on the planet. I had this big 'ah ha' movement that the UN was established to create world peace." He learned that the UN had declared September 21st as the International Day of Peace, a 24-hour period when all nations were asked to participate in a mutual cease-fire. To celebrate the day, various kinds of events were held around the world, including benefit concerts. Russell returned home determined to put on a similar event in the Twin Cities on the next International Day of Peace.

In the summer of 2005, Russell stumbled onto that opportunity. Back home in the Twin Cities, he happened upon an organization called the Minnesota Alliance of Peacemakers that was beginning to plan an event for September 21st. Russell had a feeling in his bones.

"I already knew it was going to be a concert on the International Day of Peace. Music has incredible power to affect people. It can provide the background for people being complete with each other." Working with MAP members, he booked some well-known local musicians who agreed to donate their talents. The concert ended up becoming just one of many events that MAP and its member organizations would sponsor during the entire month of September 2005.

"My assignment from Landmark was to initiate an event like this and then to give it away, so that it takes on a life of its own," Russell says. "I 'gave it away' to one of the members of our [MAP] committee. I wanted September 21st to be like Super Bowl Sunday, when at least two-thirds of the planet would stop fighting for one day and to celebrate that accomplishment. It's not a choice. It's a declaration completely free of history. I said there would be a concert on September 21st. That was my declaration and I had no reason to think I couldn't do that. I didn't know then who would show up. I just took a stand that it would happen and it did."

Russell continues to be a unique mold of talents: classical musician, handyman, business owner, and peace activist harmonizing together to orchestrate a better world. "I can fix anything," he says, falling back on his handyman skills. "Now, I want to fix the world. I'm taking a stand that in my lifetime we will have peace on the planet and we will. And I'm committed that what I say is going to happen."

**Alan at Coldwater Spring
(Photo by Michael Bayly)**

RUNAWAY TRAIN
By Burt Berlowe

Bought a ticket for a runaway train
Like a madman laughin' at the rain
Little out of touch, little insane
Just easier than dealing with the pain…
　　—"Runaway Train" by Soul Asylum

The horrible images keep coming, fast and furious, like a runaway train racing through Alan Zuya's veins: bombed out landscapes and burned-out relationships rolling past the window. Alan pushes the accelerator to the floor until the speedometer needle creeps past 100, the headlights headed straight for the freeway wall leaving the trail of memories behind…

Alan Zuya leads me into his office at the Twin Cities school where he is serving as principal. The small space is cluttered with resources, mementos, pop cans, bottles of spring water and CDs flanked by photos on the wall with a Native American flavor. Scattered about are many books on peace, justice and the environment, some of which are used as curriculum, along with his own personal journal, which he wrote while at a recent getaway in the woods. This is Alan's world, segments of his life story condensed and modified. His story has a theme song—a famous one. He mentions it as we shuffle through the pack of CDs on his desk. "Have you ever heard the song 'Runaway Train' by Soul Asylum? It's my favorite song. It symbolizes my life."

* * *

Alan grew up learning how to challenge the system. His parents were active in church, school and civic causes. His dad, a warehouse worker, was once thrown out of school for heresy. "Mom would take in children and help women who didn't have day care and lobby on behalf of day care centers," Alan recalls. "She would have children in day care before it was called day care. She was a very helping person. I learned how to be an activist from both my parents.

"Generally, I hated school. I got beat up a lot. I was tall, gangly, skinny, different. I was supposed to be really smart and it wasn't rewarding to be smart. I became introverted and involved in books and music. But I wanted to deal with being picked on. I took a job at a mill and bulked up my body strength through manual labor.

"As a senior in high school, I asked to be big brother to a young man with multiple handicaps. That got me on the road to working with children. I took a volunteer position working with a street gang. Through college and for several years afterward I mentored kids in gangs to get them off drugs and to stop terrorizing the neighborhood. Some of the youth made it out of trouble. Some didn't. Two of the gang leaders are in prison for murder. We had a partnership with the police in running a hangout place and golden gloves program for kids. One of the young men that was beating up people got into boxing, reformed and went on to national prominence. I still see him occasionally and he's thankful for the turnaround he's made. Experiences like that strengthened my resolve to be a teacher."

Alan never wanted to fight in a war, especially after he and his wife had a child. But in December of 1970, he received his draft notice and went through training to go to Vietnam. Instead, he was sent to Korea. "The war was phasing out. There were 60,000 troops in Korea on standby. I was slated to go to 'Nam and drop bombs on people. They changed my orders to make me a clerk in charge of doing efficiency reports for lifers—a position of power and a way to help others," Alan says with an air of authority.

One of the ways Alan exercised his power was as the ticket master for a secret, underground railroad, similar to the one that black activist Harriet Tubman used to free slaves during the Civil War era. The railroad actually was an army car; the "underground" a symbol for stealth. "The driver would go about seventy-five miles from Lake Charles to a gate," Alan explains. "Guards received payment of four to six beers for letting the car slip through the gates. There were some brave heroes who helped each other. They were never heard from again. I didn't know where they went. But I remember the look of hope and their saying, 'How could I ever thank you?'

"I learned how to get around the system. We saved people's lives and saved guys from going crazy from the war machine. There was this one guy whose commander wouldn't let him go home during his wife's childbirth. We got him out that night and he disappeared forever. The sergeant would ask during roll call was everyone present and accounted for. I said, 'Everyone is accounted for.' He never caught it—never noticed that any one of the 200 guys in the unit was missing. One time a soldier came to us and said, 'So and so is having a tough time.' We offered him a ride on the underground railroad. He got the ticket and disappeared.

"By that time, we knew we were losing the Vietnam War but the truth wasn't getting to the troops. Even in Korea, it was hell. Guys were making horrible decisions. There was no birth control and lots of Korean babies in the alley in the morning. It was a psycho world. I knew I had to do something. I helped create safe places for the mothers and their babies. I taught English to the Korean people. I was trying to do some good in the midst of all of the bad things they were experiencing.

"One day a sergeant said to me, 'We have guys in Vietnam that are getting bombs and mortars dropped on their heads through friendly fire. We need someone to coordinate so mortars are dropped on the enemy.' I looked at him and said, 'I understand. You want to drop bombs on the enemy, not on our guys. Reconnaissance photos show peasant farmers and children in the area. Are we supposed to drop bombs on them because Vietnamese soldiers may be underneath? What happens when we bomb and there are children underneath? I've got a third choice. Why don't we not bomb anybody at all? The war is over.' Needless to say, that was not well received.

"Morale was low because we were losing the war and our presence was being phased out. Guys were coming back from 'Nam saying 'our unit took the same hill twelve times and took sixty percent casualties and we're not there to win.' Even the lifers were discouraged about what was happening over there. A lot of them went back to Korea so they could get a Korean woman to live with. Some had two, three or four kids around. The orphanages were full of Korean children." Alan's normally low-key voice begins to rise in anger and he gestures with his hands. "They'd get a little fifteen-year-old girl on a bunk and guys would have their way with her. We had to deal with the aftermath of a woman laying there with a sock in her mouth because she's crying or hiding under a blanket after being raped and beaten by thirty guys expressing their rage. The first time I was introduced to the Korean people as an army specialist they refused to talk to me. They considered all American soldiers to be murderers and rapists. Eventually, I and some other guys created safe zones where there could be no rapes or beatings.

"The base was not a safe place for the soldiers either. There was so much fighting. There was open drug use, drinking, carousing and prostitution. Marijuana laced with Opium was allowed by the staff sergeant to medicate pain. It was pure hell. I became very angry at my country and the behavior of so many soldiers."

When two of Alan's best friends became war casualties, he had had enough. He wrote a twenty-eight page letter to his commanding officer expressing his feelings. Using a flashlight given to him by a platoon sergeant, he stayed up all night composing it. "I'll never forget the way he looked at me after reading it and said, 'Okay I'll support you.' That meant he was going to help me channel it to the underground so I wouldn't end up in prison. Basically, I was protesting the war. I named it for what it was – 'the killing fields.'

"Once the letter left my hands, I knew I was risking everything. I was so afraid for my life that I would stay awake for days straight doing 'buddy watches.' There were rumors of guys bayoneting other guys in their bunks. You had to be afraid of the other soldiers. I didn't know if I was courageous or in-credibly stupid or both. I prayed to God that I had the courage to fight this evil."

Alan's voice softens when he reflects on perhaps the most poignant of his army experiences—the months he spent in the Seoul City orphanage. He re-members "sitting with children with dreadful ailments and holding them in my arms and crying for them. There were sixty to seventy kids crowded together in a room. There was no heat and it would get damn chilly and they would have to huddle together to keep warm. They had huge open lesions on their body and when they came to you for a hug you could smell the filth and stink.

"We organized Koreans to come into the orphanage and take care of the children. We had twenty to thirty of them coming in every week teaching the kids songs, bringing them food and supplements. All they got was a bowl of rice or cabbage. That whole experience was a powerful life-changing event for me. I still see images of the kids crying."

Runaway train never going back
Wrong way on a one-way track
Seems like I should be getting somewhere
Somehow I'm neither here nor there…

Alan was able to leave the military after two years, but his life of combat had only just begun. "It was a different world I came back to. At the airport I was spit on and called names. When I came home, my marriage was a mess. I had missed the first few years of my child's life. I had to work hard to turn my anger around. And often it flared—a deep rage where I would put my hand through walls and tear things apart. I never hit anybody. But I wanted to. Any kind of frustration or rejection would precipitate it. My wife tried coping with it but didn't understand it. We became intimate strangers. We've been separated more than five times and I've seen seventeen psychologists and psychiatrists to process the pain. At one point she said: 'I want the man I married, not this man.' Things were not going well at work either. And I didn't have a lot of friends. Then my twenty-one-year-old daughter ran off with a man my age who didn't speak English and they disappeared. I figured out that she was with vice lords. I called 9/11, and went in with the police and got her.

"When you go through traumatic experiences, you lose your innocence in order to survive. That's why I behaved so differently—that and the fact that I had so much anger. I was raging against the machine."

Alan vividly remembers the flashbacks that began soon after his military service ended. "They came on strong in full force—horrible nightmares of war, shootings, beatings of children, you name it. Then came the shaking, sweating, striking myself with fear. People didn't understand it. To them, I had gone over the edge."

During a six-year period, Alan tried to take his life seven times, only to stop at the last minute. Once he was about to jump off a bridge when "the voices inside of me said, 'Don't do it.' The last time in a fit of rage I pushed my car to 110 miles an hour and headed right for a freeway wall. At the last minute, I had second thoughts and slammed on the brakes. I turned the car around and drove to a nearby hospital to seek treatment.

"I was originally diagnosed with Christ syndrome. I thought of myself as all-powerful. Later, psychiatrists said I had bipolar disorder. When I didn't take my medicine, I had fits of anger. I've been institutionalized several times." Currently, Alan is taking lithium and is under psychiatric care. He claims to have his disorder under control.

* * *

Amidst all of the turmoil of his return home, Alan found a way to achieve his career goal—to teach children to resolve conflict peacefully and become better citizens in schools with an alternative educational approach. In addition to classroom teaching, he started a private school and became principal of a public school that is an international peace site symbolized by a peace pole that stands prominently in the schoolyard. Engraved on its four sides in eight different languages is the message the children were learning every day: "May peace prevail on earth."

At the same time, Alan never forgot his dissident roots. His tendency to buck the system got him into frequent trouble with education officials. He sued the Minneapolis Public Schools after they closed a neighborhood school. He calls it "a classic example of leaving white schools open while black ones closed. We lost the case. But we booted out school board members who had favored the closings." Eventually, Alan became a spokesperson for the Save Our Schools movement.

"The one thing the military did for me was to make me into a leader not afraid to speak out. I had suggested some changes in a school where I was working. For doing that, the principal put me on a silencing order and said, 'You will do what I say.' He and the school's vice-president called me in and said that no matter how much passion I had for my ideas, they wouldn't change. I looked at them and said in a fit of rage: 'I really don't care if this place burns down.' Then I walked out the door and never came back.

"I was fired from another school after nine years on the job. The school's parents were concerned about my leaving and held a meeting to discuss it. The superintendent found out about the meeting the next day, came into my room, slammed the door and asked me what I knew about the parent meeting. He accused me of defying his authority and got within four inches of my face. The hair stood up on the back of my neck. I said to him, 'We disagree. We have different values.' 'You're defying my authority,' he yelled, so loud that people could hear it through the walls. Later, I got a call to go to another school. We ran the school as a democracy. It seems like you always shoot the hero—the leader. I'm no hero. But I did try to lead with democracy. And many of the changes that I advocated when I went against the system have become policy after I left at some of the schools."

At the aforementioned school where he worked most recently, Alan seemed to have found his niche, as well as a more open environment. He held a Powwow and Black Expo to celebrate diversity and emphasized the child-centered, independent learning style. But in early 2004, he again ruffled feathers by complaining about school board policies, causing him to part company with the school. He was once again out of a job, unable to do the kind of work he loved best.

Since leaving the job, Alan has been reading, reflecting about his career, spending time with his four children and embarking on a renewed life of dissent and social change. He still has a lawsuit in progress against a public school system. He has also found a way to integrate his rebellion with a sense of spirituality.

"Why have a democracy if you don't have dissent against what the system is shoving at us?" he asks. "I am a patriot—an informed patriotic American. [President Bush] claims to have Jesus on his side. The Jesus I know helped women and the poor and was against prejudice and was peaceful. I have lived according to those principles.

"I tell people to make decisions that will make a positive difference for peace whether it's against or within the system. There will be consequences for taking action but also rewards. My actions have had consequences but it was worth it for the rewards. I will always see the images of the soldiers I helped to escape, their crying and weeping good-byes, and be happy that they could re-unite with their families. When it came to the point of decision I couldn't sit still. If people respond that way, it will change their lives forever."

* * *

On the wintry December day that I had my second interview with Alan, I immediately noticed something different about him. He had a bear claw tattoo on his left arm and hand—a Native American symbol for strength, courage and wisdom. That story begins and ends with an American Indian he is fictitiously calling Smith.

Smith was Alan's bunkmate in Korea. They would have engaging and supportive talks and Alan learned a lot about Smith's heritage. When Alan's stint in Korea ended, so did his close relationship with Smith. The two went their separate ways and lost contact. Then in the summer of 2004, Alan discovered Smith's whereabouts from a American Indian friend in Minneapolis. "I found Smith at the reservation where he was living. I hadn't seen him for thirty years. It was an awesome experience. My history was affected by Smith. He opened many doors for me. One of those doors led Alan to his current passion: leading an effort to open a Native American charter school in the Twin Cities area.

"I've always had an affinity for American Indian culture," Alan says. "I had read the book *Bury My Heart at Wounded Knee* many years ago. I reread it recently and it blew me away. It inspired me to visit the Wounded Knee site. I saw relics of the battle and where it had taken place and met some Indians there. When I got back home, I had the tattoo done as a way of showing my solidarity with the American Indian people."

The tattoo is one visible image of that solidarity. There is another. An Indian elder used the Lakota words "Akechita Zuya" which mean "solider, warrior, scout, searcher, " to describe Alan. Those words have become the tattoo on Alan's soul — the signature of his life.

Runaway train never comin' back
Runaway train tearin' up the track
Runaway train burnin' in my veins
Runaway but it always seems the same

Chapter Three
Freedom Riders

INTRODUCTION

The Freedom Ride is a sign that it's time for the people to rise up and again become a force for freedom.
  —Rev. James Lawson, speaking at a Freedom Ride stop in Minneapolis.

On October 4, 2003, in various cities around the country, some 1,000 immigrant workers boarded buses to reenact the concept of one of the most significant events in American history.

The Immigrant Workers Freedom Ride, patterned after a similar action during the heyday of the civil rights movement, took place over twelve days, crossing the country from west to east, traveling 20,000 miles through more than 100 cities. It culminated in a massive rally in New York's Flushing Meadows Park attended by more than 125,000 cheering supporters. Among its most significant stops along the way was a visit to Washington, D.C., where the riders marched through downtown and met with members of Congress to demand full civil rights and better working conditions for immigrants.

In the years since the Freedom Ride, the issue of immigrant workers' rights has literally exploded onto the American political scene, reaching a crescendo during George W. Bush's second term.

The battle over immigrant rights is waged on many different fronts: from the volatile Mexican border to the streets and barrios of our towns and cities and the hallowed halls of Congress. It pits several conflicting factors against each other: the post 9/11 concern for national security versus the traditional desire to be a welcoming safe harbor for visitors; the need of immigrant workers to fill certain jobs against the fears of those who may become unemployed as a result; and, in some cases, the age-old struggle of tolerance versus discrimination.

Immigration is an issue that engages strong, deeply-felt sentiments and political action. After the U.S. House enacted sweeping legislation in early 2006 that would clamp down on illegal immigrants and the people who help them, multi-cultural communities around the country erupted in protest. About a million supporters of immigrant rights marched through the streets of Los Angeles, the biggest demonstration that city has ever had. The marchers—ordinary immigrants alongside labor, religious and civil rights groups, stretched over twenty blocks. Meanwhile, thousands of high school students walked out of class in Los Angeles and elsewhere to show their dissatisfaction with the Congressional action. Similar actions followed in various cities around the country. All of this prompted one organizer to say: "There has never been this kind of mobilization in the immigrant community ever…It's the beginning of a massive immigrant civil rights struggle." Congresswoman Cynthia McKinney called the mobilization "the new civil rights movement."

The huge demonstration of immigrant power seemed to have an impact in Congress. Soon after the L.A. march, the Senate approved a compromise bill allowing for a guest worker program for illegal immigrants and taking away proposed House penalties against those social service agencies that assist them. When efforts at a further legislation between the two Houses stalled, protest efforts resumed, including a huge rally in Washington, D.C. and a May Day immigrant boycott. More and more, it appeared that immigration would become one of the most riveting and decisive issues in the next national election and beyond. And while immigration did take a back seat to economic stress during the 2008 presidential campaign, it remained a topic of considerable discussion in the media and in affected communities. Latinos turned out in record numbers to help elect Barack Obama to the White House, due in part to an organizing effort that began with the immigration reform demonstrations and built into its own movement—a potent force that will almost certainly demand some changes in immigration policy in the months ahead.

As divisive as it has sometimes become, immigration is as much about commonality as about differences. Everyone in America comes from immigrant stock. Somewhere in our past, all of our relatives came here from somewhere else—whether on a ship through Ellis Island, or by vehicle or foot across an international border. Regardless of how American each of us turns out to be, we cannot ever totally escape from our immigrant past.

The stories in this chapter are about immigrants of all kinds: people who have migrated to America themselves or are descendants of those who did, all of whom have been or may still be on actual or symbolic freedom rides, traveling their own personal roads to emancipation and social action. What they seek is more than just a welcoming space. They yearn for and have fought for the freedom to be what they want to be, to be able to pursue their dreams, but also to find a way to heal their wounds and help others do the same—to be catalysts of a caring culture in the United States and sometimes in their original home-land as well. What they are doing will not solve the conflicts over race and immigration. But it could open up new avenues of understanding, compassion and transformation for everyone who has come to America.

Marv speaks at peace rally
(Photo by Michael Bayly)

THERE'S MARV.
WHERE'S THE REVOLUTION?
By Burt Berlowe

I've known (former Senator Eugene) McCarthy for thirty years. He'll step out of a car, and I'm there to listen to his poetry. He'll say: "There's Marv. Where's the revolution?"

—Marv Davidov

Along the highway that leads from Minneapolis to the Deep South, the Freedom Ride bus is rolling again, re-enacting a famous civil rights trip of four decades ago. This time, the faces on board are more than American blacks and whites. There are immigrants of many cultures sitting alongside each other, chatting about the journey, singing songs of solidarity and justice, making history once more.

For much of the trip, the passenger's attention is focused on the slim, white, balding man at the front of the bus. Microphone in hand, Marv Davidov is entertaining the crowd with stories of his first Freedom Ride. For eight hours, on two different buses and at rallies along the way, the veteran activist takes center stage, bringing alive compelling events that changed America and his own life forever.

* * *

Young Marv Davidov was in a daze has he stumbled across the Detroit school yard on his way home. The images were still fresh in his mind: National Guardsmen camped on campus, guns drawn, battling the crowd of black youth outside his classroom window as teachers scrambled to handle the panic, while in other parts of town the mixed smells of gunpowder and mace hung over fragments of broken glass and shattered dreams.

This was not the first time Marv had seen the violence. As World War II was waged abroad, armed conflict was raging in the middle of America. Blacks and some whites who had emigrated from the South primarily to work in the auto industry were now fighting each other in the streets of Detroit.

The race riots had rudely interrupted the once-quiet Jewish neighborhood where Marv lived with his family. Both parents were immigrants—his father from Russia, his mother from Romania—who came to the U.S. through Ellis Island and settled in a Detroit neighborhood dominated by middle and upper class Jewish families. His dad worked in a Ford plant; a cousin owned a community supermarket.

The riots often frightened Marv. But they also fortified what was already an inherent sense of and sympathy for injustice. "When I was ten or eleven years old and I was babysitting in the neighborhood, I had a sliding scale based on income," he recalls. "I always had a feel for people who were victims. I remember in about fourth or fifth grade an anthropologist from Columbia University came to speak at a school assembly about why blacks were not inferior to whites. I was so excited, I ran home afterward. I always knew that. But here was the evidence.

"I remember my high school history teacher giving us book reports to do. A wealthy friend in class was reading Tom Payne's autobiography by Howard Fast. It was the height of the Red Scare in 1948. The teacher said, 'You can't read that. Howard Fast is a Communist.' The student argued with the teacher and had to go to the principal. He came from an important family. So I read the same book. It reinforced my identification with working people and their struggles. I had other experiences like that and saw what racism was, and it had a deep impact on me.

"When I was in third or fourth grade in Detroit, one of my classmates from a wealthy family invited me to his birthday party. His grandmother told him I couldn't come to the party because I was 'a dirty Jew.' I ran home and told my mother what happened and asked how could I be dirty since I took a bath every night. I also learned that all rich people aren't bastards. The morning of the party, a black chauffeured limousine pulled up with my classmate and his mother inside. The kid had complained to his mother about his grandmother and to make amends, they had come to pick me up for the party.

"There was lots of anti-Semitism at that time. During World War II, you could only buy property on the lakefront on a point system. If you were Anglo-Saxon rich, you got the most points. Blacks could never buy property there, nor could Jews or Catholics. I said to myself even as a little kid, 'this hurts. No child should have to experience what I experienced. When I get older, I will do something about this.'"

* * *

"The Army radicalized me," Marv says, referring to his stint in the military during the Korean War era that marked the beginning of a half-century of dissident activism.

"We were sent to Fort Riley, Kansas for sixteen-week basic infantry training in 1953. During the sixth week, one of the soldiers in our platoon had jumped the boat and didn't make it to Korea to shoot the 'Gooks.' Several of my fellow soldiers were ordered by the sergeant to beat up the slacker. I objected, saying, 'Why are you going to let that sergeant make an unthinking mob out of you? Let's talk with him and find out why he didn't go to Korea.' The general had said that 'We're going to make you trained killers obeying every order without thinking.' I said, 'I know what happened because so many people in Germany, France, and Russia obeyed orders and there was terrorism and six million Jews were sent to the gas chamber. I don't think we should do this.' The sergeant paid no attention to what I said.

"Our military officers were backing Joe McCarthy at that time for finding communists and queers in the state department. I told my entire division about the evils of McCarthyism from a liberal point of view. Our sergeant was mad at me because I wouldn't shut up in classes. I had to do thirty all-night KP duties as punishment. But I was winning people over because I wouldn't stop no matter what they did to me. I was organizing without knowing what it was. Eventually, the sergeant said to me, 'you'll never make it this man's army.' I said, 'You may break my body, but you can't break into my spirit.'

"I re-enlisted in counterintelligence. I was an anti-Communist liberal named a group leader for an intelligence analyst program at a counterintelligence school. They were delivering right-wing anti-Communist propaganda to us. I resigned and was sent to Fort Campbell, Kentucky. I once asked for emergency leave to attend to a family problem. They wouldn't give it to me, so I went home anyway. My punishment was to clean a room. I refused. I was court-martialed for being AWOL and sentenced to thirty days in the stockade, a GI prison."

When Marv returned home to finish his education at Macalester College in St. Paul, he had a rude surprise awaiting him. The administration had put a hold on his file. "The dean told me, 'We understand you've had some difficulty in the service. If you want to return to the military, you have to go visit a Veterans' Administration psychiatrist.' I went to the doctor and he wrote a letter to the dean that said he wished he would have had the courage to do what I did and to let me go. They were trying to take the ethics out of my soul. It was a result of McCarthyism. I was learning how society works."

* * *

At the Ten O'Clock Scholar in Dinkytown near the University of Minnesota campus, Marv Davidov spent many a night in the late 1950s watching the performance of a skinny, young nasal-voiced Jewish folkie named Bobbie Zimmerman (later to become Bob Dylan). Marv had more than a musical interest in the singer. He knew him as a friend and neighbor. The two lived next to each other above Gray's Drugstore for a couple of months. "Dylan and (Spider) John Koerner performed at parties I went to. We had a culture of artists, writers, poets and other people into racial politics. Any night, you could find any one of eighty people you want to talk with."

Marv became close friends with a black artist named Mel Geary, rooming with him for a year in 1958 and 1959. Marv was a freelance art dealer and modeled for art classes. One particular experience with Geary stays with Marv to this day. "One day, we were going to have dinner and plan an art show. Mel didn't show up and called me from jail. I went down and bailed him out. He told me he had been out in front of our apartment drinking a can of beer when he saw a couple of white cops and ducked behind a bush. I asked him, 'Why did you duck?' He said, 'Because I'm black, Marv.' We talked much of the night. He told me what is it was like to be a black man in Minneapolis in 1958."

Experiences like this confirmed Marv's sensibility to injustice. He joined the Student Peace Union and Students for Integration. In 1960, he picketed at a

Woolworth's store in Minneapolis to support the Greensboro (North Carolina) sit-ins that eventually opened up segregation in that department store.

"On June 7, 1961, I was hitchhiking from my parents place to Dinkytown. As I was walking to the campus, I saw David Morton, one of the people involved in the sit-in. He told me about a meeting going on right then about Freedom Rides. If I had been there a little later, that would not have happened, and my life would have gone in a different direction. I went with David to the meeting. There were about ten CORE (Congress on Racial Equality) representatives in the room. They were going to Jackson, Mississippi to support the Freedom Rides. When they first asked me to go along, I hesitated. They said, 'Go, man. You'll make history.' I went to a bar that night and talked to forty friends about the trip. They said it was violent down there. But they all agreed that one of us should go and it should probably be me. I decided to take the chance.

"Later, our group of seven, six of us from Minnesota, who were going on the trip held a press conference near the Greyhound bus station in downtown Minneapolis. All of the media was there. I was the oldest of the seven at twenty-nine. The youngest on the trip was eighteen. It was an all-white group.

"The next day, we were in Nashville for an orientation given by black student leaders and for a peace march. We waited in the Negro waiting room in Jackson and sat at the lunch counter. There were rumors that everyone would be taken to a Mississippi state prison. We were arrested with about 100 others. We were put in a cell block where we met our attorney, a black man named Jack Young. He warned us that we would be convicted by an all-white jury. We were, and we got four months in jail and a $200 fine, which I refused to pay. We were driven to Parchman Farm, a 20-thousand acre prison farm. It had desegregated cells for the first time in history, so we were all able to be imprisoned together."

On the first day of his confinement Marv lay on his bunk in the Jackson jail cell listening to the freedom songs wafting through the bars. For hours, he was entranced by the black prisoners and clergy reciting and singing gospels about their struggles. At first, this had become just a way to pass the long lonely hours of confinement. But gradually, the spirituals penetrated his soul. "I felt a surge of human solidarity with people of a different race, people I didn't even know," he recalls. "At that moment, I knew there was no other place I should be on earth. I decided then that I knew what I would do for the rest of my life.

"We all won our freedom with a little help from our friends. Entertainers held concerts around the county to raise money to bail us out, along with some 350 others after forty-five days. When we were released on bail, we were brought back to Jackson where a poor black church had a banquet for us. I thought, 'They're really poor and look at how they're treating us.' When we returned home, there were hundreds of people to meet us. A car caravan took us to a mayor's reception room for a press conference. The whole world was looking at Jackson. It was a major watershed moment in civil rights history. The last day we were in Jackson, 3,000 people from the community came together, and we sang 'We Shall Overcome.' That song is the most meaningful when you're taking risks."

* * *

In October of 1962, in the wake of President Kennedy's Cuban missile crisis, Marv joined a year-long Canada-to-Cuba peace walk sponsored by the Committee for Nonviolent Action. "I joined the walk in upstate New York," he recalls. "In the North, sometimes we would camp out in people's backyards. In the South, it was too dangerous to do that.

"When we reached Georgia in late 1963, twenty-five of us walking with signs about race and Cuba got beat up and shot at and cattle prodded. We were jailed in Macon, Georgia for four or five days, then in Albany, Georgia for two months for daring to walk into the white downtown where Dr. (Martin Luther) King and 1,700 others had been defeated with violence and high bail fines, leaving Albany in shambles. We had black men walking next to white men and women, singing about Cuba and race as we walked along the highway. We were an open target and you never knew what would hit you. We were all arrested and sentenced to spend two months in jail. We fasted in jail for about thirty days then were released. We were told that no integrated group like ours would ever cross into downtown again. We offered a compromise where we would walk one square block into downtown and meet up with some local blacks. That was originally turned down. But a few days later, our offer was accepted, and we walked into downtown without resistance. We had dealt the racist police chief a major defeat.

"A year later, I was back there visiting some friends and I went to see the chief, and we talked about our previous walk into downtown. He said, 'I don't think you accomplished much.' But by then the Negro community bus boycott (after the Rosa Parks incident) had been successful. There were Negro bus drivers and negro cops. The chief thought we had nothing to do with that. But we had everything to do with it. We made history with that walk. We had shown that radical nonviolence at the right moment in history could win a victory."

Marv's civil rights activism led him into other peace and social justice endeavors. He worked with the American Indian Movement, welfare mothers and farmers. He also began to question U.S. involvement in Vietnam and did draft-resistance organizing in Los Angeles. During a radio show appearance, he urged soldiers serving in the war to "immediately desert and we'll get you to Canada." Soon after that, he was visited at his house three times by FBI agents. Nevertheless, he did take one deserter to Canada under risky circumstances and made a public statement that "I am ashamed to be an American."

"Beginning in the mid-1960s, the FBI categorized me as being dangerous to the U.S," Marv explains. "In my FBI file it says that I am nonviolent but in touch with revolutionary groups—all of which isn't true. They were probably referring to the work I have done with the American Indian Movement (AIM) or the draft resistance organizing I did in Los Angeles, or my involvement with black people, welfare mothers and farmers."

After some antiwar activists urged focusing on the involvement of U.S. corporations in war, Marv learned that Honeywell, a large international corporation with its main headquarters in Minneapolis, manufactured the anti-personnel bombs that were being used in Vietnam.

Marv, along with some twenty-five socialists, Catholics, feminists, students, labor unionists, veterans and others got together to form the Honeywell Project as a vehicle for protesting the corporation's bomb-building activity. In September of 1969, project members demonstrated in front of Honeywell's general offices. Leaflets containing stark photos of cluster-bomb victims were given to shareholders entering the meeting. During the meeting, one protestor stood up to say that it was illegal, immoral and inhuman for Honeywell to manufacture armaments for mass destruction. The protestors also attended a city council meeting and demanded that a zoning law be enacted to remove Honeywell from the community. On December 12th, leafleting was done at all the plants, followed by rallies. Protestors and their friends began to buy Honeywell stock and secure voting proxies in order to become a reform movement inside the corporation. The proxies would allow them to attend meetings and speak up.

One day, Marv and 3,000 other demonstrators assembled in a neighborhood park and marched to Honeywell with proxies for one of their members. The police were called and came in riot gear as windows were smashed and security guards used mace. Activists asked the CEO of Honeywell to call off the police, which he eventually did. But in the meantime, the Honeywell meeting came apart and adjourned after fourteen minutes.

Following that major demonstration, the Honeywell project founders sponsored a retreat in Wisconsin attracting activists from various antiwar and anti-corporate groups around the country. They formed a watchdog organization called The Council for Corporate Review (CCR) and asked Honeywell to create a committee on corporate responsibility with community members. Honeywell refused.

In 1971, Clergy and Laity Concerned About the War and the American Friends Service Committee conducted a campaign to stop Honeywell's bomb production. A year later, during a corporate war crimes investigation held at the University of Minnesota, there was testimony about weapons production and involvement by the Campaign for Nuclear Disarmament.

The following year, Honeywell began to respond with a public relations offensive, defending itself against the allegations. There were more antiwar protests, Honeywell demonstrations and speak-outs throughout 1973. But with the end of the Vietnam War, the protests dissipated.

Three years later, The Honeywell Project suspended its activities, but controversy over it continued. The project had been monitored by various law enforcement agencies that had planted informants inside the project from 1969 to 1973 and gave information to Honeywell management and to the U.S. Senate Intelligence Committee. An apparent FBI reference to Davidov described him as "a self-professed instructor of revolutionary nonviolence and an anarchist." In 1977 in Minneapolis, the American Civil Liberties Union sued Honeywell and the FBI, charging them with conspiracy to deny the constitutional rights of antiwar groups, including committing burglary, rumor mongering and infiltration with agent provocateurs. A judge ordered the defendants to provide the names of paid informants and to pay a $70,000 fine. The U.S. government got Honeywell to send half of that fee to the American Friends Service Committee for its program to aid cluster-bomb victims and to remove and diffuse the bombs. All of the protestors, including Davidov, were acquitted of trespass charges filed by Honeywell, although some of them were branded a threat to national defense.

Between November of 1980 and April of 1989 there were 2,300 arrests made relating to the Honeywell project, one-hundred trials, six acquittals and fifty dismissals. Activists spent a total of three years in jail. In June of 1999, Honeywell, unable to sell its weapons-making program, moved its plant from Minneapolis to Morristown, New Jersey, replaced by another weapons manufacturer and protestor target—a company called Alliant Tech, where Marv and others continue to demonstrate regularly to this day.

Marv's further list of activist accomplishments is lengthy and impressive. In the late 1970s, he helped start the Northern Sun Alliance that subsequently stopped Northern States Power Company from building a nuclear power plant in Wisconsin, and marched with Minnesota farmers to protest the construction of high-voltage power lines, again landing him in jail.

In addition, Marv joined the Berkeley, California Vietnam Day Committee and the military draft resistance movement; staffed the Black Hills Alliance, which protects the Lakota Indian tribe from energy exploitation; and most recently, founded the Midwest Institute for Social Transformation (MIST) a nonprofit organization that promotes social change through education on nonviolence.

For the past several years, Marv has been teaching courses on nonviolent action through the Peace and Justice Studies department at The University of St. Thomas in St. Paul, a significant accomplishment considering the socially conservative nature of the Catholic college. In recent months, his determination to stand up for justice has threatened his job at St. Thomas. The college had invited Nobel Peace Prize winner Desmond Tutu to speak at a planned event but then uninvited him when they were told that he had made anti-Semitic remarks in a previous speech—a claim that proved to be unfounded—and the department head, a woman named Chris Tofolo, who had invited Tutu, was fired. Marv was part of a movement to protest the decision through an impressive letter-writing campaign. The college re-invited Tutu, but he refused the invitation unless Chris Tofolo was reinstated. She was not and Tutu gave the speech elsewhere.

At the time of our interview, Marv had recently surpassed a half-century of peace and justice activism, including work with many of the most famous radicals of our time. He continues the frugal, independent, progressive existence he has always treasured, choosing to devote his life to activism rather than raising a family and holding down a regular job, even though it has often meant a hand-to-mouth existence. "The world takes care of me," he says. "I'm supported by the community. When I'm in need, friends have come forth with money and support."

Marv is now a revered elder in the peace and justice community. He has been honored with the (Noam) Chomsky Award For Social Justice, has been featured in many media interviews and films, and is currently writing his memoirs. He is still a constant presence at protests and rallies, continues to receive invitations to speak and to run for political office (which he has turned down), and maintains contact with a veritable who's who of past and present peace activists. As an acknowledgement of his reputation, he still gets threats against his life and, as far as he knows, is still on file with the FBI.

At age seventy-seven, Marv is showing signs of wear and tear. His remaining twin flocks of hair are pure white on the edges of a balding pate. His voice is raspy from years of smoking and speaking out. He is on kidney dialysis and on the waiting list for a transplant. "But I don't let that stop me from doing my work," he says. "I will never retire from this. It is my life."

Like many older activists, Marv sees his main task as paving the way for the next generation to take over and build the movement. "I have realized that we can't change society in its current form," he says. "We must have a drastic change in government from the way it has been for the past fifty years. We need to build a revolution. It is probably a hundred years away from happening. That's every reason to begin today. When I'm teaching I tell stories about my experiences and say to the kids, 'When we were your age, look at what we did. You can do that.'" One of the stories Marv tells nowadays drives home that message:

A few years ago, I went with some of the original Freedom Riders to Jackson, Mississippi to visit the prison we had been held in forty years ago. They opened the cell block and we all walked in together. Then everybody joined hands and sang freedom songs on Jackson TV. The government proclaimed Freedom Ride Month with city council members, a black mayor and cop present. Then we went to the courtroom where all of us had been tried. Students from the University of Mississippi came to do a black history project with each of us. A black elected official we met said to us, "We would not be sitting here except for the risks all of you took." Later, friends would say, 'Thanks for what you did for me and my family.' I said, 'I did it for me first. This is what I believe. I had to act.'"

Lu marches for immigrant rights
(Photo courtesy of Lu Samaniego)

LU'S FREEDOM SPEECH
By Angela Andrist

I was kneeling down, cleaning floors. I wondered, "What am I doing here. I am not trained for this job. In the Philippines, I was a professor with a PhD.; here, I am cleaning floors for minimum wage, $5 per hour."

—Lu Samaniego

Shortly after the Immigrant Workers Freedom Ride, I interviewed Lu Samaniego following his church service at the Church of Christ in Rochester, which also served as a meeting room for his Local 21 union meetings. We sat under red white and blue banners that edged the ceiling, and near a union sign on the wall that read:

Freedom to Choose

No Freedom - No Choice - No Voice - No Future

We All Deserve Better.
Local 21 – H.E.R.E.

Lu was neatly dressed in a light gray suit with a brightly colored tie. Several gold rings adorned his fingers and sparkled like his eyes behind his glasses when he talked about his life experiences. I was anxious to hear about his Freedom Ride. I soon realized, however, that it was his activism in the Philippine Islands decades ago where his real freedom story began.

He was born Luvimino Sunio near a small village in the Sagay, the oldest of twelve brothers and sisters. After the Japanese occupation of the Philippines, his parents left him with the Samaniegos, a childless family that owned the house they shared. Lu was three years old at the time. His natural born father relocated to a settlement farm and received twelve acres from the government to grow corn, cotton, mangos and coconut trees. In Mindanao, eighty percent of the people were family farmers. Lu's "foster" parents raised him. He enrolled in the seminary and went on to major in philosophy and theology. Lu never heard from his biological family again until he was in college, when he received one letter from them telling him, "We left you and want you to treat (the Samaniegos) as your parents." He took Samaniego as his surname.

That was the last contact Lu had with his biological parents until he invited them to his ordination from the seminary to become a Catholic priest. This would be the first time he had seen them since they abandoned him when he was three years old. They were the only members of his family to attend his ordination and his first Mass in 1963.

Lu served as a priest on Negros Island from 1964-68. While studying with the Jesuits, he became involved with social and community action. He worked with the sugar cane workers and in mills with various activist groups. Lu witnessed the "haves (Haciendaros) and have-nots," who were the poor, exploited laborers. He organized a group in 1967 and got the media involved documenting injustices all over Negros Island. The bishop then assigned him to be an urban development leader. Liberal parties met in Quiapo while President Ferdinand Marcos had soldiers terrorize them during their meeting by tossing hand grenades. Lu became more involved with activism shortly after President Marcos created the "New Constitution" and declared martial law to perpetuate his power.

Lu spent most of the 1970s and 1980s denouncing the government as an enemy and repeating the slogan: "Down with Imperialism and the Bourgeoisie." He created an acronym, DOPE, "D" for Deprived or Depressed, "O" for Oppressed, "P" for Persecution, Poverty or Poor, and "E" for Exploited. When the bishop told him to "simmer down with the activism," Lu refused, claming that he had seen the poor and oppressed. He had seen people killed. He had to speak out on their behalf. Many of Lu's fellow priests hated him for standing up for his beliefs. "I was alone," he says. "I thought the Church was supposed to help the poor." Disillusioned, he left the ministry. Meanwhile, some of the priests that agreed with him donated money to build settlements in the mountains, gave land to farmers, and built schools and clinics.

Free from the restrictions of the cloth, Lu stepped up his efforts against the government. He joined the N.P.A. (The National People's Army), rallying priests and political activist groups to action. Many of the participating priests were apprehended or killed or escaped into the mountains. The climax was the assassination of Benigno Aquino on an airport tarmac.

President Fernando Marcos had to declare martial law due to the unrest in the streets everyday near the presidential palace. Lu mobilized chapters all over Manila, including drivers, students, teachers, and doctors. His activism was recognized throughout the Philippines and he was on "Marcos' list of 10." (Like a most-wanted list.) He told his family, "I am not afraid if I die for the cause!" He coordinated with fifty-six churches to be liberated from Marcos and martial law, holding meetings at the church where he had been a pastor, organizing rallies and offering food—while taking time out to earn a master's degree and PhD in Theology at the Manila Theological School and become a professor.

Lu recounts an incident while teaching in Manila when activists and citizens stormed the presidential palace. "They tore the barbed wire down with their bare hands. They were disappointed when they found out that Marcos had been airlifted to Clark Air force Base and then escaped to Hawaii. The chief of staff didn't want to follow Marcos. Soldiers were sent to EDSA Highway, where millions of Filipinos stood praying and blocking the tanks. They begged not to be shot down as helicopters flew overhead. The tanks stopped moving and the helicopters landed. The soldiers said, 'We are with you.' 'We won't kill you.'"

The American Embassy had been closed, and not until martial law ended with the Aquino Administration did Lu get his petition approved. Lu had waited twenty years for the immigration department to process his papers so that he could migrate to the United States. He felt stressed by the small window of opportunity to get processed and from a lack of money. He was finally interviewed and arrived in his port of entry in September of 1996. He had a temporary working VISA with his passport and received a green card within a month.

Lu lived free of charge in a hotel managed by his sister-in-law in Rochester, Minnesota and had a difficult time adjusting to the harsh winter. "Knowing only new family members, I missed my three children in the Philippines and became lonely after three months. I had no work, no money. Friends and clergy at the United Church of Christ offered me fellowship and used clothes to wear. I was surviving only through the generosity of others. I felt like a beggar. In the Philippines, I had an office with a secretary and maids. I had dignity.

"When I finally got a job, it was at the Salvation Army, sorting clothes through Green Thumb, an organization that helps seniors look for work. One day while I was kneeling down cleaning floors, I wondered, 'What am I doing here? I am not trained for this job. In the Philippines I was a professor. Here I am cleaning floors for minimum wage, $5.00 per hour. In the Philippines, this would be a low job, a janitor.' I found it was different in America. I enjoyed my first dollar."

It looked like Lu's life would turn around in 1997 when he became a resident pastor C.P.E at a Minneapolis hospital. "It's like a chaplain. I felt at the level of the doctors." He left the hotel where he was staying and got his own apartment. He attended the weddings of a son and daughter back in the Philippines. But when he finally returned to the U.S., his position was gone. Once again, he had to start over. He took a job as a food service worker at the Mayo Clinic. "I was not trained for the food service job and bungled the job. The only thing that kept me going was telling myself, 'God wants me here.' I accepted it as another field for me."

The long, tedious hours Lu spent bent over piles of dishes in the Mayo Clinic turned out to be a blessing in disguise. In his spare time, he became a union activist, attending meetings at the local Church of Christ. That eventually led to his taking over as a pastor at the church.

When his union was looking for people to go on the re-enacted Immigrant Freedom Ride (Hundreds of people went to Washington, D.C. to meet with their members of Congress about the need for comprehensive immigration reform), Lu jumped at the chance. He recognized the Freedom Ride agenda as "legalization, a road to citizenship, reconciliation of families, civil rights and organizing the workers. Educate immigrants, get in touch with their problems in the short term, and get organized in the long term."

Lu witnessed his co-workers, including many Latinos, "vanishing" at work. "I see, I feel, I know it's real. They are coming to me. Respect us, our dignity as human beings. Human dignity IS the American Dream. Don't manipulate us during election time to get our vote. It takes time to become a citizen; meanwhile, we're paying taxes. Don't count the $100-$300 rebate; that's just temporary. No rebates, except for the wealthy. Political process is a long change. It must start at the local level. In the Philippines, when people were fed up, it turned into violence. Terrorism in the Philippines is a police matter. Fighting terrorism is not new anymore in the Philippines. We experienced bombing. I saw Muslim rebels destroy bridges, mega malls, schools and banks. In the streets of Manila, in broad daylight, teachers were kidnapped and killed. I tell the Americans don't tell us the way you want it according to YOUR image. Leave us alone. Give us the money, but leave us alone. We are not beggars, thank you. We are a democracy.

"In the Philippines, I am 'Luvimino,' which stands for the three islands, LU (Luzon), VI (Visaiyan), Min (Mindanao). The Americans colonized us. In America, I am not Luvimino. I am Lu, Luey, Love. America is a nation of immigrants whether you like it or not. We are building America through justice, equality, peace and prosperity. The American dream!" I pictured this as Lu's freedom speech.

At that moment, Lu opens his King James Bible and, as a way of explaining the Christian principles that have guided him, reads his favorite inspiration from Philippians 4:8. "Labor is honor. To work is honor." He zips up his Bible in a case embroidered with the last line of the poem "Footprints:"

When you saw only one set of footprints…it was then that I carried you.

Nicole Ly at work
(Photo courtesy of Nicole Ly)

I CAN DO THIS
By Angela Andrist

Nicole Ly is living proof that you can't tell a book by its cover. She speaks softly, almost inaudibly at times and seems uncomfortable with strangers, although her smile could easily light up a room. The day I meet with her, she is dressed in a plain navy shirt, and her dark hair is pulled back, exposing a mole in the center of her forehead. But hidden beneath her shy, plain-appearing demeanor is a fighter. Behind the scenes, this young woman has been a powerful leader in her native Hmong community. Her journey of slightly over two decades has already demonstrated hope and inspiration to all those she has encountered along the way.

Nicole's parents emigrated from Laos to a Thailand refugee camp during the Vietnam War. The government wouldn't let them go back to Laos, and most Hmong had to get sponsorship to come to America. Fortunately, Nicole had a great-uncle in America who sponsored her family.

Born in Philadelphia, Nicole moved with her family to St. Paul in 1980 before she was a year old. She was a middle child, seventh oldest of ten brothers and sisters. Her mother assumed the traditional role of raising the children, while her father worked for a St. Paul food production company. Being a bridge in the middle is a role Nicole has played in many capacities.

Nicole's early influences centered around family. Education has been important for Nicole and her siblings. As a child, she would blame herself for not fitting in at school. If she only studied harder and learned better English, then maybe the kids wouldn't perceive her as different, with an accent. It was hard to fit in when her family was poor, "in and out of borderline poverty, living in a crappy apartment building," she recalls. "Children should not have to worry about money problems, about not being cold at night." She chuckled about wanting to fit in with new clothing styles, but she was happy just to get clothes passed down to her from older siblings.

Nicole had a great deal of support from her family and the Hmong community. (She explains that the Hmong word for *cousins* was like, "Your dad's cousin's kids, twice removed….") She focused on getting good grades in school and making her parents and siblings proud of her, "to give back to them."

But some of her experiences in school were less satisfactory. She had a "bad history teacher" who "spent only twenty minutes talking about the Vietnam War," even though her school in St. Paul and the adjoining neighborhood had a huge Hmong population. She did not question the teacher at first. Then she got mad. "I could do better than that!" she thought. She went to the University of Minnesota Morris to become a history teacher. But she was again disillusioned once she realized that she would still feel constrained by "the system." She switched her major to Human Services.

That decision influenced Nicole's future path. She fostered her love of Hmong history through other channels. She traveled to China to study Hmong culture and work with Hmong youth. "It was transformative. I learned about the French/Indo China war." The statistics astounded her, that Hmong history goes back 5,000 years, and there are over seven million Hmong people living in China. She hadn't connected with the idea of Hmong being in China. She could only understand about twenty percent of what was said by the Hmong people in Ghanzou Province of Southern China, due to the different dialects. She learned about Hmong heroes that led revolts. She climbed a mountain and stood where a battle had taken place surrounded by a stone wall. Touching the wall made it all real for her. She was saddened that mainstream American and Hmong youth had missed the rich history of her people and their fight against oppression. "People don't want us to be here, but we work through it and have the strength to overcome. It's amazing."

Nicole's passion focuses on anything that affects her family: health care, Medicare and education. She is disturbed by the cuts that have taken place in those services. Her sister is in college and can't get financial aid. She worries about money, instead of studying, and may have to switch schools.

Language remains one of the biggest barriers for Nicole's family. Her mother took classes for the citizen's test at the Jane Adams School for Democracy and was confused by the language difficulties. Nicole went with her one day to help translate. She found that the same things that confused her mother confused both Hmong and non-Hmong immigrants.

Nicole thought there had to be a better way. She got her fellow Humboldt High School students to work with the immigrants as part of a community service project. Students translated and took care of the kids, while the parents attended class. Nicole is credited with bringing Humboldt to Jane Adams. She admits liking Jane Adams' philosophy of "Everybody is a learner *and* a teacher. It's about knowledge and cultural exchange." She also loves the idea of the different generations working together. "I always learn from others, especially in the Hmong community. I learn about culture and history. I want to inspire people at the grassroots level to get others to do things, to get off their butts! To quote Gandhi: 'To be the change that you want to see.'"

Nicole is currently a Hmong community and political organizer for Progressive Minnesota, whose mission is a commitment to bringing about social and economic justice through community organizing, education, coalition building and elections. The hardest part of her job "is getting the Hmong community away from social service and into activism. With huge state service cuts, it's not a priority for them to vote. They're focused on getting food and shelter. It's about teaching them to fish. It's ongoing and not about one issue. I want them not to say what is bad, but teach them how they can change it. I get others involved, get groups organized. I explain the system, who to go to, which officials, school board or leaders."

Nicole draws her inspiration from other Hmong leaders like Senator Mee Moua from the St. Paul's East Side, the first-ever elected Hmong politician. It impressed her that Mee Moua not only campaigned to the "white folks;" she reached out to the Hmong community in her district and furthered political awareness. Nicole gives credit to her predecessor, Pa Kou Hang, who helped to get Moua elected. "These are strong women. They try to balance between the Hmong community and mainstream America. Respecting the old ways *and* the new ways. We need both ways."

Although Nicole doesn't want to be a politician, preferring to stay out of the spotlight, she knows the future of her community is about politics as a power source. It is now understood that to get things done, mainstream leaders need the Hmong community's vote. That's hard to do that when such a small percentage of Hmong people get involved.

At Progressive Minnesota, Nicole was part of the biggest voter mobilization in the state. "They got a lot of Hmong to vote. It is important to build political power for the Hmong community."

Nicole was the only Hmong representative to go on the 2003 Immigrant Workers' Freedom Ride. She described the Freedom Ride as a group of immigrants that went to various cities speaking with people already involved in or just learning about immigrant issues. The purpose of the ride, she said, was to get change done at the federal level to enhance rights in the work place, civil rights, citizenship and family reunification. "By not having more representation on the Freedom Ride, the Hmong community missed a huge opportunity, especially since St. Paul has the biggest Hmong population in the nation."

For Nicole, the most interesting part of the ride was listening to the personal stories of those on board, such as one from a woman who had not seen her children in over four years.

She believes that another wave of Hmong immigrants will soon be coming to this country from the refugee camps in Thailand. The need for help from community services and families will be a priority. At the time of this interview, she was planning to participate in a Hmong fundraising event where elected officials, including Senator Moua, and the Hmong community would get to know and support each other.

One stereotype/myth Nicole would like to change is that the Hmong are just here to receive services from their new country. "We've contributed to America. We've given back through economics, culture and family values. Thousands of Hmong have been 'educated' in the American system and have become doctors, lawyers, teachers, and elected officials."

Nicole draws most of her strength from her family. Her eyes light up as she talks about their accomplishments. Her second-oldest brother, with only a ninth-grade education, got a college degree in computer science at Metro State. Her sister went back for her GED *and* raised six children, five of them now in college or postsecondary school. She's been a role model for Nicole, both as a successful mom *and* career woman. Another sister has inspired Nicole to work with youth. She credits another brother for pushing her into college, showing her the way through the system to apply for grants and scholarships. Nicole's life is about action. She sums it up best in four words: "I can do this."

LIGHTING THE WAY

By Angela Andrist

...as immigrants, we're supporting the economy. We're not here to destroy it, but to build it...If they really say this is a country of prosperity, why don't they give us an opportunity to do it, experience it, to fulfill our dreams and our goals?

—Oscar Hugo Roman

Oscar was packing boxes again. He was leaving his small apartment in the western suburbs of the Twin Cities to move in with his mother in south Minneapolis. He had to leave shortly for church to practice for a concert later that evening but was anxious to show me some lyrics he was working on.

In his apartment was an electric keyboard on the floor next to a few half-filled boxes. He grabbed a notebook off his keyboard with notes and lyrics. His couch faced a television with a shrine of photos of family and friends. He picked up a tablet full of pictures he had sketched of beautiful tropical sunsets, faces, abstract objects and religious artifacts. Many of the pages had different sayings such as: *Our life is like a flower. Today it was born...tomorrow is gone.* "We must live each day to the fullest, as it may be our last," Oscar said.

He rummaged on a shelf for what he called "his thoughts," written both in English and Spanish. Another collection of writings and drawings contained a multicolored watercolor painting that read, "God's idea of good is hope and help and assurance of salvation. He will never withhold peace, help, hope and power...to trust him no matter what." This was by a favorite author named Joni, a quadriplegic woman. The last sketch was of a hand holding a candle. "Lighting the Way!" it read in bold letters. He wrote in Spanish underneath "Encendiendo un hombre. Apacionado por terner mas de Dios."

As he shared his thoughts and artwork, he talked about destiny. His knowledge of world affairs, conspiracy theories, metaphysics, and spirituality seemed far beyond his twenty-one years and limited education. He referred to the world to come after 9/11 when terrorists—he called them "enemies of the United States"—destroyed our symbols of power, the Twin Towers, the Pentagon, and they tried to destroy the White House. He then expounded on the future of this country.

Thinking about the future and his own convictions were years away when his father left him, his mother and siblings in Mexico when Oscar was three years old. He was again abandoned when his mother left him to work in America, cleaning, ironing and doing odd jobs in warehouses. He gives his mother credit for building his strong and independent personality. Coincidently, Guerrero, the town he was from in Mexico, means "warrior."

His brow furrowed as he explained that his grandma, aunts and cousins had raised him. Oscar felt they were "bad" people who treated him like he wasn't part of the family. He had to be strong and prove himself. All the kids around him were hanging out, lazy. As an impressionable teenager, he could have chosen smoking, drinking and/or being in gangs. Gangs would have been the easy choice. Instead, Oscar wanted to be a role model for his three younger brothers—to show his relatives he could become something. He worked hard in school in Mexico, got the best grades and planned on going to college. He wanted to follow his dream of being a teacher of biology or music. He embraced the love of science, ecology and geography; he dreamed of becoming an astronomer, exploring the universe, planets and stars.

Oscar's uncle, his only role model, was a talented carpenter in Mexico, who built houses and furniture and fixed electronics but was also an artist, who painted and wrote poetry. This artistic side would be the palette for Oscar's self expression, motivating him to study hard, do whatever it takes to succeed. Instead of going to college in Mexico, Oscar immigrated at age seventeen to the United States in 1999 to finally be with his mother.

"I spoke no English," he recalls. "My older sister, Patricia, who was already in the U.S., would interpret for me when I wanted to buy things at the grocery store. I didn't like being dependent on her. One day, she told me that she was sick of talking for me and I would have to learn to speak for myself. I went to school for one year as a freshman in high school and learned to speak English. I actually feared for my life around gangs, and had trouble adapting to the diversity in school. I was scared of being in the middle of white people, black people and Asian people with me speaking Spanish. When I would experience discrimination, I said, 'It's not about your size, your color, or the color of your eyes, it's about down here in your heart, and up here in your head.'"

Oscar chose not to follow the gangs. It took him only one year to learn to write, read and speak English. He shaped his grammar skills over the next three years. Unfortunately, he was forced to drop out of high school after his freshman year to help his mother and half-sisters, and send money back to his brothers in Mexico.

Oscar's dream to establish a career "hit a big wall" that he couldn't break through. He had no Social Security number for governmental financial aid and paid double tuition as a foreigner with pending immigration status, due to the changing environment between the United States and Mexico after 9/11.

After working for two years, he decided that graduating from high school was still part of his dream. He worked in an Independent Study Program to get his diploma. Part of his school requirements enabled him to work on an English grammar project. His ability to communicate and work with other students so impressed his teachers, they gave him a job as an assistant teacher. This finally seemed like a step in the right direction, until they chose to lay him off due to reduced federal funding from lack of enrollment. To financially help his mother, he has since found a delivery job at a company that sells organizational furniture and shelves. A delivery job seems far from his path of teaching and exploring the universe.

But this young warrior did not lose his spirit. "If you fight, you'll get what you want…if you don't get it, just keep on fighting. Just don't give up. When one door closes, a window will open. Even though things get worse during your journey, when you find barriers and obstacles, just kick them and punch them, and get them out of your way; keep on moving and don't ever give up. There is always hope."

Oscar further talked about the plight of the immigrant. "I want the government, people, the Congress, to know as immigrants, we're supporting the economy. We're not here to destroy it, but to build it. This country has been built with immigrants. If they really say this is a country of prosperity, why don't they give us an opportunity to do it, experience it, to fulfill our dreams and our goals? I want them to know there are good and bad people. I consider myself one of the good people. I never did anything to this country. I'm a good citizen. I consider this to be my country too, because I take care of it. I really want to go to school and make a career. I want to make a difference for the country, and for my community, my minority community. I want to make a difference, to support our country for the future, to help others, to be a role model for my sisters and to make my mom proud of me.

"With my capacity, my intelligence, I know my dreams are reachable. I can get there. I'm not afraid of school or learning a new subject." He draws upon his church and his music for inspiration. "Music is my passion; it's in my blood…It gives me strength to go on." He taught himself to play the guitar at age thirteen by learning three chords from a pastor at another church, who inspired him to play. He is now the music director at his church and has a band. He plays the guitar, piano, accordion, bass, drums and other percussion instruments.

Oscar has a philosophy about his journey. "Life is your destiny to go from point A to B, but sometimes we end up at point F. There are only two paths in his life. When someone knocks, I answer. When someone calls out my name, I answer. When I search, I will find. I'm just not sure how long it will take."

As he walked to the door of his half-empty apartment, Oscar picked up a black-and-white picture of a park path he had photographed. On the back of the photo in a frame he also made himself, is the following:

Although our journey is long and we may find suffering along the way... our hope awaits at the very END...of the road...hang in there. Jesus is there with you....Oscar H. Roman.

Chapter Four
Freedom Fighters

Belma Demirovic on a built replica of the Old Bridge in Mostar, Bosnia-Herzegovina (Photo courtesy of Belma Demirovic)

THE TREE INSIDE THE BUILDING
By William Wroblewski

So much suffering was put upon us. What was done to my family and all Bosnian families was unjust.

—Belma Demirovic

Leaving their families and horse carts near the road, three men stepped to the door nearest to the entrance of a typical, Soviet-style apartment building. The nameplate below the peephole indicated the first name Goran, a good Serb name. One of the men rapped his tired, dirty hand on the door's hard wood.

The pounding woke fifteen-year-old Belma Demirovic from her sleep. It was 8:30 a.m., and her parents were gone for the day. Her brother had left for good, and she was home alone. She opened the door, and standing in the threshold were mysterious men, the one in front very tall and wearing a jacket of the old Yugoslav Army. His deep blue eyes seemed to jump out from his tan face. A pack of filthy children watched from nearby.

"Good morning," the man said.

Belma greeted him, nervously hiding her lanky frame behind the open door. He adjusted the rifle hanging over his shoulder and asked, "Are there any Muslims living in this building?"

She told him she didn't know of any, one eye tracing her Serb uncle's name her father had placed on the door, a practice that was becoming more commonplace in the dissipating numbers of Muslim homes in Banja Luka. They allowed her to close the door. A moment later, the men were gone.

"Generally, any good nationalist Serb would have told of any Muslims that were living around there," Belma says now. "They just happened to ring the wrong door. Had they known who I was, they would have evicted my family from our home."

Unexpected visitors were becoming a routine in Belma's neighborhood. It was 1995, and elsewhere in the country bombs were falling, entire towns were on the move, and ethnic cleansing was being performed at a level not seen in Europe since World War II.

Yugoslavia, a communist nation known in particular for its industries, resources, and its grab bag of Roman Catholics, Orthodox Christians, and Muslims, was dissipating and its people facing an uncertain future. With this uncertainty came cultural, political and economic conflict, ultimately leading to war throughout Bosnia in the early 1990s.

For decades, ethnicity and religion were of no consequence in Yugoslavia, but in the post-communist days, it meant everything. For an ethnically mixed Bosnia, this meant that three groups claimed rights to one land, and while some sought to resolve this in a peaceful manner, others found bullets and grenades more appropriate. While many Bosnians still struggled to grasp what had happened to their beautiful land, 250,000 civilians were killed and 1.2 million displaced.

In the supposed UN safe haven of Srebrenica, a systematic and deadly operation of Serb militias was forcing Muslims from their homes. Despite the protection of Danish troops, close to 8,000 Muslim men and boys fell victim to Serbian ethnic cleansing. Once the world learned of the events that took place in Srebrenica in July 1995, they described them as genocide. The white, pristine snow that covered the land was splattered with the blood of thousands of children and elderly who were besieged by the Serb forces and who firmly believed that the world would not let these atrocities happen.

On that summer morning, Belma saw things that reaffirmed her belief that the city of Banja Luka would never be the same and that the place she called home was no longer hers. After the visitors left her doorway, she dressed herself and stepped outside. The sun was shining, the sky was clear, and the trees on the street swayed in the morning breeze. Yet, there was something noticeably different about this place.

"Pigs were on the front lawn," she recalls. "People with horse buggies were scattered about. This sight was surreal. These people somehow appeared overnight. They came unannounced."

Belma was witness to a mass exodus of ethnic Serbs expelled from their land by the Croatian army. Many of the estimated 140,000-250,000 peasants and soldiers were slowly flowing in the direction of Serbia, transecting Serb and non-Serb areas of Bosnia. Along the way, many families stopped their journey in search of a new place to settle. Some has stopped in Banja Luka, and were now eating lunch and resting their horses on Belma's lawn.

Soon, it was Belma's turn to leave in search of a safe place to live in the United States. More than a decade has passed since her departure, and even today she struggles to accept what happened to her family and her home. Her experiences have given her a deep understanding of conflict and of people facing similar situations elsewhere. Had the Bosnian war never ignited, she may have been a doctor back in Banja Luka. Instead, she went West, where she is now an American professional dancer and human rights activist with a compelling story to tell.

* * *

Banja Luka is the second largest city in Bosnia, a hilly and wooded community of a quarter million people bisected by the Vrbas river. The city's name dates back to the late fifteenth century, when much of this region was under Turkish control. It was a quiet city where ethnic Muslims lived side-by-side with sizeable populations of Croats and Serbs, as well as smaller groups of Kosovars and other ethnic minorities. "Both of my parents were successful," Belma says. "They were typical folk who worked hard, lived and loved life, and always looked toward to a better future. We lived modestly, but I felt we had everything we wanted."

Belma's mother was a technician who worked with electronic blueprints, and her father managed imports and exports for an automobile manufacturer. His job allowed him to travel outside of Yugoslavia, frequently taking business trips to Austria and Germany. Several times a year, Belma's family would take beach vacations on the Adriatic Sea or skiing trips to Bosnia's numerous ski slopes. As a child, Belma spent many weekends relaxing in her uncle's cabin outside Banja Luka.

The Demirovic home was in an apartment building fifteen minutes from downtown Banja Luka. As a child, Belma's playmates included Muslims Serbs, and Croats. Their parents worked in the same factories and offices, and most cultural differences were whitewashed. Belma and her friends considered themselves, simply, Yugoslavs.

Talkative and smart, Belma did very well in school, and her family had high ambitions for her. She spent most of her childhood with her grandmother, Mina, who watched over her while her parents were at work. Belma helped her grandmother make pies of all kinds—spinach, meat, cheese. While making the flaky crusts, she and her grandmother would slowly roll out the dough by hand, often consuming an afternoon. "When we would start to make the dough, there were things Grandma would say to bless it, to make it turn out good," Belma remembers. With dough between their fingers and the oven warming, Grandma would briefly say a blessing, "Bismilla."

At this time, Banja Luka was home to seventeen mosques, whose minarets pierced through the trees and rooftops of the city's skyline. Over the years, particularly with the onset of Communist rule following World War II, religious traditions faded, though older generations and small, rural communities quietly held onto them. To Belma, Islam was part of her culture, not a religion. "We were religious during holidays and special occasions, but that's about it," she says.

Belma and her parents did not follow the rules of the Muslim faith. They grew up in and embraced a secular Yugoslavia where "brotherhood and unity" had no religious or ethnic undertones. But Belma's grandmother's generation was more in touch with tradition. Belma says, "Grandma didn't complain much, and she tried to make the best of everything. I know she wasn't happy that being Muslim was unpopular, but she didn't let that bother her too much; she just wanted access to the things she wanted to provide for her family.

"When I was very little, I sometimes prayed with her. This helped with occasional boredom during the winter months, and I learned to say a few prayers in Arabic—with a heavy Slavic accent. I didn't know what these prayers meant, but I think Grandma knew. I thought of religion as something Grandma and Grandpa did. It didn't affect me in any real way. But I liked the tradition aspect of it: Like many people, my grandparents found comfort in the rules of their faith. And I accepted Islam as just something that Grandma and Grandpa did. I now realize that I had found comfort in hearing the 'Allah,' as it brought peace to my grandparents' lives, and it helped them believe in the goodness of all people." That was a lesson that Belma carried with her throughout the tumultuous years in Bosnia and in her later life in the United States.

* * *

Yugoslavia began to unravel with the secessions of Slovenia and Croatia in 1991. A referendum in March of 1992, supported by Bosnia's Muslims and Croats but boycotted by its Serbs, declared the independence of Bosnia and Herzegovina from Yugoslavia. Elsewhere, in the governing halls of Belgrade and Zagreb, some leaders in the forming sovereign powers of Serbia and Croatia were unofficially developing their own plans to split Bosnia in two, creating homogenous Serb and Croat areas to be annexed by their respective states. It became clear that to nationalist Catholic and Orthodox Christians, Bosnian Muslims were a boulder in the road, the "Turks" that needed to be controlled, expelled, or even terminated.

In Bosnia, rural Serb populations began moving into cities either at the urging of Serb leaders or after being expelled by Croats, pushing Muslims from their homes. The rise of Serb nationalism, and the aggression it heralded, trapped Bosnian Muslims into a corner, where their desire to maintain a multi-ethnic society collided head-on with the Serb agenda.

The streets of Sarajevo became a lightning rod of conflict and would remain that way until the war's end. In 1992, as Sarajevo Muslims, Croats, and Serbs peacefully marched through the city in support of a peaceful, inclusive Bosnia and Herzegovina, they were bombed from the mountains surrounding the city. Sixty-eight people were killed, and dozens injured. Serb forces pounded Bosnia's cosmopolitan center with shells and bullets from April 1992 until November 1995. Showers of gunfire and blasts of mortars became a frightening reality for the city's residents as they attempted to survive the war years.

The aggression toward the Muslims in Banja Luka was different, though no less oppressive, than the sniper shots that rained in from the hills surrounding Sarajevo. As the Yugoslav economy came to a halt, many Serbs from the countryside made their way to cities in search of work, also serving the Serb expansion plans being drafted in Belgrade. Banja Luka's ethnic makeup was changing.

Soon, Banja Luka became an important part of the new Serb Republic of Bosnia. The takeover of Banja Luka was both a strategic and symbolic victory for the Serbs. In fact, Serbs soon set up a mint in Banja Luka and started printing a new currency in that city.

In Belma's eyes everything was changing so fast, it felt like she had been transported to a different galaxy. What used to be known as the Yugoslav People's Army was now the Serb military. The area's energy, natural resources and even manpower were soon put to work in the Serb war effort. Shortly after the war in Bosnia started, Banja Luka was lacking everything—from food and fuel to clothes and supplies. The new government was rationing supplies and energy. Cities were plagued with outages and shortages, and most conveniences of modern living had disappeared.

Short supplies, high demands, and a soaring unemployment rate required families to quickly sell off luxury goods, such as the family car, to purchase expensive fuel and food for the long blackouts and cold winters. At the peak of the blackouts, in the winter of 1993, Banja Luka went forty-three straight days without power.

"I can remember that as if it were yesterday," Belma says. "We had no electricity, no radio and no television. To accommodate for lack of refrigeration, people started building shelves outside their windows so they could keep their food cold. Our homes were very cold without heat. We had no laundry driers. And if we did, what were we going to plug it into? We had all this laundry that could not be dried."

Belma's father installed an old wooden stove in the living room of the apartment, drilling a hole in the wall to pull the chimney through. He managed to buy wood and store it in the garage, but it was all of low-quality; green and wet, and did not burn very well. The stove's black smoke would crawl up and stain the walls, leaving black soot and a scratchy smell in the apartment. Every summer, Belma's family managed to repaint and disinfect the walls. "You couldn't keep looking at the walls. It was nasty," she says, scrunching her nose and shaking her head.

"I remember the summer my dad got fired and basically put under house arrest for three months. My dad is not the kind of man who spends much time inside. He works all the time. Seeing him locked inside our home for three months was hard on all of us emotionally. He was getting depressed because he didn't know what to do. He felt he couldn't protect or provide for his family, and we could all sense it. The income wasn't coming from anywhere. These circumstances made my adolescent years difficult. I remember wishing for everything. Like most teenagers, I wanted things and I had no access to anything."

In her high school class of thirty-five, Belma was one of two Muslims. Enrolled in a pre-med program, she had an internship at the local hospital, where she helped nurse Serb soldiers coming in from the front lines. Belma was afraid the soldiers would find out she was a Muslim, and she was in constant fear of a classmate divulging her ethnicity to the patients. "It is a fear you have in the back of your mind," she explains. "We were teenagers who hold grudges for silly reasons, and I could never be sure that no one would point out my ethnicity or what kind of reaction that would provoke." She covered up her nametag to hide her identity.

"I used to study six hours a day. I used studying to tune out the war. But I also daydreamed about how great it would be to study medicine without a war hanging over my head. At that time, I didn't study issues of human rights and conflict, I lived them."

Throughout the war, Bosnians had little knowledge of what was going outside of their own neighborhoods. The struggle of day-to-day survival left them with no time for books or newspapers. "My dad would hook up car batteries to power a radio," Belma says. "But the signal was too weak. We had no access to real information. We felt isolated."

What was going on was one of the largest and most violent population shifts in modern history. As a result of the war, nearly 1.4 million people were on the move, either to other villages or cities, or exiled to refugee camps throughout Europe or new homes in the United States and elsewhere. Many unfortunate families, often villages at a time, wandered lost through the thick hills, unsure of where they were going or if they would even survive.

After completing high school, Belma's brother Dženet faced a mandatory military draft, a proposition that would have made him a forced laborer on the front lines, digging trenches, hauling supplies, and taking bullets for Serb forces. He hid for months in their grandmother's house. In Serb-controlled Bosnia, a young man had to hide from the Army but would have no problem purchasing a bus ticket and simply leaving.

This is one of the many paradoxes of forcing the creation of an ethnically homogenous state, a process that trapped Bosnian Muslims between the eager hope of a new life elsewhere and the deepening sadness of leaving what for generations they had called home. "There were organized ways to export people out of their hometowns," Belma says. "This strategy was a key part of ethnic cleansing—you provide the oppressed population with means to leave, and by doing so, they help you cleanse regions. And in the process, you force them to pay extraordinary sums of money for their escape."

In August 1995, the family had scraped together enough money for a bus ticket to get Dženet out of Bosnia. After a week of being held by Bosnian Serbs, he found himself in a Hungarian refugee camp, one of the only places in Europe still accepting those fleeing the Balkans.

By November, the Dayton Peace Accords were signed, and the fighting had subsided. But the mood in Banja Luka remained tense, and the edgy weight of uncertainty lay in the air. Belma recalls, "It was still very unsafe. People continued to walk around with Kalashnikovs (Soviet-designed assault rifles) hanging off their necks. Muslims were still being kicked out of their houses because of their ethnic background. There were no jobs. Things weren't getting any better."

For Belma's parents, both without any income, the need to leave was growing stronger. "They had lived there for fifty years, and their families had lived there even longer," Belma says, "But my parents no longer knew anyone in our city."

With Belma's brother resettled in the United States, the family decided to leave and join him in Minneapolis. They left late one Saturday night in September 1996. Friends came over to say goodbye, and they ate dinner at a relative's house. Belma and her mother walked home together, crossing the Zeleni Most, or Green Bridge, that connected the banks of the Vrbas. Belma took out a camera and tearfully snapped a final look at the green hills they had walked countless times. "It felt very surreal," she remembers about leaving. "I felt a part of me was being taken, and it seems like with every step I took, I knew I couldn't go back. It felt like my life was disappearing from underneath my feet."

The Demirovics hitched a ride out of Bosnia in the back of a van owned by a Serb friend; his name alone was an advantage that would reduce the risks they faced on the journey. The path was long, twisting and dangerous. The main roads were barricaded, bombed, or mined, so the yellow van that carried Belma and her parents out of Banja Luka was navigated through the winding, often lawless back roads of rural Bosnia. "There was a lot of fear because we knew we could have been pulled over at any moment and harassed, killed even," she says. "We knew our life was on the line. In such a lawless state, there was no guaranteed security, and those with weapons could do with you as they wished. This fear was made worse by the fact that we had all lost trust in people. Four years of war and impending terror made us fear and distrust everyone." A trip that would have taken five hours before the war became an overnight twelve-hour journey through roadblocks and war zones, avoiding cities when possible. The ride was bumpy as they crossed over rivers and hills, the green forests showing their first hints of brown in the September sun.

Towns they drove through, including Prijedor and Tuzla, were torn apart by the fighting. Buildings were razed or coated in the pockmarks of ammunition fire, and dazed chickens and other livestock wandered lost in the roads and fields. "Entire villages were burned. In Banja Luka, the mosques were blown up, and a few houses and businesses here and there, but nothing like what we saw there," Belma recalls. "We went through northeastern Bosnia, where entire areas had been flattened to the ground. It was very eye-opening and scary. It looked surreal in a way, even though I knew such large-scale destruction had occurred in many parts of Bosnia. I simply didn't know what it felt like. When we did stop, we didn't want to talk to anyone. I felt detached from towns where we stopped; they looked like war-ravaged ghost towns I used to see in the movies. But in my gut I still felt that this was my home; maybe not this particular town, but this war-caused destruction was in my backyard."

* * *

In Minneapolis, Belma found the transition to American teenage life a difficult one. Much of her time in Bosnia had been spent studying and helping at an ill-equipped hospital. Now, she found herself frequently sitting outside a Dairy Queen, blankly watching her classmates gossip and flirt. "I remember being exhausted all the time and having this feeling that this wasn't my life. I didn't want people to know that I was from Bosnia because it separated me from everybody else. After living through a war, I felt like I didn't belong anywhere."

Belma struggled through her first job, working the counter at a local sandwich shop. She would come home from work, peel open a dictionary, and devour the important new words she had learned on the job, words like "bacon, baloney, and dough." A string of similar jobs followed, including as a cashier at a discount department store. She even tried in-home sales selling cosmetics and knives; her English was good, but she knew so few people outside her own family that her appointment book was consistently empty.

In her last year of high school, Belma studied advanced English at the University of Minnesota, and one year later enrolled as a college freshman. It was here that she found a job working in a community involvement office on campus, where she helped to create a program for students looking to do volunteer work. She quickly made friends and began to like Minnesota. Having lived through a brutal war, Belma's mind had opened to the issues of human rights, conflict resolution and peace.

"When I first moved here, I didn't want to think about Bosnia or deal with the loss of family, friends and home." Belma says. One of the few reminders she had of home was a red thread with knots along it her grandmother had made for her, a small precious keepsake she carries in her wallet. "She prayed over it to see that I stay safe, and that God keeps me from bad things. I've been carrying it ever since."

One summer day, Belma attended an international music festival in Minneapolis' Loring Park. She watched an Eastern European Gypsy band in complete amazement. Soon she began dancing and signed on as a performing member of the Ethnic Dance Theatre, a local company reviving folk music and dance from all over the world. Her years spent dancing in downtown Banja Luka paid off, as she was able to quickly pick up the rhythms and movement of this music. Belma found acceptance and comfort in a form that embraces tolerance and requires an understanding of ethnic and social differences. In that way, ethnic dance was an extension of both her dealing with a difficult past and embracing her newly found politicization. "It struck me how comfortable I was with it," she says. "I had found a niche. It provided an outlet to connect with this society."

As she became more comfortable and politically aware, Belma began to address what had happened to her, her family, and her home. Following college graduation, she spent seven months in 2002-03 working in Bosnia through a human rights internship. She worked at the International Organization for Migration (IOM), the same organization that brought Belma to the United States. "I was looking for a way to go back to Bosnia and work there," she explains. "Since leaving Bosnia, I had gained new skills and I wanted to contribute. I also knew that I could contribute more in Bosnia than in other places, given my background and cultural understanding. This was both a personal and professional decision."

At that time, IOM was coordinating a massive population swap between Hadžići, a Serb town, and Bratunac, a Muslim town near Srebrenica that lost many of its men and boys during the massacre in 1995 and had its remaining women exiled elsewhere. The historic residents of these towns were cleared out, and by the end of the war, they had essentially switched populations. Hadzici became a Muslim town, and Bratunac a Serb community. With the war over, many wanted to return home, and a proposal to fund reconstruction and the return of original populations was being prepared for the European Commission.

Belma was assigned to fundraise for the project. She began by meeting with officials and other international organizations. "Part of my job was to do community needs assessments and find out about resources that already existed," she says. "We needed to avoid overlapping work with other organizations and work in partnership as much as possible. International funding for reconstruction and return of refugees and internally displaced persons was running out."

A lack of funds and a limited understanding of what these populations needed tossed Belma into the streets of Bratunac, meeting with women in local community centers and schools. "I wanted to talk about numbers, and get a general feel for the people with whom we hoped to work." She met with them to gather facts and ended up collecting more than she had bargained for. "Many of these women were raped and had seen their family members murdered or tortured. And I wasn't ready for these exchanges. I had seen the aftermath of war in Bratunac and Srebrenica. Brutal violence and destruction of life had become these women's daily reality. Their trauma was palpable."

In these meetings, the tragedies of the war that escaped the residents of Banja Luka were now sitting across the table from Belma, no more than five feet away and staring right into her eyes. "That population was hit particularly hard," she says. "In Bratunac and Srebrenica, no Muslim men are left. The husbands, brothers, fathers are gone.

"The women I met had a lot promised to them by the government and the international community, and very little of that was being fulfilled. They felt cheated. And when I came to meet them, they were distrustful. I understood their attitude and wished I could do more to meet their needs."

After months of resettlement work, Bosnia's new reality began to set in with Belma. The reminders of what her life used to be before the war were starkly opposed to her daily experiences in the new Bosnia. The realization that the Bosnia of Belma's childhood no longer exists provided closure to her years in Banja Luka and the opportunity to continue to look forward in her life. "It is difficult to explain, but I lived with a belief that maybe someday I could go back to this place I call home," she says. "Going back to Bosnia made me realize that place now only exists in my memory, and I came to accept that."

As Belma separated herself from her childhood home, much of the international community was putting the remnants of the war aside as well, as aid flows began to dwindle, the number of sponsored returns dropped, and the international community all but rolled out of the region. Belma is quick to refute explanations of the Balkan conflict that place deep-rooted historical ethnic conflicts as central to the instability. Many suggest that in modern Balkan society, these histories themselves caused the spillover of simmering ethnic animosity and conflict. "That argument upsets me," she says. "The situation is not that simple."

Growing up, one of Belma's best friends came from a Serb family. Her friend's father was called to the front lines to fight, and he did so for the duration of the war. "But," Belma says, "he did not believe in that war. He had nothing against Bosnian Muslims. He went to war because he had no choice. He had to provide for his family. This deeply rooted ethnic conflict was primarily a tool of political opportunists. Religion and ancient hatreds are used because they are easily manipulated, and people associate with those things fairly easily."

Belma points out connections between what happened in Bosnia to conflicts elsewhere. "The more I read about other conflicts, even in places as far as Rwanda, the more I see they are similar. In Rwanda, ethnicity was similarly manipulated like it was in Bosnia. I can understand that people can identify with a particular group for various reasons—religion, ideology, race, etc.; what I don't understand is how one goes from associating with a group to becoming a ruthless murderer of others.

"Thousands of innocent civilians were kept in rape and concentration camps across Bosnia. Torture, rape and beatings were a daily routine. Many times the guards knew the camp prisoners—they could have been their neighbors, a colleague or a classmate. Yet unspeakable atrocities were committed against these civilians. And this is the scary part about us humans. We function well when we believe in something; when we are driven by our belief, we are capable of much. But what happens when our quest becomes torture, mutilation, mass killings and extermination of a group of people? I know I am not the first to ponder this question, but I have yet to find an adequate answer and to understand what causes people to commit such mass acts of targeted violence."

In respect to Bosnia's war, much of Belma's frustration is aimed at the international community for not intervening sooner. "The human aspect of international military intervention appears to be minimal," she says. "It was quite clear what was going on in Bosnia and that civilians were the primary targets. It also seemed clear that Serbs were in possession of weapons from the Yugoslav People's Army and using them against civilians. The politics are complicated and dirty, and I can see why the international community would have wanted to say out of this conflict, but they did not. Diplomatic interventions started shortly after the war began and proved to be irrelevant. However, the civilians needed to be protected. I find it hard to believe that European leaders allowed for such brutal ethnic cleansing to take place, but they did. They watched it happen.

"Part of the problem is that we have a sheltered and limited understanding of violent conflicts. The majority of people in the Western world who believe in the international community and who have the power to make decisions don't know what war is. They don't know what war feels like. They don't know what war smells like. They don't know what it is like to be a civilian living in a war zone. This leads people to believe that they have the luxury of taking the time to go to numerous conferences and seminars and debates, and go through 200 peace agreements. Another significant factor is that a war is a profitable enterprise. And those who profit from it have developed a strong lobby."

Despite the hell Bosnians faced throughout the war, the peace accords brought a certain sense of normalcy, at least on the surface. After a long period of short supplies, limited food and destroyed infrastructure, cities began to liven. People ventured out into the streets, no longer needing to avoid strangers or to execute a cower-and-dodge method of walking that had been common practice in Sarajevo. Shops and restaurants began to fill with goods and patrons. Many Bosnians tried to carry on with their daily lives as they did before the war.

Belma knows that the international community, if it chooses to, can serve the interests of conflicts' victims. That is why she was drawn to the work of the Center for Victims of Torture (CVT), an international human rights organization that works one-on-one with torture victims from all over the world, offering healing services, including counseling and access to adequate social services and medical care. Belma has worked in CVT's development department since returning from Bosnia in 2003. Her work at CVT goes beyond raising funds. She has interviewed potential interpreters and takes part in mock counseling sessions, often playing the role of the client. Her past, she says, makes the interviews that much harder.

Belma recently returned from a week-long trip to Azerbaijan, where she was part of an election monitoring delegation from the Organization for Security and Cooperation in Europe (OSCE). She joined forty-seven other Americans and hundreds of others Europeans to meet with election officials and oversee the voting process in this former Soviet state located in the Caucasus, on the Caspian Sea. This small county has a history of corruption and political violence, and this election was no different. The OSCE reported that election processes included ballot-box manipulation, voter intimidation and suppression of opposition parties.

On Election Day, Belma visited polling stations and spent the night monitoring the recording of ballot counts, which were performed by hand. Much of the process reminded Belma of things she had seen and heard about during her childhood in Yugoslavia.

"The counting was fraudulent," she contends. "They spent a lot of time filling out forms with fake numbers. The process operated like a Communist apparatchik (a devoted member of an organization). It takes time for democracy to take root in a society. To a degree, it is something that has to be homegrown—the people have to embrace the entire process and not just the ballot-casting action. And in Azerbaijan, this doesn't exist. In college, I studied various theories about sponsored democratic development, and I of course had my doubts then, but witnessing elections in Azerbaijan made it clear that democracy cannot happen overnight."

Belma's personal history has become the fuel for her quest for basic democratic rights of people around the world. "I don't know if I feel betrayed as a Bosnian in thinking about the Bosnian War. But I do feel betrayed as a human," she states, her voice wavering with tired frustration, "How could this happen at the end of the twentieth century?"

Belma has been preparing for her entrance exams, and hopes to go to law school to study human rights law. And she hopes to continue the work she is a part of at the Center for Victims of Torture. She feels strongly about providing rehabilitative services to survivors of war and torture. "We all stand a lot to gain when survivors heal and restore their potential," she says.

* * *

Sometimes while walking through the changed streets of Banja Luka, Belma visited a wooded park near her old apartment. She stepped off the sidewalk and onto an unmarked path that led to a clear area in the grass. "I remember walking there when I was a girl. I knew exactly where each stone was, and I could avoid them without looking down, as I had walked that path thousands of times. And I thought how bizarre, that nothing had changed, in the sense that the dirt is still in the same place. Yet everything has changed so much, so many times.

"I felt very strange in Banja Luka; deep inside me, I knew I belonged there, but when I looked around it was clear that I didn't. There were all the familiar places and none of the familiar people. I still struggle with the loss of 'my city,' but I find comfort in my memories, which no one can take away from me.

"I recall taking a stroll down a street near my former Banja Luka apartment I call 'Chestnut Alley,' walking where I used to gather wild chestnuts beneath the trees to make hair dye. I would boil the soul out of nuts and then rinse my hair with that tinted water. It would give my hair a very nice red shine. The edible chestnuts were delicious, a wonderful snack for fall evenings with friends. And you could have fun with them. You could buy roasted chestnuts from street vendors. And then with soot on your fingers, you tell your friend she has something on her face, and then you would wipe two fingertips from your nose across the curve under her eye and she would have a black mark on her face for the rest of the night."

Today, trees mean something different in Bosnia. Banja Luka was not bombed and burned, but the war's physical scars remain in the streets of Sarajevo, Srebrenica, Mostar, and countless towns and villages across the countryside. In these parts, where the ethnic cleansing was aggressive and destructive, Belma has witnessed what she calls the "Tree Inside the Building Phenomenon."

She remembers a tree in Sarajevo she passed nearly every day on her way to city center. The tree grew from the rubble of a bombed building, spreading its limbs from a pock-marked crater where an apartment building once stood. "It is a bizarre sight as you can actually look inside this building and see where the bathroom was," she says. "There were ceramic tiles on the walls. This gives you a glimpse of the life that at one time existed in that building. There is no human life in the building now; instead the tree's growing inside it."

Surreal and absurd, the chestnut, as well as oak and birch trees stretching out of the rubble of mosques, hospitals, shops, and homes, taking root in the remnants of atrocities of a decade ago, seem to rest in the peripheral vision of the people living in their shade every day. These trees, as Belma sees them, serve as an allegory for the Balkans in general—numerous problems and strange occurrences surround the people, but these go unnoticed as people carry on in their daily survival modes. These trees speak of history, culture, ethnicity and economy.

"I recognize that it is difficult to deal with painful experiences and memories, and many people simply don't do it," she explains. "But I think that if we don't, we will always have abandoned trees growing in places where they shouldn't be.

"The complexity of Bosnia's situation may have affected me differently than other people, as I tried to connect its opposing aspects, to connect all the dots and make sense out of them," Belma once wrote. "My work has provided me some comfort in thinking about Bosnia, as I know that many committed individuals are trying to make things better. Nonetheless, I fear that Bosnians as a people will leave a number of important issues unquestioned and unaddressed—just like the trees that continue to grow inside the war-destroyed buildings... [an] unnoticed and unquestioned phenomenon."

**Ahmed speaking at the Center for Victims of Torture celebration
(Photo courtesy of Center for Victims of Torture)**

I NEVER CRIED
By Burt Berlowe

Ahmed Tharwat stands at the microphone on the lawn of the Center for Victims of Torture reading from a piece of paper he holds in a trembling hand. His words, articulated carefully through a Middle Eastern accent, paint shocking images of a painful past brought back to life; the colors mostly red and yellow, black and blue. As Ahmed's story unfolds, a hush falls over the stunned group of spectators gathered on the edge of the University of Minnesota campus to celebrate the Center's twentieth anniversary. On a day dominated by formal speechmaking, Ahmed is giving the audience much more than a bunch of rhetoric to chew on. He is handing them his soul.

It's 1968. Ahmed is a sixteen-year-old freshman at Cairo High School. The so-called "Six Day-War," between Israel and Egypt has caused anti-government protesters to fill Egyptian streets. At Ahmed's school, students have been let out of class early to join in the protests. Ahmed feels glad that school got out early, not fully realizing the serious circumstances encompassing the upheaval in the community. He is not interested in joining the protests at that time and is looking for a short cut to get home.

As Ahmed is walking, a soldier with the secret police approaches him and asks where he is headed. "I'm going to my home," he replies, continuing his brisk pace. The solider then grabs him and places him in a line with students who had been in the protest. The officers begin cursing the students' parents. Instinctively, Ahmed speaks softly in defense of his parents.

The colonel then orders a guard to take Ahmed to an empty, dark room filled with bugs and a wicked stench. Ahmed assumes it is an effort to make the daily quota officers must complete each day. Instead, the officer begins beating him with a billy club.

For forty-five nonstop minutes, the brunt of the club lands with a jarring thud again and again on Ahmed's nearly bare body. Bent over on his knees on the cold, hard floor, he helplessly absorbs each blow administered by the brutish soldier. The putrid, damp smell permeating the room stings his nostrils and leaves a foul taste in his mouth. He is unable to raise his battered hands to swat at the horde of insects crawling over his bare arms. His only movements are the twisting from side to side, the facial contortions—the jerking and pulling in of the muscles as they meet the end of the large black stick.

"I was vulnerable, helpless; I had no protection. The colonel never looked me in the eye and never spoke a word. The pain was relentless; it just went on and on. My body swelled so bad I looked like I had gained twenty pounds. My skin began to peel. I eventually lost all association with my body. I never cried. I wasn't trying to be heroic. I couldn't make a sound, I couldn't scream, nothing. I was morally humiliated."

Desperately, Ahmed tries to divert his attention away from the pain, fleeing the agony through an open chamber in his mind. He imagines himself painting a wall many colors—red and yellow, black and blue— moving the brush up and down, back and forth in distracting, repetitive detail. It is the only thing that keeps him from a total mental breakdown.

After what feels like forever, the beating suddenly stops. The colonel just walks out like nothing happened. Ahmed believes he is alone in the room, until he notices that the guard that brought him to the room is in the corner crying. This was the only heartfelt expression from his captor. It touches Ahmed emotionally, staying with him as he struggles his way home. It helps carry him through the first intense night of pain and confusion and ensuing nightmares that haunt him for years to come. "I had nightmares of police or other authority figures having power over me," he recalls, "and I'm helpless to do anything about it."

Beyond the enduring physical trauma, the beating had another kind of impact on Ahmed. It planted the seeds of a growing anger against authority and abuse of power. He began to participate in protests against the Egyptian government's handling of war, which also was his initiation into political dissent. He recalls that "there were lots of protests. People were asking for change."

* * *

Ahmed grew up in the shadows of the Middle East conflict. He was one of eight children in a large family raised in the cozy farm town called Delta. "I had a very secure, innocent childhood," he recalls years later. "My parents operated a village school. My dad was the principal and several uncles were teachers. They also farmed the land. My dad made no more than seven dollars a month. It was a depressed area. But people fished and produced what they needed.

"Our village was peaceful. But all around us, the country was consumed with war between Egypt and Israel. It seemed like there was always war. In our village, we could hear the guns and bombs off in the distance. It was scary.

"We moved to Cairo in 1966 when I was fourteen years old. It was the end of the monarchy in Egypt and the military had overthrown King Farouk. They just told him to leave and he did. It was an unceremonious departure. There were lots of raids going on in town. I went back to the village with my brothers while my parents stayed in Cairo. The '67 war was devastating for everybody on a macro level. People would demonstrate all the time. Things were in turmoil."

Even as he was still recovering from the '68 beating, Ahmed would once again become a target of physical violence. He was drafted into the Army and assigned to a non-combat job. His problems with authority surfaced quickly. He couldn't follow orders and cooperate with his superior's demands. In response, he often found himself in the brig with other so-called criminals, where his rebellion got him into more trouble. "The other prisoners would ask me to do something for them and, if I didn't do it, they beat me up. I couldn't report it or they would beat me up again."

When Ahmed's military service ended, he decided to leave Egypt, find a job and begin his life again. In 1977, at age twenty-five, he left for the United States. He settled in the Uptown neighborhood of Minneapolis where one of his brothers lived. His other seven siblings remained in Cairo. At the time, he recalls, there wasn't a stigma attached to being an Arab-American, "at least no more than any other 'hyphenated American.'"

Nevertheless, Ahmed was constantly concerned about how he might be accepted by other cultures. "That attitude changed when I got a puppy," he says. "When I would take my dog for walks, I would meet people from many different cultures who also had pets. One even had a puppy with the same name as mine. It was better than a class in diversity."

Ahmed wanted to do something to further the capacity of all races and nationalities to better understand each other and to get along. He secured an MBA degree then became a teacher of multicultural marketing at St. Thomas University in St. Paul. He also began hosting a public television show called "Open Arms," which is part of Muslim-American television. He calls it a variety show that covers topics ranging from "what is going on in Iraq to what kids are doing in the streets of our community," with a lot of human-interest stories about Arab-Americans. He has not shaken his problems with authority, instead choosing to take an academic path that allows him as much personal freedom as possible.

The bitterness of Ahmed's torture experience has never left him. But he has refused to live as a fearful victim. He believes that would satisfy the perpetrator's need for power and control. He also has rejected the temptation to harbor feelings of anger and revenge towards the man that beat him. Instead, he is interested in exploring the psyches of torturers and what makes them commit such horrible acts towards their fellow human beings.

"What was in him, a grown-up man to make him so cruel and unfeeling towards a child?" Ahmed asks, reflecting on his torturer. "What happened to cause him to behave this way—and the other torturers too? I want to understand this; I want to know why the man who tortured me did so, and in general, how one can torture another."

Ahmed believes that torturers are victims too, due to the brainwashing they receive. "They also live in fear because they must follow the chain of command or risk being abused themselves. My torturer was a victim of his sadistic obsession with violence and his intoxication with power. I was physically paralyzed. He was morally paralyzed.

"I believe that all people inherently have within them compassion for those who are victims of a system of socialization that is mostly no fault of their own. After all, what are your options? You can either be angry and act destructively, or forgive and interfere with their plan to make you angry and to have power over you."

This does not mean, however, that Ahmed condones violence or torture.

To the contrary, he has been an outspoken critic of U.S. policy in Iraq and in prisoner detention centers, as well as of the coverage of those issues by the press. In particular, he is upset with the torture inflicted upon Iraqi detainees by Americans at such places as Abu Gharib and Guantanamo Bay. "I'm not surprised that it happened," he says. "There's lots of abuse of power. The media only gives American citizens 'snapshots' and 'sound bites' of these events, devoid of the context that only human eyes and minds can record and convey. Is it a good thing to be ignorant? Is it harmful to not know the whole truth? Could our American elitist psyches handle the truth?"

Ahmed's life story and his willingness to share it for the first time are testimonies to his desire to speak truth to power. His few minutes at the CVT microphone were also powerfully cathartic. As he said afterward: "Being able to finally tell my story was empowering and liberating."

But even the telling of his story has not totally healed Ahmed's wounds. He found that out when, on a recent trip to Cairo, he decided to revisit the site of his torture. "I went back there in order to talk to someone to find out what has happened since. I realized that even thirty years later, I can't go back to that place."

FIELD OF DREAMS
By Burt Berlowe

It was one of those oppressively hot central Minnesota days when the heavy, moist air sticks to your skin and wears on your whole body, making the ninety-degree temperature seem at least ten degrees higher. By noon, the midsummer sun had scorched the farm field red and parched the five-foot-high corn stalks that spread for miles and miles.

Ten-year-old Ana Castillo, drenched in brown sweat and besieged by nagging pain, grimaced as she stretched out a weary, sunburned arm, reached up to a corn stalk above her head, plucked a tassel off the top and dropped it into one of the two heavy baskets tied around her waist. As she plodded forward, she turned her head and, letting out a deep sigh, looked warily down the seemingly endless rows that lay ahead. It would be a long time until sunset.

Ana wasn't alone on the field that day. Her actual and expanded family of laborers was spread across the vast acres of earth, battling the elements to make a day's wages, only to return to the primitive living conditions in the migrant workers' camp. Although Ana was new to the fields, she had, at her young age, grown quite used to the hard life.

* * *

In the tiny Mexican ranch town where Ana was born in 1980, across the border from Texas, residents farmed, raised cattle and rode horses. "We got our water from a well, had no outdoor plumbing and our electricity would shut down all the time," Ana recalls. "We lived in a brick square two-bedroom house with a lot of people in it. I had seven brothers and sisters. It was crowded. There was a lot of poverty in our town. My parents were better off than some other residents. My father was mayor of the town and had a mechanic shop at home. We were comfortable.

"In our small town, everybody helped each other. Everyone there was your relative. Extended family meant a lot. My father didn't live with us and often left us children with an aunt. I remember thinking, 'Why wasn't he there?' Everybody in the household grew up being a little insecure. There were so many of us that no attention was paid to anyone. We all had chores to help with. I learned early to work around the house. I learned how to cook real young.

"In 1989, when I was nine years old, my father had a friend invite him to come to Minnesota and pick asparagus. He said we'd make a lot of money because the whole family would work together and get one paycheck. We contracted with a canning company in the town of Owatonna that raised asparagus." The Owatonna migrant workers were paid every two weeks at a rate of $4.15 per hour per family. Ana's dad would sometimes do jobs for other people in the camp and buy old cars and fix them up and sell them in order to make extra money.

Ana vividly remembers the long days spent in the fields "Each row was two miles long. There were usually about 150 of us working at once. We would go down each row with a basket, sometimes two at once on our waist, tied with a belt. My younger brothers, from ages seven to eighteen, would help carry the baskets which weighed around thirty to forty pounds each. We had to be bending down and picking with our hands. I wore a lot of clothing so as not to get sunburned. But then I was really warm on the hot days. We worked from 5 a.m. to 7 p.m., taking short breaks and drinks of water brought to us when we finished a row. I wanted to rush my break so I could complete a field before the sun went down, so I wouldn't have to come back the next day.

"The hardest part was making it home, lying down and getting up the next day stiff, sore and burned up from the sun. Often, I didn't want to get up in the morning and go into the fields. And after I got home there were always chores to do. But when we were working, we tried to have as much fun as possible. Everybody took care of each other. We ate together. We laughed and told jokes. We competed against each other for who would collect the most pounds.

"Asparagus grew with the sun. It grows a foot or two high. I would pick until my hands were full. When we finished the asparagus, we then had to tassel corn five feet tall in suffocating heat in rows three or four miles long. The rows were so crowded with asparagus and corn and pickers that I would be constantly brushing against the leaves and they would make me itch and cut my face.

"We were not allowed to get out of the field unless it was lightning. We would even work through rain. We used to wear yellow rain suits, but if it rained really hard we would be soaked and our shoes would get so full of mud that we couldn't walk in them, making it difficult to get through the fields. We knew that the sooner we finished a row the sooner we could sit down before others could finish. There were people who couldn't take it and would walk off in the middle of a row and go wait in a car. I constantly felt like I wanted to go home. But I couldn't."

Going home didn't mean total relief from hardship. Grass Camp, where the migrant workers lived, consisted of twenty-six brick homes with two units per building. The nine-member Castillo family was packed like sardines into a unit that had only one room, no air conditioning, hot water or toilet, only bunk beds for furniture and a tiny kitchen. The floor was cement and there were brick walls. All of the residents shared a restroom in the middle of the camp. "It was a hard adjustment to make, showering in front of everyone," says Ana. "We also didn't have drinking water. We had to buy it." The crowded conditions did create a sense of extended family among the immigrants, who would take care of each other's children. But, says Ana, there was little time for play. "We were told, 'You come here to work, not for luxury.'"

The Castillo family worked hard for three or four months a year over several seasons in Owatonna then moved to Texas where Ana started school. It wasn't an easy transition. "I was the only Hispanic in the whole school. I felt really left out and preferred to be at home. I was taken out of school in March so we could work in the fields. I wouldn't go back until November, when I had to make up all of the school work, often staying after class or going to school at night. Through a special migrant program, I was able to attend an alternative school. It was a two-day trip from home, nine of us in a van. And we wouldn't stop along the way unless it was absolutely necessary.

"We never had the time to take any electives, such as sports or computer classes, or to be in any extracurricular programs. I never learned to swim, ride a bike or anything others could do. I saw other girls being cheerleaders and thought I was never good enough to be anything because we didn't have money. No one would eat with me in the cafeteria, and children on the bus would make fun of me, saying, 'You're a wetback.' From teachers and counselors, there was always a lot of, 'You're not good enough. You can't do it, you're Mexican. You're an immigrant. You should never come to school anyway.' They didn't want to work with me. They thought it was a waste of their time. My response was, 'I'm going to show you that you are wrong.'" And she did just that, completing high school credits at age sixteen, although she never had a formal graduation.

Ana worked in the fields in Owatonna until 1993 when she was seventeen. The family then packed their meager possessions and headed for North Carolina to pick peaches, earning fifty cents for each thirty-pound bag. Their first check was $3.60 for a day's work, even though Ana's father was a crew leader. To make matters worse, Ana itched so bad from physical contact with the peaches that she left that camp and went back to picking asparagus. Recalling the North Carolina experience, she makes a statement that could generally apply to her family's labor history. "We worked so hard, and we were never paid enough."

When Ana was ten years old, she had made a promise to her mother. "I told her that someday I would earn enough money that she would not have to work anymore." After years of toil in the fields, in factories and at fast food restaurants, Ana has kept that promise. She went on to get a degree in social work and a position as regional manager for an agency in Owatonna that helps migrant workers find work and have a stable family life. In a way, it is a job that takes her back home again.

* * *

The steamy summer day finds Ana in a familiar place, roaming the Owatonna farm fields. Only this time, she is on the outside looking in. Pausing momentarily to survey the scene, she then wades into the crowd of migrant families. She walks with workers for a while, showing them how to detassle corn stalks she now can reach without effort. Or she waits for migrants to come her way then pauses to talk to them, asking "How is the work going? How do you feel about it? Do you need a school for their children? Or a place to live for your family?" When she's not in the field, Ana is in her office, helping an immigrant who can't speak or read English fill out documentation papers or apply for a visa.

"Because I used to be a immigrant farm worker, I know what these families are going through," Ana says. "I can motivate them to change their lives. My goal is to make them understand that it is hard on children to move state to state and not have stability. One of the most difficult frustrations I have is when the children don't attend school because they have to help in the fields or at home and their parents don't want to let go. Some parents have been able to obtain academic degrees, hold good jobs and enroll their children in school. But many want children to be migrants. They won't accept change.

"They will go back to what has been routine to them. I tell them, I used to be in your shoes. I know how hard your life is." I try to be a role model. I call them. I bother them. 'I tell them you can learn English and we'll pay for it.' We try to reach them where their priorities are. We are the first response to their needs. There isn't anywhere else for them to go."

Ana is quick to point out that conditions have improved in the farm fields in recent years because of the influx of new technology. "Machines are taking over a lot of the work. They can pick the corn, for example, so people don't have to detassle. All they have to do is inspect. There have been other advancements too. Camps now have hot water and day care, and workers make $6.50 an hour."

At the same time, the migrant workers, most of whom are in large families, have plenty of challenges to overcome. The new technology has meant that fewer human hands are needed, reducing the number of jobs available. Immigrants still work long hours in all kinds of weather and with no guarantees of how well they will do or how long their jobs will last.

Furthermore, in Owatonna, a mostly white, middle-class town, ingrained traditions and attitudes are planted as deep as the corn stalks that line the surrounding farm lands. Many of Owatonna's longtime residents have had a hard time adjusting to the influx of immigrants into their community. They don't want immigrants to come to the U.S. even if they are legal. Rather than trying to accept the change, they have fought against it, with divisive results. Ana explains: "I've heard comments from some of the immigrants that they have to leave when the season is over. It turns out that was in response to what they perceived as racist comments made by some of the older residents here. Those comments include allegations that the migrant workers are here for the welfare payments and to take away resident jobs and that they want to live for free off taxpayer money.

"We explain that the migrants only want to make a living and they are doing work that helps put food on everyone's plate—work that no one else will do. But many of the residents are stubborn. They won't listen to any other point of view."

At the time of this writing, the Bush administration had budgeted to eliminate federal funding for Ana's agency, a move that could put them out of business. "They say that we aren't effective," Ana explains, her voice rising a bit in anger. "We are effective in the way we've changed the lives of a lot of people, giving them the motivation to believe 'I can do this. I really can.' We have seen some real changes.

"We're trying to find some ways to get the funding restored. If we don't, all of our 200-person staff will be unemployed. The bigger question is what happens to the people they serve. They have no place to go. They will be homeless, forced to find any way they can to do farm labor, the only kind of work they know how to do. There are farm worker programs everywhere. But we all get funded from the same program and do the same thing. This funding cut would eliminate all of them or make us ineffective." In response, Ana was planning a trip to the nation's capital to talk to Minnesota congressmen about this issue.

Ana's years of struggle have only strengthened her confidence and resolve. "If I get laid off," she says, "I will be going for a master's and maybe a Ph.D. in social work. I want to be a social worker because of what I've been through.

As I look back over my life so far, I come away being positive. I know that hard work motivates me. I value everything I've done and shared with others.

"If my father hadn't shown me the value of work I would have thought of life as a given. It's not a given. You have to work hard every day. But my father was optimistic. He saw the life they had and said he didn't want the same for me. Now, I don't want my children to have to go through what I did. I want them to have something better than I had. With all of the barriers, some of us are not inspired to do anything else but be immigrant laborers. I see myself as a motivator to help others to do whatever motivates them. Because I'm female, because I'm Hispanic, I had to work harder at everything. I hope I can be an example for other Hispanics. If I can do it, anybody can."

*Ana Castillo has recently left the agency she was working for in Owatonna. They do not know her whereabouts.

PILGRIM OF PEACE
By Burt Berlowe

Father Joaquin Mayorga's road to peace leads into the soul of Colombia. It meanders past simple huts and rolling fields where peasant families toil for daily survival and a semblance of dignity, while small children stalk passers-by for pesos and handouts amidst gathering storm clouds of chaos and violence. For Fr. Joaquin, it is a familiar journey; the desperate faces of the poor are profound reflections of his own past. He does not walk past them, but rather with them, extending an outstretched hand, engaging smile and strong shoulders for the taking.

Joaquin's journeys often begin and end at the small, inconspicuous church where he ministers to the down-and-out and lifts them to new heights. Operating out of the church, Joaquin has rallied the parishioners into a formidable force for change in one of the world's most troubled but overlooked countries.

* * *

"I'm here to promote peace in Colombia and around the world."

Joaquin's words come to me through an interpreter as we sit in a meeting room at the Resource Center of the Americas, a Central America-focused facility in south Minneapolis. It is Joaquin's first trip ever to the United States courtesy of the Colombia Support Network. He will be speaking at several events around the Twin Cities, promoting the work he has been doing to bring peace and stability to his home country.

Joaquin can easily walk in a poor man's shoes. He was born into an impoverished family in 1960 in the southeastern area of Colombia. He was the only child in his large family to finish secondary school.

"I grew up during a time of two big events in the region: the migration of Latin Americans and a burst of the theology of liberation," Joaquin recalls. "At a very early age, I realized the need to struggle for the poor, the excluded and the oppressed. I wanted to place myself on the side of those who are poor and in need. I always wondered what caused poverty.

"I also wondered what was the best path for my liberation. I found that path in religion and decided to become a priest. I went to the seminary where I became known as a revolutionary. I think I am a revolutionary. But I never believed in using guns or any kind of weapons to solve conflict. I believe in the power of the word and the power of organizing and in popular sovereignty for the people as a tool for the struggle for liberation."

For many years, Joaquin's home town was governed by two families who used municipal funds for their own benefit and wielded an iron hand over the population. In response, an insurgent guerrilla organization known as the National Liberation Army (NLA) decided to intervene politically and militarily to remove and punish the people in power. Joaquin learned that there were guerilla groups in Colombia and eventually met with Christian leaders of the NLA and other revolutionary leaders like Che Guevara.

NLA is a rebel group formed in 1964, inspired by the liberation of Cuba that tended to use military force to get its way. Many priests in Colombia became members of NLA. Joaquin eschewed a formal membership but pledged to join the struggle for liberation of poor people, albeit without the use of weapons. "I recognize that NLA has contributed to liberation of the poor in the country," says Joaquin. "But they have done it at gunpoint. I prefer using the power of organization and dialogue and by exercising sovereignty."

Joaquin has been called "a pilgrim of peace." Through his work as a priest, he has connected with a lot of people from different groups, enabling him to organize peasants into community leaders. In 1992, during a time of violent turmoil in the country, he led area churches in an effort to form a movement that said, 'Let's bring down war.' Its greatest achievement was to help turn the country to peace and popular elections, to take our peace into the streets.

"Bringing peace to Colombia is a hard and difficult path," Joaquin says. "Many peace leaders have been killed. Sovereignty is being pressured by politics and by the army of the paramilitary. Despite public opposition, the government voted to increase its armed forces.

"In December of 1997, we started getting all the people in the church together to determine what could be done to find a peaceful solution for the political and military conflict and to give the government back to the people. After many meetings, we decided on several actions. The first of those was an attempt to free the mayor of the town who had been captured and held hostage by the NLA. Through dialogue and negotiations with the NLA we were able to get the mayor freed. After that, we petitioned the ruling family to explain their corruption. It turned out that people wanted the mayor to be free, but they did not want him to continue in office. After many meetings with the mayor, he refused to resign. A town meeting was called to vote on whether he should resign. When ninety-five percent voted for his departure, he had to accept the decision. This empowered people a lot, and they went on to establish three objectives: social justice, the exercise of popular sovereignty, and the building of peace."

This peace process addressed political corruption and military action where the population found itself in the middle of the war between the paramilitary and guerillas. In some cases, the popular confrontation with the military went through the NLA. "The people do not want the solution to come through war," Joaquin says. "That's why the municipal assemblies of voters are getting together and finding peaceful solutions and cooperation. We want to generate and keep momentum going.

"The problem in Colombia is not only war and arms groups but social injustice and economic differences because of political corruption and sanctions. But so many groups have turned to war to solve problems. The government defends itself through war. And its armed forces have been the cruelest assassins we have ever had. To make things worse, the guerillas have organized to change the country through weapons."

The fiercest enemy faced by Joaquin's populist peace army is not from his home country. "The U.S. is a major source of our misfortune," he bristles. "Its government has been sending millions of dollars down here and directing the war supposedly to battle drugs and terrorism—an effort they call Plan Colombia. That money is being used to strengthen the war that our government is directing that uses illegal armies against the people. This war is really due to other interests, among them the riches of our country: oil, gold, coal, many other minerals, which different American companies want to benefit from. The free trade agreement of the Americas gives the best advantage to multinational companies.

"There are several things that can be done. We have to work together. Citizens of organizations in the U.S. and Colombia and Latin America must realize that the first step is to get together in honesty and sincerity to find out what's really going in Colombia and Latin America. We need an organizational brotherhood between your country and mine. And we need to build empowerment of people in our countries, to take away the power from those who direct the war and Plan Colombia. We also need to stop economic and military actions because of Plan Colombia. We need to build a new order nationally and internationally based in peace, social justice, solidarity, and love so that we can find useful solutions to poverty and war. We want a relationship with America that has the respect of our people.

"As part of a new approach to international partnership, an organization called the Colombia Support Network has been promoting a Sister Cities project. It includes brotherhood and sisterhood Christianity through all different forms of organizing and ways of social expression via universities, churches, various organizations, and political leaders that we have in our country."

Joaquin has learned to walk with two major forces: revolutionary struggle and traditional Catholic teaching on the way to Colombian liberation. He believes that "education is the first step, but we also need to build sovereignty."

It is not an exaggeration to say that Joaquin has risked a lot for the cause of peace. His life has been threatened many times. On three occasions, he barely escaped an assassin's bullet, experiences so awful he chose not to talk about them. Yet he has no plans for any special measures of protection. "I have placed my life in the cause of the liberation, in the hands of God, and in the trust and support that people give me. I always travel with a sense of solidarity and the hope of changing the world into one of happiness and peace."

*Soon after this writing, Father Joaquin was forced to leave Colombia due to threats to his life.

Tom Ivory
(Photo courtesy of Tom Ivory)

LAW WITH A HUMAN FACE
By Burt Berlowe

In the Nigerian town of Nembe, it was business as usual—the nasty, noisy business of secession. Inside his family's one-story, wood-paneled house, six-year-old Thompson Ivory had become used to the federal troops marching past his door, the sporadic gunshots rattling the windows, the general chaos of civil unrest. But on this particular evening, the violence hit especially close to home.

"There was war all around us," Thompson recalls years later. "A lot of people were executed and shot from my town. The secessionist soldiers would come into our homes unceremoniously and grab from us whatever caught their fancy, including foodstuff. Men were taken from their homes and told to take a walk on the pier where they were shot and fell into to the river. My mother was a strong woman and resisted them. I thought it was a miracle they didn't shoot her. Then one night, federal troops were advancing in town and we heard the gunfire. I could distinguish the warring forces by the sound of the gunfire. As usual, my mother would react to the shooting by going prone on the floor. But this time, just as she moved, a bullet hit the headboard of our bed and landed right where she had been. By the break of day, federal groups had taken control of town and the rebellion was crushed. But I have never forgotten what happened that night."

Thompson grew up in the shadow of the African revolution. "I remember as a little child seeing different soldiers from the Biafran Army take over the area until federal forces came to liberate our town," he says. Members of the Igbo tribe in eastern Nigeria which brought about the Nigerian civil war that lasted between 1967 and 1970. I was made to understand that our people did not support the secession because the Igbo were considered domineering and we were afraid as a minority that they would dominate us. Our people felt they would be better off in a united Nigeria than under the Republic of Biafra," Thompson explains. "The rebellion was crushed and the war ended in 1970. There have been successive military governments after Nigeria's independence that were brought about by coups and counter-coups. But whether military or civilian, the result hasn't been good for our people. We have no benefit from so many natural resources on our land. All minerals are federally controlled by law.

"There's lots of instability in many of our countries. People get into power and refuse to leave. We've never had an effective system for proper democratic change of government. There are coups and counter-coups, and religious and ethnic conflicts, and civilian demonstrations and strikes. Church bombings happen all the time."

In the Africa of Thompson Ivory and his neighbors, struggles for survival are tempered by traditional sense of community. "We are fisher people (living) in the midst of many rivers," he says. "The Nimbi tribe we belong to is one of at least twenty ethnic tribes within the Niger Delta. My family was considered aristocrats within the structure in town. We traditionally think in terms of extended family relationships that go beyond the nuclear family. Boats were the only means of getting from one place to another. Family members and other residents would crowd into the boats, often at great risk. We have one of the longest bridges in that part of the world. We travel everywhere by boat. There is no land travel to my hometown. Every year, there are casualties from boat mishaps. Once, our boat was overloaded with relatives, and it tipped over. I ended up picking my drowned younger sister out of the water.

"Most people in our community lived in poverty in huts. Often, there were as many as eleven children in one room. We have this communal system and could stay with each other's mothers or fathers with no restrictions. Everybody was responsible for one another. I remember sleeping on mats in various families' houses. We would tell stories at bedtime under the moonlight and in our kitchens—fairy tales, folk tales, stories of heroic deeds and history. Storytelling was very important. We used rituals like painting our faces with ashes or stuffing salt into your mouths. That could go on for several hours. We always had to do chores, and the neighbors could discipline each other's children. Each person was responsible for every other one. It left me with a wonderful legacy of community-mindedness and respect.

"At the same time, there was cross-cultural integration. We were into the American lifestyle, the jean-wearing culture. We dressed and spoke and tried to behave like Americans. In Africa everybody wants to be an American. But they cannot get the full details of American life. They get a warped picture—a pseudo thing. They don't really get it right. For one thing, people in the U.S. work and play very hard. Back home, we don't have such a culture. It's more easy-going. There's not much regard for time.

"Where you are from in your own nation matters a lot in Nigeria. You could tell where some people are from by their looks or how they dress. I am told that I have the looks of an Igbo man, but it is difficult to tell where I am from. I tell people not to worry about my place of origin; it suffices that I am a Nigerian. I believe that the emphasis on place of birth is one of the banes of Nigerian nationhood and the genesis of retrogression. To a large extent, it is who you know that determines what you get. In my case, for example, I met my wife when she came to an all-night Christian vigil. I set my mind on marrying her in a ceremony in the tradition of the African white wedding. My parents, accompanied by religious leaders, visited her parents with some drinks. Then they told them, 'We have discovered a flower in your house.' That is a sign of the married couple's intention to live together by sharing drinks. There was a celebration where I paid a dowry for gifts to my wife. We were married in formal ceremony in 1998."

Thompson briefly left his wife in Africa to come to the U.S. for his Hubert Humphrey International Fellowship program at the University of Minnesota. She later joined him for a while in his Minneapolis apartment. During my interview with him at the University's Human Rights Center, where he was finishing an internship, Thompson told me that he eventually wanted to return home to Africa and put his U.S. study time to good use. "Everything I do is with the best interest of my people in mind. I hope to establish links here that I can use back home."

Growing up amidst stark deprivation made a deep impression on Thompson. "I have always wanted to be a lawyer from childhood so I can fight for rights, redress wrongs and help people to better their lot. At one time, I wanted to be a pilot, retire at thirty-five, read law and settle down. But after being admitted to the North American Institute of Aviation, I couldn't afford the fees. So I abandoned that dream and turned to studying law. So I read law. I have been influenced greatly by my Christian faith and family background. My father always had non-relations living with us. I was always around people who were kind and willing to help others in distress. In our African communal life, one person's problem is our problem. I grew up hurting for those in need and wanting to do something about their plight. I figured that being a lawyer would help me do that."

When he first tried to pursue new his dream, Thompson found out that even his aristocratic upbringing didn't automatically open doors. He had hoped to enroll in prestigious Keys College in Lagos, but after he applied, his name somehow disappeared from the college files. "My father was not an influential person," he says. "I was a member of a one of the smaller ethnic groups. There were three dominant ethnic groups, three dominant tribes. Mine was outside of that. It takes influence to get into such good schools. Even if you are qualified on merit, your name can disappear from the list." Thompson might have given up had it not been for the encouragement of his father, who said to him, "You can be whatever you want in life without that college."

Thompson did get his law degree at the University of Nigeria in 1987. He then went to work in national compulsory youth service projects in Africa's largest city for about a year to learn more about its culture. In the process, he worked at the firm of a prominent lawyer in the areas of human rights abuses, such as robbery and land disputes that were rampant in Nigeria. "People were picked up by police on community complaints, locked up, denied bail. I had to go to court to get them released. They were being denied any privilege of a free citizen. Sometimes, people would be locked up for years for petty crimes and not let out on bail. The cells were crowded and in very bad condition. I went to court to fight for these people's rights and to prevent citizens from getting picked up by police who were acting like a debt-collection agency, using their power to coerce people to pay debts so they could get a percentage."

Thompson wants to continue to fight for the common people of Africa. "One of the great needs we Africans have as a people is leadership. Everybody in public office just wants to get what they can out of their position. They use the government as a way to make themselves 'fat.' They don't have public service in mind when they vie for public office. I want to change that, using myself as an example. That would have to be done through a political position. I would start trying to enlighten people to know their rights and to stand up for themselves. The financial temptations are many, and I must not give in to them. I must fortify myself against them. Leadership must know how it is going to be effective. It must be ready for opposition. If I'm going to try to solve the problems people face, I will have to be strong against that opposition.

"I may eventually run for the state house of assembly or one of the federal and local councils. I want to bring improvements and changes. Politics in

Nigeria is a money affair. If you don't have money, you don't stand a chance. Money is worshipped in Nigeria almost like a god. They don't care how you got it or through what value system. Money means everything. People will cling to anything that will make money. People in power buy votes. They buy allegiance and loyalty with money, while the general population is near starvation. The poor never had it so bad economically. And yet, people are afraid to rise up. I want to speak for the hungry. I want to make sure that money affects the lives of ordinary people rather than end up in someone's pocket."

Thompson is aware of the dangers he may face if he attempts to campaign for and serve in public office. "Our minister of justice was assassinated in his house!" he exclaims, his voice rising with concern. "If you want to fight against the establishment, you must be ready to lay down your life. There's nothing they won't stop at. When you have enough contacts, it is more difficult for them to eliminate you because they would be afraid of the stink it would cause. And people are afraid to rise up.

"Nigeria is rich. It can pay its own debt. Our money is being mismanaged. Africa has a vibrant population. Most of its blacks are intelligent but have nothing to excite their intelligence. We have never had a government that channeled our people's ingenuity into something useful. Since government has failed to create the necessary environment for profitable employment of our virile people, they naturally quite frequently turn to crime to survive. We are inventive, but we have no government backing. I have many good ideas for making Africa better if I can get the backing. They need a leader. I want to be that leader.

"There are many things we can do rather than just pumping money into private pockets. I want to work with the Nembe Development Foundation to carry out projects. I would get together all of the intellectuals I can and discuss problems. Then, I would go to the people for solutions. Enlightenment would begin a process of change and transformation. If we can mobilize and educate people they can become instruments of that change.

"I've been involved with the Christian Lawyers Fellowship of Nigeria. We promote the practice of law in a godly fashion through principles of honor and integrity. We work on human rights issues in prisons. We've taken a stance on national issues such as Nigeria's relationship with Israel. I speak to law students frequently. I'm also a Christian lay minister. I have the calling of an evangelist. I speak in many churches and conduct crusades, retreats, and special programs in my own church. We have extended family relationships we are responsible for. For example, lots of people stay at my place from other tribes. I have had as many as thirteen people in my three-room apartment. I like to spread the word to them. I call that 'practicing law with a human face.'"

Thompson completed a non-degree program at the Humphrey Institute at the University of Minnesota, specializing in human rights expected judicial process and leadership and a master's in public affairs degree from the University. He has given presentations on human rights, social justice, conflict resolution, and developmental issues in Washington, D.C. and other U.S. locations. In the Twin Cities, Thompson has spoken at schools, churches and other locations about his experiences in Nigeria, has challenged aimless immigrant children to rise up to change their lives and make a difference in society, and has fostered cross-cultural relationships.

In August of 2003, Thompson and his wife gave birth to a baby boy. The following year, he received the Arthur Naftalin Award for Public Service, given in honor of a former mayor of Minneapolis. He is currently a principal partner in the law firm he founded in 1992, T.A.G. Ivory and Company in Lagos, Nigeria, and continues, as he puts it, "to mentor the younger generation of his colleagues in legal practice as well as people in schools, churches and elsewhere about their civic rights, duties and responsibilities, and to be engaged in work and projects connected with the propagation, protection and enforcement of human rights throughout the world."

**Roelof and his wife Anne on the shore of Lake Superior in Wisconsin
(Photo courtesy of Roelof Nel)**

SHADES OF GRAY
By Burt Berlowe

It was a bright summer day in the Mozambique countryside. Roelof Nel was on a church outing in the midst of a poor, black community. As he and his fellow visitors walked the streets, swarms of small children followed close by, grasping for attention.

When the group paused to rest in a sandy area, Roelof strummed his guitar and played with some of the African children. One of the children, unable to speak English, found a unique way to talk to Roelof. He drew an image of the guitar in a piece of hard sand then carved his name in it. Then he picked up the sand and handed it to Roelof. The sand ornament cracked and vanished quickly in Roelof's palm. The gesture has stayed with him since.

* * *

Roelof grew up in a black and white world, white on top, black on the bottom. Ever since his childhood in apartheid-torn South Africa, Roelof had been bumping against issues of class and race. As a European African boer (Afrikaner) in a segregated world, his primary relationship with blacks had been to be their boss.

"I was raised primarily in a small rural town called Louis Trichardt, 500 kilometers from the capital city of Pretoria (my birthplace) close to the Zimbabwe border," he recalls, speaking with a profound British-like accent. "It had about 20,000 people, mostly whites with money, mixed with a few of the poor. The greater metro area around it was largely black, and there was some mingling of races in the town. If you walked around the area on a normal day, you'd think it was a black town. Actually, it was expensive to buy houses there so after the fall of apartheid it remained mostly segregated. Before 1994, only whites could vote. No blacks were allowed to live inside the town. They could shop there if they had a pass but had to be out of the white area at night. Most would do unskilled work like cleaning houses.

"I grew up thinking apartheid was the right thing. That was what they taught in schools. Lots of people believed that whites are the superior race. I was raised to think that blacks were there to serve you, to wash our dishes, do the laundry, cut the grass. We had servants in the house. We thought it was a way to provide them with jobs. The mindset was 'I'm the boss. They've got to do what is I say because I'm white.'

"My native language was Afrikaans. English became a second language in fourth grade. My dad owns a construction business. I remember once my dad and I were at the Pretoria Café before we moved. The police came and people started to run, including some of the blacks working for my dad. They were employed by him doing renovation jobs. I couldn't understand why anyone would run away from police. They were supposed to be good guys. Later, I learned that it was because they didn't have pass books. Dad saved them from jail.

"There was a big income gap in salaries between the races. For instance, my mother, a trained teacher at a black school, made about twice as much as a black foreman. In her job, my mom had black colleagues. When we would go shopping and she would run into her colleagues, they would always get a hug. She really was concerned that black children were getting an inferior education. The superior feeling we had was never hate. It was just a result of a class system."

The race issue in South Africa then was a time bomb literally waiting to explode. Roelof's home community had its own town council that was under the control of a government under siege from the rebelling African National

Congress (ANC) military wing. "I remember when I was young being close to the border where land mines were going off and bombs were being dropped by the ANC. They were after petroleum depots and the like. We were being told in school to look out for the mines.

"The purpose of the bombing was to start a revolution. The military became the government after 1994, organized by Nelson Mandela, who was previously imprisoned supposedly for life. They were the revolutionaries who started a movement overthrowing apartheid. We (whites only) had an election to decide if we wanted to stop apartheid. There were a lot of sanctions against South Africa by European countries and the United States. The sanctions, combined with the ANC operation's outcome, were people saying, 'we want to stop apartheid.'

"I remember a lot about the revolution; big protests, 'toy toy' dancing, which was like a peace walk, mostly blacks and some whites together taking a stand for human rights. I was scared of it. It was confusing to me. I kept thinking, 'Why are we so segregated? Is this really right?' Sometimes, I would think it was right, and sometimes that it wasn't. At times, I wondered why I couldn't go out and just change it."

The first real sign of an attitude shift for Roelof came during his college years at Pretoria College where he was studying agricultural research. His grandfather had a farm nearby that Roelof would often visit. Blacks were working and staying on the farm harvesting corn, potatoes, and fruit trees and raising cattle, sheep, and African goats for local consumption. Roelof grew to love the wide-open spaces, fishing in the dam, enjoying nature and the openness of the countryside.

Roelof's interest in working the fields later led him to a job at Makhatine Flats, a flat piece of land sixty kilometers from the sea, surrounded by mountains. "There was a big dam and nearby irrigation system for small-scale farmers. I worked at an agricultural research station for six months. I began talking to black farmers, working closely with them. I noticed that they were people with good ideas. And we were being paid the same as they were. It was no longer a case of having an attitude that I was rich and they weren't. After that, I worked at another research job for rich white tobacco and black cotton farmers where I interacted with both cultures. My thinking continued to change. It was hard to make that transition in my attitude towards blacks when everything you've been told in the formulative stages of life all of sudden doesn't seem right anymore.

"I began reading the Bible and figuring out some of its messages. I had been raised as a Christian at a time when many of the churches were segregated and language was a barrier. I grew up in an area where many blacks had their own language as part of their culture. The Christian message focused on giving people their rights and having feelings for those who are struggling. It is very much about compassion, realizing that it's not so important what you have yourself, but how happy people are around you.

"I remember one evening when a black came up to me and said he was a missionary and didn't have a place to stay. I found him a place. With that act of compassion, I was opening myself up in spirit. He stayed in my house one night, then I took him back to town the next day. I realized that we were both Christians, that we had mutual respect for each other. It was a spiritual experience.

"At that point, I began to change my own way of living. I had previously been a bad kind of rebel, drinking a lot with my friends and not caring much about the world. I was a party boy in college. It was a miracle that I passed my classes. I began to realize I was hurting my parents and everyone around me, that drinking was an expensive habit and I wasn't making much money. I gradually phased it out and learned how to better handle peer pressure. I got my agriculture degree and became more serious."

One of the first times Roelof left his home country was in his second year of college. He hiked with friends up to Vicrotia Falls, one of the world's largest waterfalls on the border of Zimbabwe and Zambia. "We came to a place where blacks were making ornaments. We pitched our tents and stayed with some black people. We got along well with each other. I was actually in the minority as a white person. It made me reach out further than I normally would and discover it was not as dangerous as I had thought.

"I loved traveling so much I decided to go on a working holiday to England. The one-year work permit only allows the traveler to do non-professional work. The tables turned and I was now the worker and "they" (the rich English men) were the boss.

"I worked on a farm in England with fruit pickers from Eastern Europe, picking strawberries. It was tough, physical labor and, for the first time, I experienced the irony of being a slave, and I thought about that a lot. I came to understand how the blacks felt. I could get out of that situation because of my education, but they couldn't. I got tired of being a field laborer. I quit and became a security guard patrolling the innards of a large office building, as a lot of rich people came and left."

In 2002, through the International Agriculture Exchange Program, Roelof received a call from the Institute for Agriculture and Trade Policy (IATP) in Minneapolis, inviting him to do an internship with them in agricultural marketing and commerce. It would be his first trip to the U.S., and he wasn't quite sure what to expect. "Most South Africans thought America was THE place," he says. "I was trying to find my little space there."

Roelof found that space as an intern with IATP. His duties included packaging and selling Peace Coffee and copies of the Institute's published book *Renewing the Countryside*. At the same time, he began pursuing his main interest, learning about U.S. development and how it compares to that in Africa. He also became an activist, attending some antiwar protests at the downtown federal building. He calls those demonstrations "our toy toy."

Living in the U.S. has made return visits to South Africa increasingly difficult. "I found it hard when I went home to visit; people don't have that same kind of compassion there. There are high crime rates. Rape is terrible. Black on white, white on white—all of them. I don't personally feel a sense of danger, but I feel concerned about my women friends and what could happen to them. I have friends who were robbed and raped. There are racial tensions because of economic policies, lack of water and electricity. Government promised a lot and hasn't delivered. There's a thirty percent jobless rate. People can't afford water. You drive through the streets and there are fifty people on corners coming up to you begging to wash your car or anything else they can do to make money. And people still have servants there.

"I am really against apartheid. I want to do something to make a difference when I go back home. It could be on the economic side, in politics or government policies. When I went back there recently, it was still a different world. There were a lot more poor people. One town had a black mayor and town council. There was a small black middle class and a few rich ones. But the majority of people were struggling. There's lots of privatization. Even the water is privatized. In the townships, you have to walk to the river to get water. If you don't pay for it, you don't get any. On the road between my hometown and Pretoria, there used to be one tollgate. Now, there are three or four. And the toll went from two rand to a hundred rand (about ten rand in a dollar).

"The government is trying to get more investment but hasn't created jobs. Municipal workers in my home town went on strike. A black councilman shot two of them. I read the African newspapers and a website about this conflict. It was quite shocking. We need to change to a new way of thinking. A very old generation grew up with apartheid and is caught up in their ways. Younger people need to be instigating change. You ask the people, 'Why are you saving food?' They say, 'You never know when there's going to be a war.'

"I am interested in changing people's minds. We need to change one mind at a time. My brother and mom both understand what I want to do. My dad is the hardest mind to change. He has a strong personality. We've had a lot of conversations. I had a lot to say he didn't agree with regarding the role of whites and blacks in South Africa. I have spoken to friends in South Africa about this to try to generate some new ideas. One idea I have is to get each of them to sponsor one of their black servants and pay for one of those kids school tuition that would stay with the kids for the rest of their life. And they would learn that not all whites are bad. Kids are going to grow up and remember that someone looked after them and gave them an education. Some of my friends have e-mailed me and said they are going to try to find a black they can sponsor.

"Africa now is too much about making profits and about people being slaves. There's much more that can be done. Through the World Bank, we can give money to Africa. We need more people with more money helping those with less money, plus a lot more trade with the European Union, stopping misuse of money where the banks give loans that have to be paid back with interest.

"I would like to eventually get into a government position in South Africa to help any way I could to get people to trust each other and to trust me to be their leader. If you want to make change, you have to be a leader. I will go wherever in Africa I can to make a difference."

Following his tenure at IATP, Roelof completed a master's degree in applied economics at the University of Minnesota and married a Minnesota girl. "I still dream of going back to South Africa," he says, "although I feel I can do more for my family here in the U.S. I am worried about my parents and the families they support through employment. The jobless rate in South Africa is growing and finding work has become increasingly hard. There are many people that are stuck with skeletons of apartheid—the aging population, the 'bosses,' and the undereducated."

While at the University, Roelof encountered an ironic twist on the issue he dealt with for so long. "I wanted to do research on bank loans to the poor in South Africa but couldn't get funding. I was told that because I am not black, there was no money available. It makes me sad that the color of my skin inhibits me from helping those the color of my skin has suppressed for so long."

Chapter Five
Community Builders

INTRODUCTION

"Community" is all of us together, working for the common good.
—Dick Bernard, former president of the Minnesota Alliance of Peacemakers
and retired staff person of the Minnesota Education Association

The many social movements that come under the umbrella of the compassionate rebel revolution promote a wide variety of causes, tactics and participants. But they all share one thing: a connection to community. In fact, all social change activism, whether by groups or individuals, originates and lives in one or more communities.

We define "community" in the broadest, most-inclusive way. It can range from two people gathering on a street corner to millions around the globe coming together in a common cause. It can also be synonymous with neighborhood or defined by ethnicity, race, religion, workplace or lifestyle. You've all heard the expression "communities of color" or "community of nations," or what about "global community" or "community of man." Basically, wherever you have people, you have community.

Most people love their communities and want to maintain, improve, and defend them. Out of that urge comes the drive for social action. In the process, community building often takes place, either through the development or renewal of an actual physical space or the improvement of an organizational structure. It is through that process that political and social movements are made and strengthened.

We have seen powerful examples of this throughout history. The American Revolution, fostered by small groups of citizens in town squares and backyard gatherings, led to the building of a national community and set a precedent for the decades to come.

The major movements that have followed: for women's rights, civil rights, peace and justice, and the preservation or transformation of neighborhoods all have been largely about community, as have the countless efforts of individuals and small groups working for social change.

In the previous two chapters of this book, we have seen how individuals can come together over issues of war and peace, immigration, and human rights, and, in so doing, build the strength of the movement, organization, and/or place they are working from. In this chapter, we feature people who have built and strengthened communities of all kinds, and, in the process, transformed the American landscape. Their compelling stories help us to understand the importance of community in our daily lives.

*The full context of this quote can be found at OutsidetheWalls.org/blog. June 10, 2009. #38, "Seeing Community."

Bob Milner at National Night Out
(Photo courtesy of Wendy McCormick)

HUMPTY DUMPTY IN OVERALLS
By Burt Berlowe
With contributions from Heidi Rivers and Wendy McCormick

It was April 5, 1968, and the response to the assassination of Martin Luther King the day before had turned America into a war zone. The simmering rage and frustration of the black community had exploded into a barrage of turmoil and violence that would eventually spread to over 100 cities over the next five days.

That afternoon in Chicago, rioters took to the streets on the west side of the city, breaking windows, looting stores, and setting off numerous fires, resulting in a dozen civilian casualties and the destruction of 170 buildings, leaving more than 1,000 people homeless. It took some 11,000 federal troops to finally bring order.

In a peaceful but tense part of Chicago, near one of the city's poorest neighborhoods, the Sears-Roebuck building was being evacuated, many of the 14,000 employees streaming to the parking lot, scrambling to get out of the path of the storm. Among the people leaving the building with a friend was Bob Milner, a clean-cut rising young executive who was visiting on business, dressed for the part in his customary dark-blue suit, attache case at his side.

While most of the evacuees headed west to the freeway traveling to their homes in the Chicago suburbs, backing up traffic for miles, Bob went in the opposite direction, following a service road that would eventually lead him to his residence several miles away. As he came to a stop light, he noticed a group of young African American men walking towards a car with some elderly people in it. They stopped, grabbed a hold of the car, and rocked it back and forth.

Disturbed by what he saw, Bob honked his horn and called out to the youths, "Leave them alone." The group of young men left their original victims and moved towards Bob's car. His passenger instinctively put his hands on his head and ducked down underneath the seat as a brick was thrown through the car window. Bob remained upright, leaning slightly into the steering column.

The youths pulled the driver's side door open and tried to drag Bob towards them. He grabbed the wheel forcefully and hung on, refusing to be moved. Then he looked at his attackers and said, "You've got the wrong person."

Bob forced his muscular 250-pound frame against the door and stepped out. He stared directly into the eyes of one of the youth and a strange feeling came over him. "I felt like we had been staring at each other for 10,000 years," he recalls. The young black man returned Bob's glare momentarily then turned and walked away, his companions following behind. A broken front window was the worst of the damage to the car or its occupants. But the experience of that day would shatter Bob's view of the world. The ride home began a new life for him, a long journey from which there was no turning back.

* * *

"There have been many turning points in my life," Bob says, reflecting on his stormy past. "When I was young, I was active in sports. Because I was the biggest kid I became the baseball catcher. Playing sports saved me from pursing a life of crime. I was close to becoming a professional player signing with the Cleveland Indians when I tore cartilage in my knee."

In college, Bob was a young man with a promising future. He was chairman of the homecoming selection committee for the alumni association, president of about ten campus organizations, and married the homecoming queen. After graduation, he went to work for Burlington Industries, the world's largest textile corporation, designing and selling products and creating marketing programs. At age twenty-four, he was one of their rising young stars, managing an office in downtown Chicago.

Bob and his wife lived on the twenty-seventh floor of a high-rise on an exclusive street called Marine Drive overlooking Lake Michigan. The elite neighborhood was right next to one of city's poorest communities. But Bob paid little attention to the urban blight that was practically in his backyard. "I never noticed the poverty behind us. I would drive through my underground garage to my office space every workday, totally oblivious to what was going on in the world. I played golf, had an unlimited expense account and was entertaining almost every night. I went into fancy restaurants and they would usher me to a table for three-martini luncheons with buyers from Sears. I normally didn't drink, but this was what you had to do if you wanted to advance in your job."

Sometimes the conversations Bob had with co-workers or clients took an unexpectedly nasty turn. "The day JFK was assassinated, I was at work walking down the hall when the news came. The president of our division said, 'It's about time they shot the S.O.B.' They pretty much felt the same thing about Martin Luther King. I would be at lunch with buyers and they would talk about how King was a troublemaker. I thought he was probably a nice guy but that he talked too much and that trouble seemed to follow him wherever he went. But I really didn't care much about politics or race. I was part of the problem not the solution. I only cared about money and prestige."

That all began to change on the fateful April night in 1968. Shaken by his encounter with the youths who attacked him, Bob drove back to his apartment to pick up his wife, pausing to let her vacuum the glass shards from his hair. He grabbed a set of knives to take with them for protection. As they were pulling out of their parking garage, a friend drove in next to them, and, noticing the smashed car window, asked what had happened. "When I told him about the assault," Bob recalls, "he said, 'Would you like a gun?' I said, 'Yeah.' The only other time I had used a gun was shooting skeet. I had mixed feelings about having the weapons. I was glad to have them to protect myself, but I also couldn't stand to have them. Those kinds of paradoxes have happened time and again in my life."

After the attack, Bob began to reach out to whomever he came across to find out what their viewpoint of the world was, what concerns they had. He left himself open, he says, "I didn't want to argue back. I just wanted to understand.

"I would stop people I met on the street and ask them: 'How do you see the world and why do you see it as you do?' Generally, I talked to people who looked like people I wouldn't have normally talked with or known or who looked different than me and whose lives might be very different from mine."

When he heard that a black student group staged a sit-in at the bursar's office of Northwestern University in May of 1968 to campaign peacefully for black studies and greater black student recruitment, Bob called the office directly and spoke with the group's leader, a graduate student named James Turner. Turner offered his view of the day's newspaper stories, giving Bob insight into how he would read between the lines of a typical newspaper story.

Bob has come to believe now, looking back, that many people took on pieces of Martin Luther King's dream in the days following the assassination. At the time, Bob found himself wrestling with trying to see the world from a new or different perspective. He realized just how oblivious he had been to much of the world in his quest to succeed in the corporate environment he'd stepped into after college. As he searched for understanding, he also began to search for ways in which he could make the world a better place.

"I didn't feel good that I thought I needed a gun that night," he says, "I wasn't afraid, but I wondered why there were people angry in the streets. And then, following close behind that: what could I do about it? What skills did I have that I could use to make a difference?"

Bob began to look for common ground, not only among people individually, but between the public and private sectors, government and corporations, hoping to develop a conversation that would result in development and application of solutions to issues like poverty, job opportunities, housing and education, to try to create a more equitable and just society.

"I was coming from the business sector, working in a corporation. I wanted to get corporations to feel their sense of social responsibility to the society that birthed them. I wanted to get groups together to create a different kind of society. I called it Enlightened Capitalism."

Bob organized several meetings hoping to stimulate collaborations and ideas that he was developing and that were in a very formative stage. "In the end, I think I was looking for more from other people, and I think they were looking for more from me than I was prepared to provide."

After a "falling out" with his Burlington boss over his extra-curricular activism, Bob gave up his high-salaried position, his dark-blue suits and three-martini lunches. He took a job with a small company selling furniture fabric. He also got involved in electoral politics for the first time

At one of his Enlightened Capitalism meetings, Bob had met a man named Victor DeGrazia, who invited him to work as the finance chairman for Abner Mikva's campaign for U.S Congress from the Hyde Park area of Chicago. Bob calls Mikva "one of the most compassionate, honest, intelligent and genuine people I've ever met. He was an extraordinary human being. In fact, Abner was probably the only person that I could have or would have worked for at that time."

One day in 1968, Bob's then-wife bought him a colorful paisley black beanbag frog about 12" long that was stuffed with grass seed. She had found the frog in a Chicago specialty gift store named The Emporium.

"I really liked the frog and wanted to find out who made it," Bob recalls. "It was like I was driven to it. I went to the Emporium and asked the owner (whose last name was also Milner) where he got the frog. He wouldn't say because he didn't want another store in the area to sell the same item. The Emporium prided itself on carrying unique and novel gift items. Being blocked didn't deter me."

A year later, Bob found out that the frogs were made in Minneapolis. Shortly thereafter, while on a business trip to that city, he took the opportunity to visit the place where the frogs were manufactured. The shop was called Things, and the frogs were a part of a line of products called Amiable Animals. Things was in many ways like the Emporium, but sold much more down-to-earth, natural products such as seeds and herbs, incense and dried flowers and paper, leather and glass products.

"It was during the counterculture era and this was a typical shop of that time. I thought of it as a 'hippie place.' I was dressed in a suit. The employees there all had long hair and the smell of incense and marijuana was in the air.

"I said, 'I want to meet whoever made the frog.'" To Bob's surprise, someone with a beard and long hair came toward him and said, 'Why do you want to meet him?' Bob said, "Because I really like the frog." The bearded man responded: "If you really like the frog, why don't you buy them all?" Bob was taken aback and said that he'd think about it. He ordered some samples of the products: a big and small frog, a frog in togs, an octopus, a snake and a whale, and promised to ponder the offer.

* * *

Bob tossed and turned on the hospital bed, gasping for air again and again. Six months after the frog visit, he was hospitalized with severe bronchitis. After two weeks, he was released, but readmitted shortly thereafter, with bronchial asthma, a childhood chronic ailment that had been reactivated by the bout of bronchitis. Over the next twenty-two years, Bob had close to 150 emergency trips to various hospitals resulting in nearly 100 hospitalizations.

Bob recalls some of his first struggles to breathe in Chicago: "Once, I couldn't even walk to my car and had to stop and lean on a pole unable to move. Two gals and a guy helped me across the street. Another time, I was starting to drive from Chicago to Dubuque on a sales trip and nearly fell out of my car. I ended up taking an ambulance to the hospital. On another occasion, I was driving to Elgin, Illinois, pulled over to the service road and fell out of my car. A guy fixing a pick-up truck took me to a tollbooth where an ambulance was called to come and get me."

In those days, Bob recalls, some people didn't take things like asthma seriously as a physical illness; they would assume an emotional cause. Often, people like one of Bob's new bosses, would say, "Fight it. Keep going." When Bob tried that he wound up in the hospital, gasping for air again. On one sales trip, he almost died from an attack. He decided then that he really wanted to get to the root of the problem.

"I began to think that my symptoms could be psychogenic or psychosomatic, or even socioegenic, that I had a weakness in my system, sort of like when one part of a city affects the other. We live in a very unhealthy society. If we want to be in denial that people are suffering, starving, and not working, and are outside the system, then we have to realize that the system is unhealthy, like it's a body. In order to be healthy, we need to recognize the cause and how we deal with it. The whole became important to me. I realized that if the world isn't healthy, then I'm not. I needed to work on creating a healthier existence within myself and outside of myself."

Bob's friends and family, aware and concerned about what felt like personality, attitude and significant world-view changes in him, as well as his health condition, were pleased when he decided to get an in-patient psychological evaluation to see if his asthma was psychosomatic. Despite his physical discomfort, Bob exhibited the kind of compassionate rebellion during his institutional stay that would come to characterize his life.

"There was a common room in the ward which housed group meetings as well as serving as a TV lounge. It was a large room with lots of very tall windows that looked out on a beautiful park. The windows were covered with heavy, dusty curtains and you couldn't see the park. Since many of the patients there were suffering from depression, I felt it would be very helpful if they could get some sunlight and a good view.

"The staff didn't see it that way and didn't respond to repeated requests to even open the curtains. I felt compelled to take the curtains down myself. From that point forward, everyone enjoyed the beautiful view of the park and the trees."

Bob had brought a record player with him that he would play in his room. His roommate was suffering from amnesia, but when he heard the first notes of Bach's "A Little Night Music," his hands would rise and he would start to conduct the piece, even with his eyes closed. Other patients started coming by to listen to music in Bob's room. This became an unintended challenge to the staff, says Bob, and they took the record player away. "So, some of the patients and me decided to sort of strike so we could get our music back. Eventually, what happened was that they made a separate room into a music room. We had a place to go to listen to music after that. It was great."

Bob also formed powerful and touching connections with some of the other patients there. "There was a young woman who never spoke to anyone. One day I said to her, 'Why do you not speak anymore?' and she replied: 'I'm afraid if I say something, I will have said all I have to say and there'll be nothing left to say.' I said, 'Is that true?' and she said, 'Yes.' Then I said, 'See, you did have something else to say.' As the conversation went on, she introduced me to the music of James Taylor and his song 'Fire and Rain.' We became friends.

"I had a lot time to think while being evaluated in the hospital. I began to think that what was outside in the world was crazy—the Vietnam War, bigotry, division of rich and poor—and my being oblivious to it all. I decided I would make a change. The world I'd been living and working in wasn't for me anymore. I was going to buy the frog company. I wrote the contract for it in the lobby of the hospital."

Bob got out of the hospital on a day pass and hitchhiked to see the frog company's Chicago sales rep, Barrie Byrd. He got a ride that day from one of Jesse Jackson's bodyguards. "Barrie and I picked out new fabric for the frogs, which made them much more appealing and fresh, which eventually helped to increase the gross sales from $11,000 to $30,000 the next year."

Bob's changing attitude towards his life threatened his marriage. "My wife and I weren't getting along. We drifted apart. She was unhappy that I had changed so much, that I didn't do the things I used to do. I decided I didn't fit in my old world and was going to leave it.

"That decision left me homeless after I left the hospital. I hitchhiked to a studio of a photographer friend, and lived there through a winter, sleeping on the plain, white pine couch—quite a change for someone who once lived on Lakeshore Drive."

On some nights that winter, Bob picked his way carefully along the icy sidewalks of Old Town to look at his new company's line of frogs through the window of a store called Granny Good Fox. "I was running this small company from Chicago, but it was really running itself up in Minneapolis, managed by a woman named Marilee DeLauriers, the only employee, who'd worked for the prior owner."

When Bob had bought the company, he named it the Peaceable Kingdom. The frogs were the Amiable Animals, migrations from the Peaceable Kingdom.

Bob migrated too, that spring, setting out for Minneapolis with a suitcase full of frogs and hope for a new start.

* * *

Bob's asthma continued to plague him when he arrived in Minneapolis in 1970, eventually leading to fifteen hospital admissions and over thirty emergency room trips in the next two-and-a-half years. At the same time, his small company was being run out of a big closet in Marilee's small apartment. When Bob bought the company, it had relied on people sewing the fabric frog skins in their homes. The skins were then turned into beanbags when they were filled with grass seed by Marilee in her apartment, who would also close them with a closing machine and glue on their googly frog eyes. Bob continued to work in the same way. However, that year, the business moved a number of times, from that small apartment to a basement in a house on 4th Avenue in South Minneapolis.

Eventually, Bob met a young man by the name of Eric, who Bob called the Long-Haired Laughing Boy. Bob had no place of his own to live at that time and moved in with Eric and his girlfriend and her brothers, where Bob slept on the floor, head to toe with the brothers across the length of the apartment. They all soon came to work with Bob at the Peaceable Kingdom.

"While I was in one of the wards of the old Hennepin County General Hospital, Eric found a place to move the company to. It was the Fawkes Building on Loring Park (in Minneapolis). I rented a pie-shaped room for $50 a month. I slept in the back and the company occupied the front of the space. I remember being awakened in the morning by the sound of the mail being dropped through the mail slot in the door. I really felt like I was being birthed in that room and the mail was the food being dropped through the chute."

Bob has a great deal of gratitude for the man who rented him that space, John Brendan. "John was very kind to me. He was one of the first people I met who was deeply involved helping people through chemical dependence and addiction.

"The Fawkes Building at that time was a magical place. There were people doing all kinds of creative, artistic and alternative things there. There were two guys making yantras (which are) Hindu meditation wheels in the basement. There was a photographer at the top of the building and a sculptor on the same floor as I was. At the same time, there were also older, more mainstream businesses in the building like the tie factory, a small neck-tie manufacturer, complete with an assembly line of older women and wall full of *Playboy* centerfolds for the men who worked there."

One of the frog skin sewers, Helen Carlson, gave Bob a little pom-pom caterpillar with a floral wire antenna with colorful seed beads at the tips. One day, he went to the beach in northern Minnesota and saw ladybugs, and when he came home, he tried to paint little dots on the pom-poms to make a ladybug. When that didn't work, he put little eyes on the pom-pom and he called it a "bump." Pairing that with the caterpillar, he said, "I had little bumps and little buggers. I thought they were adorable and so did Barrie Byrd, our rep back in Chicago."

These pom-pom creatures were glued to magnets, the first of this kind of novelty gift item and the first of the refrigerator magnets, which have become now a staple household item. Bob put them on a paint can and found that to be a great point of sale display, perfect to act as both a shipping container and a display case.

One day, Bob went down the stairway from the Peaceable Kingdom, under John Brendan's office, to the School for Social Development in the Fawkes Building. He wanted to find out if they could handcraft some bumps. A woman who was waiting there, Marge Micelli, asked what he was doing. He said, "I'm here to see if they can make the little bumps," and showed them to her. She said, "We can make them for you." "Who are you?" Bob asked.

Marge Micelli was a coordinator at Meeker-Wright Community Action Program in Waverly, Minnesota. She had three people who could make the bumps, working in their homes. Within a month, she had ten people working. In a couple of months, she had as many as thirty employees.

Meeker-Wright Community Action Program was trying to create work initiatives in economically-depressed rural Minnesota, and eventually, a group of workers formed a producer's cooperative called the Crow River Crafts Co-op. This group grew to over 300 people in the next several years and consisted of people who lived in five counties across the region. They contracted to make upwards of two million pom-pom creatures a year for Peaceable Kingdom in their homes. The bump and the bug grew to become little bears, little lambs and eventually over 100 designs including holiday items and people designs and even vegetable creatures.

Providing work opportunities to disabled, disenfranchised and economically challenged people became a way of doing business for the Peaceable Kingdom. And it worked for the business as well as the people involved.

"Sales started taking off and the magnet creatures became an international craze," Bob says. "In the first two months, we sold $30,000 worth of items. Peaceable Kingdom grew rapidly to a $700,000 business. I realized that we had a product that could be a huge thing. I was living my dream. I was more interested in serving the people who were working there than in making money, which took me back to one of the reasons why I left the corporate world and that was because all the corporations seemed to be interested in was making money and not dealing equitably or fairly with their employees and/or the communities in which they were housed or came from. My business became an experiment in how we can meet social responsibility working with a population that doesn't normally get work. I was on this quest and wanted the seed to spread."

In the meantime, Bob continued to endure many more hospitalizations and emergency room experiences with his asthma. Medications for his asthma would also affect him in ways that even the doctors didn't understand. "In the hospital, I was put on massive doses of IV steroids for asthma and then pulled off of them without anyone knowing the consequences. It caused me tremendous mood swings and bouts of depression. The worse part was that I was the one who had to discover this pattern and convince the doctors that it was caused by the medications. Even now, patients are not often prepared for the mood swings that can occur with their asthma medications."

Bob continued to try to work, sometimes holding design meetings from his hospital bed. For him, the business was also a welcome distraction from his health challenges, and designing little pom-pom creatures often took him out of his physical pain. At the same time, the other people working at the Peaceable Kingdom stepped up when he couldn't.

"There were all these young people working in the business who'd come out of dealing with difficult family, personal or chemical dependency issues; kind of lost kids, really. They ran the business when I couldn't. They came to the door and we gave them a job. We didn't turn anyone away in the early days. We just made another place for them at the table, so to speak."

Peaceable Kingdom grew and was marketed by independent sales reps in the U.S., and in other countries from Europe to Japan. Along the way, Bob met a producer from England, who wanted to make an animated film series based on Peaceable Kingdom product characters. Bob wanted a portion of the proceeds from the enterprise to go towards social good, to be a part of the overall plan and structure of the business. This was in 1976, well before other enterprises were thinking along these lines. "I thought then, and still think now, that when business reaches a certain point, it should be about a greater social purpose along with its business purposes, as long as it conducts its business in ethical ways, even moral ways. This animated series would have given me international exposure but I turned it down."

By 1978, Bob says, the Peaceable Kingdom had gross sales of nearly a million dollars and had no long-term debt. "We had no written contracts with anybody: not the suppliers, the producers or the sales reps. Everything was done on high ethics and goodwill dealing."

Late that year, Bob began negotiations to acquire the Fawkes Building, which housed the business. He connected with an old acquaintance who he thought shared a common vision for a better future for one and all, and brought her to see the building with the idea that she might become a partner in its purchase. A feasibility study was done to see what it would take to acquire the building and, at the same time, Bob got other tenants to protest the lack of upkeep of the building, which was beginning to fall into disrepair. Feeling secure that matters were in good hands, Bob went to National Jewish Hospital, a medical and research center for respiratory diseases, to have his asthma evaluated, and to try to find some better ways of managing the chronic illness. He was told to expect to stay anywhere from six weeks to six months at the facility in Denver, Colorado.

"During the time I was gone, the business ran like clockwork. This was before e-mail or other electronic communications, but we stayed in touch well with a system of review, weekly reports and good communications."

But while Bob was away, the building was sold and he was completely left out of the deal. Shortly thereafter, the plans for the new owners included raising the rent for the space for Peaceable Kingdom to three times its previous amount. And soon after that, Bob received notification that the Peaceable Kingdom would be evicted from the building when the owner's son became the manager.

In the summer of 1979, Bob had a fall that crushed several vertebrae in his back. Many of the Peaceable Kingdom employees had left to pursue other dreams, and the long-term effects of his chronic conditions began to have an impact on him. He had developed cataracts and diabetes from using asthma medications. All these things, combined with the prospect of having to move from the building, weighed on him, and Bob initially reached out to try to find a partial business partner to help. Instead, he was contacted by an acquaintance of the Peaceable Kingdom's accountant who pressured him to become an equal partner and then to sell the business outright. Bob faced the agonizing decision of moving his beloved business elsewhere, or sell it.

"We sold the company for less money than we had in the bank. We essentially gave it to him (the new owner). I was broken. I would frequently break into tears. It was the end of a dream. Peaceable had always been more than just a business for me. It had found gifts in people who thought they had none. Throughout most it, I never thought about money. We were for people before profits. We worked with discarded people and materials. Through our work, the definition of social responsibility had expanded tremendously. We found out that business had the power to be a creative force in making change."

* * *

In 1980, while at a cabin in northern Minnesota, recuperating after the sale of his business, Bob heard a story on the radio about a woman whose daughter was killed by a drunk driver with multiple previous arrests for that crime. The story touched him and he reached out to the woman, who was trying to start an organization to deal with awareness of this issue. Her name was Candy Lightner, the name of the fledgling organization was Mothers Against Drunk Drivers. Bob wound up donating the cost of printing some of their first petitions. This was the beginning of Bob's re-entry into the world, as he became active in more non-profit organizations that needed someone to help them get their message out.

"I found that there were many voiceless populations and organizations trying to do good work who were being misrepresented or not represented in the media. I found that increasing public awareness of these people and organizations was something I could do."

Bob helped establish Mothers Against Drunk Driving in Minnesota and worked with MADD both nationally and statewide for twenty years, doing much of their early publicity. He created a candlelight vigil that became the national model for MADD. He also learned how to create audio documentaries and produced some materials for the University of Minnesota to raise awareness of the issue of drinking and driving.

Over time, Bob became involved with over eighty grassroots groups and causes, including the Nuclear Freeze Movement, the American Indian Movement's mascot issue, and Hispanic and Southeast Asian organizations. The enterprise that he created out of all of this was another small business called Decent Exposure. It was his way of keeping the alive the vision of betterment of the larger society that grew out of his Chicago days.

"I worked on developing the concept of what I call the Creative Design and Development Center, where artists, business people, and visionaries could come together to create projects, products and programs to better the human condition and to build more humane enterprises. I also began to network and organize people and organizations around the idea I was starting to call Harmony. I proposed that these groups stage music events that could create opportunities for large-scale food drives and other beneficial, cooperative efforts. Now this is a regular part of many concerts."

* * *

Bob steers a golf-cart down the dirt path that bisects spacious Theodore Wirth Park in Minneapolis, where the annual Juneteenth Minnesota celebration is taking place. Wirth Park, with its rolling hills, glistening lake, and sprawling golf course, sits on the border between the affluent inner-ring suburb of Golden Valley and the deprived neighborhoods of North Minneapolis, as if striving to be bridge between the two opposite ends of the social spectrum.

As the midday sun beats down hard, Bob drops off a passenger, then picks up and embraces a young black man he will take to the other side of the park, past the rows of exhibitors, musicians, and visitors that line the street and fill the woods. Dressed in his trademark blue jean overalls, bushy mustache and ponytail, Bob has been acting as the Juneteenth taxi service, driving around repeatedly that day looking for people weary from the heat who need rides across the park or to waiting cars or buses several blocks away.

Juneteenth is a national celebration marking the end of slavery in America and is planned and attended largely by African Americans. Yet Bob, a white man from south Minneapolis, has been a major force in the event for many years, serving as its vice-president and a chief advocate and promoter. His involvement with Juneteenth led him in 2004 to initiate the Freedom to Vote Project, an effort to mobilize minority voters in that election year. Freedom to Vote grew to include some 125 Twin Cities partner organizations. It was part of his ongoing commitment to dedicate his life to "giving voice to the voiceless," bringing positive stories from minority communities into the public eye and encouraging all people to co-exist in peace and end social injustice.

In recent years, Bob has focused on building community in another way, through his work with National Night Out, a project of the National Association of Town Watch. National Night Out is a nationwide event held on the first Tuesday in August where neighbors gather on their streets and yards to get together, share a potluck, and help to prevent crime through getting to know each other. Bob has worked with the City of Minneapolis as the media relations and public awareness contact for the summer event. During that time, Minneapolis has become one of the most active National Night Out cities in the country with more than 1,100 events held citywide, along with more than 200 locations throughout the state.

"Building community is a first step in building harmony," Bob says. "We're often at odds with each other and need to reconcile the differences within and between ourselves. There is nothing impossible to achieve, just improbable, and improbability is easy to overcome when people come together in harmony to work and act for what they believe in. We can deal with differences after we are united. Our differences can energize us."

* * *

In 1992, after years of suffering and treatment, Bob's asthma suddenly disappeared and has not returned. But he continues to face severe medical conditions as a result of his diabetes and long-term cortisone use for asthma. He has suffered two strokes in the last three years, the last one requiring that he start kidney dialysis. Yet he continues to work on National Night Out, Harmony, and the genesis of a Creative Design and Development Center. He currently lives in the Corcoran neighborhood in south Minneapolis with his wife Wendy, an award-winning children's book author, and a stable and supportive force in his life.

"The fact that I am here is a miracle," he says. "There's some force that moved in my life that has given strength. At the same time being as helpless and dependent as I have been for so long has made me conscious of the need for interdependency."

Bob believes that people need to get involved in their own lives and take responsibility for their own, their children's and their grandchildren's futures, and not leave it to others, like the leaders they choose, to take responsibility for them.

"Each of us, and all of us together can create a far better future than the one we've inherited," he says. "I believe that the future for coming generations will be different and better. There will be less emphasis on material wealth, and a greater emphasis on social cohesion and spiritual development; less emphasis on competition, and greater attention paid to cooperation and collaboration."

Over the course of Bob Milner's life, there have been some constant themes that have guided his thinking and his actions. Throughout the constant upheaval and struggles, he has remained faithful to the notion that people should be with and for one another. He believes strongly in the idea of "power with" as opposed to the idea of "power over," and in his own life this is what has allowed him to survive and thrive. "Alone, I was often helpless and if it wasn't for the kindness of others, helping friends, and often helping strangers, I would have drowned many times over."

In 2008, Bob had a severe stroke (his second in three years). He's calling it "the perfect stroke" because he survived it well, and it helped close up questions he's had since that fateful day he was attacked in 1968: "What skills do I have to make a difference in the world, to make it a better world?" and "How can I understand what makes people think the way they do and do the things they do?" Over the years, as he experienced new things, he has always examined the affects of those things on himself and/or others. Whenever he made mistakes, and he admits he's made many, he tried to learn from those and to apply what he's learned to his life and to better the lives of others.

Bob believes that he holds a valuable philosophy for the future. He calls it "Dynamic Evolving Harmonious Synthesis and Synergy" or "Harmony" for short. He believes, if it is applied in healthy ways, it can be a practical and pragmatic way to end strife and war and to create healthier relationships within people, families, communities, countries and throughout the world.

"The thrust of Harmony," Bob says, "is to unleash the creative energies of people so that the focus of the world will shift from competition to cooperation and from destruction to creativity; sharing in the world's abundance instead of fighting over perceived rare and diminishing resources."

Nowadays, you can still spot Bob Milner a mile away. Years ago, he bought a pair of overalls at Ragstock for a quarter and they helped him deal with sudden weight gain that was a result of medications he took. He still wears overalls everywhere he goes. The suspender-like shoulder straps hug his rotund body and, along with thick, white hair and a mustache, are a trademark statement of his independence as well as a constant in his ever-changing life. (He bemoans the loss of his ponytail during a recent surgical procedure.)

"I have this memory of the times I would sit in my office or at home sorting boxes of paper trying to piece together my life," Bob says. "I realized that nobody can do that for you. You have to put it together yourself. I'm like Humpty Dumpty," he says. "I'm always putting myself back together again."

Ann Benson at home in Merriam Park
(Photo by Chante Wolf)

NEIGHBOR TO NEIGHBOR

By Burt Berlowe
Interviews by Tony Simon and Arletta Little

People across the country have responded to the war and occupation of Iraq by unifying with others in their neighborhoods and towns in unprecedented numbers to work for peace and justice....Meeting and working with our neighbors on our shared visions for the future has strengthened our communities and empowered us to work together toward a brighter tomorrow for our neighborhoods, cities or towns, state, country, and world.

—Minnesota Neighbors for Peace

Anne Benson settles into a large, overstuffed chair in her living room underneath a sewn quilt above her head, a crowded, motley bookshelf standing nearby. She is casually dressed in jeans and a large sweatshirt, with straight brown hair and no makeup, a fitting testimony to her laid-back, unassuming nature. Across the room, her persistent cat Dusty fetches a cloth ball and tiptoes it back to his master.

There's a whole lot more to Anne than immediately meets the eye. Behind the quiet, inauspicious demeanor lies a multifaceted woman: mother, wife, Celtic music enthusiast, music teacher, gardener, and activist whose passion for peace has engulfed the streets, sidewalks, and prim houses around her.

Anne's neighborhood, called Merriam Park, stretches from the Minneapolis-St. Paul border well into the midst of the capital city. Its western edge touches the Mississippi River and the Sri Chimnoy Peace Bridge that spans it. The latter connection is particularly significant for Anne. From it, she would build a bridge across her spacious neighborhood, resting on the trestles of commitment, community and the longing for a more peaceful world.

* * *

September 11, 2001 began as a typical day for Anne. After dropping off her son at his high school, she had arrived at her job teaching music at a Catholic elementary school in her neighborhood. As usual, other teachers had brought their students into Anne's class for their daily music lessons.

Then about halfway through the hour, a teacher suddenly poked his head through the door: "Something really big is going on in New York," he blurted out. "There's been a bombing or something." Every time there was a break, Anne found a TV to watch. But it wasn't until much later that the real impact of 9/11 hit her.

"I wasn't scared. I didn't feel threatened. What got me going was not so much that there was a terrorist attack on us, but our government's response to it. It was this opportunity where all the world was on our side and everybody was rooting for us and we had the good will of the whole country, and all of a sudden—'You're either for us or against us.' President Bush was dividing us right away, trying to make everything into good and evil. That was just wrong.

"After 9/11 I started going regularly to the Lake Street Bridge vigil. At the bridge, I learned about political talks and peace events, which I began attending, culminating in a national peace march in Washington, D.C. in January of 2003."

The week after she got back from D.C., Anne attended a training on Iraq by Phil Steger, director of Friends for a Non-Violent World in St. Paul. What began as a fascinating informational session turned into a life-changing experience for Anne. Steger was attempting to create a groundswell of opposition to the war. One way of doing that, he suggested, was by having house parties, inviting neighbors over to discuss their opinions about the war and what to do about it.

During the training, Anne happened to be sitting next to woman named Rachel. "We were talking during the break, and we realized that we lived in the same neighborhood (Merriam Park). Rachel had actually grown up Republican and originally had no particular feelings about the first Gulf War. But now she had an eleven-year-old son and she thought about mothers who had lost their children to war and how they were parents just like we are. It became obvious to her that this war was bad and that Bush wasn't doing the right thing.

"Rachel and I began talking and discovered that we had both noticed a lot of 'Say No to War in Iraq' lawn signs going up in our neighborhood. We knew there was support for our point of view out there, so we decided to try to get our neighbors involved.

"I believe it was Phil's idea to invite people who had a sign in the yard to come to an organizing event. We booked a room at the library. Then we went door to door in our neighborhood. We shoved a couple hundred papers under doors inviting people to come and meet about the war and what we as neighbors could do about it. Within two days, the fliers had been left at every house that had an antiwar sign."

The first meeting of what was to become Merriam Park Neighbors for Peace (MPNFP) was scheduled to take place at the community library. There was such a huge turnout that they exceeded the fire-code capacity at the library and were asked to leave. They reconvened at a nearby church. At that first meeting, predawn maps were handed out to people so they could distribute to every house in the neighborhood flyers about a second meeting. That next gathering was held just five days later. Steger gave his Iraq training to a large group, which included Minnesota Congresswoman Betty McCollum (representing St. Paul) and St. Paul City Council member Jay Benanav. Among the actions taken was collecting signatures petitioning the St. Paul City Council to pass a resolution against the war.

The group continued to meet on a weekly basis. Within a few weeks, they decided that they would organize a peace march in St. Paul. They called it a Neighbors March for Peace, reaching out not only to individuals and families, but to churches and labor unions. As the march proceeded, people joined in spontaneously—couples with baby strollers, shoppers coming out of stores, joggers stopping their run to walk instead. "It (the march) really brought out the neighborhood," says Anne.

"This march was a real test for the peace movement in the Twin Cities because days before it was scheduled, the U.S. started bombing Iraq. The war had begun. Everyone was wondering if anyone would show up for the march, or if folks would just think, 'What's the use?' But the march was a huge success, with people turning out in droves, making it one of the largest demonstrations during that time period.

Activities around 9/11 and the onset of the Iraq conflict led to the formation of many Neighbors for Peace groups in the Twin Cities and elsewhere around the country. After the initial surge of interest and the continuation of the war, the outburst of early enthusiasm began to wear off for some people, and attendance at subsequent Twin Cities NFP groups faded significantly. Merriam Park Neighbors fared better than most, experiencing a smaller decrease in interest. Months into the war, a core group of about twenty-five people were still involved. Five years later, the group continues to meet twice a month. Over the years, they have sponsored (often in conjunction with other NFP groups) many community peace events such as speakers, films and vigils. "Our group is still together largely because we're all good friends," Anne says. "We all share this wacky sense of humor, and we all come from diverse places that have so much to add to each other's experience."

* * *

Merriam Park has a list of PEACE goals that could apply generally to the NFP movement. They include the following:

Participate in the political process
Educate ourselves and others
Actively serve our world
Connect and cooperate with other communities or efforts
Energize, equip and empower our members and organization

On their website, MPNFP has a quote from author Howard Zinn that sums up what they are about:

Don't look for a moment of total triumph. See it as an ongoing struggle with victories and defeats but in the long run the consciousness of people growing. So you need patience, persistence, and need to understand that even when you don't 'win' there is fun and fulfillment in the fact that you have been involved, with other people, in something worthwhile.

HOW TO START A NEIGHBORS FOR PEACE GROUP IN YOUR AREA

By Tony Simon, founder of Seward Neighbors for Peace in Minneapolis

Peace isn't abstract. It can't be captured by concepts of how it looks or what it means. Peace begins and abides as a lived experience, starting with oneself and the wish to share it with others.

Due to its size, diversity and proximity, the neighborhood can be a profoundly efficient and effective tool for making peace.

Here are some ideas to get you started. These are things that actually worked for people.

- Look for signs, stickers and other evidence that indicates which neighbors might be interested in a Neighbors for Peace group. These could include yard signs, campaign signs for pro-peace candidates, signs promoting local initiatives, encouraging alternative energy, etc.
- Look for peace flags or similar decorations.
- Look for bumper stickers on your neighbors' vehicles. This is often the most popular venue for personal expression.
- Once you've identified those in your area who might be interested in a neighborhood peace group, draft a simple letter that introduces yourself, briefly describes your ideas and intention for convening this group, and invites them to participate. You'll want to have secured a date, time and venue for your first meeting to include in your letter. Depending on the proposed attendance, you may want to hold the meeting in your home, at a park or coffee shop, or in a community building.
- In the letter, you may want to identify a particular issue to discuss at the first meeting. Be sure the issue has broad appeal. You don't want to risk alienating people by making the group's focus too narrow. It's good to get started on the right foot by being active and productive at the first meeting. Also, it will show others that this group really will take action and be a presence.

Muriel Simmons (Photo by Dawn Vogel)

COMMUNITY IS WHERE THE SNOW CONES ARE

By Jacque Blake and Burt Berlowe

Summer in Minneapolis is a fleeting three months jam-packed with community events, activities, and warm weather treats. The sun moves closer to the earth, melts away the winter mindset and refuels the body and mind with energy and playfulness.

For many years, the Phillips neighborhood in south Minneapolis did not fully participate in the summer fun. Crime, violence, and drugs, submerged by the ravages of winter, exploded onto the streets at the first sign of spring and spread as the temperatures rose. Even as Phillips moved forward with spirited summer activities, a winter-like pall hung over a community chilled and numbed by fear, anxiety and depression. That is until social and community activist Muriel Simmons moved into the neighborhood with her coalition, her family, and an old-fashioned snow cone machine.

Each of us authors visited Muriel individually at her home in Phillips, a spacious old house that had been boarded up and condemned, but has been beautifully refurbished. Transforming this house into a home was only the beginning of Muriel's mission for the Phillips community. She has almost single-handedly turned the distressed and impoverished neighborhood into a safe and viable home for many to enjoy—a seemingly inconceivable feat for anyone. But Muriel is not just anyone.

* * *

Muriel grew up on the East Coast as her parents' only child. "My parents were community-minded people," she recalls. "We lived in Baltimore. I would go with them when they would go door-to-door collecting for the March of Dimes. My interest has always been in children, family and neighborhoods."

Even as she has grown into a life of activism, Muriel has had to battle constant health problems. When she was in her early thirties, she was diagnosed with Thalassemia Minor Disease, also known as Coolies Minor. Coolies is an inherited disorder that originated in the Caribbean—similar to Sickle Cell Anemia. Medications aren't helpful and there is no cure. Muriel also has Lupus, Parkinson's disease, and Epilepsy. She had a double radical mastectomy at age thirty-three. During the next three decades, she underwent twenty-six surgeries. The fact that she is still going strong today into her late seventies is a testament to her inner strength and ability to conquer adversity.

When Muriel was facing her most recent surgery, one of her daughters talked her into coming to Minneapolis to see an oncologist at the Sister Kenny Institute of Abbott Northwestern Hospital. Muriel feels fortunate to have given birth to four children in the midst of battling her unstable and often debilitating health.

Muriel married a military man and lived in Norfolk, Virginia, working with family services and the Red Cross for about ten years as a minority affairs omubsdman for the area. She raised her children largely alone, because her husband was in the military and spent the majority of his time on sea vessels. Being a military family, they frequently changed residences, and wherever Muriel went she was active in the community. But in the process she says, "I lost hold of my children. It was like trying to grab a hold of a horse after they've left the barn. I was a jumping jack between my family and the streets. After military duty, I focused more on my children. I came to the realization that what I was seeing in Baltimore was happening everywhere."

Needing income, Muriel took a job driving a tractor trailer carrying boxes. "It was something I always wanted to do. I went to school a long time to be a truck driver. I drove truck for ten years and it was heaven. I was really fed up. I didn't understand what was going on in the world around me. Driving the trailer was spiritual experience. I woke up in a different place every day without a phone and no one to talk to so I found myself in conversations with God. I also found out that the United States is a beautiful country."

Muriel had five children at the time. When she was on the road, the two oldest ones stayed behind attending a job corps program and living on campus. For the last year of her trip, she carried her infant child Barbara with her in the trailer, feeding and changing her at stops along the way, even though it was against regulations to have children on board. When that burden finally became too difficult, she quit driving.

* * *

In 1994, Muriel moved to Minneapolis as a single mom to have surgery and visit her married daughter. "I was down to my last dime. I came to Minnesota to get back on my feet. I tried to get involved on the northside of Minneapolis where they were revitalizing neighborhood houses. I was an outsider and had no pull, no voice. No one wanted to hear what I had to say. I saw solutions but they weren't interested."

Three years later, Muriel and her family moved into a bright, spacious two-story house on busy Portland Avenue in the midst of the Phillips neighborhood. After a prolonged struggle to secure the house, they were glad to be finally settled in. They weren't aware of the problems in their community. It didn't take them long to find out.

"The first morning we were here my son said to me, 'We can't live here.' I said, 'What do you mean?' He said, 'Do you know what's going on here, look over there.' 'What are you lookin' at?' I asked. He pointed through the window. 'They're selling drugs out of those houses,' he said. I looked out and saw people lined up around the block and young men standing on corners. I was shocked."

That was a preview of worse things to come. "We had gunfire 24 hours a day, multiple gangs, and traffic in prostitution," Muriel says. "Turns out this had been going on for years. The criminals would get arrested, serve their time, and come back to the same neighborhood where they left off. I thought 'somebody has to do something about this.'"

Muriel quickly stepped back into her role as community activist. "I met face-to-face with drug dealers on my block to get the message across. I have outlasted them by the grace of God."

With the help of her son Bryan, whom Muriel calls her "arms" and "legs," she approached neighborhood residents and businesses, pestered politicians and police, contacted other community activists, and literally spoke to anybody who'd listen to her plan to revitalize Phillips.

She began by working directly with neighborhood kids to change their outlook. "We would take fifteen to twenty kids—toddlers to teens—to do a neighborhood clean-up and then take them to McDonald's afterward for a treat. Everybody else in the neighborhood had been too busy to do that. We also would get senior citizens together from neighborhood high rises and walk around the neighborhood talking about it and observing. Many of the seniors were afraid of the young people on the street. So we would have the seniors confront the youth. In one of the towers we couldn't get the residents out without police escort. We would go out at five or six in the evening up to thirty at a time to take back the neighborhood. We would see drug dealers on the block ahead of us on the corner and would talk about how they don't live here. If they stared at us we just kept going. We wouldn't cower in front of them. We did that for about two years. And it made a difference. The neighborhood got better. A measure of success was the number of wheelchairs and walkers that would be out on any day around the neighborhood.

"At that time, we were under the umbrella of a community organization called People of Phillips. I helped start a block club in my area. When the city disbanded People of Phillips the neighborhood was broken into four areas. That's when we formed the Phillips West Neighborhood Organization (PWNO)."

As one of the founders and president of PWNO Muriel developed important relationships with large corporations and organizations in the neighborhood such as Honeywell, Wells Fargo Bank, Abbott-Northwestern Hospital, The Swedish Institute, the Phillips Eye Institute and Saint Mary's College, as well as the Zuhrah Shrine Center and Messiah Lutheran Church—all of whom supported the community in varied ways. For example, the Shrine Center provided space for the annual winter social that Muriel and Bryan created. It began as a small get-together in her home, but when it outgrew the space, they moved it to the Messiah Lutheran Church. Over 500 people now pack into the Shriner's Center for the event each winter. The aforementioned corporations help pay the expenses and many of their employees donate their time.

Muriel and Brian involve themselves in many community events in Phillips and elsewhere, including functions like the Fourth of July Art on Wheels parade, the Longfellow Community Street Fest, a Richard Green Community School fund-raiser, annual National Night Out gatherings, and the Juneteenth festival at Theodore Wirth Park in north Minneapolis.

Muriel's home became the first McGruff safe house for children in the neighborhood, then expanded to include any needy person who came to visit. "I make my home a safe house for anybody. I help people who come to my door, people on the street. They call on me and I share with them whatever I have that they need even if it's just a place to rest for a couple of hours. I also did a welcome basket containing neighborhood information for all the new homeowners in the community.

"A lot of people don't put things in perspective. They always flip it into something bad. There are still problems here but they are quiet problems. There has been business development that has changed our commercial strip on Franklin Avenue. Drug dealers are not hanging on corners as much. Now they have cell phones. You'll see a car stop, another one pull up behind them, they make an exchange and then they're gone. It's nothing like it used to be."

In addition to leading neighborhood crime prevention efforts, Muriel has served on a committee to revitalize Lake Street, a main thoroughfare on the south edge of Phillips, and has worked to get low-interest loans for home repair, all of which contribute to the image of the neighborhood, and ultimately who hangs out there.

Now that she has helped change the reputation of her own neighborhood, Muriel wants to hold a conference of all the community organizations in the state coming together in workshops sharing ideas. "Everybody has basically the same problems they just handle them differently. There may be a smaller community that can help a larger community on the other side of the state. It's a vision in progress. I've talked to Neighborhoods USA and the NRP (Minneapolis's Neighborhood Revitilazation Program) about hosting this with Phillips West. I want to get it off the ground next year. It should give people some hope from all the bad stuff that's going on out there."

* * *

Traveling everywhere with Muriel, like one of her own children, is an old-fashioned snow cone machine. She makes and sells thirty-five flavors of snow cones (or snow balls as they are sometimes called) at community events, as a way to meet and connect with people in the neighborhood. "When I lived on the East Coast, we had a snow cone machine. Lots of families needed to make extra dollars in different ways. Some made candy apples, for instance. In the summer we got snow balls from friends of ours that had a store and then put in a bid for their snow ball machine. We made the syrup and many delicious flavors. It was 'have machine will travel, make a buck.' The machine has kept my family together. I've had three generations of children and grandchildren helping me." Those helpers include some of her seven children and twenty-nine grandchildren.

Muriel has been both a day care provider and adopted parent to several of her grandchildren. She takes care of some of them while their parents aren't available. "Sometimes they stay for a week or month. I've have had some for nine months."

Muriel's grandchildren call her 'grandma mom.' She adopted the youngest child named Charlotte from her daughter who had chemical abuse problems. "When she got pregnant the first time I suggested she get into treatment. She fell off the wagon when she was close to having that baby. I have been raising the baby (she was two years old as of this writing). My daughter came to visit the baby and said she would come back but didn't. She lost her parental rights eventually. I am raising Charlotte here. Neither of her parents is currently able to take care of her but I have high hopes that that will change. I'm still on the board of Phillips West. But I can't always go to the meetings because I'm doing child care. Somebody has to give these children some loving."

During a second interview, Muriel conducts a tour of her house—a graceful turn-of-the-century home fronting on one of Phillips' busiest streets. There is a classic, old-fashioned look to the living room, with its dark red sofa and soft back chairs spread out across a hardwood floor. The dining room cabinets are full of antique glassware.

We go upstairs past a children's room that looks very much like a nursery school play area and on to a small, cluttered attic where she pulls out a series of picture boards with photos of many community events she has participated in. The walls are full of leadership awards she has received for her neighborhood work. She proudly flashes a proclamation from the mayor of Minneapolis declaring her birthday as Muriel Simmons day in Phillips. Back downstairs, inspirational quotes, poems, helpful hints, and cards from the children are displayed in plain view. One of her favorite quotes says, "Drop life's baggage and move on." "I don't want people to go around and get a case of the 'blues' or the 'blahs.'" she exclaims emphatically. Her pride and joy are the make-believe butterflies and angels she hides around the house. She points out two of the brass butterflies sitting on top of ceiling chandeliers. "Butterflies are friends," she says.

As we talk with Muriel, we realize her beauty, strength, compassion for people, and passion for the community. She's a tall woman, her hair pulled back showing the soft glow of her face—a face with only a few gentle lines that hardly illustrate the fact that she's endured years of hardship. Her eyes are deep and determined. Her body is erect, confident, and proud. Her hands, shaking from Parkinson's, are broad—her palms illustrate an arduous lifeline. It is easy to imagine all the work they've done, including making snow cones for thousands of people over the years. Her smile is comforting—maternal, like a grandmother holding her first grandchild. She adorns herself with subtle but attractive jewelry. Muriel is especially proud of a framed picture of herself in somewhat younger days when she was wearing her "locks." In it, she depicts a congresswoman, a goddess, a look-alike of Coretta Scott King. It is a fitting symbol of her contributions to her extended community.

We had the opportunity to meet Bryan's three children who alternately live with him and their grandmother. We asked the children to share something they like about their grandmother. They all said they appreciate that she always has time for them, and not only allows, but also encourages them to share their feelings with her, and that she "walks her talk." Before they left the house, each of them kissed and hugged her, and said, "I love you grandma."

Child care commitments have caused Muriel to cut back on some of the appearances at neighborhood events. But she still gets out and about a lot when the weather permits with some old and new helpers and the proverbial snow cone machine in tow. This past summer, for example, she and her crew were a popular attraction at a church festival, a back to school cook out, and an event at a local social service agency known as The Open Door.

"I will keep doing it," she says, "as long as there are people to help me run it. I maintain the snow cone tradition because it brings my family together. Nothing else matters if my family isn't together and happy."

Mary Heuer
(Photo courtesy of Angela Andrist)

DEFYING THE ODDS:
TRIBUTE TO A NEIGHBOR

By Angela F. Andrist

On a summer day about five years ago, my neighbor Mary Heuer drove her car through the back of her garage. "I wanted to step on the brake, but I stepped on the gas. I remember I stepped hard and the harder I stepped..." Defying the odds of gravity, her Dodge balanced on the cement foundation, having catapulted her back wall into her maple tree. She crawled out of the wreck with only a scratch on her knuckle. Not bad for a ninety-six-year-old.

Mary defied the odds for more than a century, ever since she became an American. Her family emigrated from Norway through Ellis Island, looking for a better life. They bought a forty-acre farm with a ninety-nine-year lease. After losing her mother at age thirty-three, little Mary was sent to a foster home and lived with her foster parents, working on their farm in Pine County near Sandstone, Minnesota until she was seventeen.

Her first experience behind the wheel came some eighty years ago. "My foster dad drove me to town in his Model T. I took the car out to drive one time when I was in my teens, without permission, and I didn't know how to turn around. Every time we'd have to stop or turn, he'd always look down where he was going to put his feet on the brakes. You don't do that now; your feet automatically go there. I drove a mile to the schoolhouse to turn around to go back. I knew how to drive it because I watched him. I thought there was nothing to it."

Although she ended up spending most of her life in the Twin Cities, Mary initially felt like an outsider. She met her husband, Arnold Heuer, of German descent, while she was attending sewing school in St. Paul. She had fond memories of this kind-hearted man, but it was difficult being Scandinavian in a tight-knit community of Germans.

"The Germans, when they came over to this country, the men walked ahead of their women and belittled them, and Arnold was something like that. He was brought up with German ideas. Many of those German girls had their eyes on Arnold, and they wanted to know who he was taking out. They found out it was a Swede, and asked him, 'Why would you pick a 'Swede'?"

Mary fought sexism and discrimination but kept her self-reliant drive, even though she had little support. "I went through life thinking I was the ugly duckling. I used to think I was never as good as the next one, why everyone was better than me. I think it's stupid because there are a lot of people worse than me that do more dumb things.

"I wished I had gotten a better education. It's very important to learn the three Rs. I didn't look forward to college or anything because my foster parents couldn't afford to hire me out to stay in town. It was five miles to town, and I had to walk. I couldn't take a horse and buggy. I walked to school a mile. I liked school. I could have studied harder, but I was more interested in drawing and stuff like that. I like to draw, especially in geography. Once my teacher thought I did a good job when I made a freehand drawing of South America. I drew the country Chile and I forgot the Balkan Islands. I put them in, all the countries. I put in the cities and the capitals and she sent it to the State Fair. I didn't get anything, but she thought it was good for my age. This was in direct defiance of my foster dad, who said that women were meant only to cook and sew and keep house.

"I wanted to also play the piano. My stepmother's father taught music, but I had no way to get there. When I was down here in the Cities working, that's when I started to go to the Coliseum on Robert [Street] and University. It was a bit place…it was a dance hall. I'd rather dance than eat."

Mary moved her interests to the outdoors, planting flowers, but even that was met with resistance. The memories decades later linger with strong emotion in her voice as she recounts. "My father-in-law got me upset when I was planting flowers. The flowers were a lot of work. He would say, 'Plant something that would be worth something around here.' My husband was the same way." She smiled and continued. "Until someone came around and complimented me about my flowers, and then he took the credit!

"One day, my foster dad told me what to do, and I said, 'I will try.' And he said, 'No. You should say, I will do it.' And I felt hurt about it. I thought when I said I would try, that was enough. I thought, he wasn't my father and should not be telling me that, in that tone of voice. I didn't like that. But I realize now that he may have actually reinforced my drive for life, as a doer."

Mary's perseverance overshadowed her meager beginnings and didn't stop her dreams. "I was happy because I wanted a home more than anything. Deciding to build a home, after we were married, was one of my biggest accomplishments. You know what it means when you start with a shoestring. It means you don't have much money to work with. I didn't have money to start out." She'd often told her youngest daughter, "It's not what you make, it's what you save that counts." Mary never believed in taking handouts, which was further demonstrated by her creative frugality. "I always wanted money so I wouldn't have to depend on anybody. I wanted money, but not the love of money. It's great satisfaction when you can help yourself without bothering anybody else. I always believed in not letting the government pay for me. Like some of them say, 'Let Uncle Sam take care of me.' I don't feel that way."

This practicality was one of Mary's earthly gifts, but her faith in God was her foundation. Other than her family, her faith was her most prized possession. "Any child that has any faith at all, that is the most wonderful thing. If you don't believe there is a God, you can do anything and get by with it. That's what kept me on the straight and narrow. I knew there was a God, and I knew if I did anything wrong, I would have to answer [to] Him someday."

Mary's attitude towards religion started as an innate faith affirmed by one miraculous moment decades ago. When she was living at home as a young girl with her dad, she would go down by the train tracks, getting rides from what she called "the men on the carts that go up and down." One time, wearing laced-up shoes, her foot got stuck in the tracks crossboards. She could see the train coming down the line. As she struggled to get her foot out, a woman suddenly appeared, untied her shoe and pulled her aside to safety. Mary referred to the woman as her 'guardian angel.' "I never saw the lady before, didn't know where she came from and never saw her again."

Mary stayed active with her church and her presence transcended to the neighborhood. She was its hub. She was the first one seated in her folding lawn chair on the barricaded street for National Night Out. She watched the children run and play, draw pictures, and present her a neighborhood birthday card signed by many on a giant poster board. She was present at her neighbor's going-away party for a son fighting in Iraq and at the celebrations of a high school graduation, a birthday or a wedding.

Nevertheless, she claimed to miss the closeness, the ease of listening to gossip on party lines, when neighbors knew each other well. She though most everyone stayed to themselves. I wonder if she realized how much she meant to all those in her community.

The day after an ambulance came and took Mary away, two young boys that lived behind her came to our front door. In tearful voices, a surprise coming from "cool" preteens usually seen on skateboards and bikes, they were worried about what had happened to her. "She broke her foot and is doing fine," we said, and the compassion lingered between us.

Living over a century should have been enough to prove Mary's tenacity, withstanding the struggles of injustice through the decades. However, she more than just endured. She taught and inspired us by remaining agile, retaining her independence and managing her own home (still drawing income from a renter on the top floor). She only needed a bit of assistance from her children and the support of her neighbors. Our being there for her was the catalyst that bound us as a caring group, sharing the latest "Mary story" every time we would speak to each other over the fence or at the grocery store. She provided us an opportunity to slow down from our fast-paced lives to "take five" and share our artistic endeavors, promotions, travels and family celebrations. She was a modern day storyteller of our clan—modeling how to savor the memories.

Mary had a willingness to keep learning at any age. She was a gifted conversationalist, and her interest in current events demonstrated that growing old doesn't mean just remembering the past. People at any age often say, "Oh, I'm getting too old!" But Mary's strong convictions and vigor encapsulated a veritable Fountain of Youth. This atypical woman centurion defied the stereotypes of aging. She taught herself to ride a bicycle in her seventies and didn't stop driving until she was ninety-six. In her nineties she re-cemented and painted her basement floor, disposed of an old toilet by smashing it to bits with a sledgehammer (so as not to incur the cost of having it hauled away), and swept snow on her walk for the mailman.

Mary lived to be 101. Her advice for living a long life was "clean living, strong faith, a good family and health." Mary taught us to stand tall on our own, to smell each blossom, save each small seed, and not be afraid, even during the hardest times, to lean on others for support. She bridged the generations and showed that at any age, one can be an important part of a community.

Juan Linares at Plaza Latina in St. Paul
(Photo by Jacqueline Mosio)

MARKETING HOPE
By Jacqueline Mosio

What does commerce and economics have to do with being a rebel or with compassion? I've always had a slight bias against business, to tell the truth, and often felt that people involved in business don't view the world in quite the same way I do. Living in Mexico for over twenty years, however, changed my mind on the business of business.

Commerce, trade, markets, and exchange of goods are the stuff of daily life in Mexico, where it's still possible to see vestiges of ancient economic forms such as barter, trading patterns among indigenous villages, and, of course, commerce in the markets. Anyone who has visited Mexico more than superficially has encountered the vibrant Mexican markets. What I learned about commerce in Mexico is that when it's carried out on a person-to-person level in a spirit of honesty and with respect on both sides of the transaction, it's an essential and satisfying facet of life.

Now let's take a jump back in time and geography to East Lake Street in Minneapolis in the 1970s and '80s. The city's once-prime commercial corridor is abandoned and run down. Some stores bravely hang on, sharing the street with thrift shops and massage parlors. While crisp, efficient modern malls are booming out in the suburbs, areas like East Lake are in steady decline.

Fast forward to today and take a drive down the same Lake Street. Small shops with colorful, original windows and inviting signage line the street. Buildings are decorated with colorful murals; others are painted in brilliant hues. There's movement all along the street and in and out of the shops. What happened to transform the area? What brought about this revitalization?

Immigrants did—specifically immigrants who organized themselves around a common purpose and worked with civic groups and city government to make their dream a reality. The Mercado Central figures as the first big dream project to appear on East Lake. It was a major force in the economic comeback of the area and now serves as a model for other ventures in the Twin Cities, in greater Minnesota, and in other states as well.

The person who was closest to its origins, the one who nurtured the dream into its three-building, forty-eight-shop, seven-restaurant physical reality was Juan Linares, an immigrant from Mexico. His efforts helped members of the Latino community identify their abilities, skills, and desires and organized them to get what they wanted.

* * *

It's a chilly January day, but inside Plaza Latina on the East Side of St. Paul, Mexican music heats up the atmosphere. Patrons stop by the shops and beauty salon. The tables at Café Mi Pueblo are filled with the lunch crowd. As he sips hot coffee, Juan talks about his part in creating the Mercado Central and the East Lake Street comeback in Minneapolis and the Plaza on Payne Avenue in St. Paul.

"People emigrate from Latin America for economic reasons. They have hopes of something better for their kids—college, a profession," says Juan. "What makes economic sense, then, is to give them opportunities to create things that work, to create measurable success. The way to do that is by engaging a community's members on their own interests and vision, exploring that, building relationships—giving folks the opportunity to excel, and showing them that success is not dependent on schooling."

Juan gets passionate in a quiet, intense way when he talks about what the immigrants bring to this country. "They have a skill, a gift, maybe to sell, cook, or run a restaurant. All of this benefits the community. It makes economic sense for the government. Look, money circulates among us five, six, seven times. It's good for the local economy. We show we can support ourselves. There's less dependency on federal dollars—that's healthy. When you pay taxes to pour money into communities that remain poor and have crime, it doesn't make economic sense. But when you give opportunities to people to be part of the solution, things change.

"One of the lessons I've learned is that you engage people by not just helping them develop their own capacities to grow and do what they are good at, but by letting them be the main agents of change. It's in their best interest to do that."

As Juan talks, it becomes clear how deep his commitment is to helping establish the fledgling Latino business community. But it's not so much a commitment to an idea of justice as it is a commitment to a relationship with people, to the individuals, who in their turn, commit to learning, growing, and taking on the responsibilities of a business venture. The reason he has been so instrumental in these revitalization projects is that he engages each person and, in so doing, encourages, empowers, and emboldens them.

When Juan first moved to Minnesota in the 1970s, there were only a handful of Mexican restaurants in the Twin Cities. The Mexicans who migrated to work here settled on the West Side of St. Paul and a few other areas. Ingredients for Mexican cooking were available at only a few stores in those neighborhoods.

"I was clueless when I arrived. I had just graduated from college," he says. "I didn't speak more than a few words of English. It took me six months to feel comfortable even opening my mouth." He moved to Minnesota because his wife at the time wanted to be near her family.

Because Juan had a green card, he didn't have any legal barriers to immigration, but besides learning English, he had to understand the system. "I finally figured out the social services system, but all I wanted was a job. I had a business degree and thought I'd have great opportunities. Not so simple. I waited tables and worked at hotels. I managed a Burger King for a year."

Then Juan began working with Catholic Charities as a bilingual service coordinator. The last ten years of his twenty-five years with them, he was in charge of Latino outreach, a position he requested. With the amnesty decreed for immigrants in the early '80s, Juan saw the needs of the immigrants who were becoming citizens. Then came the 1986 welfare reform.

"We had been helping people with services," Juan recalls, "but I knew a lot of them were going to lose assistance or become homeless when welfare was cut because they had such low-paying jobs. So I began managing drop-in centers where we provided meals and social services such as job referrals, housing, transitional housing, clothing, furniture, and financial assistance and advice on a daily basis.

"But at the end of the day I was always faced with the question: Are we really helping people? There were more issues than just giving someone a dollar for the bus. A colleague challenged me, saying, 'You've got to get out of the needs and begin to confront people. Find out what it is they want to do here.'

"His comment really agitated me. I realized I didn't want to work at the level of handouts any more. Immigrants have so much to offer. They want to be part of the community in a meaningful way. But we needed organizing. So I went to the Gamaliel Foundation, a leadership training institute that works through faith-based communities. After that, we started Sagrado Corazon parish in Minneapolis. Once we had a place to meet—a sanctuary space where religious needs were being met—the community grew.

"Organizing through faith-based communities gives people a space to start to understand how they can act in public life. We see how we can, in the name of social justice, reclaim or at least begin to challenge what is not just. We build community from the inside out. We explored our community's assets by doing a talent and capital inventory. This is an important tool. It tells us who we are and what we have. When we did the inventory at Sagrado Corazon, we saw we had people who were interested in starting their own businesses. This was the core group for the Mercado Central Cooperative."

Creating the Mercado Central took three years and involved a coalition of various organizations led by Project for Pride in Living (PPL) to recondition three old warehouses. It was inaugurated in 1999 and has impacted commercial development in the area. The Mercado also serves as a small business incubator and cultural center.

Juan pauses to greet one of the Plaza Latina business owners then continues with his story of economic development Latino-Minnesota style. "Here at the Plaza, we again started with a church community in St. Paul. Our community was growing significantly in terms of participation and numbers, and they asked, 'Why can't we have a Mercado Central?' So we did the abilities and skills inventory and found out people were very serious about having a development here. This was in 2002. We had an economic summit. Thirty-five people participated. We did the training—classes on starting a business, writing a business plan, leadership—and implemented the plan.

"Plaza Latina was an easier project than the Mercado Central and became a reality within a year. It's an association rather than a cooperative and, for the time being, they are renting the building. This project has really had an impact on the neighborhood in the years it's been here, prompting other immigrant-owned businesses to come into the area.

"Immigrants and immigration policy are in the spotlight again with federal and state Legislatures proposing bills that are restrictive in their effects and anti-immigrant in their intent. I'm on the ground level in contact with people. There is a fear. 'What are we going to do?', they ask. But we need more than ever to say 'Be calm, don't panic.' I can't guarantee a positive outcome. I just say wait, stay put, stay calm. How do we continue our forward momentum if we are under attack? This makes my job more challenging, providing help and guidance and keeping people from panicking. We can lose too much.

"Immigration law needs reform, but the specters raised by the current anti-immigrant proposals are grim. If people abandon their shops and businesses because of tougher, more exclusive immigration laws, what's the gain—the return of empty buildings on a desolate Lake Street?"

Juan recently took a detour in his organizing to work for two years with a foundation whose mission is reducing poverty in communities in eight states. He worked with immigrant Latino communities applying the lessons learned from the Mercado Central and Plaza Latina. "I did the first step," he says. "Now they are in the process of implementing this work. I learned that to build powerful communities, you have to begin by building relationships in the community around self-interest and increase the relationships through networks. When I began my work, I organized one at a time. That's how we started the church, the Mercado and the Plaza. It's not a prescription process. It's about building communities from the inside. That's how you help people recognize that they have what it takes to be the producers producing change, producing their own communities. I have to engage folks by building an intentional, trusting relationship. So when I go to Idaho and I'm working for an organization, the first thing people see is the checkbook. The foundation has money and people were saying what they thought we wanted to hear.

"Forget we have any money, I'd tell them. How would you do this? Folks started talking about how they would want to do it. The next step was to tap into their interests, intentionally build relationships, and help individuals become their own agents of change. People are afraid to come out of anonymity, to stop being invisible people. This is easier said than done and there are no shortcuts to this. The first lesson is to help individuals see themselves as the leaders, as the producers of this change. Otherwise it's just providing social services."

As proof that he is walking this talk, Juan is currently working with the Plaza Latina partners, the East Side Neighborhood Development Company on a project to create prosperity for East Side residents and business owners.

* * *

Café Mi Puebla is quiet at midafternoon but people are still dropping in, including non-Latinos from the neighborhood. "Not to recognize this powerful labor force and understand what industries immigrants work in—what would happen if all the immigrants walked off their jobs for a few days?" Juan says. "Talk about power—we do have the power. We just haven't recognized it. This social capital has no price. That's what I organize around—that we have no price. We are what make things go around."

In the time since the interview, the café has been sold to La Loma Restaurant and Catering, another Latino business. Juan points out that while the original owners wanted a business, running a restaurant was not a good match for them. He worked with them to purchase an auto mechanic shop in the neighborhood. "This is part of the business process," says Juan, "and that's what we're here for—to help people do what they are best at to support themselves and contribute to building the community's prosperity."

It takes a community to have a market. A market requires the participation of individuals with experience, preparation and training in business. A market creates a viable economic structure that supports families and opens a space in the community. A market forges ties with the greater community and creates community consciousness. This is how things go around. Immigrants bring their language, culture, experience, and dreams, and they find a way to plant them here and watch them bloom.

In his store, Super Precio, which recently moved from Mercado Central to a new location across the street, Fernando Lugo is doing inventory, which is quite a task. The gazillion items for sale include health products imported from Mexico to novelty key rings and jewelry to Mexican flags. "It's a problem counting each thing," says Fernando, "but I have to do it."

Fernando moved to Minneapolis with his family from Los Angeles six years ago. "I started working in construction and painting, but I saw there weren't many businesses so I decided to open my own here at the Mercado Central." Now he has three stores. "This is an idea I had. Sometimes it seems like I'm dreaming," he says. "Immigrants come in order to do things. We want to work and take advantage of all the opportunities to develop our ideas. Fernando sees his store as making a "better community for all the others. This is what motivates me. I'm also trying to support the community by participating in organizations. I want to give back. I've had great opportunities."

Among the opportunities that helped Fernando be successful with his store was the training provided to the Mercado's business owners. Juan Linares was key to setting these up. "He's one of our best and an example for all of us," says Fernando. "He's done so much for all our community. He's a good person."

While Fernando attends to some customers, I wander around the store. I'm intrigued by a line of items I recognize from Mexico—magic powders, perfumes and soaps. There's a soap to keep enemies at bay, one to break hexes and protect auras; and another soap to bring financial security, wealth and success. Ah, if only it were that easy.

*Juan Linares is currently working as an independent business consultant.

Bonnie Urfer (Photo courtesy of Bonnie Urfer)

DOWN ON THE FARM
By Madeleine Baran

On a lazy summer afternoon, Bonnie Urfer stared out the windows of her office at a garden below, perusing the rows of asparagus, tomatoes, flowers and raspberries, as she talked about her lifelong commitment to anti-nuclear activism. The patch of land around her, she is quick to point out, is a living example of what she has devoted her life trying to preserve.

Bonnie lives and works at the Anathoth farm, a community of about a dozen peace and environmental activists who live off the land and hold it sacred. She helps run Nukewatch, an activist organization that produces a newsletter for its more than 2,000 subscribers.

Located on fifty-seven acres in rural northwestern Wisconsin, Anathoth Community Farm is an intentional community, dedicated to peace through nonviolent action. Founded in 1986, and placed in a land trust in 1992, the farm's five homes include two that are off-grid (one made of straw bales), two greenhouses, and lots of low-tech, energy-saving devices. The farm has evolved into a model of sustainable living. The homes were built with donations, and ongoing costs are paid by their current occupants. Nine people now live at Anathoth with a large extended community of supporters.

Inside the Anathoth office, alive with bright hardwood floors and quotes from Martin Luther King, Jr., and Gandhi hanging on the walls, Bonnie explained how she went from being a troubled child to a leading anti-nuclear activist.

"I think I was born this way, actually," she said, in a girlish voice that contrasts greatly with her strong, stocky build. When Bonnie was growing up, she was always thinking about another way of living beyond her violent alcoholic family home in a working-class Milwaukee neighborhood. Her father and both grandfathers were alcoholics, and Bonnie's childhood in what she calls "the land of beer and bowling" provided her first glimpse at oppression.

"My mother and my grandmothers worked all the time, twenty-four hours a day mainly to serve these alcoholic men who terrorized them into those positions. I looked at the injustice of my father's power within the family structure and knew that it was wrong," she said. Early on, she made a vow to herself, "that I would never participate in the abuse of power when I could make my own choices."

In grade school in the late 1950s, Bonnie participated in "duck and cover" preparations in case the Soviet Union dropped a nuclear bomb. "I was told, 'If you're ever outside and the bombs go off, you'll see a flash, and then all the fallout is going to come out of the sky. It'll be just like ashes. If that happens, go home and take a shower, and in three minutes you'll be fine,'" she said.

But Bonnie was not convinced. A few years later, in high school, she still could not shake the images of a nuclear catastrophe. She painted mushroom clouds in her art classes.

The enormity of the nuclear problem attracted her, and, when she moved to Madison in the late 1970s to escape her violent past, she accepted a job as a circulation assistant at *The Progressive* magazine, and quickly fell into a circle of social justice and anti-nuclear activists.

"It was an automatic path to just do the anti-nuclear work because I can see in this whole country, for the most part, it is ignored," she said. "It is so serious. It is so deadly. It's gonna' kill us, and it's so horrendous that maybe people can't face it. I think always, from the time I was a little kid, I felt very affected by the reality of it, a little snippet here and a little snippet there. You put it all together, and we're talking about big bombs. We're talking about something that can wipe out life on this planet as we know it within twelve minutes."

Before Bonnie began working at *The Progressive*, the federal government took the magazine to court over its decision to print a controversial article about H-bombs. After the legal fight, Sam Day, managing editor at the time, left the magazine and started *Nukewatch*. Bonnie got involved, and traveled across the country with Day as her mentor "talking all the time" about nuclear issues.

Bonnie began working at *Nukewatch* in Madison, using her two-year degree in commercial art, and soon took over production and graphic design of the newsletter. At the same time, she began to get more involved in direct action, crossing lines and trespassing on nuclear sites and sitting on nuclear missile silos. Sam Day retired from *Nukewatch* in 1992, and Bonnie took over as director and moved the office to the country outside of Madison.

Bonnie increasingly felt the need "to just use my body as a tool for peace and justice." She started getting arrested and served time in prison. Most of her friends did not engage in direct action and could not relate to her newfound passion. In search of a community where she could feel more supported, she moved, taking *Nukewatch* with her, to Anathoth Farm in 1996. "As soon as I came up here, I felt like I was home and that I would live here for the rest of my life," she said, smiling.

Two anti-nuclear activists established Anathoth Farm in the early 1980s to provide a supportive community for activists committed to direct action. All of its residents have been arrested dozens of times. Their approach is simple. As Bonnie explained, "I don't like this weapon that's in front of me. I'll engage in nonviolent resistance in opposition to it, no problem." She is fast approaching 100 arrests and has served almost five years of prison time, mostly for trespassing on the private property of nuclear sites. Most recently, she served eleven months in prison for cutting down antenna poles at Project ELF, a Naval communications center in central Wisconsin designed to communicate with nuclear-armed Trident submarines. The prison sentence was in addition to a $7,500 fine. She refuses to pay fines connected with nonviolent resistance and has numerous warrants for her arrest based on that decision. Bonnie spends her time in prison drawing and painting, using watercolors surreptitiously sent in by a friend and a paintbrush made using strands of her own hair.

Bonnie lives in a two-room house across a field from the main area on the farm. The other Anathoth residents are nearby in five different houses. Only one house, which serves as an office and general gathering place, has running water and an indoor toilet. Outside, a solar-powered summer shower and sauna stands across from a two-acre garden, which provides most of the community's food. None of the members earns over $7,500 a year, a conscious decision that allows them to avoid paying federal taxes which fund military spending. Some members work part-time doing construction or a job in town. The community's main expense is $4,000 in annual property taxes for the land, which is owned by a trust. Bonnie said she earns enough to get by from the small donations and a meager salary *Nukewatch* receives.

Bonnie believes her living situation is more than just a convenient way to do activism. It also offers an alternative to the world of technological comfort, provided in part by nuclear power that most Americans take for granted. In a post-nuclear age, she argues, wealthy nations will have to eliminate some of the same luxuries the farm has already discarded. "If these reactors are shut down, we might have to work a little harder," she said. "We might have to actually install solar panels. We might have to turn our lights off. We might have to turn our TVs off. We might have to change our lifestyles." By living such a lifestyle while nuclear energy is still available, Bonnie hopes to show others, like visiting students and activists, that another way is possible.

Although Bonnie has spent most of her life protesting nuclear weapons, nuclear power and radioactive waste, she doubts that her activism will have much of an effect. Instead, she freely admits that she embraces direct action for personal reasons. "The bottom line is, it's extremely selfish," she said. "I do this so I don't go crazy. While I don't think that anything I do has much of a chance of changing anything, not to do it would make me feel like such a criminal and an asshole that I have to do it to keep myself emotionally sane." In the end, it comes back to her childhood. "I grew up in so much violence," she said. "I cannot now participate in it. I just cannot."

In a dozen years, Bonnie will reach the age most Americans retire. However, unlike the average worker, she will have no pension, no health insurance and no steady income. For some people, this would provoke alarm, but Bonnie has a simple solution. "Retire in prison: nonviolently resist war, environmental destruction, nuclear weapons and power, and do artwork instead."

Allison Weeks-Ewoldt and Dave Ewoldt
(Photos courtesy of the Ewoldts)

LIVING ROOM REVOLUTION

By Stacy Larsen Stafki

Nestled among the rolling hills of Bellingham, Washington sits an unassuming white house with peeling paint. The front porch has three modest chairs and a bulletin board filled with upcoming events and listings of rooms for rent. As you walk through the door, it is like you are going to an old friend's house for dinner. The house is warm and welcoming and the hosts are multitasking. "Welcome to ECO Bell, help yourself to a cup of tea." Like most parties, there are old and new friends here, but this is no ordinary barbecue, this is Monday nights at ECO Bell, and the revolution is sitting in the living room.

This is not a revolution of gas masks, rallies or marches, but of community and systemic change. Little by little and person by person, ideas and lifestyles are changing, and that change will affect the world. The vehicle of change is the newly created nonprofit organization, Attraction Retreat, whose community hub and intentional community is known as the EcoIntegrity Center of Bellingham (ECO Bell). In a little less than a year, the world of Attraction Retreat is spreading, and attendance at the community discussions and potlucks is growing in numbers.

The hosts for the evening are the co-founders and directors of Attraction Retreat, Allison Weeks-Ewoldt and Dave Ewoldt. Every Monday night, Attraction Retreat hosts a community potluck/barbecue to discuss what is on the mind of the Bellingham community. Most nights, you never know what the topic will be or what direction the discussion will take, but it is always a great opportunity to meet your neighbors. In the past few months discussions have included an online chat with Michael Moore about his movie *Fahrenheit 911*, a dialogue about local currency, and a visit by an indigenous Burmese man to talk about the atrocities happening to his people. The community events at ECO Bell are just one part of Attraction Retreat and their holistic philosophy, which, in turn, is part of the contemporary radical green movement that states: "Peace on Earth requires peace with Earth."

Allison and Dave may be new to starting a holistic retreat center, but they are old hands at creating systemic change and caring about others and the planet. Allison started her own elementary school and has worked in many others, while Dave has been involved in community, social and political activities. Attraction Retreat is the result of their many years of frustration with society and the desire to build a new life.

While living in New York, Allison was taking classes in Project Nature Connect and discovering a new consciousness that led her to the realization that her life lacked integrity and she needed to live what she was teaching. "I was living the American Dream. I had everything my mother had always wanted for me, but I was not happy. My natural attractions kept pulling me towards Washington state." She and her family moved to Camino Island, Washington in the Puget Sound. She began teaching classes and counseling clients in the Natural Systems Thinking Process (NSTP). After awhile, she said, "the growing, horrifying awareness that my 'dream come true' was contributing to the demise of our planet grew within me."

Allison decided to follow her natural instincts and open a center where people could heal themselves and the planet. At first, she and Dave tried to start a retreat center on San Juan Island, but after traveling to Bellingham, they decided to settle there. They began offering classes and EcoTherapy, utilizing the wide selection of wonderful parks in the city. In November of 2003, they moved into the Eco-Integrity Center and created Attraction Retreat as a non-profit organization dedicated to helping create a just, sustainable and peaceful world by empowering individuals, building healthy and mutually supportive communities, and educating for sustainability and social justice. They created three branches under Attraction Retreat that addressed different issues but could be all be used together to create real systemic change.

Each of these three branches is guided by the Natural Systems Thinking Process. They are (1) EcoTherapy and Life Coaching services, (2) The Eco-Integrity Center of Bellingham (ECO Bell) and (3) The Holistic Living Institute. Each contributes to the Attraction Retreat mission, and, when woven together synergistically, have the potential to make a powerful contribution to the creation of a more just, sustainable, and peaceful world.

Why do we need a new thinking process? What is wrong with the one we have?

As Dave says, "The mindset that allows the destruction, exploitation, and squandering of the Earth's resources is the same one that allows war, domination, and subjugation of our Earth Mother's children. The Natural Systems Thinking Process can help you overcome this insanity and regain your senses. It is a psychological tool for the health of both nature and people's inner nature. It can help overcome all types of addictions, including overconsumption. It will help increase your feelings of self-worth through self-empowerment, help you see through the myth that progress and growth are synonymous, and restore inner peace by decreasing stress, depression, and feelings of isolation and encouraging the building of relationships with others and the environment. We use NSTP in every aspect of our lives, to solve disputes in our household as well as to build consensus and democratic governance in meetings."

Allison asks, "How do you feel when you walk through an ancient forest, sit perched upon a mountaintop, or enjoy the quiet of dawn by the seas? Most of us feel much more relaxed, peaceful and content than we do in our hectic daily lives. As part of nature, we instinctively know how to communicate with the rest of creation. We have at least fifty-three 'ways of knowing' our multiplicity of senses that we have inherited to help keep us fulfilled, healthy and in sustainable balance with the rest of the web of life."

Dave and Allison realize they can't change the world by themselves. They have an advisory board of community members to help with making decisions, fundraising and outreach. They are also part of Sustainable Connections, a business network that supports a sustainable economy.

When Allison and Dave were deciding on a location for Attraction Retreat, they thought about a small piece of land in the country with a barn they could use for teaching classes. Instead, they decided to show people that permaculture and nature healing can be done in an urban setting and to model the idea of community living: They wanted to live with like-minded people trying to make change. They purchased two houses that could hold up to nine people. Each house would have composting toilets, solar power, and a gray water recycling system. They planted a garden designed to be a sustainable permaculture demonstration site, providing enough food for the household and extra to trade with neighbors. ECO-Bell is just the start of their community. They want others to purchase homes and expand the community, to make their abode an activist hub and meeting center.

* * *

Laughter is coming from the living room, and there are people playing some sort of game. It is part of a permaculture training class offered by the Holistic Living Institute. The Institute's mission is to "reflect the interconnected nature of reality. Since we come from the Earth and depend on it for our very sustenance, we require a healthy planet in order to be healthy ourselves." Allison and Dave's teaching style is experiential and hands-on. They want people to get out in nature and look for and experience relationships. They offer classes in Organic Psychology, Urban Permaculture and Processes for Social Change. By the end of the day, your head is swimming with new ideas on how to make your life more sustainable and leave less of an ecological footprint.

EcoTherapy is the third branch of Attraction Retreat. Dave and Allison have been working on their Ph.D.s in applied ecopsychology/integrated ecology from Greenwich University. They believe that many of our personal health-related problems are tied to our disconnection with nature. "We seldom recognize that our greatest troubles—our rampant personal, social and environmental crises—directly result from this estrangement from our natural origins." Instead of sitting in an office, Allison and Dave meet their clients in a local park or even a backyard. They teach methods to bring people out in nature to improve relationships, increase well-being and maximize potential. "Most of the people are slightly skeptical at first, but they come back from the session looking at the world in a different way," says Dave.

Attraction Retreat is playing a much-needed role in the current anti-consumerist movement going on in this country. When people understand how they are connected to the Earth, they can make more responsible choices in their lives. Dave and Allison are not only talking the talk, but living it as well. They are giving people the social/community and personal tools to make choices to lead an ecologically responsible life. "When you live with integrity and community, your life is very rich," says Allison. "What will it take for us to face the reality that the American Dream is killing us and then do something about it? Attraction Retreat is teaching people how to develop the strength and resolve to just say 'no' to the war against nature and our human inner nature. This change will not happen overnight, but with more people living in a harmonious and sustainable way, it will happen and it will last."

Attraction Retreat recently moved its center from Bellingham to Tucson, Arizona, where they are continuing their work building sustainable communities. Their mission remains one of "catalyzing personal empowerment and transformation and environmental sustainability." One of their current mottos comes from a quote from former U.S. Interior Secretary Stewart Udall. It reads as follows:

A land ethic for tomorrow should be as honest as Walden's Thoreau and as comprehensive as the sensitive science of ecology. It should stress the oneness of our resources and the live-and-help-live logic of the great chain of life.

George Siemon
(Photo by Carrie Branovan)

ORGANIC REBEL

By Patricia Cumbie

Getting to the tiny town of LaFarge located in the Kickapoo River Valley of Wisconsin feels like a leap of faith. The roads are so hilly and twisted that the scenery beyond every corner is unknown, but each turn in a new direction reveals evermore breathtaking landscape: meadows of wildflowers sprawled out in the sun, inviting and cool woodlands, green hills swelling with livestock. This is dairy country in all her fertile and magnificent glory.

After I take the umpteenth fifteen miles per hour turn, the land finally shows the way to the ridges and hills where Organic Valley, America's largest organic producer cooperative, has its rather unlikely headquarters—miles and miles away from any readily available labor pool or convenient transportation. Yet the cooperative, which began in 1988 as the Coulee Regions Organic Producer Pool (CROPP), has led to a powerful renaissance of the family farm, not only in its local area, but nationwide.

The region shows all the signs of resurgent economic prosperity. Neatly maintained farmsteads and homes thrive within the towns and countryside, sustaining an active alternative culture devoted to living lightly on the land.

Vernon County, where LaFarge is located, is home to a newly expanded natural-food co-op, a Waldorf school, and a facility for natural healing among many cottage-industry massage therapists and chiropractors. New arrivals co-exist peacefully with the area's long-term agrarian neighbors. It's an amazing turnaround and a story of hope for a part of the state that had been economically devastated by a forced relocation of the populace in the '50s due to a failed damn project, and by the subsequent farm crisis of the '80s.

Organic Valley started with a founding group of seven organic farmers who were disillusioned by what little they were making for their labors. So they sought to change that dynamic by forming a cooperative they could own and control to better their position in the marketplace. The co-op is now 750 farmer-owners strong, posting annual sales of $240 million in 2005 on their milk, cheese, eggs, vegetables and meats. They are a leading force in the organic food industry, maintaining an annual growth rate of twenty percent for almost a decade.

Anyone sizing up the co-op's foremost leader, George Siemon, on first glance would never peg him for what he is: one of the natural-food industry's most astute chief executives. He's got shoulder-length strawberry-blonde hair, wears a necklace of wooden beads, and walks around the office in bare feet. He looks more flower child than CEO. His business card says: "CEIEIO," as in the "Old MacDonald" ditty.

As I enter the farm, people are busy preparing for the Kickapoo Country Fair, an annual outdoor event hosted by Organic Valley for the community. George is calm as he prepares to play host to hundreds of people ready to descend on LaFarge for what is the region's event of the summer.

George allows the sun to beat down on his face while the wind blows his wispy hair as he talks. He sits cross-legged most of the time and his occasional hand gestures are as laid-back as his looks. George is elegantly plainspoken and speaks with conviction, but a slight Southern accent adds another layer of charisma to his down-home hippie persona. Meanwhile, the wind gusts up here on Organic Valley's verdant ridge impart a sense of urgency.

George might make light of his role sometimes, calling himself Organic Valley's CEIEIO, but he's really the changing face of agriculture in America—one that encompasses biodiversity and sustainable and regional food systems that support local economies in rural communities. Under George's leadership, Organic Valley has proven that real people with a heartfelt desire to change the old-school values of agriculture can be economically successful even beyond their wildest dreams.

For many people, including farmers and consumers, Organic Valley is a model of the future of agriculture wherein people and the environment are respected. Through the efforts of the cooperative, consumers around the country can connect with organic, high quality food via its national brand, while the food maintains a strong connection to local markets through its members' business with regional processing facilities. It's this kind of burgeoning regional food system that has many benefits for the environment, local economies and even food safety.

George became a dairy farmer in the '70s because all he ever wanted to do was work outside. Since then, he has had to reconcile his fundamental desire to get his hands in the dirt with his equally fierce determination to create new ways of doing business that benefit the family farmer.

* * *

Flash back to 1989. George is thirty-six years old; it's autumn on a Wisconsin farm. He's dressed in outdoor work clothes and a jacket, wearing a cap that makes him look rakish and sweet. He holds a squash aloft, and his smile is triumphant. This is a man in his element, and it is evident that this newly harvested squash is something of a miracle to him. You get the feeling he is holding a soul in his hands.

A year after Organic Valley was founded, George began a process of searching and struggle. As a person with a strong back-to-the-land ethic, he was conflicted. Could he give up peaceful days caught up in the natural rhythms of farm life close to his wife and children? Or should he apply his skills for the greater good, giving other family farmers hope that their way of life could be preserved?

"When I first got involved in the co-op, I was resistant. I was happy on the farm. It was important work too, pioneering organic farming. But I was really encouraged by the vision of co-ops, and I got lots of support from co-op elders. It enthused me, and I felt I should get involved," George said. Eventually, he came to see that his passion and commitment to farming didn't have to split his heart, that there were ways for it all to come together. "It felt like big work I could give myself to. I realized my work coincided with my spiritual life. With my communication ability, I could do a lot on behalf of farmers in Washington, D.C. I could serve more people."

The people needed him, but so did his family. "My doing this is not what my family expected. It was hard on them to give me up and have to share me. Anyone who gets involved in something like this, it's not an easy thing.

"I had to face the reality of what my dreams meant. Good ideas usually come with a workload," George said. "I believe the ultimate thing is to prove that it [business] can be done differently, and just start to do new models rather than fight the old models. I've never been one to fight the status quo. I just ask, 'What's the better alternative?'"

So he set out, in his words, to "de-boogie man" what a successful company can be in American culture.

What's kept George away from his beloved farm in the Bad Axe Valley in Wisconsin is his call to envision of a better way of doing business on behalf of the family farm. By giving up farming himself, in fate's interwoven irony, George has helped contribute to hundreds of other farmers staying on the land and strengthening their own communities.

* * *

Long before George ever made his way to Wisconsin where he would meet up with his future as Organic Valley's CEIEIO, long before he would ever articulate how to create a place where fairness could be better served on a dinner plate, he was actually well on his way to the fulfillment of his destiny.

George grew up in the suburbs of West Palm Beach, Florida. His childhood was positive, and while his family was not well off, he wanted for nothing either. His parents, who ran an office supply business, were sometimes challenged by their outdoorsy and spirited son, but he didn't lack for affection or instruction. He remembers feeling a strong urge to protect and love the Earth even at a young age, and today identifies himself a naturalist. "I had a real deep nature wonder to me. I realized it wasn't right to hurt nature. I was always very sensitive to the violation of nature."

When he was fourteen, the Everglades in his area got bulldozed to make way for orange groves. George said, "I felt a sadness for all the relations that were so harmed so Minute Maid could grow oranges. My attitude then was almost sour toward corporations at an early age…now I see it's a disease of times changing and lack of land use planning. I lived in a place where things were getting destroyed, that would never come back. I had a concern that the next generation would never experience the things that were dear to me."

George also kept a small brood of chickens that he cared for throughout his childhood. Every three or four days, he would head over to a neighbor's house juggling a handful of eggs, careful not to break them. He felt the joy of sharing the fruits of his labors. "I felt so wealthy to share something that I'd been given," he said.

The strong feelings George felt for these things ultimately led him to farming, growing vegetables and raising livestock when he became an adult. He got a bachelor's degree in animal science from Colorado State University but didn't feel motivated by academics. He was inspired by the natural world and the wisdom to be gained from elders.

"My first real heroes were farmers and old people. They've really fascinated me, their connection to nature, their understanding of nature, reading the leaves, reading the caterpillars, reading everything you could imagine, guessing what the weather's going to be. So right away I was able to connect my nature-ness to farming. I was fortunate to run into a lot of old-fashioned farmers. So I picked up ideas like wit and common sense. Common sense became my study.

"Common sense is to believe that you have knowledge within yourself to sense or feel or understand things without the full engagement of your intellect or your past experiences. Common sense is the lead-in to what you call intuitive thinking. One of the things that's impressed me in the role of being a CEO is how valuable intuitive thinking is. CEOs have to be very intuitive. Compare that to what my thought had been before, that a CEO is very nonintuitive. Very objective, you know, demanding. Not compassionate. But in truth, the best CEOs are very intuitive and find all the reports and business plans, feasibility studies very fussy, and confusing compared to having a real deep sense of what, when, and how. What's impressed me about business is how valuable intuition is. It's not as objective and cold as I thought it would be. Actually, it's quite subjective."

George honed some of the ideas that propelled him to think differently about the character of business by bird watching and raising animals. He believes nature has been his strongest teacher, and learning from it would benefit anyone. "I believe that we should teach bird watching to all our kids because people get way too narrow in their eye-vision, which will give you tunnel vision sooner or later. Your head follows your eyes if you haven't noticed. So if you're always looking down, pretty soon that's your perspective on life.

"You've got to have enough vision, enough functional behavior, and enough foolishness to really succeed at something like this." George points from the picnic table he's sitting on toward the Organic Valley offices. The building, which looks like a barn, was built in 2004 and was constructed using green and sustainable building materials. The staff of 250 people can enjoy such perks as natural lighting (an average of one window for every two people), gorgeous views of the Kickapoo Valley, and a cafeteria that serves organic meals every day for reasonable prices.

"When we started the co-op, it was phenomenal. It's been amazing how farmers who have no business background outside of the business of farming were very good at facilitation. Their common sense skills were very, very valued as business leaders." It also didn't hurt that George had been raised in the language of family business.

"My family very much valued family business. I distinctly remember my grandpa saying, 'Malls are bad for community.' And he was right by the way. This was in 1964, before they even really got started. So it wasn't a very big leap for me to go from family business to family farms."

For George, it's also not a big leap to think that a cornerstone value of cooperative business is its cultural impact on communities. "Family business is all about culture. All about distinct character in a distinct region," George said. He gave an example: there could be 2,000-cow farms in your community, or you could have a number of forty to sixty cow farms that yield the same dollars, have the same acres. But the 2,000-cow-farm might hire workers at a low wage, putting them up in substandard housing. "Compare that with fifty grandparents with a swing in their yard, who were on the volunteer fire department, the church boards, and now you're jumping out of the economic realm into a cultural realm. You're talking about your ability to go to your grandfather's farm and swing on a swing, versus a 2,000-cow farm with low-wage people doing the bulk of the work. It's a different culture. While it's obviously very subjective and not the easiest to talk about, to me, it's about culture.

"It's about the sense of place family farms have. They are people's homes. A lot of people are born and raised there. They care for the place like it's their mother; it's something deep to them. It's not just an economic model, there's too much heart there. I believe those family models have more compassion."

It is George's conviction that it's not just errant CEOs that are responsible for the lack of equity in corporate America, but how wealth is distributed in the first place. "CEOs have taken a lot of bum raps—not that they haven't deserved it. But shouldn't we be looking at the corporate structure? The stock market? The way we pay people? All kinds of things. With the stock market, the next quarterly report is what counts, and when you have employees and CEOs with stock options and bonuses all based on stock value, guess what you run your business for? What's your business unit? Doing what you do or your stock value?

"CEOs are driven by these short-term goals with their own wallets involved. The managers, the stockholders, the board of directors are all telling them that all that matters is 'my value.' Not your morals or how you do it. So I feel like our business model in the United States is not properly aligned with what's good for this country, what's good for the people.

"Most CEOs wake up in the morning and the first thing they do is check their stock price, without much thought to how the business is doing or its service levels.

"What's really unique about a co-op is that the owners are the people who benefit from the business activity. Within the cooperative, owners benefit from the service they give, not from their stock value. So you've gone from a stock-value-driven perspective on business to a value-delivered perspective and that is a radical difference.

"Organic Valley decided to build in LaFarge, Wisconsin because it was important to continue to support the community that nurtured it. We made a declaration. We're a co-op, we stay a co-op, and we're going to stay true to the people who founded us. We're not going to move. Our function is to be who we are and stay who we are for here in the future and the next generation."

Which leads George back to the common-sense approach to fair business. It starts with consumers thinking for themselves and making their own decisions. Rather than fight an entrenched, outmoded system, create one that works for you and your values. He believes that the consumer-powered direction people are going in the natural food movement in particular is the kind of thing that will ultimately cause reform in business. It's something he feels optimistic about.

"I'm just thrilled to see the organic movement, the slow-food movement, the gourmet movement, help people regain their relationship with food. We have a country where we spend the least amount of money on food than anywhere else in the world and yet we think food is too expensive. We spend the most on medicine and we don't relate our health to the health of the plants, the things we eat, the soil; so I'm really encouraged that there is a reawakening relationship to food." George sees it everyday with the kind of feedback Organic Valley customers give the farmers.

Last year, Organic Valley created a pack of Earth Dinner cards with questions about food to encourage dinner time discourse. "By the time you've gone through an Earth Dinner and gone around the table at dinner with four rounds of questions, it's shocking how deep food is in people's psyche. If I asked you, 'What are your favorite memories of food?' It will stir all kinds of things in you.

"People can make consumer choice a big deal. They can start to make choices about how they want to treat themselves and treat the earth through their food purchases. It's a very simple, personal and profound place to take control."

This is something George has thought about a lot about over the years and has recently put down on paper. He's created a pyramid of food awareness called the "Organic Food Relationships—Steps of Fulfillment." It looks something like Maslow's Hierarchy of Needs pyramid. Abraham Maslow was a humanist psychologist who developed a theory that when basic human needs are met (food, shelter, etc.), people will have the ability to progress and act on social needs in their lives until they achieve what Maslow called self-actualization (at the pinnacle of the pyramid).

In George's food-relationship pyramid, federal oversight starts at the bottom (including the United States Department of Agriculture's certified organic label), and ends with "having your hands in the earth." In the layers in between are various steps of personal action, including cooking with whole foods, supporting humane business relationships, and having a direct relationship with a farm or the Earth. All of these activities hinge on consumer choice and their support for them. He believes Organic Valley is part of a larger movement that is building holistic thinking in many areas. "There's no doubt there's a whole lot of working models now that are coming together for a major shift in our society."

* * *

We head back indoors where a sense of optimism prevails. Down the hallways glowing with natural light, we pass people hard at work at their desks, doing their part on behalf of the farmer-owners. Tomorrow, they'll all get together to celebrate at the Kickapoo County Fair. When George arrives at his office, his assistant hands him a stack of papers. He notices the message light on his phone is blinking. A voice surges through its intercom. Good ideas come with a workload.

George stops to take a look outside his window. "Once you have the seasons in your blood, you look and think, 'Today's a good day to combine corn,' or something like that. I still live the life inside." He sits down at his desk with strength and grace; he's used to using his body to set to work. He might not work the land anymore, but its meaning and rhythms are as close to his purpose as his heartbeat.

Earth Dinner cards can be downloaded at www.earthdinner.org.

Hilary Abel with products
(Photo courtesy of Hillary Abel)

CIRCLE OF HANDS
By Burt Berlowe

"Ay Nicaragua Nicaraguita..."

It was a warm Granada, Nicaragua day in the summer of 1989. A group of forty women had formed a cozy circle and begun to sing together; white and brown hands clasping each other; English and Spanish voices blending into one; collective souls sharing tears of the moment. For one of the American women in the circle, Hilary Abell, reaching a helping hand across cultures would become more than a spontaneous act of bonding. It would become her way of life.

Hilary was one of five children born into a middle-class family in the conservative Chicago suburb of Winnetka. She learned the meaning of cooperation at an early age, having to get along with her four siblings. Her baptism into social activism came when she was part of an Episcopal church youth group that ministered to the homeless in the Chicago inner city, where she "learned some sense of social justice." Later, she traveled with an Amigos de Las Americas (Friends of the Americas) group to help build latrines in Mexico. Her pivotal experience was a trip to Nicaragua in 1989 with a group of professional women and students from Princeton University, where she was majoring in religion and politics and studying liberation theology.

"I went to Granada, Nicaragua (a sister city to Princeton) and observed firsthand the results of U.S. imperialism, how we were illegally supporting the Contras and providing them with bullets that were killing children. It was a very profound experience. I saw the way poor people organized at the grassroots and formed their own sugar and coffee co-ops, some of which did economic and social development. In addition, women's groups worked on issues of health care and human rights, despite the fact that the U.S. government was undermining their organizing effort. It was a profound experience in democracy, illustrating that the whole is greater than the sum of its parts, and that we can all do more together than we can alone.

"There was this Nicaraguan women's group: the Mothers of Heroes and Martyrs—mothers of victims of war. That was a turning point for me—watching U.S. women working alongside poor Latino women and forging an incredible bond. Each of them told their story of how this experience had affected them. Those of us from the United States apologized for our country's actions against the population. Then we all stood in a circle singing songs and crying together. We sang a song called 'Ay Nicaragua Nicaraguita,' about love of country and people and the sharing of a just society. I ended up making many trips to Latin America after that."

Hilary continued her Central America advocacy in New York City through an organization called Neighbor to Neighbor that promoted human rights in El Salvador, including a boycott of Salvadoran coffee to protest American policy. While working for the Massachusetts-based fair trade company Equal Exchange, she was involved in a pioneering project that helped support co-op development for small-scale coffee farmers. "In Colombia," she recalls, "I visited a coffee farm where they turned rabbit droppings into compost. They grew about forty kinds of fruit, and the family got ninety percent of their food from the farm each day. As a suburban girl, I had never seen this level of self-sufficiency and sustainability.

"In Peru, I watched Quechua families pick coffee together, using indigenous traditions of rotating from farm to farm to make the heavy work of harvesting lighter. They were very poor and lived in adobe houses with dirt floors. Only a few of them had electricity. Yet they developed a childcare center and their own schools with paid teachers. They had a strong sense of community, possibility and progress. The common opinion is that poverty equals despair. But these poor people are organizing to make things better."

These compelling experiences guided Hilary on to a new and lasting path. She went to work for the Hesperian Foundation, a nonprofit publisher of health care materials used in poor countries, and then for TransFair USA, the nonprofit certifier of fair trade products in the U.S. That ultimately led to her current job as executive director of Women's Action to Gain Economic Security (WAGES) headquartered in the San Francisco Bay area.

"WAGES was started in 1995 by a couple of social workers interested in issues of women's empowerment and economic security for immigrants," Hilary explains. "They wanted to start a co-op that would raise incomes and improve working conditions for immigrant women. They set up a house-cleaning cooperative to provide work for Latina women, while using environmentally friendly products and waste conservation. We are one of the few worker co-ops in the nation that exclusively serves immigrant women."

The WAGES program has created three successful co-ops: Emma's Eco-Clean, Eco-Care and, the newest one—Natural Home Cleaning Professionals. Members clean private homes and small businesses for pay and benefits well above what most immigrants make after coming to the U.S. "What excites me about WAGES," Hilary says, "is that it promotes principles of fair trade in the domestic service sector. We create businesses that are worker owned and controlled, so the worker-owners have a say in company policies and develop leadership skills in the process."

Members of the WAGES co-ops also contribute to the community around them. "We're a leader in the use of clean chemicals," says Hilary. "That has a positive effect on consumers and the community. And we are visible businesses. Some of our members belong to the local chamber of commerce and interact with other business leaders. We are also mission-and social-change driven. We teach democratic values and practices and are equally concerned about those principles as we are about making money for the co-op members. The WAGES co-ops are an example of collective entrepreneurship where workers become business owners. This is part of a broader movement towards a more sustainable economy and a community-building process. We are turning the (standard) economic model on its head."

Chapter Six
The Care Givers

INTRODUCTION

One of our compassionate rebel buttons says, "I care, therefore I act." It tells us that caring is the key that opens the door to active social change. We are most likely to act on those things we care deeply about. And it is that caring that keeps us going when things get rough.

In order to create a more caring culture, we need to lead by example. There are literally millions of people who perform acts of caring everyday in the world. These range from small, random acts of kindness and compassion to large humanitarian projects which show the generous side of many Americans.

The problem with many of these well-intentioned actions is that they are temporary. Once the immediate need is over, people tend to fall back into their old habits, and the change they brought about may not last. To get a true picture of the caring culture, we need to look at the less spectacular but more consistent actions that citizens do, especially those that can turn into real social change.

There is a substantial difference between random acts of kindness and compassionate rebel acts. Let's suppose you run into a homeless man on the street who asks for a handout. A random act of kindness would be to give him a few bucks or buy him a bowl of soup then send him on his way. A compassionate rebel would go further, wanting to know why the man was homeless, how there could be beggars on the streets of the world's richest country, and what could be done about it. When they turn that curiosity into action, they begin to change the world.

Traditionally, the word "caregiver" brings to mind people who take care of children or those working in medical and social service professions. We are expanding that concept further to include anyone who gives of themselves in pursuit of a cause they care deeply about, and in so doing, helps to create a caring culture. The people in this chapter are especially profound examples of the power of caring and giving.

Diane Knobel in New Orleans
(Photo courtesy of Diane Knobel)

KATRINA CALLING
By Burt Berlowe

It's the week after Katrina hit the Gulf Coast and the previously onrushing water has receded, leaving in its wake tracks of mud and black mold rancid under the torrid Mississippi sun. Diana Knobel stands on a cleared patch of land, stunned by the sight of once-proud homes that have fallen off their foundations, their parts lodged in the muck. Nearby, survivors linger forlornly on curbs and street corners. Hordes of kissing bugs, blown off course from the storm, swarm relentlessly around Diane, sticking to her skin. Her aching feet and shoulders feel damp to the core. She seeks a shady place to rest, but the few remaining trees have lost all of their leaves and offer little protection from the muggy heat. She wipes the beads of sweat from her forehead with one hand and with the other grabs hold of a handle on her truck and hoists herself into its bed to finish unloading the pile of boxes and supplies that will go to local food shelves and churches. Diana is finishing one leg of a missionary journey into the soul of America. Many more still lie ahead.

The long, winding road that brought Diana to the poorest areas of the Deep South at a time of national crisis began many miles and years ago in a much different time and place but with definite signs of things to come.

* * *

Born to Survive

"My childhood was not pretty," Diana says, reflecting on the psychological and emotional trauma that plagued her formulative years virtually from the moment she was born. "I was conceived on the campus of the Minneapolis Institute of Arts. Mom had been having an affair with a professor on campus. Her parents forced her to get married, and that lasted about five months. They were separated before I was born and divorced soon after that. I was put up for adoption and spent three days alone in the hospital waiting for my mother to make her final decision before she took me back. The warmth and comfort of the womb were replaced with the sterility and clamor of bells and whistles and nurses around the clock.

"I grew up in the student housing projects of the Prospect Park neighborhood in south Minneapolis. Mom was going to school. I was the only child. When I was about four and a half, she met and married my stepdad at a neighborhood Methodist church. My mother was ill-equipped to juggle marriage, childrearing and schooling due to a previous head injury she'd received in a high school water skiing accident. She didn't perceive the signs of my trauma or stress, nor could she provide me with a healthy emotional upbringing.

"Years later, through alternative and traditional therapy, I realized incest was a part of my childhood ever since I could remember and stopped when I was about ten years old. Most of my childhood is a thick fog of sadness and despair. Because of incest, I felt shame and unworthiness. I suffered from depression and anxiety most of my early life. I learned to cope by using marijuana, alcohol and cigarettes starting in my junior high confirmation classes.

"We were a hypocritical suburban family playing out the competition with the Joneses. There wasn't any communication or clarity in my family, and I was highly susceptible to outside influences and shamed into being cool by my fellow confirmation participants, all of us dazed and confused by the double standard '70s. The one thing I wanted desperately was to be accepted and noticed. That was a big part of getting me through those years.

"My parents finally divorced when I was sixteen. The animosity and tension between them was so palpable you could cut it with a knife. My own lifestyle was not helping. My boyfriend was supplying me with weed and alcohol even after I broke up with him and moved across town to another suburb. I was trying to decide what I wanted out of life. When my parents split up, I went with my mom. She had a night job. I was forced into responsibility I wasn't ready for and without any adult guidance. It was the time I felt the most abandoned. I went down a slippery slope of taking advantage of my freedom, partying, skipping school, with an illusion that everything was fine, that I had it made. What more could a teenager ask for?

"In our family, whatever happened in our house was to be kept a secret. We were to present a front that we were an upstanding 'Kodak family' despite the divorce. I pretended everything was okay. I would be at home when I knew my mom's call was coming and then would duck out. 'Getting away with anything' was one of my most destructive tendencies. The price of freedom was also a curse that developed into a survival mechanism, a measure of entitlement. I knew that the Kodak world was a farce and began questioning reality without any adult feedback or sounding board, which only intensified my ingrained feelings of worthlessness.

"I decided to test the limits of my understanding of right and wrong. I was going to break the rules while playing the Kodak game of keeping up appearances. I broke them big time without anyone ever suspecting. I held my own by doing strange things, like getting high in French class when the teacher left the room or cheating with a few of the cool students who knew how to get away with it.

"In the high school where I transferred into after the divorce, I found a true friend of African American descent. She couldn't believe my boldness, and we made each other laugh a lot. Both of us came from dysfunctional families and bridged our differences with shared pain. She was one of the most popular girls in school and, because of our friendship, I had a modicum of status. I was figuratively adopted by her family as one of the only honorary white persons allowed to experience their side of suburban racial divides.

"That lifestyle was physically foreign, visceral and as real as one could get. Yet I was accepted beyond anything I had experienced growing up white middle class. My friend's home had roaches, piles of dirty dishes and clothes on every surface. I admired her determination to escape this reality as much as I was determined to escape my sterile understanding of the world through education and surviving beyond our families' limitations.

"My friend's older sister was into drugs, fraud and prostitution, and got me to shoplift fancy dresses for her so she could resell them. I was high from the adrenaline rush of breaking the rules. Yet I was hollow, empty inside, and looking for something real. I subconsciously let my guard down one day and got caught. I got a slap on the wrist and my parents were notified and I was given a drug evaluation. That was my cry for help, a real wake-up call for me. I joined an AA (Alcoholics Anonymous) program. I still found less serious ways of breaking rules such as speeding. I smoked and drank a lot of coffee and lost a lot of weight. Yet, all of this time my soul had my back. It kept tapping me on the shoulder and asking, 'Why are you doing this?'"

* * *

Born Again

Diana wondered why the young man she had just met seemed so happy—why he was constantly beaming with a beatific smile that lit up the room. She was in the midst of her own search for a happiness she had not yet found in the early years of her life. When she asked why he was so happy, he said he was 'born again.'

"I had been breaking rules, having sex, partying. I wanted to go from being lost to finding meaning in my life. I had a twenty-four-hour conversion after listening to a group of young Nazarenes explain the answers to my soulful question, 'How can I be saved?' I confessed my sins and received Jesus. I gave up partying, sex and feeling lost. It was a spiritual experience that marked a significant passage to changing my life for the better. It made me believe that someone might be listening to me, unlike my parents who lacked interest in me and let me slip through the cracks. Knowing that Jesus cared about me and wanted me to succeed was such a relief. When I purged the past and the questions burdening me about why I had to suffer such a miserable childhood, I found space for something new. I found a relationship with God. Later, I met a woman praying in the park and she invited me to her church. It was a radical evangelical, right-wing Christian church. They gobbled me up and filled me with their dogma. I enrolled at North Central Bible College. I plunged into Bible training and became the best Christian I could become."

But even as she immersed herself in the "born again" experience for two years, Diana felt creeping doubt. "At the peak of my new life, I was a Bible-thumping Christian standing on downtown streets evangelizing people. I was told that's what you were supposed to do to be a good Christian. I liked breaking the rules of society and conformity to perceived social standards. It felt bold and exhilarating to brave the fear of rejection for Christ. But I wasn't sure I believed in what I was doing. There was something about it that nagged my conscience. It seemed a little too pat, a little too sterile—even dishonest. Who were we to tell others how to best live their life in order to prevent themselves from going to Hell? I was disillusioned by the hypocrisy of the Christian double life, saying one thing and doing another, believing that you had to be in this special Christian box to be saved. That box turned out to be too small for me. Once again I felt my soul tapping on my shoulder questioning, 'What are you doing?' It was the beginning of my questioning God and the church. I started unwinding from the right-wing evangelical experience and left the Bible College."

Diana set out to restore her faith in humanity and to rediscover her place in the world. She made pilgrimages to various churches and cathedrals in Europe where Christianity was ancient and enduring. "I was seeking others who wanted to break away from strict rule of dogma and religiosity. I checked in with my soul as my guide. That is the one thing I took from my days in the Bible college, was the belief that I wasn't alone in the world and that there was wisdom that spoke to me from on high. It spoke through my soul, and I listened."

While backpacking across Europe, Diane met and eventually married an Englishman. They returned to the U.S, where she planned to finish her college education and embark on a new phase of her life. "I was learning how to be a wife, how to make money, how to live within the mixed cultural worlds we both came from. I didn't realize how different my American upbringing was from my husband's. Four years into our marriage, I gave birth to my daughter who became my second salvation. She was born prematurely weighing barely over three pounds. She thrived because I stayed with her for the three weeks she was in the hospital. I held her constantly. I sang to her. I prayed a lot. I knew how to pray. In two years of Bible college I did a lot of praying. I learned to be a prayer warrior.

"I determined to do my mothering like I did everything else—radically. In those days, women weren't staying home with their children. They were all interested in climbing the corporate ladder. I took the hippie mom track and stayed at home. We bought and remodeled a house in North Minneapolis. When our son was born, our marriage was beginning to weaken under the pressure of living in the inner-city with its escalating crime rates, housing depreciation, and eight challenging years of remodeling. We knew we had to make some changes and ultimately became a part of the white flight out of the inner city. We found a HUD house on a five-acre lot with a barn in Lino Lakes, Minnesota and moved there in 1993 with a four-and two-year-old in tow. We set up a hobby farm, raising goats and sheep for six years, and spent our spare time in remodeling and renovating the house. Our third child came in 1995 to complete the family."

Raising three children and the toll of living under constant construction, financial hurdles of living on one income; along with emotional, spiritual, and philosophical differences led to growing marital conflicts between Diana and her husband. In 2003, they divorced after eighteen years of marriage. He stayed on the property. She moved back to the city, settling in St. Paul. They would split parenting time with their children while undergoing a two-year custody battle.

During this period, Diana gradually began to find the path that would ultimately define her life. "Despite my own wrestling with hereditary mental illness, addictions and feelings of not fitting into any set society mold, I had produced three healthy happy children. As they began to grow, my nurturing experience came together with my understanding of the gospel, and all the spiritual training I received only deepened. Being a stay-at-home mom, working so closely with nature and the farm animals gave me an incredibly powerful chance to develop my spiritual gifts. I was, in essence being born again."

* * *

Call Waiting

One day, while moving some boxes in her new home, Diana unpacked her Bible. It reminded her of a prophecy she had received during her born-again years. It said she was going to get married, raise children, develop spiritual gifts and do ministry. She had accomplished the first two. The last two were works in progress. She had begun to use alternative healing, turning to acupuncture and yoga to treat a sinus infection, a back injury, and bouts of depression when standard medication failed. She was on a full-fledged quest to develop her whole self. In 2001, she enrolled and graduated from an Unconditional Love and Forgiveness class and went on to teach people how to get in touch with their inner selves. "I was ready to sprout my wings as a spiritual being. I came to embrace mysticism. I believed I was breaking through my past and it no longer had to haunt me."

Then Diana's life took another strange twist. She fell in love with a woman named Lynne. "I am not a lesbian," she says. "But I now understand what it means to be bisexual. When I wrestled with my attraction to this woman, I once again pushed boundaries and trusted my soul to guide the way. We had a tumultuous love affair for four years that opened wide the doors for intense introspection and inner healing for both of us."

Thankfully, the strong ties to her children only deepened as Diana shared honestly and openly the radical decisions she was making. As her children were entering their teenage years, they only respected their mother more for going to extremes to find meaning in life. This proved to be an important and incredible opportunity for the children to juxtapose their traditional suburban lifestyle with their dad and experience a more radically alternative lifestyle in the city with their mom. Her relationship with Lynne would soon turn toward a dramatic journey that would move Diana ever closer to fulfilling her prophecy.

In the spring of 2005, Diana had just graduated with a B.S. in visual and technical communications and the art of persuasion and decided to take the summer off, contemplate options, and focus on what to do next. In late August, the family went on their annual camping trip to Lake Superior south shore near Herbster, Wisconsin. "There, the children, and our friends who come along, unplug from the world and commune with the spirits of land, water, fire, and sky. I consider myself an 'empath'—someone who senses. I feel my body has radar that tunes into people's feelings and receives energy from outside of me. I can be doing the dishes right as rain and a storm cloud comes over me and I sense things going on in the world. While I was on the camping trip, I had periodic feelings that something major was happening on the Earth. When I got home, I knew something was wrong because my body felt like lead. Then the television showed people crying out for water. I found out that Hurricane Katrina had just hit the Gulf Coast."

A few days later, Diana went to visit her friend Aria, a mystical woman who owned a small New Age store called Stonehenge in the Uptown area of Minneapolis. "As I was climbing up the steps of her front porch I said to Aria, 'My body is all out of sorts, my brain is muddled and I feel so much dread. It must be Katrina.' She said 'I feel the same thing.' We were feeling a 'calling.' We sat on the porch of her store and looked at each other for a moment. Then Aria said 'I feel like shutting the shop down and bringing water to those people crying out.'

"I got huge chills and goose bumps. I had a vision where I saw myself driving a truck. We became silent again into our own worlds. We wondered how we would take care of the things we would leave behind if we made that trip. Then, in an instant, we made up our mind. We prayed and called upon our souls, all of our spiritual guides and ancestors, and asked, 'Please guide us.' We feel like we're supposed to take water to people on the Gulf Coast. Help us find the connections.' I had come to a crossroads of who I was and what I was supposed to with my life, what my contribution would be to the world. That led to my jumping fully on board with Katrina."

Diana, Aria and Lynn began to make plans to go to the Gulf Coast. With Aria's help, Diana created an e-mail mailing to people they knew asking them to contribute time, money and supplies. They then developed a list of what they would need. First on the list were a truck and some water. They found a local company that was willing to donate 12,000 pounds of water. They took the donation and rented a twenty-six foot Ryder truck to carry it.

"We wanted to go directly to New Orleans, but we had heard that we wouldn't get through, that trucks were being turned back. We ended up going instead to one of the hardest hit areas on the coast in Biloxi (Mississippi). It was September 3rd of 2005, four days after the storm happened. As we were leaving the truck rental facility, I got a call from a Minnesota artist Quito Ziegler in New York. She said 'I have a truck to loan you. I read your requests on the e-mail and I wanted to help.' I couldn't help question the humor of the universe at that moment. We turned the rental truck around and took it back to Ryder. The executive who had offered us the water paid his staff to stay overtime for us and waited until we could get across Minneapolis, pick up the donated truck and come back to the dock where the employees were waiting to load the water before they went home for the weekend. We had all the water balanced in the back of the truck and still plenty of room to gather waiting supplies. We knew then we really did have the blessing of the universe."

* * *

Answering the Call

Diana and her troupe were inundated with offers of help in many forms. "We set up drop-off sites. Before long, our truck was filled with pallets of water. The outer walls were embedded top to bottom, front to back with larger-than-life photos taken by Quito Ziegler for the purpose of documenting various immigrants around Minnesota—a testimony to diversity that we were proud to take to the Southern Coast. Later, we duck-taped 'Power to the People' with a huge peace sign on the back of the truck. Throughout the next several months, the truck would become the symbol of our commitment and compassion."

The day the three women left for the Gulf Coast in the truck and a Ford van, they welcomed to their team an Indian husband and wife, Guru and Sudha, who had been heavily involved with the Tsunami relief efforts the year before. "We all took turns driving. Guru was an expert at using the Web to access information and would call ahead to find others willing to donate supplies along their planned route.

"Two huge crates of organic apples were donated in Wisconsin, along with an amazing amount of squash, and bags and bags of sweet corn from another roadside stand. One generous group of people drove sixty miles from

St. Louis and waited twelve hours for us in a Wal-Mart parking where they donated food, water and baby supplies. We arrived in Biloxi on September 5th.

"Here we were: two lesbians, a bisexual, and a heterosexual couple—three white women and an Indian husband and wife. We made an amazing working team together, sharing decisions, practicing consensus and nonjudgment of each other's cultural differences, lifestyle preferences, shortfalls, and short tempers. It was an amazing experience.

"Before we left Arkansas, Sudha warned us to pull off the road and get gas cans to prepare for gas shortages that lay ahead. We took the next exit that led to a tiny town three miles off the Interstate. It was Sunday and everything was closed. We knocked on doors asking people for a gas can without success. We didn't know that you just don't walk up to people's homes in the South.

"One woman gave us the number of the town sheriff. After sounding extremely miffed that we had troubled him on his time off, he called a man who owned the only town hardware store to see if he was inclined to open his store and sell us a gas can. The man took time off from celebrating his wedding anniversary to let us purchase gas cans, rope and a few other supplies. We later found some pickle barrels that we could fill with gas.

"Just over the border of Mississippi, we nearly caused a riot when a manager of a gas station allowed us to pull ahead of a long line of cars waiting for gas. It was a tense moment of trying to explain to a very strung out security guard woman with a gun that we were not trying to cause trouble. We didn't dare try to fill the barrels there.

"When we got to Jackson, Mississippi, a pastor who offered to be our escort was waiting for us and took us to a gas station heavily guarded by police to keep riots from erupting. The police looked the other way, allowing us to fill up our barrels, one with diesel for the big truck and the other with gas for the car.

"After leaving Jackson, we began seeing the damage of the storm's rage. Huge trees were snapped in half in the line of 100 mile per hour winds that had ripped through the area. Debris was all over the sides of the road, and periodically we would have to swerve and miss branches that had fallen off the cleanup trucks. When we got to the outskirts of Biloxi, the pastor introduced us to a city councilman who graciously provided lodging with his relatives. It was about 9 p.m. We had been on the road for twenty-six harrowing hours.

"Early the next morning, driving into Biloxi, we saw horrible damage. Trees split apart, debris, garbage, people's lives still hanging in the trees marking the high-water line. All of the roads, buildings, and vehicles were beginning to dry out. Survivors and returning evacuees were feeling pinched. There was a run on gas so ferocious that the supply couldn't keep up with the demand. In

Biloxi, the water had receded. But there was a lot of residual damage, migration and uncertainty. Electricity was off in many places. There were downed power lines; huge chunks of asphalt lying around; twisted metal wrapped around trees, poles and fences. There were trees uprooted everywhere. Piles of machinery had pushed the tree branches into the street, and we had to skirt around fallen limbs. Casino barges had been washed up onto shore, colliding into houses, knocking them off foundations, slamming into ancient massive oaks, being forced to a halt by the root systems holding against the force of the storm. The water had reached twenty feet in some places. Countless cars, trucks, and boats were left abandoned in strange places not even imaginable unless witnessed firsthand. The destruction was worse than any man made war or catastrophe, only nature could be so totally powerful. The only thing halfway clear were the main roads.

"Coming out of Biloxi, trying to find a place to stay, we were told of the 6 p.m. curfew. Helicopters were buzzing everywhere. It was like a military zone. All kinds of official vehicles, including the National Guard, Homeland Security, the armed forces of every kind, and the media vans were on the road going from place to place. We had to cross the only bridge standing to get into Biloxi. There were long lines getting out and into the East Bay of Biloxi with many signs telling which exits were blocked and which were checkpoints. You could see that the other bridge off in the distance along the coastal highway was completely torn up, with concrete sheets pointing into the air like dominoes waiting to be pushed over. We were guided through military checkpoints to the church waiting to receive our goods and help us unload. A film crew from a news channel was there and interviewed us.

"We unloaded the truck and took time to meet survivors, recuperating from what it took out of us to get there and taking in the shock of what we were witnessing. In any spare time I was filming what was happening. We had previously determined to stay put as long as they allowed us to stay. It was important to me to get as much footage as we could before we had to leave.

"Our first major decision of that day was deciding if we should give all of our supplies to the one church we stopped at first or spread it out to other survivor bases. It was totally shocking to see how many supplies had poured in prior to our arrival. Knowing that we would be heading back through areas inland devastated by the storm, some of us wanted to save some supplies for a chance meeting or operation really desperate for what we had in our truck. Some of the team just wanted to be done with it right then and there. A fair amount of general supplies—water, toilet paper, diapers and food—the things the church had a generous amount of were held back on the truck to pass out on our way back."

The weary, shell-shocked Minnesota team decided to check out other areas in Biloxi before leaving. Diana recalls how on the other side of Biloxi, the predominantly white area, an out-of-state Christian organization had set up a stainless steel kitchen with an abundant supply of equipment, pop-up canopies for rain protection and shade, and lots of supplies coming into their camp. "We didn't feel needed there, so we went back to a relief site in East Biloxi operated by an African American Baptist church. They had a makeshift outdoor kitchen that was feeding about 500 people a day, set up in someone's front yard across from where we had first unloaded supplies into the church. The survivors improvised everything. They were stringing up tarps and washing an assortment of pans and pots in a rusty tub. The whole operation was run by African American resident survivors and returning evacuees. We asked those in charge, 'what do you need.?' They gave us a list.

"We went back to Jackson to get these specific supplies with the cash donated from Minnesotans. We wanted to make a difference for this neighborhood imbued with resolution to recover and restore some semblance of sanity.

"We had to find lodging as the curfew was fast approaching. There weren't any motels within a two-hour drive, and we couldn't stay with the pastor's family anymore. The only place we knew that could possibly have plenty of room for us without taking lodging from those who desperately needed it was called Camp Sister Spirit. We didn't find out until much later that Camp Sister Spirit was a hated lesbian women's retreat center in the midst of Ku Klux Klan territory and that we could have been putting ourselves in great danger by going there. The residents of the camp, in years past, patrolled the land with shotguns; it was that bad.

"By the time we got to Hattisburg at about 11 p.m., there had just been a random shooting over some food dispute. We had no idea the perilous position we were headed into. At any time, a group of vigilantes could force us to give over our supplies. Thankfully, we were guided into no serious mishaps but got terribly lost later that night. As we pulled into town, the headlights illuminated absurd and frightening images of the remnants of metal buildings twisted and wrapped around trees. This major town had no electricity, and there was a 6 p.m. curfew as well. Yet we hardly passed even a police car. There was no one on the streets when we got there nor as we drove for miles through the city. We found out that Camp Sister Spirit had lodging that could house fifty people. They also served as a battered women's shelter and a potential relief center for emergencies.

"The closest town near the camp was called Ovette. We stopped a man in a van alongside of the road to ask for directions. He just happened to be a county surveyor who knew the area. He explained that the road leading to the long driveway to the camp would be impassible with our big truck and that we should stay somewhere else until daylight. We continued on until we found the Ovette gas station and general store. Guru offered to stay with the truck, assured us he was fine if we needed to find more comfortable digs and waved us off to go find the camp in the van. It was 1.a.m. All the road signs had been blown off. The stress was getting to everyone. We argued about where we were. It was possibly the worst night of our lives. We just completely fell apart. We got lost for two hours on the back roads of 'God knows where' and finally ended up at an abandoned gas station around 3 a.m. We pulled over to sleep as best we could—three miserable gals in a Ford Ranger. We hoped sunlight could show us things differently.

"We didn't realize the danger Guru might be in. We didn't know the extent of the racism problem until we pulled into the Ovette gas station at 7 a.m. the next morning to start over in the daylight with the directions we were given. We were strangers with this strange truck covered with multiracial art, and we had a black man with us who was openly asking anyone who listened how to get to Camp Sister Spirit. It was like being in some extreme white racist B-horror movie. There were men looking at us with pure unabashed hatred. I had never in my entire life experienced such distain and mistrust. An older woman approached us and said, 'You need to leave here as soon as you can. You are not safe here.'

"Two women led us out of the gas station towards a church off a main highway about seven miles from Ovette. They didn't ask us a lot of questions, just seemed to want to show us how to get to Camp Sister Spirit. A half an hour later, we arrived at Camp Sister Spirit, pulling the big truck into a neighboring driveway.

"We all climbed into the Ford Ranger and headed down the driveway of Camp Sister Spirit. We were greeted by a pack of dogs and a woman calling them back. Having a pack of dogs was the best security they had against invaders. After hot showers, some food that was cooked up from what we brought, much sharing of stories ensued. We all got our first good night's sleep in four days. The camp had suffered lots of damage from Katrina and we had to constantly be on the watch for venomous snakes, spiders, and large flying cockroaches. But it was peaceful and intoxicating to be within the forest of the Deep South. We talked about the tensions of the community and the camp and they invited us to return to use their camp as a base. We had made a commitment to take supplies for the East Biloxi community kitchen, and we still had another hour-and-a-half drive to get to Jackson where we could find those supplies. We said tearful goodbyes.

"We were on the road for about an hour and came into Magee, Mississippi, where we eventually made our way to a hardware store to get supplies. While we waited in the parking lot, a car with two women pulled up and one of them had a copy of a flyer we had handed out at a Red Cross center asking for donations and with a picture of the truck on one side. One of the women said 'Our church has been collecting supplies for you for a week. Just an hour ago a group of us got in a prayer circle and prayed for you. Please come to our church just outside of town.'

"When we got to the church, it was like a festival with twenty to thirty people lined up cheering for us. In the parking lot was an assembly line waiting load everything they had been collecting for a week. The church basement was brimming over with boxes, suitcases stuffed with supplies and crates of canned food and bottled water. It was a virtual gold mine of relief. Within a few hours, we had a truck filled to the gills. They kept asking, 'what else do you need?' They even took us to the local mill and allowed us to top off our diesel on the big truck. I remembered that the kitchen in Biloxi needed propane tanks. A few of the church members went home and took off the tanks to their outdoor grills and insisted we take them. It was incredible.

"What we really needed was a place to sleep that night. We were about to contact a motel when a woman at the church insisted that we stay at her house. It was a recently constructed mansion, a huge, luxurious house. We were put up in the guest wing and fed a grand Southern breakfast the next morning. It was Southern hospitality to the max."

Weeks later, Diana returned from that Baptist church to bring much-needed supplies to an African American church that never had received any free supplies from white people. "This great, incredible generous offer of Christian compassion was an exciting testimony to the goodness of humanity, when really, this white church was afraid to go the hour and a half to the inner-city of the coast and get messed up in race relations or face any of the horrors of the destruction. They prayed for someone else to do their dirty work. They didn't feel the need to even reach out five miles across some imaginary demarcation of territory to help another church close to home. I had to remind myself that at least they did give us incredible supplies that got distributed to the people who needed it in Biloxi." That was Diana's first extreme taste of the homophobia and racism that marked the entrenched attitudes of the rural areas of Mississippi.

On the way back from Magee that first trip, with a full truck of supplies from the Baptist church commissioned to deliver to the poor survivors of the hurricane, Diana's team stopped for gas at a place called McDaniel's General Store. There were a couple of women with children in a truck. "We asked them when was the last time they had any food. 'Seven days ago,' they said. All they got from FEMA was ice and water. These rural people hunt and fish and put everything into a freezer. Their freezer was wiped out in the storm. We gave them eggs, butter, milk, and filled the back of their truck with other supplies and some toys for the children. Everyone felt like it was Christmas."

Lynne, Aria and Guru needed to get back to their lives in the Twin Cities, leaving Diana who was unemployed at the time to find other helpers as well as the resources for a return trip. Within twelve days, Diana had created a ten-minute documentary of their first trip and found another team of two men and a young woman who followed the truck re-creating the first run. They had enough funds to get the truck there and back but had to find a way to stay afloat while they were there. They loaded up the truck and car with another generous offer of 12,000 gallons of water, and donated paper products, coffee, bikes, mosquito repellant that could be thrown into the swamps, and other basic supplies. They went straight to deliver supplies to Camp Sister Spirit. "There were four of us as a team. I had an effective team of young people who wanted to change the world. There was no ego. They had no trouble letting me lead. They just wanted to get their hands into the dirty work of service. They provided lots of muscle, willingness to go the last mile, and we laughed all the time."

On the second trip to Biloxi, Diana and her new crew left some pedal bikes for people to ride as there was no gas for cars. They found a Salvation Army quarter-mile-long warehouse that had shipped in supplies from all over the world. They also began to take stock of the many other Christian-run organizations that were stockpiling supplies and were only too happy to get food out to where it was needed. "We all were having an incredible amount of fun while doing the hardest and grittiest of jobs: constantly loading and unloading a truck of supplies, driving for hours to and from supply centers and churches in the heat, and being smack in the face of injustice after injustice, knowing we were only making a dent in the larger scheme of things.

"Back in Ovette, people's attitudes began to change by necessity. In the beginning, just after the storm hit, there were no supplies except from Camp Sister Spirit. For a moment in time, there was a laying down of 'isms.' Everybody understood that we were all connected. Over the next three weeks, a new community emerged. We brought water from one of the various warehouses to Camp Sister Spirit and from there to give to the Richton Fire Department. Before water treatment had come back to the area, local babies were getting dysentery. They were able to drink electrolyte formula we brought from Minnesota. People who would never before have crossed the boundary into Camp Sister Spirit came in and humbly asked for food.

"But it didn't last long. The hatred and mistrust came back. Recovery was long and hard for most of these people who did not get government help. To this day, Ovette and Richto haven't gotten the proper help they need. They'll be working on roof repairs and debris cleanup for years. The deeper issues can't be washed away by hurricane winds. There's much work to be done to heal race relations and economic issues of the Deep South."

Diana's team was running out of money and didn't know if they could make any more trips to the Gulf Coast. Around that time, an organization called Mission From Minnesota had heard about what Diana was doing. They helped finance some of the expenses of her trip so she could return. FEMA was there providing well-paid contracts for hauling water, ice and lots of debris removal, but they had no distribution system for food.

One night, another truck came into Camp Sister Spirit to deliver supplies driven by two young Jewish men. They had heard about the food distribution center through the grapevine. They were from a collective of all Jewish relief efforts based out of the Henry S. Jacob (Camp Jacob) camp. The mayor of Utica, Mississippi donated warehouse space in town and many of the African American residents volunteered to work along side Jewish volunteers who came from all over America to help set up a major hub of receiving shipments of water and supplies. It was the best run of all the warehouses Diana had encountered. She called it "a mini-Wal-mart." She left the camp not only with an abundance of supplies but also with a thousand-dollar check from its owners.

Diana and her team became primary food runners in the Gulf area, their radically decorated truck a recognized and generally accepted vehicle of public service. Together, they made twenty-six trips by truck with an estimated worth of $500,000 of bottled water and various supplies distributed to African American churches not receiving aid from the Red Cross or FEMA.

"Food supplies were drying up ten weeks after the storm. People were still coming in from all over wanting to help, but a shift was occurring. Once, in Biloxi, I was contacted by two 'Day Traders' working in oil commodities from New York. They had been told I was going into the interior and helping communities who were in need of supplies. They wanted to get a piece of the action. They drove three hours to Richton, and we met at a gas station, where I was to lead them to a church to drop off their supplies. When the two men drove up in a SUV, I was surprised at how little they actually brought.

"They asked 'how long are you going to be here?'"

"I said 'I've tapped out all of my resources and will have to go back home in two days.'"

"How much do you need to stay on the road a week?" they responded.

"I remembered the thousand dollars I received from Camp Jacob. I replied quickly 'I need a thousand dollars.'

"One of them reached into his pocket and pulled out this wad of money. And without a blink of an eye, he peeled off ten one-hundred-dollar bills and gave them to me.

"I fell in love with Mississippi. But most of the white people there scare me. They are flag-waving, gun-toting, shoot-first-and-ask-questions-later kind of people. Once I was with one of the founders of Camp Sister Spirit. She took me out to the main road, the very same one where we were lost trying to find the camp. She got out of the car and started spray painting on the road over the words: 'nigger don't let the sun go down' and 'fuck all niggers' that had been written there overnight. This was one of many routine times over the last twenty years she had done that. She said to me, 'You don't know a whole lot about the South do you? You know, we could get shot at right now. We've probably got a shotgun pointed at us from over there,' as she pointed to a ramshackle shanty house with a Confederate flag waving at us an eighth of a mile down the road. 'You're in the Deep South, home of the Ku Klux Klan. This is the reality down here.' I took my camera and scanned the houses within rifle range. It was too late to be scared. I had been filming the whole time, driving an obnoxious identifiable truck all throughout the area for weeks by then. That was the first time it really hit me. The Civil War is still going on in people's lives here.

"One day, we drove back from Utica and I was totally surprised. Lynn had come back and brought a woman healer and lots of fruits and vegetables. Lynn had been to the Minneapolis farmers' market and, because of the goodness and generosity of some of the vendors, she loaded up the trailer and truck for Sister Spirit.

"I was getting weary and missing my children terribly. Lynn encouraged me to go home and let her take over the truck. I had promised to do one more trip. We were lured into Louisiana for the first time since the storm.

"It was the beginning of October. We were unloading the truck when I was approached by this young African American pastor, the son of the woman who called her aunt in Richton, Mississippi, asking for supplies for her devastated community church. That aunt was Miss Mildred, the matriarch I took directions from regarding which churches to deliver supplies to. The church pastor, Reverend Eden, asked if he could take some supplies for his church in New Orleans. Officials had just opened the city to returning evacuees, and his church, which had been spared by the flood was capable of facilitating a center there. I was shocked to learn that the Red Cross or FEMA had not been set up in New Orleans to help and welcome home evacuees from the storm.

"We headed straight back to Utica, as they were closing up their operations by then. We brought back a full truckload and filled up their fellowship hall. We were completely shocked to see the abandonment of an entire city. All the military and security personnel overwhelmed us because that first weekend in October of 2005 not many residents had returned and the only place up and running was the French Quarter. Reverend Eden knew people would return in droves. We were convinced that his relief operation needed more food and supplies. We set out to get one more truckload. The people of the Jewish operation were overjoyed to empty their warehouse with our help, knowing their supplies were finally reaching New Orleans.

"Lynn wanted to take some supplies to the Houma Indian tribe in another area of Louisiana. It was time for me to go home. I left the truck in her care and, for the first time in ten weeks, went home to regroup and figure out what to do next. Mission from Minnesota gave me about $600, which I had passed onto Lynn so she could make one more grand run, loading up the last of Camp Jacob's supplies.

"I went home noticing how strange it felt not to be driving the truck every day and doing relief work. It was like coming back from another country and no one knew anything about where I had just come from. It was like I came from another planet. I met with Mission from Minnesota once I got a few days rest and shared with them the opportunities that were available to choose from. We could work in rural Mississippi and help Camp Sister Spirit, or go to New Orleans and work with a Methodist church. The next phase of relief work was all about bringing volunteers down. Mission from Minnesota agreed that with Thanksgiving coming up, it would be a great time to go back.

"We were the first volunteers to a visit a church in Central City New Orleans, one of the city's worst neighborhoods. Because it was on the high ground, it didn't have much destruction, yet the damage was far deeper than physical structures. Across the St. Charles Avenue from Central City is the affluent New Orleans Garden District. Central City housed the servants who took care of the people in the affluent white neighborhood. At the height of the civil rights movement, the whole area of Central City was a booming economic haven that lasted up to the Reagan era, when Central City started to decline because of the national economic slump and reallocation of priorities.

"The educational system in New Orleans is extremely unequal and deplorably lacking in resources, which has led to generations of crime and poverty in its neighborhoods, especially Central City. There is a saying around that neighborhood, 'Once you've passed Barrone, you're on your own.' As you leave the stateliness of St. Charles Avenue and head away from the river, Barrone is the third street you cross to arrive at the church. First Street United Methodist Church sits on Dryades and First Street, the next street from Barrone. Gentrification is taking over this area, forcing long-term residents to make hard choices resulting from rising taxes, unfair insurance premiums and escalating rental fees.

"Reverend Eden knew that he had to make a difference right away to capture the hearts and minds of the community. He had a vision to reach out into the community and serve the people as a means of living the gospel. Because of his stance on inclusiveness, and service to all, he received resistance from some old-time members of the congregation that didn't want their church filled up with mess and confusion. Out of that chaos, great service ensued and amazing volunteerism opportunities emerged, for many who would walk through those doors from the initial boost the first group from Mission from Minnesota provided.

"Reverend Eden still tells the story of how Lynn and I are First Street pioneers. To this day, I have grown much attached to Central City New Orleans and have come to accept First Street United Methodist Church as my second family. Two and a half years of steady forging of friendships and reciprocal restoration and recovery happens with everyone's soul who takes the time to participate in a volunteer recovery operation. The experience of service, meeting the lovely people of New Orleans, engages the soul on a level nothing in our routine lives will ever match."

Staying on Call

Diana went to the Gulf Coast ten times, including a visit of five months living in a blue hippie bus parked in an unclaimed lot across the street from the First Street church. The corner of the lot was dedicated as an international peace site on Thanksgiving of '06, with a community ceremony blessing a peace pole planted with the intention of "no more shootings in the area." The peace pole is still standing, the bench is intact and the plastic garden rocks people can sit on are still in perfect shape. There has been no graffiti or vandalism on that consecrated ground. There have been no shootings or stabbings within the immediate area since that Thanksgiving Day. Efforts are under way to purchase that lot and officially dedicate the peace pole park to the community as green space.

The longest trip Diana made to New Orleans was from January to June of '07, where she spent much of the time filming her documentary. What she experienced there disturbed her so much, she decided not to return after spending the summer months with her sons in Minnesota. "I didn't feel effective anymore. I literally tanked out. As an empathic person, I felt the stress and emotional upheaval all the time. I felt I would have a better chance of making a difference by concentrating on fundraising from Minnesota, finishing my documentary, and earning some academic credentials and using that for leverage to gain attention for the cause of continued relief efforts."

Back in St. Paul, with two children now living in California, and the other enrolled at the University of Minnesota, Diana is launching a new career. She maintains a spiritual healing practice, while consulting, speaking and producing documentaries. She continues to work on a master's degree in a self-designed interdisciplinary program researching the concepts of cultivating soul connection as individuals and the effect on the collective consciousness in response to chaos and disaster. She would like to use her experience with Katrina to help organizations deal with crisis—to make effective sustainable social, economical, and policy decisions for the common good and future generations.

Wherever she ends up, Diana will always remain emotionally connected to the memories and the friends she has maintained through her Katrina experiences. "Of everyone I worked with in two-plus years, about a quarter are still involved and three quarters went back to lives elsewhere. We've all been affected and touched by something greater than ourselves in the services we offered. I felt like I was a missionary with an apocalyptic vision. That time snapshot, right after the storm, gave us a taste of the end of the world and the possibilities of a new tomorrow. And because of that experience, our lives will never be the same. Most of the volunteers I interviewed intend to return to communities of privilege and remember the plight of those entrenched in a system that ignores people of color and the economically disadvantaged. I believe we will continue to make a difference in our home communities and serve justice in a variety of capacities.

"The tenacity among people to live in the homes and neighborhoods of the Gulf Coast where they were born and generations had lived was incredibly powerful. I realized that I too could develop such roots back in Minnesota. I want to believe the collective efforts of Minnesota volunteers have been making a difference on the Gulf Coast, yet there is so much work left that hasn't even yet begun. The challenge is how do we convince people outside New Orleans to care about what goes on there."

Call to Action

Diana recently returned to the Gulf Coast to assess the progress of the rebuilding. Here is what she found:

"Our government has not given the attention or resources to alleviate the problems on the Gulf Coast. There is no administrative vision for how the city will be reconstructed. Residents are now just starting to slowly rebuild after two-and-a-half years of governmental hurdle after hurdle. Too many evacuees were not able to receive funds they had coming due to complications with procedures, policies, and lack of training or understanding of the system. Many houses are slated to be demolished. Many of them are worth restoring.

"Some of the poor people who left during the storm have come back. They have nowhere else to go. If you're going to be down and out, you might as well be home on your own turf. Yet, most of that turf is uninhabitable, and all the high ground is packed with two to four families living under one roof. Meanwhile, most of the middle class people who left haven't come back. If you're middle class from East New Orleans, why would you come back when there is no electricity, there are empty shopping malls and hospitals out of commission, where there isn't any economic future to invest precious remaining resources? The super-rich have largely returned. They can afford to have houses on the higher ground, and they possess the resources to rebuild where flooding occurred. New Orleans will be sopped up by big money that wants to put casinos on the land and turn even the poorest areas like the Ninth Ward into meccas of white consumerism.

"Much of the funding that was poured into New Orleans is held up in layers of bureaucracy. Many of the volunteer efforts to date have been concentrated on gutting homes. There's no money from the private sector for reconstruction of buildings except on the commercial end. There is very little effort underway to address the emotional reconstruction of the people who have been devastated and aren't getting satisfaction from the government and a historically corrupt system. There is suffering day-to-day among the residents beyond what most people could imagine. While levels of domestic abuse and addiction are incredibly high for all New Orleans residents, there is no official mental health training or post-traumatic-stress program for the police like the one that was given to the first responders in 9/11.

"There's a need to rebuild schools. Eighty percent of school buildings don't have air conditioning, half didn't have working kitchens because of years of neglect and corruption and money not channeled properly by the bureaucratic power structure. Most of the thousands of volunteers who have been to New Orleans from churches, social service agencies, and universities who have shipped students down on spring breaks don't understand the whole picture and have little understanding of the how incredibly important the wetlands are to the success and survival of New Orleans. All their collective efforts are in vain if they don't fix the wetlands. The truth is we are all affected by what happens to our fragile ecosystems all over the world. If we can find ways of restoring the balance here along the Mississippi, and start in New Orleans, I believe we can do it in the rest of the world. I'm eager to participate and to learn how that story will be written.

"Fortunately, I did discover clusters of compassionate rebels in New Orleans. People are coming out of the woodwork from all over the world to rebuild the city in a new way. It's the establishment versus the anti-establishment. The anti-establishment, including the many organizations that are working there, need connection and an acknowledgement of community ceremony and ritual that transcends race and class. We need a huge, whole-scale revolution in New Orleans.

"Katrina challenged my belief systems. It was shocking to find out how much racism, elitism and the stereotypes I initially carried. I'm a much better person for having encountered and faced them head on. I want to go back to Mississippi again and interview some of the people at Camp Sister Spirit to follow up on what happened to that community. I also want to see what I can do from Minnesota in finding funding, showing the documentary, speaking out on issues of race and privilege, and other creative ways to support the cause. I will never be done with New Orleans. It will always be a part of me—a second home and a second family.

"When we were emptying the big truck in the unusual Southern heat of September of '05, there were bugs crawling all over everything. I'm not fond of things crawling on me and I detested sweating. But the purpose of serving was so much greater than bugs and sweat. I've learned how to disconnect from my ego. I'm more connected to my soul. That connection gives me hope. I've been witness to some amazing things—both the power of love and the power of fear and knowing what each can do. I became a clean and sober person from the trauma. I experienced looking for healthier ways of dealing with stress than distracting myself with addictions.

"What's really missing is cultivation of the soul—how to nurture the soul of New Orleans back to its full glory. It's not about religious revival, but rather about a need for radical healing on a broader scale.

"Cultivating our soul's intelligence as a collective priority in all that we do is my focus for the second part of my life. Without being taught to cultivate soul awareness, listening to and following our soul's guidance, the alternative that guides us is ego. Soul is based in love. Ego is based in fear. Everyone needs to know how to cultivate his or her soul."

"We have laid upon future generations the huge burden of solving the crises we have created. The evolution of change necessary for humanity to find answers to these problems is going to take a lot of spiritual, intellectual, emotional and political resolve. Accepting that what affects us over there also affects everyone over here is a huge leap forward. Those that have more privilege than others have great power, and it's up to us that realize this to make sure that the system allows others to achieve equal opportunity and resources as well.

"We need a revolution of caring. My role is to help carry that revolution forward. We can no longer separate social movements from economic and cultural injustice because they are all connected. I can't turn my back on what I know about environmental degradation, racism and elite privilege. I receive such joy and sustenance from being a part of something bigger than myself. I feel it's just beginning. I plan to collaborate with people who are carving out a new way of being, creating a caring culture. That's what I'm about—finding a way to influence social change that gets people to care. We as human beings have the capacity to care deeply. My desire is to awaken that latent tendency into our everyday existence. A key ingredient in that formula is service.

"I am hoping I can capture something meaningful with my documentary. A huge part of my maturation is coming away from the addictive chaos, conflict, and quandary, allowing this fertile information to bubble up into something organic and channel the energy into a medium for mass communication. I need to be away (from the Gulf Coast) to do that.

"I struggle with the fact that I haven't yet made any effective lasting change. American society and cultural norms haven't changed because of what we did around the Katrina work. But we were incredible witnesses to what the power of selfless service can do to diminish the power of fear. We witnessed the best and worst of the human condition exposed, and people putting egos aside and coming together. What I've seen in the last few years is a spiritual understanding and acknowledgement that there is something more than what our senses perceive, something that allows for miracles to happen. When we collectively come together on a spiritual level, magic happens and hope abounds despite the obstacles. That means doing the work of healing ourselves, unloading the past and making way for the present to fill the God gap. In order for all of us to get spiritually fed, we all have to unload the metaphysical truck.

"I want to witness what happens when people connect to their souls and then collectively operate from an awake, clear, healthy collective conscience. When we do that individually and then join together with our intention and attention on the common good, we can circumvent tragedy and unnecessary suffering. We're in the eleventh hour. I believe we're going to respond. We're going to all unload the truck, grow an abundant garden of possibilities, herd ourselves in a new direction, and make a healthy world putting the puzzle pieces together. I have tremendous hope."

**Ephraim with his wife Meghan and daughter
Lily Marie at a Burning Man event
(Photo courtesy of Ephraim Eusebio)**

BURNING MAN
By Burt Berlowe

In a corner of Ephraim Eusebio's living room, a baby is being born, pushing out of breach and uncertainty into the joy of newfound life. The mother is steadily holding a pail of milk and a wrapping around her midsection. The father, looking on, finds his own rebirth at hand amidst gradually brightening shades of gray and white. It is all a fake image, painted on canvas and hung conspicuously on the wall. But for Ephraim—its creator—it is a mirror into his soul.

A few feet away from the large painting, Ephraim sits at a table surrounded by various works of art, musical instruments and an ambience of well-kept natural woodwork, a scene repeated throughout the two-story house. Ephraim, a slightly built Filipino, is by any measure a Renaissance man—artist, musician, real estate agent, philanthropist, activist, and caretaker of the planet and its least fortunate members. But beneath the many talents and engaging demeanor, Ephraim continues to battle demons that have shadowed him since childhood.

* * *

At first glance, Ephraim's early childhood seems to have been idyllic. His parents emigrated here from the Philippines so his dad could get a medical degree. He grew up a Quaker and learned to sing in those churches. Both of his parents were serious musicians, and Ephraim began playing the Suzuki violin at age seven. Often, the three would play classical music together. But their life away from the sweet melodies was less harmonious.

"It was tough emotionally for my parents to move here," Ephraim says, "and it took them some twenty years to get immigration status and citizenship. Then there was a question of marital infidelity that scarred the parent relationship. I shouldered a deep-seated guilt and blame for my family's problems. For years I was scared to speak about it."

Ephraim also had to endure the hardship that came with the color of his skin. Growing up in a mostly white neighborhood, he experienced racial slurs in school, in restaurants, on the streets, even when he went away on vacation. "People looked at us with such hatred just because of our race. Because I knew kung fu, people assumed I was Asian," he bitterly recalls. "It just blew my mind. I felt very sad about it. There were words like 'Chink, Gook, Jap, Spik,' and Japanese jokes. There was a Japanese stigma around that time, a perception of Orientals as being Communists. There was the assumption that we were good at math or that we couldn't speak English or that you had to speak louder or slower when you talk to us. My dad experienced discrimination at work. In turn, he developed racist thoughts. He would talk about black people in negative ways. We'd all get mad at him and ask how he could say anything bad about blacks when we are also oppressed and seen as no better than them. All of this made something in me want to live equally with other people. I wanted to know all aspects of society. It bolstered something in me that wanted to fight."

One day, a student leveled a racial epithet at Ephraim on the early elementary school bus, and his two older brothers came to his rescue, ganging up on the perpetrator. "From that point on," he recalls, "I realized I had protectors and a support system. I really grew from that. In the first grade I became a leader. The color thing didn't matter. If someone said something they knew they were in trouble. In second grade, I organized a SWAT team of about eighty boys, sort of like a big gang. I was the leader, the captain. It was about belonging with people who wanted to belong, like myself, and it got bigger.

"Then something happened that changed my life. I helped organize a fight against retarded kids so that I could make others feel worse than I did. Kids were on the playground dumping on each other for fun. It wasn't so much fun watching it in slow motion like a general on the hill, so I joined in. Later, I became disgusted with the whole thing and left the SWAT team. I realized that something I created to give people a sense of belonging became an opportunity for some to take off on others because they thought they were better than them. That was the whole thing I was supposedly fighting against. Partly to assuage my guilt, I later worked with developmentally disabled people at schools and community centers. This was my way to make amends, to get sufficient understanding, to see those people as part of me. I knew that attacking those people would be like attacking myself.

"During my teenage years, I was popular. But I was disgusted with status quo popularity, what it meant to act cool, and I rebelled against that. The clique I hung around with was kind of subversive and didn't think the same as other people. I abused drugs and alcohol. My grades slipped. I didn't care about academics."

In the midst of this youthful angst, Ephraim found his artistic bent. He liked literature and art. He won a scholarship to a prestigious Midwestern arts school, majored in studio art and displayed at galleries. "I learned that there are all kinds of ways to make art," he says. "I came to believe that I am here to do some kind of art work. My expression on this planet is through visual art—painting, sculpture, media, photography. I also discovered that I didn't like mass-producing art with others. I wanted a place to create that I could call my own."

With that in mind, Ephraim became an independent real estate agent, hoping that his access to properties would facilitate his search for an arts space. "One reason I went into real estate was to open doors and creative avenues to having a space I can call my own, where people can meet and listen to music, view art, watch movies—a sort of cooperative." Until that dream comes true, Ephraim's century-old house is his art studio as well as a place for the guitar and drums he plays in an alternative rock band called The Hated View.

"I love music," he muses. "My first radio was a Mickey Mouse model that I got when I was four years old. I would also go around with a transistor radio, listening to bands like Wings and falling in love with that music. I make drums out of anything I can find. There are times when I feel so connected to the musical instrument I almost feel impure, like with masturbation. It's a liberating place to go."

It is no coincidence that the prominent painting on Ephraim's living room wall is about giving birth. His life has been profoundly affected by the relationship with his wife and daughter. His wife Meghan is a massage therapist and former youth worker, studying to be a nurse. They met in Jackson Hole, Wyoming in 1995 and were married three years later with their one-year-old daughter Lily Marie present. Ephraim talks about the special bond he has with his wife. "Our relationship means always being present. She has helped me to open up, to experience the full blame and pain of the past and cope with it. We can show each other the darkest places of ourselves while striving to claim a better life with each other.

"Lily Marie has been an impetus for going into different parts of my life that I wouldn't have been willing to go to myself. When she was coming into the world, I went into protector-provider mode. I wanted to make sure she didn't make the same mistakes I did when I was kid. I immediately put that big weight upon myself to be a perfect dad, never yell in her presence, be there twenty-four-seven, to be Superman for my baby. But looking around at the world then I felt helpless. It seemed like a very angry, nonsupportive place, not a good place to raise a baby.

"My perception of others was not to trust them. I didn't have a great relationship with anybody at that time. I used different vices to escape, such as drugs and alcohol and sex, mainly alcohol. I'd average a couple of drinks a week. I would drink six packs at work. I thought that was the norm. I'm definitely a different person now. I've given up the drugs and wild behavior. I've forgiven parts of my past."

As part of his new life, Ephraim has become a unique kind of realtor. He started a charitable giving program wherein he committed a percentage of every sales commission to support a worthy nonprofit organization, and he has volunteered for some of those groups. "My mission is to make a positive difference in the world," he says, "to get people to think about sharing—to realize that we have so much to share in this world.

"I believe we should change how we treat our bodies and how we treat our planet. This Earth we live on gives us life. Everything is integrated. We should be caring for the Earth as our guardian. Our goal should be to be able to love ourselves. The more we love ourselves, the more we can extend love."

Ephraim adopted this philosophy largely from another life-changing experience, his attendance at Theopolus Divinity School. "There," he says, "I began seeing myself reflected in other people's faces and discovered my inner power and innocence. Previously, my existence was built on guilt and blame. Yet I always believed I could be otherwise. That's what made me a rebel. As part of my search for ways to deal with that, I found out about the Theopolus program. It uses yoga to move emotions through body and has helped me a lot. I have learned the power of innocence and love. I still have a fear of failure. I'm still processing a lot of the guilt and blame. But I realize that I have to let it go. It's part of my path, finding what I'm made of and coming to peace with it."

In recent summers, Ephraim has been on another kind of journey. He travels to The Burning Man event in the sweltering Nevada desert. There he meets and interacts with people from around the country who have come to retreat and bring odd works of art. "I have a cathartic experience every time I go there," he says. "I find a piece of my soul. I go there to work on my personal transformation and have fun doing it."

Ephraim driving his vehicle in the art car parade
(Photo courtesy of Ephraim Eusebio))

Ephraim's oddest and most practical piece of art is a car he made from scratch that comes from his Burning Man experience and reflects his commitment to a better world. It has a diesel engine that runs on waste, vegetable oil and string. He and Meghan have decorated it with artificial green turf and shag carpet, with children's toys on the dashboard and a roof rack on top. They call it a Turfmobile. "When other people see it, it makes their day," Ephraim says. "It gets lots of attention and promotes interaction."

Ephraim has twice visited the Philippines, spending time with relatives there. The first time he went "home" in 1989, the country was in a constant state of upheaval. "The hotel we stayed in was later taken over by a military coup. There was lots of poverty, shanties and garbage everywhere, canals where waste water goes through. But there were also a lot of beautiful, happy people."

Although Ephraim plans more visits to the Philippines, he won't be returning there for good. He has found a comfortable place to be within the confines of his home, his family and his work. His improved frame of mind is reflected in his art. Compared to some of the gloomy images he once created, his paintings are now brighter and more colorful. Nowhere is that more obvious than in the large wall painting of the baby's birth. It reflects both the anxiety he felt at having a child and the joy that followed. It is indicative, he says, of a belief in human potential.

"My art now is about my family relationship and about children," he says. "I do care about children of the world. Maybe it is my inner child coming through. It reflects both my gloomy and positive side and the question I used to ask myself before I had children. My art allows me to realize my guilt and blame and practice peace without realizing guilt. It's been part of my process of opening up the past and releasing the guilt. My paintings are a conduit for that release and for discovering my vitality. I am the conduit of this work. My function is to allow it to pass through me so that I may digest each image and feeling. I open up my emotions, judgments, attitudes, opinions, what they feel like and how they manifest in my life.

"This process is my path of knowledge and of why I exist. I am looking at parts of my life that may take years to develop and understand. I surrender to not knowing what the painting will look like until the images and the answers unfold. The only thing that stops me from expressing creativity and love is the expression of fear. I release fear and guilt so I can better express myself. My long-term goal is finding ways to get to places of peace, whatever form it takes. Ultimately, my art is a message to and for the children. This is my spirituality and my gift to myself and to the world."

**Lynn Hoelzel at her clown graduation
(Photo courtesy of Lynn Hoelzel)**

GOD LOVES THE CLOWN IN ME
By Burt Berlowe

Lynn Hoelzel's voice cracks noticeably as she tries to hold back the tears. She is seated in the living room of her small mobile home in a trailer park on the outskirts of the Twin Cities. Just outside her window, a narrow blacktopped road runs through the park to a place where it fades into an open field. Lynn moved to the park several months ago to start her life all over again—to allow the bumpy road through her past to disappear into oblivion. But now, as she walks her memory lane again, the pain is almost too much to bear.

"The place I was born—I call it the Birmingham Castle. Most people think of a castle as a fairy land. I don't. It was, like some castles, a torture chamber, a ghetto of the spirit in a ghetto neighborhood. There was no God in Birmingham Castle."

Lynn remembers a Christmas morning in the 1950s at the Birmingham Castle. She and her two brothers were seated on the living room couch waiting for their dad's car to come down the hill towards their home. The youngest brother turned toward his older sister. "Is dad gonna' be drunk?" he asks with worry in his voice.

Lynn gave the standard answer: "Sure, he'll be drunk." She just hopes that this wouldn't be like another recent Christmas when he came home drunk, then went to the bathroom to vomit up his booze. They don't expect him to bring home any holiday gifts. He never has.

"My dad was a brutal man," Lynn recalls. "He didn't want my mom. He didn't want us kids. We were physically and emotionally abused, and mom couldn't stop it. She would go to bed crying. I said to myself, 'I will never let her cry again.' I would get her a present for every Christmas.

"Mother was frustrated, mean and angry. Once, I was making some juice and I put too much sugar in it by mistake. Mom yelled, 'Goddammit! Can't you do anything right?' She hated kids. She hated girls. I grew up not wanting to be a girl. I always played with boys. I had play therapy at a child guidance center. They had me make dolls out of plastic molds so that I could feel more like a girl. My fourth-grade teacher once said to me, 'You're nothing more than a baby in big girl's clothing.'

"I never wanted to go to school. I never did well there. I didn't get along with other kids. They would tease me a lot for being overweight. I didn't make many friends. When I was there, I felt trapped like I wanted to get away. On the way to school, I would jump out of the car and dash across the highway to escape. I felt like I was running from school to freedom.

"I lived in a constant state of terror. I was scared of storms, terrified of wind. My mom said it was because I once had a bad experience in a storm. I thought something else was going on. I would cry out in the middle of the night, and mother would just yell from her bed that I should, 'Shut the fuck up.' By the fourth grade, my world was beginning to fall apart. Things that everybody hated I would like. My life was reversed from what we would call normal. All I ever wanted in this world was a stable life."

One of Lynn's dad's children by a previous marriage was named Don. "Mother hated Don," Lynn remembers. "He would get high drinking vanilla cookie mix flavoring and rubbing alcohol from laundry tubs and would squirt mother with a squirt gun. Mom said if he didn't stop, she would smash an iron in his face."

When they were young, Lynn and Don usually got along well together. "I remember that we would play a game called statue maker on summer days on the grass, seemingly carefree. That was a game where someone twirls you around and wherever you stop, you become a statue."

But Don didn't function well in the dysfunctional household. He often got into trouble, committing acts like throwing rocks through windows and stealing a doll dress from a store. Law enforcement was constantly after him. "One time I remember the FBI came to my door looking for Don. I was home taking care of Bryce at the time. I was really scared. I didn't know where he was."

Don was eventually captured and ended up in an insane asylum. Lynn recalls going to visit him. "I always knew there was something wrong with him. But I didn't know what it was. He was in a straightjacket. I fed him candy bars. There were half-naked men nearby, banging cups on the bars. The orderlies unhooked his straightjacket. His fingers were orange and brown. Dad would make him roll cigarettes in those fingers just to be mean. I was told that, 'If you're nuts, you're going to where Don is.' I asked myself, 'Would I rather be with Don or be home with dad? Where am I the safest?'"

Lynn wrote a poem about Don. In part it says:

Priesthood flashing FBI badges.
A stolen doll dress not from a thief.
Vanilla ...alcohol squirt guns full of terror.
Threatening irons to be thrown. Hershey candy bars.
Straight jacket couldn't dethrone ... fake cigarettes...
The only one that called him dad only...

"My older brother's first child named Shawn had been abused by his family and came to live with us. He had night terrors and wet his pants and the bed. His mom and her boyfriend had beaten him and locked him up before they split up. Once, they sent him out to get them a pack of cigarettes. He was found walking around in the Minnesota winter with no socks on and wet pants. Nobody else wanted him. I did. But I couldn't have him. He was sent to a foster home for wayward children and was abused there.

"I was present the day he was taken to the foster home. As he left in the van, he hollered to me: 'I'll never see you again.' I was so distressed by his leaving that I couldn't find my way back home. And I didn't see him again until he was a man."

Lynn's younger brother was named Bryce. "We always had tea parties together. He would have the table set, waiting for me to come home. It gave me a reason for wanting to be home. I would constantly put myself in danger. Once, I got a stolen bike to ride and kept thinking I wanted to ride it right into the middle of traffic, right in front of a truck. What kept me from doing it was Bryce."

Lynn finally got the child she always wanted. During her senior year in high school, she became pregnant and married the dad. When she was kicked out of school for the pregnancy, she decided to put her whole life into raising the child, a prematurely-born boy named Scot. "I was devoted to that baby. I wanted to love and be loved. I would shine his little white shoes with cleanser. Those were happy days." When her baby was fifteen months old, Lynn had most of her ovaries removed and was told she could never again bear children. But in 1970, another boy, Jake, was born "although I had just one piece of an ovary left." Scot would suffer from ADHD (attention-deficit-hyperactive-disorder) and problems with the school system throughout childhood, and, as an adult grew apart from Lynn.

* * *

By April of 1975, Lynn's world was totally falling apart. She had a breakdown and was diagnosed with psychotic depression. Her tormented mind was blown up by shock treatments. "When I came out of there I wasn't a piece of when I went in. Part of me was gone." She was hospitalized for thirteen weeks. Anti-psychotic drugs were injected into her to numb the pain. She was given 100 milligrams of prolixin every week and up to 2500 of depacote. Her psychotherapist was a reputed doctor considered an expert in his field. Lynn's experience with him changed her life forever.

"For the next twenty-five years, my doctor imprisoned me in drugs that kept me in psychoses. I trusted him. He appeared to be devoted to my welfare. He told me there would be no side effects from the drugs. He felt that what he was doing would save my life. My husband Paul believed the doctor was my knight in shining armor and that if anyone could help me he would. I gave all my power to this man. I gave him full reign to pump drugs, and pump he did.

"The side effects were bad. I couldn't read. I couldn't write. When I read, words floated off the pages, everything moved. I couldn't even drive or walk to the grocery store. I couldn't move my neck. I just sat in a rocking chair all day and rocked myself. I missed out on being with my children who were riding bicycles and flying kites. I gained 100 pounds and went from a size eleven to twenty-eight in ten months.

"Sometimes I tortured myself getting in the car to visit our son Scot and his wife out of my love for them. It's what kept me going. I had nothing else left. Paul had a breakdown and kept getting worse. Once, he was pushing my empty wheelchair out of the hospital emergency room and threw it across the parking lot. He walked out on me five times in two weeks. I didn't know who he was anymore.

"One day, Paul never showed up at work and we didn't know where he was. I couldn't call a doctor and had no friends or family nearby. My kids had turned their backs on me. I sat there in my rocking chair and I cried out to a God I had never known. For me, there was no God. My doctor was a god. It turns out Paul had taken large doses of Tylenol and Nyquil. Fortunately, he recovered, but our relationship didn't. He had been the only person that understood my rage. We had a sacred bond. But it had been broken, and I didn't know if it could be restored. I left him because there was no hope together. We were both drowning."

One day in 1997, Lynn was in the hospital for treatment. A huge African American doctor entered the room. He knew about Lynn's condition. "This is ridiculous," he told her. "I'm stopping this insanity now." Another doctor subsequently halted all of Lynn's drugs, telling her, "I don't think you're 'nuts.' You don't act like it. If you look 'nuts' and act 'nuts' they'll think your 'nuts.' Don't be 'nuts.' I'm going to send you home."

At first, Lynn was skeptical. "I asked myself, 'How do you know who to trust?' You trust and you make yourself vulnerable. A doctor I had put my faith in had betrayed me and left a trail of pain and wrath unmatched in my life. The medical profession had done everything in their power to discourage and destroy me. But now something within me said to finally say 'no' to the doctor who had put me on drugs. I began cutting back on the drugs until I didn't take them at all."

The aftereffects of the drugs Lynn took for half her life have stayed with her to this day. She still has tardov dyskonesia, a common side effect of antipsychotic drugs that causes uncontrolled facial movements. It waxes and wanes and is triggered by stress. "It could happen at any time," she says. She remains bitter and angry about her medical experiences and the fact that "the very people that were supposed to protect me and love me betrayed me. Pain is the base. Then anger. Then when no one hears you, it turns to rage. My reaction to all that I have been through is a sane reaction to the insanity I've lived through."

What is different now is that Lynn has found a way to turn her personal pain into a tool for healing directed not only at herself but also at the hurt in others. She has done it by uncovering a side of her personality that was submerged for so long in the quicksand of her gloom and is its polar opposite. "There's a lot of depth to me," she says, her voice lightening up for the first time. "I'm not a geek. I have only a fourth-grade education. But I have a humorous side. I can make people laugh."

A few years ago, Lynn decided to unleash her hidden talent. She enrolled at a clown college at the University of Wisconsin, La Crosse. She wasn't there long before her old demons rose up to try to shut down the laughter. "Unfortunately, I don't always understand how things work. I thought in a childish way, 'Oh goody, we're going to be clowns.' But when I got there, I stayed in a student facility with cement walls. My first thought was, 'Oh my God, a nut ward.' A woman who was to be my roommate at Clown College came to visit me. She happened to be a psychiatric nurse. I thought, 'Shit, they set me up. They'll lock me up and I'll never get out.' I had to get away. I wanted to take a car and go off a bridge. I left the biggest opportunity of my life out of a misunderstanding. I didn't graduate, but the director of the college generously sent me a graduation certificate."

Lynn now works regularly as a clown at Burger King restaurants, entertaining kids and adults alike who come in for a meal. Every other Sunday, she goes to a nursing home to do a clown act. "I put on costumes and drive around and that ain't acceptable to our society. I'm a misfit. I'm like the clown doll on the island of misfit toys waiting for Santa to rescue me. But I don't care. I am not going to make light of what God has done for me. God loves the clown in me even if no one else does."

One day, Lynn did a clown party for a little girl named Isabel. "I went as her fairy godmother. I had long hair like Rapunzel. She wanted to be a princess. I had trunks full of costumes. I took out some of them and puppets I made and did a show. Instead of just entertaining the children I had them be actors in the puppet show. Afterwards, people said they would never be able to follow that act. That was awesome," Lynn says, breaking into a hearty laugh that drives the gloom out of the small room. "Clowning heals me without question. I volunteer my time mostly. People ask, 'What do you charge?' I say, 'I don't know how to do that.'"

Lynn makes a lot of her own clowning material, including puppets and stuffed animals that fill her bedroom. Humorous slogans adorn her bathroom wall, and a ladybug costume stuffed with tennis balls hangs in the hallway. The "smile" van she drives around town is filled with puppets and clown paraphernalia, and sometimes she hauls a ladybug camper to various performances and does a "sign a bug" activity where kids write on the outside of the vehicle. She shows me a valentine box and explains how she uses it. "This monster came from the land of never being loved and wants to stomp on the contents of the box, but the love bugs are guarding it. I don't have one clown suit. I don't have one clown face because I have so many faces."

In exchanging a perpetual frown for the laughing jowls of a clown, Lynn has put a whole new face on her life and that of others, with many encores to follow. "I've come a long way," she says proudly, gazing firmly ahead. "But I'm not done making it. A friend once told me, 'Baby girl when you learn that you are not a problem to be solved but an asset, a human person to be learned from, then you'll soar.'"

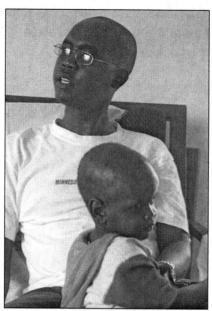

Elijah Omolo with African child
(Photo courtesy of Give Us Wings)

GIVE US WINGS
By William Wroblewski

Like many in rural Kenya, Elijah Omolo grew up in a one-room thatch hut with mud, windowless walls and a dirt floor. Inside, he and his grandmother ground corn into flour to make porridge, often the only meal of the day. His hut was five miles from Lake Victoria, the only local water source. Elijah and his brothers, along with many others in the Nyaoga community, made the daily journey to ensure they had water for drinking, cleaning and bathing. But the water they carried home was often dirty. Sewage was being dumped into the lake every day, causing typhoid epidemics and making life in his malnourished village generally risky.

Many children in Kenya, as in other parts of Africa, never went to school. Boys Elijah knew often grew up only to leave their village, hoping to find work in larger cities, such as Nairobi or Mombasa. Farmers try desperately to grow enough crops in dry, sandy soils to feed their families. But without simple reading, writing, and math skills, or agricultural know-how, most people never have a chance to break out of their poverty. The difficulty Elijah faced growing up gave him steadfast determination to improve the lives of those in his village.

Today, conditions in Elijah's village have improved. There is a health clinic. A water project brings clean water to thousands. Typhoid and malaria levels are being reduced. People are eating better. And Elijah helped make it all happen, with some help from a mother-and-daughter team from a country on the other side of the world.

* * *

On the surface, Elijah's gentle demeanor hides the rough times he has survived. He speaks with a soft voice only used after quiet contemplation. Every word he says appears to have been ruminating in his mind before he speaks it. His glasses give him a certain braininess that suits him well. At the same time, an easy laugh reveals a zest for life's possibilities.

An unusual find in rural Africa, especially in 1999, Elijah is a computer expert by trade. His technical expertise was hard to come by, and under most circumstances Elijah would never have been given the chance to work with computers. But Elijah's story is one of persistence.

After losing their parents, Elijah and his brothers and sister were raised by their grandmother. One day, while cleaning out their hut, the grandmother found some old boxes containing a bundle of pencils. An unusual item in his village, they were left by Elijah's great grandfather, who brought them back after fighting in World War I. An uncle was soon using the pencils to teach Elijah how to write. "Those pencils changed my life," Elijah is fond of saying.

Eventually, Elijah's family had enough money to send him to primary and secondary school, where he did very well. He knew that further education was essential to begin to change life for himself and others. He bravely, and quite naively, left his little isolated Nyaoga Village and headed off to Nairobi, the capital of Kenya. He stayed with an aunt who lived in a two-room rented space. He visited the successful businesses in the town center, trying to sell them on the idea that they should invest in him by giving him an education. Most sent him away. One, a law firm, said he could wait until the person in charge had time to see him. He waited in the lobby of that office from morning till closing for three weeks. Finally, the lead attorney gave in and saw him. Elijah convinced the attorney to send him to a three-year diploma program in computer technology—a newly emerging field in the early 1990s in Kenya.

With the education he gained, Elijah had the knowledge to teach others. Equipped with two outdated computers and enough startup funds from a graduation gift from the man who sponsored him, he started a computer school in 1997. His new school was popular with those looking to escape poverty by learning new skills. Elijah made a living by repairing computers and electronic equipment for Western tourists and aid workers in his small school behind a car wash that consisted of two buckets and a hose.

One day in 1998, an American woman having computer problems showed up at the school. She was Mary Steiner Whelan, a fifty-four-year-old educator and writer from Minneapolis, Minnesota.

Mary and her daughter, Shawn, age twenty-two, had just spent several months trying to work for a nonprofit organization in Kenya and Uganda. They had quit their previous jobs, packed up their home and signed up to help the nonprofit for nine months. Unfortunately, the organization turned out to be corrupt. After a futile attempt to change it, they broke away and started over again.

Mary and Shawn each took the lessons from the trip and moved on in their own ways. Shawn returned to the United States to complete nursing school, realizing that she wanted to eventually help people in Africa with health care issues.

When Shawn left, Mary decided to spend a month or so working on her second book related to the educational field. She thought this would also give her time to find another organization where she could volunteer. One day, she was out walking when a young man approached and started a conversation. He mentioned that he had seen her out walking everyday and wondered what was going on.

"Actually," she responded, "I am working while I am walking. I am writing a book, and this is my planning time."

"What is the book about?" the man asked.

"About children in the United States."

"Why don't you write about children in Africa?"

"Because I don't know enough about them."

"I do. I was one."

"Well, why don't you write your story and show it to me."

"I will," he said.

Mary returned to her room to resume her writing only to find that her computer wasn't working. There weren't many computers in Kenya in 1998 and certainly not many places to repair them in the small town where she stayed. She went to the one makeshift Internet café—a one-computer-and-telephone operation in the back of a shop. They didn't know anything about repairs, but they knew of a man in town who might. They sent Mary to the back of the two-buckets-and-a-hose car wash. There she met Elijah.

"Elijah walked out from behind the car wash with broken, crooked glasses and a questioning look on his face. I wasn't too hopeful," Mary remembers.

Elijah looked at the computer. He couldn't repair it, but his friend had a car and might be willing to take her into Mombasa where there was a repair center.

Even at this first meeting, trust became an issue. To Elijah, Mary was just another American. He admits there are mixed feelings about white people in parts of Africa. "A lot of people come to the coast for a holiday, and many are very nice people. But some do very bad things," he says.

The Westerners that villagers are uneasy about are the noncommitted aid workers who appear with promises of investment and a better life but disappear after a short period of time with no lasting change for the village. Tourists participate in the area's sex industry. Americans often don't treat the Kenyans as if they are people but rather stereotype them as backwards and use them for low-cost help or as forms of entertainment in the hotels.

So when Mary appeared, looking for technical support, Elijah didn't think much of her. Nevertheless, he was able to help. "I was just doing my job," he admits.

Mary and Elijah and his friend went to Mombasa, and the computer was repaired. As they returned, they had to wait for a ferry to cross the Indian Ocean to get to their small town. While they were waiting, a young boy held his mother's hand and rested it on the open window of the car near Mary. The mother was blind. Mary put some money into the woman's hand.

At that moment, Elijah says, he was aware of Mary's compassion, but something was troubling him. He realized that although the money may help for a while, the woman and her child will always be there, in constant need. He wondered who would help him in the future.

Elijah turned to Mary and said, "It is nice of you to give us a few shillings once in awhile, but what we need is access to information and education. We need someone to give us wings."

Mary was stunned by the statement that in part reflected what she had witnessed in her stay. Well-meaning people might give handouts, but poverty remained. Nonprofits might put in a well, build a school or give some immunizations, but poverty remained. She was also impressed by Elijah's appraisal of what was needed, information and education so that people could move forward on their own.

"I mulled over the words, 'Give Us Wings,' Mary says. "It was not giving in the sense of dependence that Elijah was talking about. It was making accessible what all humans have the right to, the tools to provide basic needs for themselves and their families. I wasn't certain what it all meant then, nor am I now, but I knew it was important."

Mary continued to work on her book. Again, she saw the young man she had asked to write his story. He handed her a one-page story, devoid of sentimentality but rather a stark account of what life was like for him as an African child.

"I was startled by the story's honesty and angst. I thought maybe this is how I will respond to this trip. I will collect people's stories, put them together in a book, and when the people in the United States read the stories, they will respond."

Mary began letting people know that she was listening to stories—that they might be in a book. The news spread. People came from all over. Some presented written stories. Some brought translators. Mary listened for hours, day after day. People invited her to visit their grandmother's or cousin's village. "I had no money to give as my funds were almost depleted. But people didn't want money. Over and over, they said thing like 'Thank you for listening. No one has listened to me before. No one has cared about us before.' Their trust and the layers of sadness and loss and horror in their lives overwhelmed me. The experience was more educational than getting three doctorates."

Then the American Embassy in Nairobi was bombed by terrorists. Things were edgy and there was little money left in her wallet, so Mary decided to head back to the USA. Mary looked for Elijah but he had left for Nairobi. She found out later that he had received word that his best friend was missing in the bombing. His friend was the son of the man who funded Elijah's education. That is how they met. Elijah went from makeshift morgue to makeshift morgue until he found his friend's body. "I felt as if half of me was gone," Elijah says, "This was the person I could dream with and believe in a future for myself and my people with. Now, there was no one who understood."

Mary left not knowing if she would ever again see the man who had so inspired her. Eventually, Elijah answered one of Mary's e-mails. He shared with her that his school was gone. It had been a rickety hut with access to one electrical outlet. When the power went out in the school one day, workers replaced the electrical system but did not install a surge protector. Shortly afterward, the school burned down. Elijah felt as if his life burned with it. "Those were dark days," he said.

In ensuing weeks, Mary tried to compile the stories that she had brought back to the USA. She realized that she didn't know the culture well enough to do them justice. So, she and a young colleague, Shannon Lacy, headed back to Kenya to learn more. "This is the part of the story when people say I wish I could afford to do that. I was fortunate. I was responsible only for myself at that time. But I didn't have much money—less than $5,000 when I got back. I set up my own little business doing training in the education field, and I had great friends who let me live with them so that I could be flexible and go back."

This time, Mary and Shannon traveled to the grandmothers' and cousins' villages—including Elijah's grandmother's village of Nyaoga. The same phenomenon occurred again—people lined up by the dozens to tell their stories. In the process, Mary and Shannon found what they call the forgotten villages. "There is a mythology that we shared that lots of assistance is reaching the people of Africa," Mary says. "All we knew is that it wasn't getting to the people we met – hardworking, suffering people with no options."

"I knew that," Elijah adds. "But, I guess coming from the USA, until you see it for yourself, it is impossible to believe that there are people who have nothing."

Mary and Shannon went home with Shawn. They gathered a group of friends together and said, "We have to respond in some way to what we know—to the information and education we received. Will you help us?" Their friends shared their personal mailing lists and planned a fundraiser.

Elijah was reevaluating his life as well. His school was gone, and he needed direction. He wanted to go back to his village but he kept thinking of the poverty, the malnutrition and the disease.

"I took a fresh look at my life again," he remembers. "I started thinking not about how I could change my life, but how much change I could bring to my home."

Through their correspondence, Elijah and Mary realized they shared a similar vision for his home community. They wanted to improve the lives of the people by using the ideas, interests, skills and resources of those who lived there. They wanted to base it on respect and accountability and staying with people until they were self-sufficient. They started planning an organization to use funds and support from the United States to help the village pull itself out of poverty. That organization became Give Us Wings.

Elijah was initially reluctant about the undertaking. "I didn't have a background in community work," he confesses. "I went into this work knowing practically nothing. I had to improvise."

First, Elijah wanted to know what his village needed the most. A series of meetings with a women's group in Nyaoga revealed that the women did not want money for themselves. "We need health care," they said shyly.

In 2001, Give Us Wings put together a week-long health care seminar, teaching eight women from the Nyaoga community about first aid, AIDS prevention, and childcare. It also sponsored a free health camp for the villagers. Today, the community can boast the construction of a permanent health clinic available to those who need treatment for HIV/AIDS, malaria, cholera, typhoid, and malnutrition, as well as for childbirth. Now, Elijah says, the women of Nyaoga are "very noisy and have the confidence and tools to meet their goals to improve life for themselves and their community."

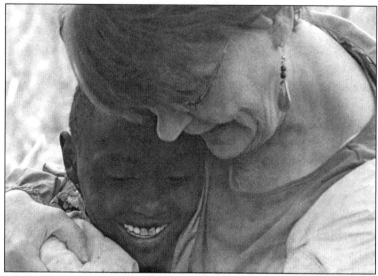
Mary Steiner Whalen embracing African girl
(Photo courtesy of Give Us Wings)

Coordinating the project was no simple task. Though Elijah was able to talk to the families he had grown up with, the villagers were cautious about the idea of more Americans coming to help the village. Many villagers had never met a Westerner, and some of the stories they had heard weren't favorable. Like Mary and Elijah's first encounter in front of the car wash, trust was still an issue.

"The initial response of some of the villagers was that of suspicion," Mary says. "They felt we were not for real, that we are looking to get something from these people, that we will not come back."

But Give Us Wings comes back every year. In fact, with local community developers like Elijah who is now the regional coordinator of Give Us Wings, the organization never leaves. Beyond a constant presence, they have learned to allow the communities themselves to take charge and make decisions.

"It is important to let people be themselves," Elijah says. "It is important to know what the community asks for. It is a way to build trust and sustainability."

At the first health camp in 2001, clinicians discovered that seventy-five percent of the illnesses in the village, including diarrhea and intestinal problems, were the result of water-borne diseases. Nearly one-third of those infected were young children. Give Us Wings raised the funds in 2007 to help bring the first phase of a clean water system to over 15,000 people in the Nyaoga area. The people of Nyaoga dug the trenches, cooked food for the construction workers and attended extensive water management training so they were equipped to make the project sustainable.

In 1999, people's stories had also led Mary to Uganda. Today, using the same community-based approach, Give Us Wings operates in Tororo, Uganda. A huge problem in that area is the devastation caused by AIDS. Scores of children roam the streets looking for something to eat and a place to sleep. "Across Africa, many children are orphaned," Elijah says. "AIDS has swept families away."

In the farms surrounding Tororo, women labor in the dry fields, trying to eke out enough food for their families. So much work often comes with little reward, and many eat one small meal a day and suffer the symptoms of malnourishment. Despite the difficulties, many rural families take into their one-room homes the orphaned children of family and friends and sometimes strangers.

In these rural areas, Give Us Wings works together with small groups in which villagers can share agricultural resources and knowledge, as well as receive training in business and economics. A pilot health insurance project is starting to impact health in the area.

In the town of Tororo, Give Us Wings is led by women's groups in the slums consisting of women who have taken orphans into their families. Thirty-two women have now moved into their own beautiful little brick homes outside of the slums and are doing organic farming and running small businesses to support their children and orphans. They are paying back the mortgages on the homes. Other town groups are participating in business and literacy projects.

In the summer of 2004 when this writer first interviewed Elijah, he had left Africa for the first time, making the journey to Minneapolis, where he had his initial taste of Western living. He notes, "Everything you have is so big!"

Coming to the United States to tell his story is important, he said. Through his stories, he hopes others across the world will understand and recognize the difficult conditions in many parts of Africa.

"I have come to realize that so many people in your country are not aware of what is really going on in Africa," he says. "But I know that they are very interested. They want to listen. So I try and talk to them."

When asked about the future for himself, his village, and Africa, Elijah is optimistic. While facing great hurdles, he keeps his concentration on the next step. He knows the problems are daunting, but he also knows there is a world of people out there who care about the needs of his village. One step at a time, with the help of Give Us Wings, Elijah is determined to improve the living conditions in his home, Kenya, and in neighboring Uganda.

After many years with no staff, Give Us Wings now has two representatives in the USA and seven in Africa. The huge amount of work it takes to help communities rise out of poverty gets done only because people in Africa and the United States, who have only met through stories and pictures, care about, trust, and work together.

Elijah and Mary, two very ordinary people from different worlds heading in different directions met, changed direction, and brought the people from their worlds to meet each other. But the real story, they vehemently insist, is not about them as individuals. "Give Us Wings is really the story of our people meeting. Many of the friends who met with us in the USA in 1999 still work as volunteers. Busy with their lives as ordinary people, they give and give and have brought others who give and give of time and money and talent. And, they would tell you, they receive and receive the joy and satisfaction of knowing that they are really making a difference in the lives of people of Africa who were brave enough to share their stories with strangers, who work incredibly hard everyday, who help the people in America to remember what is important in life. That is: to listen, compassionately listen, to each other, to allow each other time to learn, to give each other access to information and education, to work side by side—to give each other wings."

For more information, please go to: www.giveuswings.org

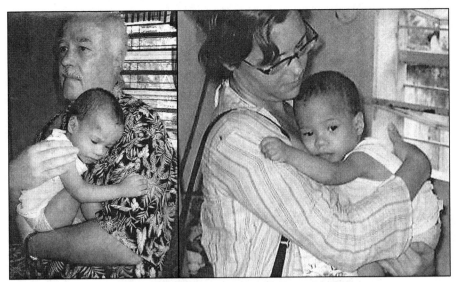

Chuck and Annetta DeVet with Vietnam children
(Photos courtesy of Chuck DeVet)

SAVING THE CHILDREN
By William Wrobleswki

The sand dunes outside of the small fishing village of Mui Ne are a pleasant surprise to those who visit this southern corner of Vietnam on the South China Sea. The hills of orange sand offer great hiking and stunning views. The uniquely exotic scenery and chance for adventure were a main reason that American father and daughter Chuck and Annetta DeVet decided to vacation in this faraway Asian land and why they set out one day to climb the rolling mounds of Vietnamese soil.

While huffing up and down the sand dunes, Chuck and Annetta met a playful group of inquisitive local children. Not used to Westerners, the kids ran up and greeted the strange visitors, eventually helping them scale the sloping hills.

The children did not ask for anything in return for their assistance. "They just wanted to say 'hello' and make friends with us," Annetta says. "One of the kids patted my dad's belly. 'Two babies,' he said."

Annetta and her father were taken by the children's cleverness, humor, and curiosity. "I wanted to talk with them, to hang out with them, to play with them. It made me smile, and I watched them take sheets of plastic and try to sled down this hill," Annetta remembers. "All I wanted to do is bring them a bunch of snow so they could know what sledding really is."

As their tourist visit continued, the DeVets began to see a different side of Vietnam presenting itself through bus windows. Hopping from resort to resort, they saw poor fishing and rice farming communities with rickety houses with straw roofs and canvas walls, supported with skinny bamboo poles.

"Just driving down the road, you see that the poverty is everywhere," Annetta frowns. Their tour guides, hoping to keep a happy view of Vietnam in the hearts of its visitors, would simply say that that was how poor farmers lived. But the DeVets wanted to know more. They began to connect what they saw out the bus windows with their experience on the sand dunes. They came to a conclusion that would turn their fledgling venture into a lifelong journey. "After looking around, we knew we wanted to help the children," Chuck adds. "And then the question became, what do you do for them? What do you do, and how do you do it?"

* * *

Born and raised near Lexington and Grand, a comfortable middle-class pocket of St. Paul, Chuck eventually moved to the more rural and quiet Prior Lake, Minnesota. Though he spent most of his professional career in the banking industry, he is no stranger to helping children. In 1970, he co-founded and became business manager of Crossroads, an innovative adoption agency still in operation today.

"We didn't do healthy, white babies," he says. "We were placing the waiting children—the older kids, the handicapped kids, the minority kids, and kids from foreign countries." That agency was also the first in Minnesota to place a child with a single parent. "There are a lot of kids who need homes out there, and one parent is better than none," he is quick to point out.

Chuck is also an active supporter of adoption. He and his wife have adopted three children. Roberto, thirty-eight, is from El Salvador; Linda, thirty-two, was adopted from Colombia; and fourteen-year-old Sumei was adopted from China.

Annetta, on the other hand, had not thought about this type of work until her trip with her father. She remembers how she felt when her father first asked her, just months away from her college graduation, to join him on a visit to Vietnam.

"I just looked at him, thinking, okay, who are we adopting now?" she admits with a smile. The trip became a bonding experience for father and daughter.

"Five months later, I was on a plane, just two weeks after graduation," she explains.

After the vacation, Annetta was hired at a local television station, editing tape and running cameras. "I was a button-pusher," she jokes. Later that year, Chuck formally decided he wanted to spend his retirement helping the children of Vietnam. He had to pull his daughter away from her part-time job at the TV station so she could be a part of her father's new venture.

On their second trip, in March 2002, the DeVets were meeting with governmental and charitable organizations when they came across Roy Montgomery, an American Vietnam War veteran who spends a good portion of the year in Vietnam working with local communities on housing construction projects for poor families. Montgomery took Chuck and Annetta off the worn tourist path to back roads, showing them battle sites from the war. These personal tours of Vietnamese history gave the DeVets a chance to mingle with local communities without the constraints and barriers enforced by packaged tours, whose guides tried to keep the poverty out of the view of visiting Westerner's eyes.

"We went to a place that we hadn't gotten to on our first trip, where tour buses don't stop," Annetta says. "We met local children, who probably have never encountered any Westerners."

Most of the world's Viet Kieu, or Vietnamese living abroad, are from the south, and send remittances to their families back home. And most American transplants, many who are veterans of the Vietnam War and many who do some level of charitable and development work, live and operate in Ho Chi Mihn City and other areas of the south. So the DeVets decided to work in the north, in and around Hanoi. They formed Humanitarian Services for the Children of Vietnam (HSCV), a small nonprofit that would coordinate access to healthcare, education, and rice to children in the Red River Delta, a part of the world where half the population is under the age of twenty-five and ninety percent of the poor live in rural areas.

One understated and unassuming issue jumped out at them almost immediately. "The issue just kind of came to us," Annetta explains. "We visited orphanages and schools for handicapped children, and a lot of them were hearing-impaired, but treated as if they were mentally ill. That stuck in our heads."

The DeVets recruited a visiting group of students led by the head of the audiology department at Brigham Young University, volunteering at the National Institute of Pediatrics in Hanoi, to donate a day's worth of time to set up an impromptu clinic to test the kids' hearing and fit them with donated hearing aids if needed. HSCV rented two vans, rallied the school's twenty-one kids and their families, and took the twenty-five mile trip to the hospital, where the testing would take place. "If we could get these children to hear, then they'd be able to learn, and they would no longer be seen as mentally ill and just stuck in a little room. It seemed to be a fixable issue," Annetta says.

HSCV coordinated a hearing aid program to acquire donated hearing aids, set up testing clinics, and fit children with the devices. When a child receives a hearing aid, his or her family is trained in proper maintenance and cleaning, and teachers are trained in speech therapy so the children are able to obtain the communication skills that had been lacking.

"At our first clinic, a quiet little girl was the first candidate for a hearing aid. Chuck says, recalling the moment with blushing excitement. "The doctor installed the hearing aid. As he was standing behind her, he said, 'Well, let's see if these things work.' Everyone stopped and got really quiet. He clicked on the hearing aid, and the little girl's eyes got big and she didn't really know what was going on. The doctor then said, 'Baaa, Baaaaa.' And she jumped up, I mean just jumped she was so scared! I have never seen anyone so scared in all my life. She turned around and saw the doctor making that noise, and she stared at him. He did it a couple more times, and she kept just staring at him.

"She turned back around, and her mother was just crying. It was the first time the girl had ever heard her mother's voice. She started to smile a huge smile. She went around to every one of us in the room and we all had to say something. And she would smile, and go to the next person. Everyone was crying in that room," Chuck says. "It was so emotional. I had never seen anything like that before."

"Another little girl, Anh, is riddled with a series of problems, her deafness only a complicating factor. She is mentally handicapped, and also has difficulty walking because her legs need braces. Anh was given physical therapy for her legs and a set of hearing aides. I turned her hearing aid on, and she started looking around," Annetta says. "We sat and waited for her. You could tell she could hear, but she didn't know how to react to it. She was mostly confused. With her mental impairment, too, she was very scared.

"I took her outside on the street. I turned the hearing aid up just a bit. With the cars passing by, and dogs nearby, she would look out of the corner of her eye. She was glaring at things, like bicycles making noises. She didn't exactly know what to think of it."

Anh's father never enrolled her in school, convinced she just wasn't intelligent. With the ability to hear, however, she had a new tool to take on the challenges of learning to talk and write.

"The last time I saw her," Annetta says, "she was writing numbers for the first time, writing letters for the first time. And she says 'hello' in Vietnamese."

When Annetta saw Anh's father again, he thanked her. "Now that he can see his daughter learning, he knows that his daughter is intelligent," she says. "He is so excited that she is in school. The whole world, at nine years old, opened up for her."

On one occasion, Chuck was volunteering with another group, working in a temporary health clinic in a rural town. "I looked out the window and saw this little girl waiting in line to see one of the doctors," he begins. "It was like her knees were going backwards. She just has these horribly deformed legs. She can't go any distance."

Chuck introduced himself to the little girl, named Van Anh, who came from the poor suburb of Hanoi, Thanh Tri. When she was younger, this girl survived a botched surgery that worsened her legs' condition. Soon, they were arranging for x-rays of the girls legs and looking for someone to fix them. It was through this process that they discovered the girl had a hole in her heart as well.

On a subsequent trip, Annetta had difficulty with the doctors. One would tell Annetta that Van Ahn's legs would have to be fixed first because if they weren't, she wouldn't be able to exercise while rehabilitating after heart surgery. A leg doctor would not perform the surgery until her heart was fixed. This same doctor offered only to fuse the joints, permanently straightening the girls legs for the rest of her life, an option Annetta could only call "unacceptable."

"It was really hard to get a heart surgery to happen," says Annetta. She eventually found a doctor who was able to offer physical therapy, message therapy and reflex therapy. Later, Chuck found a surgeon in Ho Chi Mihn City eager to look at the little patient because of the severity of her problems. This doctor concluded that the girl's heart had to be fixed first. He later joined Annetta on a trip to a new hospital in Hanoi to convince doctors to do the surgery.

Getting Van Anh's legs and heart fixed was a difficult learning process for Annetta. "I didn't know the system well enough to know that I was getting the runaround," she admits. "Now I know how the hospital system works in Vietnam. There are so many little hospitals, and each hospital specializes in this or that."

Van Anh's heart is fixed. Her series of leg surgeries began in early 2005, with surgeons from Ho Chi Mihn City working at the National Institute of Pediatrics in Hanoi, which has donated its facilities to the girl's cause. The DeVets also arranged for funds to contract the orthopedic doctors.

Problems continued to plague Van Anh's family. While trying to fix Van Anh, the DeVets discovered that her older brother, Thang, who, at four feet tall, is very small for his age, had a heart that did not beat very well. He was bedridden in the family's home. When asked why the father didn't tell the DeVets about his son, he replied, "You are already helping one of my children. It is just too much to ask you to help another one."

The DeVets nevertheless decided to help the boy as well, and coordinated the proper surgeries for him. "Today, he is running around, playing with his friends," Annetta says, "his life has changed."

Though both of these children were able to have open heart surgery at the Hanoi Heart Hospital, most families like theirs would have difficulties affording such a procedure. "They have no money," Annetta says." The mother sells fish in the market, and the father may work as a guard there. Their income is something like two dollars a day. That doesn't even buy them enough food."

This level of poverty, particularly in rural areas, also means that education is often neglected. Many schools lack the classrooms and supplies to meet the children's learning needs. Simple things, like pencils, backpacks, and even jackets are difficult to come by, which makes attending and learning in school difficult for those in the mountain areas.

A few corporations, including agricultural product producer Cargill, operate development and relief efforts in Vietnam. Cargill builds schools in poor communities, but does not offer supplies to those schools. By partnering with these efforts, HSCV equips the schools with the supplies students need to learn.

Several of the Cargill schools, mostly little two-or three-room schoolhouses, are tucked away in distant mountain communities. Many inhabitants in these areas are from the poorest minority groups: the Hmong, the Tay and the Che.

Three hours north of Hanoi, near the Chinese border, is a small Tay community with a school of 100 kids. This community is too poor and too distant to have the same amenities other urban residents enjoy. "They don't have electricity yet," Annetta explains. "They have light bulbs and fans and things. They are still waiting for the electricity to operate them."

To help with this problem, HSCV has set up a sister school program wherein schools in the United States raise money for supplies for remote Vietnamese villages. Annetta's video production experience has lent an unusual spin to the program, expanding the benefits to the American schools beyond cultural exchange with letters and photographs. By constantly shooting footage of the group's activities, HSCV is able to offer participating schools and classrooms individualized video presentations of their sister schools.

Chuck and Annetta found a school in Eagan, Minnesota, populated with young students eager to do a jump-a-thon to raise funds for their counterpart in Vietnam. "They jumped their little hearts out," Annetta says with pride. "They made so much money that we were able to supply two schools instead of one."

The DeVets are interested in filling bellies and well as brains. In the Hanoi district of Soc Son, where many poor schools participate in the sister school program and some students have their tuition paid through a scholarship program, many of the kids' families participate in a rice program that ensures a dependable flow of food each month.

Rice has always been a staple food in Vietnam, but government regulations once required farmers to give two-thirds of their harvests to the government, creating rice shortages among those who grow it and creating a need for imported rice. Though these restrictions have since been relaxed, land reallocation and pollution remain factors in creating malnutrition throughout farming and fishing communities.

Qualifying families receive twenty or thirty kilos of rice each month, redeemable the first day of every month. "Then the families come, one by one," Annetta says. "They are putting it on their bicycles; they are doing whatever they can to bring it home. If they are going to walk that far for their rice, it must be worth it."

Paying ten cents per pound for the rice, the program is surprisingly affordable.

"With very little, we can do a lot for a bunch of families," Annetta says. "It is very economical. Every dollar goes very far, luckily, because we don't have that many dollars."

All of HSCV's money comes from fundraisers and private donations. Much of the donated funds, in fact, come from Chuck himself. Because he and his family pay for the overhead, travel, and administrative costs themselves, they essentially work for free in Vietnam.

Chuck covers Annetta's expenses, and she receives no income or stipend for the work. "My dad helps me to fund my needs. So a lot of it is my inheritance," she smirks.

With the recruitment of Corey Christianson, a wanderlust-infected American the DeVets met in their travels, as a coordinator for HSCV, Annetta now residing in Vietnam, and the hiring of a Vietnamese native as project coordinator, the organization now has a staff of three in Hanoi. Today, HSCV rents a house in Hanoi where the staff stays while in the country. Most of the communities they work with are no more than a couple hours away by motorbike. This situation allows them to experience two sides of Vietnam—the polished and the provincial.

"Once you get away from the 3 million people in Hanoi, once you are out of that circle, you are very foreign," Annetta says. "When working in the communities we are going into, they are just not used to it at all. It is very easy to have a group of thirty people following us around everywhere we go."

It was the same level of curiosity that brought Chuck to this part of the world in the first place. He did not fight in the Vietnam War. At that time, he was a reservist, an artillery medic stationed in Minneapolis. But he understands the important history and relationships between the United States and Vietnam. "That was the war of my generation," he says. That connection was part of what convinced Chuck to nominate Vietnam as the destination for a father-daughter vacation.

Once there, Annetta was equally as fascinated with Vietnam. "On our second trip, we had planned on going to Thailand, Cambodia, and Laos, but once we went back there the second time, we began to wonder why we would look more. We already know we liked it in Vietnam. We really found a connection there," she says.

By having a permanent home in Vietnam, the organization can constantly oversee its own activities and is seen by government officials as a viable aid agency doing good work for the people.

The organization's interaction with authorities is often a delicate game of information sharing. HSCV often has to work through the local government authorities for access and to find appropriate families. For the most part, Chuck says, they are cooperative. "The people's committees in these little towns are very supportive of us," he says. "They do appreciate what we are doing."

The DeVets are careful to ensure that the families they work with really do need their help, and are not simply friends of the local officials. Most of the time, the officials are good about finding appropriate families.

"That is not to say there isn't an often difficult process involved," Annetta explains. "We have to go through the authorities in the correct order, or else you will upset someone. That is very important. We learn as we go. We do make mistakes, but so far the government has been pretty forgiving. You can make a mistake once, and say you didn't know. But don't make that same mistake twice and say you didn't know."

Sometimes one official can put an entire project on hold, affecting the lives of dozens of families. Once, the DeVets were working with the significantly larger Project Vietnam, an international medical aid team that sends doctors, nurses and volunteers over to conduct medical clinics in rural mountain communities. In this case, they brought over two cargo containers of medical supplies, including sixty wheelchairs. When they arrived, the supplies were stored in a warehouse overnight. The warehouse was so packed that twenty-two wheelchairs had to be kept outside.

The next morning, dozens of locals were standing in line at the warehouse, waiting patiently for supplies. Some patients were carried long distances by family members in the hopes of receiving a wheelchair and other medical assistance. While the twenty-two wheel chairs outside were distributed, they were not enough to meet the needs of those in line waiting for a local official's word to unlock the building.

The official denied permission to unlock the warehouse. Without access to the supplies, many of these people who had come down in the hopes of getting some help left with nothing. "We got in there late that night, so we got some of the chairs, but most of the people were already gone," Chuck explains, "just because some guy was showing us his authority, showing us that he didn't have to unlock that door."

This sort of thing frustrates Chuck, and makes aid work difficult in Vietnam. "It just pisses you off. This group donated all types of equipment to the hospitals, making it a different world for them, teaching them how to do it, fixing all those kids."

That particular incident, however, is unusual for HSCV because, as a small organization of only six total staff members, much of their activities go unseen. "We haven't had these problems ourselves," Annetta says. "We are small and under the radar of all that stuff. That gives us the capability of being one-on-one with the families. It keeps us grounded and in constant contact with those people we are helping." In recent months, HSCV has donated some 10,000 wheelchairs to handicapped people, some of whom have been housebound for decades, many of them victims of the Vietnam War, and has provided funding for additional surgeries for children with severe medical conditions.

By working directly with communities, the DeVets hope in the future to supply funds for medicine for premature babies brought on the back of motorbikes to the hospital in Hanoi from the rural villages.

Also, the DeVets learned that it doesn't take too many American dollars to build a modest house in Vietnam. One of the next projects in the planning stages is to find land and build homes for poor families. "It may not be real big, but it will take a family of four, five, maybe six," Chuck notes. "But, it has a concrete floor, brick walls, a metal roof and a toilet. It is pretty incredible what you can get for $650."

In Vietnam, many families cannot buy land because they do not have the money and cannot seek employment because they do not have the proper paperwork to live in certain areas. With government-donated land and planning, materials, and labor supplied by HSCV, these people may soon have a residence.

Also of concern are the many homeless orphans scavenging the streets for shelter and food in Vietnam's cities, particularly in Hanoi. Some were left by their parents who were unable to support them. Some have parents who come back at night but leave the kids in the streets during the day while they look for work. Chuck is also concerned about the thriving sex trade in Vietnam, where parents sell or rent their children, and girls leave their families to work in the brothels of Thailand or Cambodia.

With the right intervention, Chuck believes, they can help families and children make the right decisions and help them out of the poverty that creates such situations. "If we can get to those kids, maybe we can get them into a home, or maybe we can start a home for those kids. We could provide them with shelter, food, and education, to give them a chance."

These programs are in the beginning stages "It takes awhile to get things going," Chuck admits. "It's sometimes hard to know what to do and how to do it. But we are doing a lot of good over there. We really are."

This conviction is what brings the DeVets back to Vietnam every year. Chuck says that, initially, he wasn't so sure about Annetta's eagerness to commit. "I think Annetta kind of got it by surprise when we went over there. I don't know if this was on her radar," he speculates. "And now she's into it up to her eyeballs."

Now living in Vietnam full-time, Annetta shoulders a great amount of responsibility. "I'm the one in charge," she says. "If things aren't happening, it's because I am not doing it right. A lot of it is just figuring out how to get things done. But I wouldn't have it any other way. The country, it is amazing. Everywhere, I just fall in love. Every new place I go I think is the most beautiful place in the world. Then I go to another place and I say, 'That's the most beautiful place in the world.'"

Chuck believes he has been to Vietnam at least nine times. "I lost track," he laughs. He says he couldn't find a better place to do his work." Once we got to Vietnam, and saw the kids and the need, and how far a dollar would go and how much good you could do, why would you look someplace else?" he asks.

"Meeting those poor children near Mui Ne opened us up to the problems facing so many children in the fishing villages, mountain communities and cities of Vietnam. Much of Vietnam is a nation of wonderful, curious people living in the most difficult of circumstances.

"We want to do more," he says. "There is so much more to do."

Nichola Torbett
(Photo courtesy of Nichola Torbett)

WHERE WE CARE FOR THE WOUNDED
By Nichola Torbett

In the dream, there was an underground river running dark and calm through an orange-lit tunnel under the city where I lived. The concrete shores of the river were crowded with construction materials—piles of lumber and shingles, orange and white barricades and traffic cones everywhere, though the area was quiet at this time of night. In the middle of the river was the skeleton of a ship. "This is where you are going to work," said the guide who had led me down into this secret place.

"What is it?" I asked.

"It's a floating hospital," she said. "This is where we will care for the wounded."

When I woke the next morning, sometime in 2001, the question on my mind was, "But who are the wounded?" It would be several years before I understood that the wounded are all of us, and that my own woundedness was no excuse for not being part of the healing.

Like most everyone I know, my life has been shaped by having grown up in a culture of domination, violence, individualism and materialism. In our culture, at least the Anglo-American culture in which I grew up, it is taken for granted that one must look out for one's own interests and the interests of one's immediate family, using tactics of domination and control as needed to protect what is "rightfully" one's own. Efforts to dominate, control, and subjugate are so common for us that they are often unconscious. I wonder if there is anyone alive in the United States today who has not suffered under the domination system.

The effects of the domination system on my own life originate in a time long before I was born. My father was born in 1941 in Berlin. He and his sister learned to walk in a bomb shelter, and when he was not quite four years old, he stood in the doorway, waving to his best friend across the street then watched his friend be crushed when the bomb fell.

I don't know, can't imagine, what it would be like to have one's first experiences be of violence and extreme danger. Yet, there are children being born the world over into those circumstances at this very moment.

My father knows well what human beings can do to each other, and he has never really recovered from that knowledge. His early experiences have, I think, everything to do with the bitter anger and sadness my sister and I witnessed in him throughout our childhood.

I don't know either what it is like to fight in a bloody war, but I have body memories of what it feels like to have the lingering trauma acted out on me sexually by an older relative who was a veteran of World War II, when I was two and three years old. A part of me checked out at that time, so that for most of my life I have felt myself to be on the other side of a veil, able to see life happening, but unable to make real contact with it, or with other people. These are just two of the ways the legacy of violence and domination is passed down.

My father drank more and more over the years, especially after he and my mother divorced, and he sought confirmation of his dim view of humanity by reading to us from Sigmund Freud. I dreaded visiting him in the dark and gloomy house he rarely left. As often as my conscience would allow, I slipped out of the house and sought refuge in the woods that surrounded it. There were incredible moments then, sitting on a log amid the trees or building a village into the muddy root system of a fallen tree, when I felt absorbed into the world, fully a part of it. These moments of communion instilled in me a sense that some other way was possible, that my father's bleak view of a humanity forever at war with itself was not the only way.

Back in the house, my loneliness for the world was almost unbearable. I tried to connect with my father by studying his books, proving myself to be, like him, smarter than others, whom he called the "naked apes." By the end of those weekly visits, I had sunk into my own despair, though I hid it from everyone.

In my other life, with my mother and sister in town, I was also lonely. I had little interest in the girly things they loved. My mother, raising two kids on her own, was stressed almost to the breaking point, and often she would come in the door from work already raging. I developed an acute attunement to the moods of other people, always on the lookout for danger. We didn't have a lot of money, but it was important to my mother that we appear solidly middle class, so she taught us the social mores of middle class life. I learned to fake what I did not feel and could not in any way afford.

When I was thirteen, my English teacher invited me to go to church with her. Something in me recognized this as a life raft, and I leapt. I wanted to be adopted into her family. I developed a passionate crush on her, and later on both her son and her daughter, who were several years older than I. They took me to youth group meetings and events, and I tried very much to find a place there, and more than that, to feel something, anything, spiritual. There were moments, when we were singing, that I could lose my self-consciousness and feel the tones swell in my chest. At those moments, I felt connected to the whole universe just as I had playing in the woods as a child.

Meanwhile, my father was furious about this development. He read to me about religion as the opiate of the masses and accused me of being no smarter than the commoners after all. At the same time, he modeled for me the deepest reverence for the natural world. In all the time I have known him, I have never seen him kill a living creature. He would capture spiders and wasps and carry them outside to freedom rather than squashing them as I asked him to.

I stayed with the church until I left for college, where I sought out a Christian group on campus. As I listened to the often judgmental talks of the campus minister and then read a variety of religious texts in a course on the history of ideas, my faith began to crumble. How likely was it that the religion I had identified with was the one true way, as it insisted it was, when there were all these other faiths? The whole enterprise seemed deeply suspect to me. By the end of my first quarter, I was a fierce atheist. My father was delighted, and although I might have felt some loss, I threw myself all the more fervently into proving myself academically. In graduate school, in a prestigious English department, I learned to adopt a perpetually critical stance. Like a Tai Kwan Do practitioner who keeps her knees slightly bent at all times, I kept my analytic crowbar always ready. I could deconstruct anything you handed me. In this way I felt superior and safer than before, but I remained terribly lonely.

During those years, I found meaning in two places – African American literature and critical theory. My years as an undergraduate coincided with the explosion onto the scene of African-American women writers, and I was powerfully drawn to the work of Alice Walker, Toni Morrison, Toni Cade Bambara, and Gloria Naylor. Having grown up in a racist community that maintained its whiteness through cross-burning and intimidation, I couldn't explain the resonance I felt with these women, except that their evocative explorations of life under multiple systems of domination echoed my own sense of loneliness, disconnection, longing for empowerment, and search for community. I longed to know the characters in those stories and novels. I felt there was something we could have done together.

In graduate school, I was told in no uncertain terms that it was suspect for me, a white woman, to build a career around studying and writing about African American literature. Looking back at this now, I have mixed feelings. I suspect that my father's status as an immigrant—and a hated postwar German at that—had made us not quite "white" since white is something one becomes by giving up ethnicity. At the same time, there is no question that my appearance reads as white, and so I have enjoyed the myriad privileges of that designation. During those years, I was ashamed of having been called a colonist of African American culture, and I moved away from that work with regret and focused on critical theory.

Intuitively, I sensed that engaging with postmodern theory might lead me to some answers to the questions that were most urgent for me: How can we achieve real justice? Can there be difference—racial, gender, religious, ability—without hierarchy, and if so, how? Could the alienation I had felt all my life be explained by the gap between the signifier and the signified? Was it true that the resonance I felt with the experiences of African-American woman was an act of imperialism, and if so, why did I feel such kinship?

Longing to overcome my sense of alienation, I was drawn to poststructuralism's theoretical emphasis on endless play, shifting boundaries, a reality perpetually in motion. I set out to write a dissertation on literary theory and ethics. I wanted to bring my academic experience—my fascination with Jacques Lacan and Jean-Francios Lyotard—into conversation with my experience working in the dining halls, the love I felt for women who had worked all their lives at the university without feeling safe in taking a class there. Then as now, it was connection and solidarity that interested me. This project did not work. Maybe it could have had certain things not happened.

At age twenty-four, I met a lesbian who courted and cajoled me out of my closet, and with me out into the world came all the demons of my past. Years of suppressed, repressed emotion suddenly came to the surface.

Then I found out that Diane Elam, a beloved mentor and brilliant theorist, had lost her husband. I didn't know where to go with this occurrence or the grief and solidarity I felt with her. The university ground onward. The department appointed Diane's best friend, Gayle Margherita, herself in a free-fall of grief, to take over our seminar in critical theory and ethics. We were all at sea. This was not the fault of the department, I don't think. There was just no place in its highly reasoned, rational structure for random tragedy. I could not make sense of rupture from within that world. I fell into a despair so deep I could hardly get out of bed. I took incompletes in the last two classes I needed for my Ph.D., and, disillusioned, I left the academy.

Looking back, I realized that I had been trying to make critical theory into a religion, a system of belief that pointed to justice, and in the face of deep loss, that religion could not sustain me. My critical training did not allow me to consider other religious options.

* * *

At the time I had the underground river dream, I was living in the Twin Cities and working as an editor for a Minnesota-based publishing company, making enough money, and I had a smart, funny, successful group of friends whom I saw regularly, though I often left our gatherings dissatisfied, as if we'd passed near each other but hadn't really connected. In a series of romantic relationships, I tried to do everything right and say all the right things until all the unhappiness I was avoiding erupted and blew the whole thing apart. I had no idea how to be supportive of other people while being honest about what was happening in me; the two seemed mutually exclusive, so I chose to support other people until my own unmet needs became so pressing that I could not hold them in. I remembered my father's sense of human beings as inherently self-interested and dominating. Most of the time, I felt there was no room for me anywhere. I started dreaming about a bottomless abyss, about free fall. At work, I played by the rules, did everything right, was promoted; at night I went home, binged on entire packages of Oreos, and thought about buying a gun at the new Wal-Mart in town, and then disappearing into the silence I craved. The question that I courted only at night was, "What if there is no meaning? What if this is it?"

I started reading self-help and personal-growth books. So invested was I in my own image as a competent, together person that I couldn't bear to be seen in the self-help section of the bookstore, so I would quickly pass through the aisle, grab a couple of titles, and then rush to another part of the store to browse through them. Now and then, I would find something useful in one of those books, but the painful disconnection and meaninglessness remained.

Eventually, I made my way to a local Zen center. I was drawn to the open acknowledgement of suffering, and Buddhism appealed because it didn't require belief in a deity. Showing up at Sunday services was difficult, though. I found that I couldn't make eye contact with the head teacher or any of the advanced students. I felt that if I did, they would see into me and recognize what a mess I was. Still, I showed up, sat on a cushion, walked slowly around the room, sat some more, then slipped out afterward before anyone could meet my eyes. Then something started to shift in me. I began to look head-on at my own suffering.

One afternoon, I found myself in the sunny home office of a Jungian therapist whose three cats wound around my ankles as I perused her bookshelves, which included works by Alice Walker, Toni Morrison and Gloria Naylor. She made us tea in the other room. She then suggested I begin watching my dreams, writing them down so that we could talk about them.

Those dreams opened up to me a world of images and symbols that slaked my thirst in a way I'd never known. They gave me access to what Shakespeare scholars called "the green world," the wild territory that exists outside the courtly walls, outside the structures of power and the systems of domination. There, movement was possible.

That's when I dreamed of the underground river, and I woke up longing for it. The river in my dream wasn't beautiful, not at all. The tunnel through which it ran looked like a grimy interstate tunnel through a hill, lit with orange safety lights, and in that light the water was charcoal gray. Yet there was something inevitable about the current of that river, and I wanted to give in to it, to go where it led.

In my waking life, I had no sense of being led. I knew that my current job wasn't my calling, but I didn't know what else I was meant to be doing, and I wasn't sure I believed in "callings," anyway. Many years in academia had left me with a sharp critical edge and a knee-jerk resistance to all things spiritual and religious. I had learned too well that the way to succeed in this culture was to separate myself from everything by holding it all up to constant critique, and by doing so, to set myself apart from and above other people who weren't as skilled at skepticism as I was. My study of Buddhism was beginning to blur that sense of separation, but still the idea of being guided was ludicrous to me. At the same time, the idea that life meant nothing was too painful to contemplate for more than a few minutes.

In the years since this dream, I have learned how many others go home to hollow relationships and fantasies of fatal bullets. At the time I thought I was the only one who didn't know if life meant anything, who was desperate for a sense of being a part of something larger and for deeper, more honest connections to other people.

Taught to project an image of competence and control, I never talked about the despair, loneliness, and meaninglessness that swirled under the surface—except in therapy. Of course, not talking about it ensured that I never recognized my suffering as part of a cultural sickness. Instead, I assumed it was a personal failing and so was ashamed, and my shame kept me locked away from other people and from our power to challenge the domination system that ensures our suffering.

I can't pinpoint the exact moment that I made the connection between my own unhappiness and the need to challenge larger systems of domination, but I can identify some of the milestones.

In 2000, I did intensive training as a volunteer crisis counselor, and I started spending Monday nights answering calls on the county crisis line. I have journal entries written at a coffee shop where I would stop on my way to the crisis center, so I know that I was in terrible pain at that time in my life, that I arrived some nights barely able to hold myself together. Yet somehow, when the phone rang, I was able to bring myself into full presence with another human being in trouble. Some of our callers were fleeing abusive households and needed shelter. Others were homeless with no place to spend the subzero Minnesota night. We heard from a lot of teenagers struggling with sexual orientation or other questions of identity. Most of our callers were in despair of some kind, sometimes of their own making, sometimes as a result of systems of oppression and injustice, and most often from some combination of external systems issues and internalized oppression. Sometimes, we had to trace a call and send the authorities to prevent a suicide, but more often we could listen deeply enough to draw the callers back into life for at least another night. Listening to these anonymous late-night voices caused me to see the day-lit city differently. I knew some of the secrets that rode those buses and sat behind those office windows. And I knew I wasn't as alone as I'd thought.

September 11, 2001, was another milestone. Like so many others, I experienced that day as an opening into new possibility. Amidst the grief and suffering, I recognized a new sense of connection among people who passed each other on the street. We met each other's eyes, and in those glances was an acknowledgement of our shared humanity and our shared loss and confusion. Spontaneously, I drove to a Unitarian Universalist church I'd heard about, and there I found others who had come hoping for community.

When, by that night, the drumbeat toward war had begun, I was furious to see that sense of connection manipulated into hatred of an enemy. I recognize now that my reaction was less than productive. I raged. I wrote angry letters and blasted those of my friends who dared to express any fear of further terrorist attacks. I set myself up as smarter and more savvy than others, and I became another face of the domination system I was decrying.

In 2002, someone forwarded me an email containing a speech, by then somewhat outdated, by a Congressional representative from Ohio named Dennis Kucinich. The speech was called "A Prayer for America," and in it Kucinich spoke out against invading Afghanistan after 9/11. I was shocked to find a Congressperson articulating ideals of brotherhood and sisterhood, interdependence, community, and love—and from the Congressional floor! It had never occurred to me that the longings I felt most deeply could have a place in politics. Inspired, I wrote an email to the Congressman, though it bounced back several times from his inbox, no doubt full of similar notes of gratitude.

Sending that email must have landed me on some kind of list, because in 2003, I got a message informing me that there would be an organizing meeting that night for Minnesotans supporting Dennis Kucinich's presidential run. I'd never had any interest in electoral politics, but the idea of someone with Kucinich's vision running for president was more than intriguing, so I decided to go, sit in the back just long enough to see what was happening and then leave early.

You can probably imagine the rest of the story.

Standing in the middle of her living room where the meeting was taking place, Kucinich supporter Faith Kidder declared that this campaign needed to be about love, that it probably wasn't going to look like any other presidential campaign, and that our highest priority should be to generate and spread compassion and connection.

I think I must have rolled my eyes, thinking to myself, "This is politics. What does love have to do with this?" And yet some part of me recognized that this is what I'd been hungry for all my life, a vision of interdependence and deep community on both the local and the global scale. By the end of the night, around midnight, I was chairing nine subcommittees, and I had the sense that my life would never be the same. A few months later, I became state co-coordinator, with Faith, of the Minnesota for Kucinich campaign.

That campaign was a turning point in my life, and even those friends who could never bring themselves to support Kucinich will often remark that I became a different and more engaged person during that year. Neither Faith nor I had ever been involved in a campaign before, so, along with dozens of other supporters, we made it up as we went along. I was busier than I had ever been, spending my evenings and weekends going from one campaign event or meeting to another. For several months, I drove a carload of campaigners to Iowa every weekend, where we went door-to-door, talking to ordinary people about their deepest desires for their lives. Through that experience, I realized that my own longings for connection, meaning, vision, purpose and community were echoed in almost every person we visited. And yet we hadn't known about each other. Most people had felt alone with their longings and had thus assumed they were impossible to realize. Each of us had been thinking that, while we wanted connection and love more than money and power, everyone else wanted the latter, and so we couldn't act on our own desires for fear of being taken advantage of in the process.

What a revolutionary discovery! I will never forget sitting up late at night in old farmhouses where Iowan Kucinich supporters put us up, talking about the world we longed for.

Of course, it wasn't always as peaceful as these paragraphs suggest. We often fell into anger at supporters of the other presidential candidates who weren't as visionary as ours. Even within the campaign, there were divisions along gender and class lines. When a group of men started disrupting campaign meetings, challenging my and Faith's leadership and suggesting that we didn't like men and didn't welcome male leadership, we reacted in exactly the wrong way, clamping down on the meetings and regulating who could speak. In one meeting, I had a screaming fight with one of those men. It was not a proud moment. And yet, we apologized to each other, and we went on, and he and I are still friends.

Somehow, with all our flaws and rough edges, we became a community, and by the time we expected meeting attendance to drop off as it became clear that Kucinich had no chance at getting the nomination, our meetings instead were growing until we had 100 people showing up every Tuesday night to work with us on caucus trainings and mobilization. In a sense, we were doing church in those campaign meetings. To this day, I believe it was the love that drew people and love that enabled us to pull seventeen percent of the Minnesota Democratic primary vote for Kucinich despite his long-shot status. The victory that night was a victory of vision—the vision of a world in which interdependence is assumed as the basis of policy, and in which each individual is called into loving responsibility for the community.

And in that victory and all the loving, passionate communal work that led up to it, I found healing. Somehow, in the year and a half of campaign work, I lost more than 100 pounds, paid off all my credit card debt, and overcame much of my shyness. To this day, I can't explain how any of this happened except to say that I was filled with a sense of meaning and purpose, and in the movement toward that, other things fell into their rightful place.

Around this time, I noticed that my therapy sessions turned from the personal to the political. Sometimes my therapist would apologize at the end of a session because we had talked more about the cultural malaise than about me, but I realized that the two really were not separable. My own efforts toward healing could not move forward without my having found a way to engage with the healing of the society. This is what it means to live in an interdependent world.

Around the end of that campaign, when I was starting to wonder what to do next, I had another dream. In this one, I was transported to the top of a mountain, where, it was clear, I would be meeting with a group of highly creative people. The purpose of our gathering was never revealed, but the memorable parts of the dream were the intense sense of community and the gap that ran all around the meeting room, separating the walls from the floor. Through that gap, one could peer anxiously into the abyss below the mountain. Somehow, it was significant that this passionately creative group had to work in the presence of the abyss.

A few months later, I followed an impulse to attend a spiritual activism conference in Berkeley, even though I was still uncomfortable with the word "spiritual." Within two hours of the start of the conference, a radiant man with long gray hair took the podium, and in matter-of-fact language he spoke about the alienation we feel walking down the street, how alone we each are even in crowded cities, how fear keeps us from genuine mutual recognition of each other's shared humanity. There in front of a crowd of 1,300 nodding people, law professor and visionary thinker Peter Gabel gave voice to secrets I thought were mine alone, and shameful. I thought to myself, first, "I must hug that man," and then "I have to spend the rest of my life figuring out how to change this." It was clear to me that only a revolution in our relationship to each other and to the planet would save us from brutal inequalities of power and wealth, from violence, from environmental catastrophe.

Later that day, I walked back into the ballroom where the plenary sessions were held, and someone had opened the draperies to reveal the Berkeley hills. Immediately, I recognized the "mountaintop" from my dream, and I knew that these were the creative people with whom I needed to work.

And so I did. I helped Peter and Rabbi Michael Lerner found the national interfaith Network of Spiritual Progressives (NSP) from the attendees of that conference. NSP is an organization dedicated to popularizing the notion that we need a "new bottom line" for American society so that decisions—whether individual, family, corporate, or government—are made not just on the basis of what will generate the most money and power. Instead, they should be made on the basis of what will generate the most love and caring, kindness and generosity, ethical and ecological sensitivity, ability to respond to others as embodiments of the sacred, and ability to respond to the universe with awe, wonder, and radical amazement.

I worked full-time with the NSP for two and a half years. During that time, we organized a large Spiritual Activism Conference in Washington, D.C., garnering headlines in national papers that read "The Religious Left Is Back!" We also held two leadership trainings and organized a national campaign for generosity as a more effective route to homeland security than domination and control. In other words, we worked to introduce into national dialogue the notion that the way to "fight terrorism" and other forms of violence is to work to eliminate poverty here and around the world and to stand in solidarity with all the peoples of the world. At this writing, our House Resolution 1078 had been introduced in Congress, calling for a Global Marshall Plan to eliminate poverty and heal the environment as a means of bringing about security.

Through this work, I came to terms, finally, with spirituality and even religion, and I've found my way back to a Christian church that is vibrant, progressive, radically inclusive, arts-positive, and committed to making love our first priority. Involvement in this consciously multiracial, multi-ethnic community has unleashed in me a longing to be in solidarity with all people, across lines of difference, and especially with those at the margins of our society. I recently left my staff position at NSP but remain a dues-paying member as the organization continues to grow and flourish.

These days, I'm following the underground river, seeking guidance from the Source of Life every day as I pursue a number of projects all aimed at healing individuals into community. I am not sure where the river is leading, but I am interested in teaching, leading workshops on the role of spirit in our efforts to heal and transform the world. I want to prod and challenge "spiritual" people to engage with the hurting world as a natural outgrowth of their spiritual practice, and I want to prod and challenge activists, who often channel all of their pain outwards, to cultivate their own inner lives. I don't think full healing for individuals is possible without engagement with the suffering of the world, nor do I think we can heal the world without also bringing loving attention to our own brokenness, to the ways in which we have each learned from our society to dominate and control.

In that context, I have recently embarked on a new project designed to create an alternative to domination and violence. It is called the Seminary of the Street. I am convinced that what the world most needs at this juncture is an expanding corps of vital, joyful people passionately working for the flourishing of all life everywhere.

The Seminary of the Street is designed to form, train and send out into our communities just such a corps of people. It is an interfaith, intercultural, spirit-led educational institute headquartered in the San Francisco Bay area that seeks to form mutually accountable communities of spiritual warriors at work in the world, where theology, sacred texts and spiritual practices meet the challenges of living differently from day to day.

Beginning in Oakland, California this winter, the institute is offering courses, seminars, workshops and community events that foster both inner and outer work.

Our goals are collective liberation from systems of domination, violence and oppression and the cultivation of alternative communities rooted in the NSP principles of tenderness, compassion, love, kindness, generosity, recognition of the sacredness of all life, and awe and wonder at the grandeur of the universe.

For example, in one workshop, students may walk in small groups through the inner city viewing it with unconditional love and then come together to share their experiences. In another class, students might study modern-day slavery and sweatshop labor, interrogating the way their own purchasing habits inadvertently support these practices, or they might experiment with spiritual practices that root out greed and fear within themselves and find their own calling to the community.

The transformation of our external world is not possible without transformation within ourselves. Our hope is that through deep engagement with ourselves, others and the spirit, we become more and more able to lay down our lives in the service of love.

Life isn't perfect. I am just now learning how to show up fully in relationship and to hold my needs and the needs of all others as equally precious. I struggle with food addiction, and when loneliness or confusion reigns, I still head to the sugar bowl.

Still, I have traded much (not all!) of my loneliness, despair, and meaninglessness for creativity, community, and, often, honestly, sheer terror. Staying close to the underground river, to the Spirit of Life that I call God, demands that I loosen my hold on my own identity in order to be challenged, changed, and refined in the fires of community. This means, in part, trusting all the intuitive, imaginative, healing instincts that I had rejected as "irrational" in order to become the smart, highly analytical, lonely person I was. On a daily basis, I have to acknowledge that I am not in control, that I don't necessarily know what I am becoming or where I am headed, and that not knowing does not free me from the obligation to "act now for the flourishing of all life everywhere," in the words of Rev. Lynice Pinkard. The "not knowing" is, I think, what it means to do creative work in the presence of the abyss. There is danger and risk, and the creative work is impossible without it. One thing is certain: I am never bored.

If this story speaks to you at all, I hope you will find your own way to jump in. I am happy to talk with you; relationship is so crucial to this work. You can reach me at ntorbett@hotmail.com.

Chapter Seven
Speak Out Sisters

INTRODUCTION

I am woman hear me roar
In numbers too big to ignore…
—From the song "I am Woman" by Helen Reddy

Few if any of the great social revolutions of our time have had as much impact on society as the women's movement. The gains women have made over the past century have been phenomenal: in education, employment, the arts and politics, as well as in the power to control their bodies and their futures. None of that has come easy. It has taken massive rallies, demonstrations, lobbying and speaking out loudly to bring about change.

One of the biggest accomplishments of the women's movement has been the formation of empowering organizations, ranging from the broad-based National Organization of Women (NOW) to more specific, issue-oriented groups like Women Against Military Madness (WAMM) and Code Pink, who have used aggressive, sometimes militant tactics to gain publicity for their campaigns against war and U.S. foreign policy. We are also witnessing precedent-setting political gains for women in the U.S. and abroad. Chile has elected the first female president of any country. A woman is now leading the U.S. House of Representatives, and the wife of a former president almost became her party's nominee for the highest office in the land and is now our Secretary of State. The election of a woman president in America may not be far away.

Despite these and many other gains, much needs to be done to make women fully equal and powerful members of society. Women still do not earn as much as men for doing similar work. The list of corporate executives in our country is heavily dominated by men. And women, especially those of color and lower income, are still victimized by some aspects of the legal system and lingering pockets of discrimination.

Facing this realization, the women's movement of today is increasingly diverse in its tactics, ranging from militant protests to working quietly within the system; from large-scale organizing and collaborations to individual and small-group efforts; from loud, demanding voices to soft-spoken homilies of common sense, all of which fall under the umbrella of the compassionate rebel revolution.

In the ensuing chapter, we meet several compassionate rebel "sisters" who are "speaking out" not only verbally but through social action for the causes they believe in. All of them have struggled mightily along the way. None of them has given up.

Samantha with daughter Astrea
(Photo courtesy of Samantha Smart)

SPEAK OUT SISTER
By Burt Berlowe and Anne Ness

It's a midsummer day in 1968, the most volatile year in our most turbulent decade. Eight-year-old Samantha Smart is glued to the TV set as the turmoil at the Democratic National Convention flashes across the screen. She has tuned in to search for her mother and older brother, convention delegates pledged to maverick presidential candidate Eugene McCarthy. What she sees instead punctures her childhood innocence—marching and fighting in the streets, unrest in the convention hall; the intricate, battle-scarred nomination process. It is but one of many early lessons she would receive in the rough-and-tumble world of American politics and the sound and fury of rebellion—lessons that would guide her for years to come.

Samantha is a child of the 1960s, born at the dawn of the counterculture movement. She has been a rebel since childhood, embracing the questioning of authority and the need to stand up for what she believes in. Her personal revolution has endured over the five decades of her life, deepening and gathering power, much as a small stream transforms over space and time to become a raging river.

"I was politicized by the age of eight, and I owed a great deal of that to my mother who worked very hard to see McCarthy elected," Samantha says years later. "My two brothers were conscientious objectors during the Vietnam War. One of them was arrested during a protest at the Minneapolis Aquatennial parade.

"My family lived an upper-middle-class existence in the Minnesota suburb of St. Louis Park," she recalls. "My parents were active in the Democratic Farmer Labor (DFL) Party and often entertained guests from the Soviet Union. We had a Leftist progressive household. Our home was full of books and conversations of social justice issues. I read Chairman Mao's *Little Red Book* in the third grade, along with Andre Malraux's *Man's Fate*. As I became more aware of the violent dynamics of capitalism, I became increasingly critical of it.

"My mother was a working woman and professional before that was common. My father worked for a military defense contractor. He was a program manager of an area that made gun mounts for the Navy. At the same time, he ran for the city council to try to prevent the installation of a proposed Creosote plant from coming into our neighborhood. When I was seventeen, I worked as a janitor at my dad's defense plant to help pay for college, even though I felt there was inconsistency in his working for the system and for military contractors. I loved the people I worked with, and that experience on the shop floor was illuminating for me.

"My maternal grandfather was a great influence on me. He served in World War I and the Spanish-American War, and often spoke of how he wished he had fought in the Russian Revolution. He had little formal education and was self-taught, but he was brilliant and eloquent, quoting Shakespeare and the poetry of Omar Khayam. He also was an atheist who forbade his children from attending church, despite being married to my lovely Irish Catholic grandmother. He saved all of us the suffering of having to attend church. I believe that was a critical factor in my being able to truly question and search for the truth. I was raised to believe as Karl Marx and my grandfather did that religion is the opiate of the masses. That wasn't easy, considering that most of my best friends were Jewish."

By the time she was a teenager, Samantha's political views had begun to set her apart from classmates and even from her family. "I had become more radical than my family had ever been, and it began to cause problems at home. For example, I was a Bob Dylan fan. We had some of his records that belonged to my parents. I remember one day writing down some of the lyrics to 'The Times They Are A Changin'' and leaving them in my room. My mother found them and got very angry. We had a virulent argument. She was concerned that I was rebelling against authority. But the Dylan record was theirs. I felt they were hypocrites."

Samantha went off to college at Harvard in the late 1970s. The streets of Cambridge were alive with protest. Students from Harvard were marching against their own school, urging divestment of funds from apartheid-ruled South Africa. In the midst of the crowd, Samantha felt right at home.

"It was euphoric. I had always felt kind of lonely. I was such an odd person, growing up on the fringe of everything. I was glad to find out that there were so many other people like me on campus. Not that Cambridge was a hotbed of radicalism in 1980. Most Harvard courses championed oppression and upheld the status quo. I read the autobiography of Malcolm X and was impressed by his absolute militancy in standing up to systems of oppression. He became one of my heroes. I read about the Chicago Eight and the Black Panthers while I was at Harvard, but generally the school had an elitist white supremacist attitude. The establishment would try to co-opt the radicalism of some students by minimizing protests. Fortunately, we found a way around that."

* * *

It was a special night at Samantha's Cambridge residence. Her dinner guest was a new hero in her life named Mel King. She had heard him speak on campus and learned that he was a visionary and community organizer. When King announced his candidacy for mayor of Boston, Samantha, now a Harvard graduate, volunteered fifty hours a week on his campaign and wrote his speeches, a series of columns, and parts of books that he published. "He was a mentor to me. We had a symbiotic relationship. He would open his home for brunches every Sunday morning. I met a lot of powerful people there. One night, we had Mel over for dinner. Something he did there sticks in my memory. He took a walnut and divided it in half and then into smaller pieces to indicate there was enough for all of us to share in this world. He lost the election, but the coalition continued on to spur the presidential bid of Jesse Jackson and become the original Rainbow Coalition. Today, the Rainbow Coalition and Green Party have merged to assume real power on the city level in Boston. That experience was a training ground for the rest of my life."

Samantha's work and struggle in solidarity with people of color compelled her to travel to the West Indies in the early 1980s. She had high expectations about her trip and the chance to interact with the indigenous population. She became immersed in the culture and politics of the country. She traveled to

Union Island, St. Vincent, and the Grenadines, an area of some three-and-a-half square miles, a stone's throw from Grenada, and once a haven for insurgent activity.

"In Grenada, I met with people who had been involved with the New Jewel movement and the Grenada revolution, who were raging against the oppressive puppet regime," she explains. "I became interested in the Grenada revolution and discovered that there had also been an attempted revolution in Union Island in 1979. I felt like I was on a mission. I fell in love with the place. I knew I was supposed to be there, that this was my home. I left Union Island several times but kept going back and eventually moved there in 1993."

While on the island, Samantha met and married a Vincentian Rastafarian, an act that didn't sit well with the local culture. "I went through a lot of trials being accepted as an outsider and white woman in a ninety-nine-percent black society. I had trouble establishing trust, and it took years to do so.

"At first, we lived in a single-room shack that had no electricity or plumbing. Later, we built our own house. I tried to assimilate. I wore dreadlocks, covered my hair in a stovepipe hat and became a strict vegetarian. But instead of fitting in, I encountered a lot of hostility and never had many friends. I became quite political. I worked as an investigative journalist for a local paper, trying to expose government corruption in this postcolonial society. I had some great successes in bringing hidden issues out into the open, but while many people respected and approved of my work, others felt that I had no business illuminating corruption and that I should leave."

The worst threats to Samantha's well-being, however, occurred in her own home. Her husband was a vehicle for the social oppression of women and children in a master-slave society. "He threatened us with physical harm and destruction. He threatened to burn down the house. He literally terrorized us. The neighbors knew what was going on but did nothing. I would beg friends for help and they would say, 'It's none of our business.'

"One day, I decided to take the children and leave. I arranged a ruse. He had foot problems and I paid for him to have a foot operation. While he was gone, we escaped with a couple of suitcases. If we would have stayed, he may well have killed us.

"Adjusting to life back in Minnesota was hard in the beginning. My kids were teased for wearing dreadlocks. Now only my daughter has them. She is a little warrior herself. She's holding on to that good energy. Actually, they're all doing great. My oldest boy calls me a 'hippie feminist freak.' I say 'I'm closer to a yippie mama revolutionary.' I want to instill the value of being a revolutionary in my children, encouraging them to challenge injustices wherever they find them."

Out of the pain of her life experiences as a battered woman in the West Indies, Samantha began to understand the role that sexism and patriarchy played in capitalist imperialism. "I came to the conclusion that patriarchy is the root of all problems. It is the oldest form of oppression and has provided the template for all other systems of oppression that followed. Patriarchy preceded private property, industrialism, capitalism, imperialism and racism. And yet, patriarchy and the matriarchies that it subverted are almost completely misunderstood and ignored.

"I wanted to come up with some new strategies for dismantling patriarchy. The logical reaction to patriarchy is matriarchy. Matriarchy is not women ruling over men. It is a different sort of power relationship. Patriarchy is power-over. Matriarchy is power-with."

* * *

On a fall day in 2002, Samantha and a small group of Twin Cities women activists got together to discuss the upcoming International Women's Day Celebration. They wanted to plan some kind of activity for that day that would showcase their concern about the oppression of women. Samantha sent out letters to some 100 organizations, calling for a meeting to plan an event. Several groups responded, but initial enthusiasm waned when Samantha brought up the issue of patriarchy. Many of the women who attended Samantha's first meeting never came back. "I invited them to work on patriarchy. They didn't want to do it. Even some radical feminists do not want to touch patriarchy. They think that makes you a man-hater, and some feel it is a 'white woman's issue.'"

Eventually, a group of some ten feminists did commit to carry on the cause. They met regularly at Samantha's house and at libraries and decided to form an organization that would catalyze their energy. They called it Speak Out Sisters.

Speak Out Sisters grew into a powerful voice for women. It held regular discussion groups, quilt shows, storytelling and movie nights, poetry readings, a town hall meeting on Women and War, a Whistle Stop Coffee Shop discussion series devoted to popular education, and the Revolutionary Women's Cabaret that included a series of performances by women artists celebrating their sheroes. "We planned a women's economic justice project," says Samantha, "creating an economic paradigm that will infect capitalism. We developed a community gardening project where women and children planted vegetables to sustain the collective."

Samantha joined a transformative womanist radio collective—The

Womanist Power Authority—on KFAI community radio, and produced dozens of radio shows illuminating the dynamics of patriarchal oppression.

"We were more about education and transforming the dominant paradigms of thought than about protests. After going to antiwar marches, I was disenchanted with the shallow analysis that seemed prevalent. I found it more meaningful to go deeper. Speak Out Sisters was about revolutionizing women power, unleashing the formidable force of women's energy to take on the energy of the oppressor, while raising consciousness and changing mindsets. Some of our actions were considered quite radical even to some people on the Left. Still, we made progress. More and more people heard about us, and, over time, we built a mailing list of over 300. Every week, someone new contacted me to express interest. I knew we were making an impact, moving the debate further to the Left because of the resistance we encountered. That resistance showed me that what we were doing was working.

"Ideally, I had hoped that we would collectively build an alternative paradigm of socioeconomic and political reality, one that, though born inside the belly of the beast, would infect the larger system with transformative love and creative beauty. Unfortunately, Speak Out Sisters dissolved from within after about four years. I believe that it was extremely difficult for women of such diverse backgrounds to ultimately come together and do the very hard work of deconstructing patriarchy because of the hold of internalized oppression on all our psyches. We were caught in the negative conundrum of pitting racism against patriarchy without being able to collectively arrive at an awareness of racism as a manifestation of patriarchy. I recall Angela Davis coming to Minneapolis to speak a few years ago and specifically warning against over-simplifying and ranking forms of oppression. Oppression is messy, she said, and we need to embrace the confusion and contradictions and be vigilant about seeking the deeper truths.

"I call myself a revolutionary matriarchal socialist. I'm for the complete abolition of capitalism, white privilege, patriarchy and all systems of oppression. I'm not a violent revolutionary. Guns are the tools of the oppressor and, as Audre Lord said, 'You can't use the master's tools to dismantle the master's house.' I believe capitalism as we know it will eventually crumble due to its inherent contradictions and the utter brutality and genocidal violence that it thrives upon. It is our job to keep attacking it so that the disintegration happens faster."

Even though she no longer has a formal organization as a venue, Samantha continues to speak out on issues she cares about. She recently made a spirited, reform-minded, unsuccessful run for the Minneapolis Library Board.

In 2006, it appeared that the Minneapolis mayor and city council were starving the public library system by underfunding it, threatening libraries with staff lay-offs, hour-curtailment and closure. Samantha organized with neighbors to raise money to keep the libraries open and exert pressure on the Library Board and the city to maintain full funding. "For me, the library is the most important public vehicle for poor people to obtain the information they need to become conscious of the realities of oppression and also the myriad ways in which humans have organized liberation struggles," Samantha says. "Closure of the libraries meant disaster for what Paolo Fiere describes as our 'humanization.' It was painful to lose the election; however, almost 20,000 people voted for me even with my radical messaging and few campaign dollars. The Minneapolis library system went on to dissolve and was absorbed into the county system."

The demise of Speak Out Sisters and the election loss exhausted Samantha and she went on political hiatus. After two decades of being self-employed, she went to work full-time for a workforce development nonprofit, raising funds for job training and re-entry programming.

In 2008, Samantha joined Windustry, a nonprofit advancing Community Wind, a collective ownership strategy for wind energy projects that catalyzes rural economic development and represents a democratization of energy production. "I find this work fascinating because it is not just about developing clean, renewable energy, which is now sweeping the nation, but also because the decentralization of energy production is really part of the transfer of the ownership of the means of production, a Marxian ideal that is truly happening across America. I love that!"

Samantha had wanted for several years to train in martial arts, inspired by the radical fringe film by Lizzie Borden, "Born in Flames." In the film, racist and sexist oppression continued in a post-revolutionary society, and women organized into militant cadres of warriors protecting other women from attack. Samantha had hoped that Speak Out Sisters members would engage in martial arts training together and form STAPIT! – Sisters Together Anti-Patriarchal Team – to powerfully intervene in instances of oppression against women. None of the other women would go along with that idea so Samantha went ahead on her own, training in Shotokan Karate at a Minneapolis YWCA. "I love Shotokan because it represents a life path of mindfulness and physicality into a harmonious practice of discipline. In Shokotan, one does not initiate an attack, but if attacked or if another is attacked, we train to counterattack and defeat the enemy. In terms of exercise, Karate strengthens muscles I never knew I had. As a discipline, Karate evolves the mind-comedy connection to a level of intuitive control of adverse situations."

A great deal of Samantha's life nowadays is devoted to raising her children.

"My children are all completely different and completely wonderful. I am so proud to see my oldest about to graduate from college and stand at the brink of his own life as a mature, independent and skilled man. My younger son is proving to be a brilliant scholar and awesome skateboarder, and my daughter has blossomed as an incredible athlete and leader among her peers. I look forward to seeing them grow and find their own ways to change the world. They are the most beautiful part of my life.

"I find the current moment extremely hopeful as people around the planet recognize this as a moment of fundamental transformation of the capitalist paradigm, as it undeniably falters. A window of possibility has been thrown open wide. Although Speak Out Sisters, which I hoped would be my life's work, did not survive as an organization, I hope that our efforts will have been enough of a pinprick in that balloon of illusion that some of the lies will be expelled and the truth will come rushing in. Revolution happens everywhere, everyday, and I strive to radiate revolution with all that I do. I'm an indomitable optimist. Che Guevara keeps me going. He said, 'A true revolutionary is guided by feelings of love.' That says it for me."

A MOTHER'S VIEW OF SAMANTHA

By Anne Ness

We women know about coming together in grief. We know about coming together against loneliness. We know about coming together in love and in acts of committed reliable kindness. But we still crave and insist upon coming together in power for power; coming together for a specific, collective political purpose each and every time we convene a meeting of as many of us we can persuade to sit or stand together united; power for the power to recreate the world as a universal safe house for our highest aspirations and our universally neglected or forsaken human rights.

—June Jordan

When I first met Samantha Smart, I was moved by the timbre of her voice as she recited the above quotation at the very first meeting of Speak Out Sisters November 19, 2002. Since then, her vision of creating a Fringe Festival of events celebrating International Women's Day has come to be with the creation of the Revolutionary Women's Cabaret. Thirty-five women put on performances honoring revolutionary women at six different cabarets around the Twin Cities during March of 2003.

Many other events have been organized by the Sisters, including: Woman Power Convergence; Women and the Genocide of Indigenous Peoples; Women and Economics; Saturday Mornin' Gone to Market (Farmers' Market series); Potluck Picnics in the Park (picnics and park shows series); Happy Hour for Harpies and Untamed Sheroes; Talk and Bonework: a living history workshop for social and personal change; and Women's History Month events.

I have never had a lot of time for activities outside of my home. I feel grateful if I can keep my home basically sanitary and get to work on time. My children are capable of absorbing every ounce of energy I have. But I always thought it was terribly wrong when people would say, "You'll grow out of having radical politics when you have children."

Samantha Smart is a beautiful example of why that is not true. She says: "Raising children and revolution are equal; they are the same. Raising children is a way of giving your love and energy to create a better future, and so is revolution. They go together. They can't be separated." Although she suffers economic hardship as a single mother, she finds time to send e-mails and network with her friends and acquaintances keeping us informed of local events.

In her artist bio for her performance in tribute to Rosa Luxemburg at the Revolutionary Women's Cabaret, Samantha was called "a revolutionary matriarchal socialist, mother, and warrior of truth and justice…who pursues the total revolutionary transformation of all systems of oppression through the course of every day." Samantha remains optimistic that we will create a better world for our children and our children's children by honoring the oppressed and taking leadership from women of color.

Whenever I brought my daughters to a Speak Out Sisters event, Samantha's daughter nurtured them the way her mother nurtures other women. Smiling, warm and loving, Samantha always made sure we had nutritious food and a welcoming, safe environment. Samantha makes it fun to be a revolutionary.

Mary Heller at home
(Photo by Michael Bayly)

MILLIONS OF MOMS
By Burt Berlowe

Pop! Pop! Pop!

The firecracker-like retorts ring in Mary Heller's head, exploding into graphic images bursting out of her past, rattling the windows of her mind—the sights and sounds that have shaped her life: noisy clashes on a campus lawn, a teacher's spontaneous tears and a whole nation crying, a mother's alarming wake-up call, a bleeding neighbor's plea for help, pistol barrels staring out of a store window, thousands of marching feet trying to stamp out the violence.

The memories come gradually, powerfully as Mary sits in the relative quiet of her bright, airy Minneapolis home near a small community lake. She has just returned from a rendezvous with her past—a trip to the cozy Ohio town of Yellow Springs, where she first experienced the pain and uncertainty of growing up and speaking up in a volatile world.

Yellow Springs, a small university community in southern Ohio with a history of liberal activism, is best known as the home of Antioch College, an academically and politically rich institution with a Leftist bent. The famous Underground Railroad started by civil rights activist Harriet Tubman once ran through Yellow Springs at night carrying loads of runaway slaves along the river from a bank to a tavern, using moss on a tree as a guide. The story of the Railroad is part of the lore of the town and one of the reasons why Yellow Springs ended up being a hotbed of activism. The town got its name from a mineral healing spring located in a nature preserve there. People would travel miles in covered wagons to seek healing from the natural spring.

Mary remembers Yellow Springs, her birthplace, as "a peaceful place where we spent our summers riding our bikes all over town as long we were home for dinner." But in the 1960s and '70s, the peacefulness was rudely disrupted. "There was a lot of involvement in the civil rights movement and the Vietnam war protests. I recall a time when the National Guard was in Yellow Springs during riots on campus in the late '60s over civil rights issues. We weren't allowed to leave the house for a while. I remember being really scared."

Yellow Springs was a racially balanced and tolerant community—about half white and half black, with generally good relations between the two and a determination to defend civil rights. However, there were exceptions. Mary reflects on one such incident and its ramifications: "There were two barber shops in town: one that did white people's hair and the other for blacks. That was about as segregated as it got in that town. One day, an African American Antioch student went into the white barber shop and asked for a hair cut. The barber referred him to the other barber shop. That's what started the whole commotion in town.

"During that time, some of my teachers were political activists and taught us to be the same. My mom was an activist and volunteer who hosted international students and did peace and justice mission work for the United Methodist church. Dad was an aeronautical engineer at an area air force base who believed in the military."

Mary's regular exposure to social change activity around her finally prompted her to join the crowd. "I remember sitting on the steps on the state capitol in Columbus after an hour drive on a school bus. I don't remember what we were protesting. It must have had something to do with funding schools or something. It was empowering to be on the school bus with all those people singing songs. There were lots of battles to fight. That was the beginning of my activism."

* * *

Pop! Pop! Pop!

The news exploded into the classroom where Mary was spending her first year in school. As her teacher, Mrs. Henry, was explaining a lesson, a booming voice poured out of a loud speaker.

Teachers and students, may I have your attention please. I have some bad news. President John F. Kennedy has been shot while riding on a motorcade in Dallas. I repeat, the president of the United States is the victim of an apparent assassination attempt. We are suspending classes until further notice.

A stunned silence fell over the classroom. Mrs. Henry began to weep, gently at first, then harder, as she ushered the first graders out to the playground. "We all stood and cried," Mary remembers. "We didn't know what to do or what it meant. It was scary."

On a profoundly tragic day four years later, Mary was in the kitchen with her mother and visiting grandparents preparing food when the news of Martin Luther King's assassination came on TV. "I wondered how that could happen to someone so nonviolent," she recalls. "It was the middle of the night a few months later when my mother shook me awake to tell me that Bobby Kennedy had been gunned down while campaigning in California." I remember thinking that it was all so senseless. But I was too young to feel that I had power to do anything. I just kind of filed it away."

* * *

The night began like many others for Mary, waitressing and bartending part-time in her Minneapolis neighborhood while going to school. Her next-door neighbor also worked at the restaurant. Many late nights they would walk home together. Sometimes, Mary made the short trek home on her own without incident through what was generally a desirable, low-crime neighborhood, with her neighbor possibly close behind.

That was the case in the wee hours of a 1989 morning until something happened that would change her life forever.

"I came home on this night about 1 a.m. I had just walked in my house when I heard this sound:

"Pop Pop Pop!"

It was the first time I had heard that kind of sound, but I knew what it was. Within a couple of minutes there was a furious pounding on the back door. It was the neighbor who had headed home about the same time I did. As I opened the door, he staggered into the house and fell on my kitchen floor in a river of blood. He lay there moaning and giving me instructions on what to do to save his life. I quit screaming long enough to call the police. He ended up surviving but lost motion in one arm and his psyche was altered. He later left town and I lost track of him. Apparently, it had been a robbery. Someone knew he had money in his pocket when he left the restaurant. It could have been me. I realized what happens when people are shot. It's ugly. I thought, 'Something has to be done about this.' Again I filed it away"

Several years later, Mary was out for a casual walk with her two children, when she suddenly stopped in her tracks. "I noticed that across the street a gun shop had opened up. I was shocked. It was a block and a half from my house. It was around the time that crime had increased so much that the city was being called 'Murderapolis.' That is when I kicked into gear. All of the anger I had about my previous experiences with guns and violence came back to me, and I was really pissed off.

"In the past, whenever any little storefront would open in the city notices were sent out and there would be community meetings. All of a sudden a gun shop opens up without the neighborhood being notified. There were absolutely no zoning laws that said you could open a gun shop.

"That was the beginning of my fight with City Hall. I was just another stay-at-home mom and I needed others to help me organize. I put together flyers and distributed them throughout the neighborhood calling a meeting to discuss the gun shop. We had an overflow crowd of neighborhood residents, city council members and police. Mark, the owner of the gun shop also came.

"What followed was my first realization of the power of the NRA (National Rifle Association). The issue went to court. The NRA paid Mark's legal bill, and we lost. It then became a battle between the city of Minneapolis and Mark. Eventually, we were able to enact zoning laws for the first time in Minneapolis that would prohibit gun shops in the city. But his shop had been grandfathered in. He eventually lost his lease but then opened another shop nearby, the last remaining gun dealer in Minneapolis. He was not permitted to sell guns. He got around it by renting them."

* * *

Even as Mary was organizing in her own community, gun violence elsewhere had spawned a major rebellion. In the wake of the school shooting at Columbine High School in Colorado, groups of women around the country planned a massive event in Washington, D.C. to demonstrate against gun violence. They called it the Million Moms March. "I just knew I had to be there," Mary says. With her nine-year-old daughter in tow, she went to join the Million Moms.

On May 14, 2000, more than a million mothers, fathers, children and survivors of gun violence came together in D.C. and in seventy-three other communities nationwide to protest and call for sensible laws that would limit firearm use. That historic event marked the beginning of the Million Moms March movement.

"It was my daughter's first time at a protest," Mary says. "We arrived a few days before the march and walked to the national mall where they were putting up banners and preparing for the speakers. You could just feel that it was going to be a really big event. That evening, we sat in our hotel room and sewed together a banner we made that said, 'Million Moms March.' The Saturday night before the march, it rained buckets so hard I thought the event would be cancelled. But the next day was as perfect as we could have imagined. It felt like a gift.

"We walked down Pennsylvania Avenue with our banner to the White House north lawn where the media was. We stopped for a minute, and two men came up to us. They asked, 'What is going on here?' We explained to them what was happening. It turns out they were members of the NRA. But they completely supported our effort. They were doctors who had seen the results of gun violence. They ended up taking our picture. Columbine had just happened. Gunfire was claiming thirteen kids each day in the United States. The public was behind us. The time had come to make changes in gun legislation. We thought, 'Enough is enough.'

"We marched from the Capitol to the Washington mall. There were about 800,000 people there and countless more in some fifty other rallies across the country: men women and children of all ages, several generations of families, grandmothers in wheel chairs. It was glorious to have so many people in common cause.

"As we rounded the corner of the mall and looked down at the scene of people who were already there, a man came up to my daughter, got in her face and said, 'I hope you both are shot and killed today.' He might have been part of a small counter protest. We let the comment go. But that night at the end of the day of joyful protest, the last thing my daughter said to me before going to bed was, 'I wish that man hadn't said that.'" When Mary got home to Minneapolis, she helped form a local chapter of the Million Moms March.

In 2004, Mary attended an international conference on small arms and light weapons as a member of Million Moms. "We were there to take a look at the issue of child soldiers. The United States is the main supplier of firearms around the globe. Many of these firearms end up in the hands of children who are armed and used in violent conflicts in various areas of the world. A twelve-year-old with an AK-47 is very powerful. I'll never forget someone telling me that an AK-47 in Ghana is worth the price of a chicken. You can trade a chicken for an AK-47. Depending on the situation, it might be two chickens. Some 500,000 people are wounded each year from small arms fire. That's one person every single minute worldwide.

"There were people at the conference from all over the world who came to talk about the trading of small arms and what we can do about it. Million Moms was the only delegation to meet the U.S. representative. He had close ties to the NRA. We listened to testimony from different countries and had breakout sessions. There was an international arms network that met, trying to figure out how to confront this problem. A program of recommended action came out of the conference. It was really a powerful experience to be at the United Nations as one voice of many discussing the problem and developing partnerships for future work to reduce the impact that small arms and light weapons have, particularly in the world of children and with great implications for poverty, crime, violent conflict and human rights."

* * *

"Mom, come quick. I have something to show you."

It was a weekday during the thick of the Million Moms fight against conceal-and-carry legislation (giving average citizens the right to carry concealed weapons in public). Mary had just come in the door when she heard her son cry out. He led her to the porch. Mary was shocked at what she saw. "Someone had shot out a window. There were bullet holes in the glass and casings that had landed on a rocking chair where I had I rocked my kids. They probably came from some kind of common rifle." There was no evidence of who may have fired the shots. "It could have been some neighborhood kids. But the thought occurred to me that it was someone out to get me because of my work with the Million Moms. I had recently received nasty e-mails from gun owners supporting the conceal-and-carry legislation.

"We are not gun banners," Mary says, explaining the role of the Million Moms. "We support the right to own and be able to hunt. We're not crazy anti-gun fanatics that want to take guns away. Our focus is sensible gun laws, like effective background checks for small firearms and consumer safety standards. Nobody needs to own assault weapons like AK-47 copycats or hand guns. We spent an incredible time lobbying and protesting to repeal the conceal-and-carry law in Minnesota. But the gun lobby won. We did win some things such as giving churches and businesses and schools the right to forbid guns on their premises. But I don't like seeing those signs everywhere in Minnesota that say, 'We ban guns on these premises.' What kind of message does that give to people coming to our state? We shouldn't have to live in a world where we have to have signs like that. I don't want to live in that kind of fear-driven world.

"The reason why the gun lobby fights so hard is so they can continue selling guns. Because of gun-show loopholes, virtually anybody, including terrorists, can buy a weapon at a gun show. The fact that people can acquire large supplies of guns scares me. We want to close the gun-show loophole to make it more difficult for anyone to purchase weapons at those events. We also are working on gun issues on the international level to stop the proliferation of small arms to countries to supply to child soldiers. Small arms are the weapons of mass destruction. Children and women are constantly in harm's way. We're educating the public on this, focusing on children. 'Sensible gun laws mean safe kids'—that's our message.

"Lately, the Minnesota chapter has been campaigning against passage of the statewide Shoot First legislation that would give average citizens the right to shoot anyone they thought was harming or about to harm them on their property. That means that if some kid was trying to steal a bike out of your garage, you could shoot them and there would be no legal recourse. You couldn't be prosecuted. We worked to keep Shoot First from getting any legs. It was defeated in committee by one vote. It will probably be back."

Mary is concerned that the issue of gun control has gotten lost in the morass of other national and international issues and that solutions are slow in coming, that the gun rights movement is losing steam. "After Columbine, we thought we had a wake-up call. We had the march in Washington. But nobody was listening to us. The NRA is really powerful. They even make guns in different colors to appeal to people. There's a colorful one that women can drop in their purse. This is a cause that is tragedy-driven. It's going to take a massive tragedy, worse than Virginia Tech, to get people interested enough to get anything done on gun legislation. But we're not going to throw in the towel. That's what the gun lobby wants us to do. It's going to be a marathon—

a long, drawn-out battle. I know that I want in my own small way to help save children and families from gun violence. For the sake of our children we have to persevere."

* * *

Mary recently worked for a few years in the University of Minnesota Human Rights Center's international fellowship program, helping to place foreign students in internship positions. She is currently the director of two programs promoting grassroots democracy: Debate Minnesota that stages debates among candidates for political office in the state and Minnesotans for Impartial Courts (MIC) started in November of 2007 to keep the state's courts independent and impartial. MIC has introduced constitutional amendments calling for merit selection of judicial candidates, performance evaluations of sitting judges made available to the public, and retention elections to ensure that voters, not special-interest groups, have the final say on who serves as their judges.

Currently, Mary divides her work time for these organizations between her home and an office space in downtown Minneapolis. She hopes to end that soon. Turning to look out of her dining room window, she points out a small shed on the far edge of her yard overlooking the lake in the midst of a nature habitat. "I would like to turn that into my office. Look, there goes an eagle," she exclaims, calling attention to the large bird flying by the shed. "We also have blue herons and a family of foxes. It's like a rural city of animals."

Because of the nonpartisanship and time commitment of her new jobs, Mary cannot be as active as she once was with the Million Moms. "I gave five years to the Moms. I had to get paid jobs. I still give the Moms money, but I can't have a leadership role or be in protests." She does want to continue to work on gun control on an international level, believing that that will be most productive and have the greatest long-term impact.

Mary notes the similarities between her current work and her years of Million Moms activism. "All of my projects are about good government and promoting Democracy—informing and engaging people in the political process, giving power to ordinary people."

Meanwhile, Mary's children have been picking up where she left off. Her son Frankie recently went to a national conference for high schoolers who were to come with a position promoting gun control. He sponsored a position paper to ban all handguns. He also joined his mom in a 2004 D.C. march. Mary's daughter has been a peer mediator at school, helping solve conflicts, and attending lots of rallies. Both have been active in student government.

Mary notes the common thread that ties together the work being done by the two Heller generations. "It's also about taking care of people, protecting the world we live in and the one our children are going to live in."

One day a few years ago, Mary got an unusual phone call. "There was this little girl named Jasmine who was going to be taken into child protective custody. Her mother was in treatment and her father was in jail. They were looking for a place for her to go. It turns out it was my husband Frank's great niece from Connecticut. When I went to the small arms conference, I brought her home from New York. She was four years old. She was so raw. She couldn't even walk well on her own. She was behind mentally and likely had been abused. When I asked her, 'What do you have for breakfast every day?' She said, 'Cold pizza and Diet Coke.'

"We had to teach her everything, to go back and start over. We were the bridge between her old and new world. She underwent a big change here. She developed her vocabulary and grew physically. We had her for three years. She's now with a new family that plans to adopt her. I'm still in touch with her. We talk on the phone, and I visit her once a month. I'm proud of the fact that we made life better for this one child."

* * *

During a recent summer, Mary took her kids to Yellow Springs. It was peaceful there, much as it was when she used to ride her bike through quiet streets. Antioch College remains the focal point of the community and a bastion of liberal thinking and activism. There are still historic markers reflecting on the history of the Underground Railroad. And, of course, there is the spring, a constant symbol of peace and healing. Mary's big-city world of fighting gun violence bears little resemblance to everyday life in Yellow Springs. She hopes that will change—that someday, without leaving her current environment, she will truly be able to go home again.

Jodie Evans speaking out
(Photo courtesy of Jodie Evans)

SHOCKING PINK
By Burt Berlowe

Jodie Evans kept on walking—purposely, desperately through the white storm, leaving the pain further and further behind. A persistent snow fell in sheets, drenching her thin clothing and exposed skin and piling up around her ankles, making each step more difficult than the last. She had walked through towns, farm fields, pastures and mountains; past speeding cars, strolling crowds, and grazing buffaloes; through morning, afternoon and twilight. The miles came and went …ten…twenty…thirty. Her legs grew weary and burned like fire against the cold ground. But her determination burned hotter. At twelve years old, she felt free for the first time in her life.

* * *

In the intensive care unit of the Las Vegas hospital room, six-month-old Jodie couldn't stop crying. No matter how much she was attended to by the caregivers around her, the tiny tears kept trickling down her pink cheeks. She seemed uncomfortable, even scared by her surroundings. Her condition had grown critical. What little Jodie so desperately needed wasn't to be found in a baby bottle or a pacifier or a spoonful of medicine. It could only come from the warmth of human touch.

Jodie was suffering from sensory deprivation due to parental neglect that had begun shortly after birth. Living with her father, she had been constantly deprived of the attention and nurturing necessary to thrive. When she finally was hospitalized, it took many hours of special medical care to bring her back to normal.

When Jodie was finally released from the hospital, she was taken away from her father and placed in the care of a grandmother. But her childhood troubles didn't end there. Her grandmother smoked and drank heavily. "When I was two years old, I would hide under clothes in a closet, so she couldn't find me," Jodie recalls. "My mother, who had previously divorced my dad, remarried. When I was four years old, my mother and her husband kidnapped me from grandmother's and took me to their house, where I was physically abused. My stepfather was in the Air Force and believed in authority and violence. He used brushes, switches, belts. He would hit me because I had soiled and wet the bed frequently or would sit me in a corner and wash my mouth out with soap.

"Mom freaked out at being a mom. I was the oldest of six kids, so I would take care of the others. My siblings were also aching for attention. Once, my mother, in a hysterical fit, kicked me down the stairs. I was made to feel wrong constantly. I was always told that I was bad, that I wasn't part of the family because I was a stepchild. The violence in our house was just overwhelming. Through all of the pain, I was conditioned not to cry or to tell anyone about the abuse. I came to believe that this was a normal life. It was the only one I had. So I created coping mechanisms such as trying to forgive my abusers. And I developed a pattern of taking care of myself. But I still had lots of behavior problems."

One day when she was twelve years old, Jodie decided she wouldn't take it any more. She made up her mind to run away from home that day and find her grandmother who was living across the river in Colorado. Before leaving for school that morning, she stole some cash from her brother's missionary fund. At 11 a.m., she slipped out of school in the midst of a snowstorm and never looked back. Carrying only the stolen money and the clothes on her back, she walked for eight hours and thirty-three miles.

At 7 p.m. Jodie finally "dropped back into civilization," stopping in Colorado Springs, where she would take the train the rest of the way. The first place she went was a Howard Johnson's restaurant where she satisfied her gnawing hunger. As she was leaving the restaurant, Jodie was detained by military police who took her to a mental hospital at the Air Force Academy. "They wanted to send me home, but I told them I wouldn't go home because I was being abused and hated my mother. In some ways, I hurt for home. But my survival mechanism was stronger. I felt guilt for a long time after that I did that.

"The therapists at the hospital made me go to my original dad, who I didn't know very well. When I showed up there the first night, I was given a lecture and told that I had to pay my own way, that he didn't have money, that he and his new wife couldn't handle another mouth to feed.

"Dad had never contributed to my support. He was a redneck bigot. He had said things like, 'Kill all the niggers. They're lazy bums.' He would go to church, read the Bible, and then not abide by its commandments. He worked at a missile site as an engineer building material for nuclear bombs. He'd come home wearing his badge. He didn't think about anything else. I took in laundry, baby sat, worked as a maid in hotels, ran a business. I didn't go to school much. Then one day, my stepmom came home and told me she was angry about the abuse that I had suffered, and she held me. She said, 'You poor girl, you took care of me.' That experience showed me what love was, that I was cared for. I realized that 'Oh my God, the world can be different.'

"I had a rough childhood in a lot of ways. In Las Vegas, where I initially lived with my birth parents, I worked the swing shift as a maid at the Dunes Hotel, starting at 8 p.m, an hour after I got home from school, and some nights not finishing until 3 a.m. Las Vegas, with all of its supposed glamour, was uninspiring to me. It was ugly. There were prostitutes, pimps and drug dealers. As I walked to or from work, guys in Cadillacs would pull up and ask me to strip at a club. As a result, I started busing to work. I managed to get good grades and a scholarship to go to art school.

"I was pretty wild in those days, often pushing the edge. I was a total rebel. I didn't go to the school prom because I thought it was too gauche. I smoked cigarettes on the school lawn. I thought everything was stupid. I was a normal '60s rebellious teenager who smoked pot and did LSD. Basically, I was a hippie.

"I was naturally attracted to anti-establishment criticism. I realized that there was lots of abuse of power by the governing class that affected vulnerable innocence victims. In high school, I studied about revolutions. My friends and I used to joke that revolutionaries never got their way, that we just replaced one power with the other.

"When I left home, I felt like I was surrounded by lies and manipulation, with everybody into image, like what their yard looked like and who had the best car, a 'Leave it to Beaver' culture. I didn't believe in love. I thought it was stupid. At the same time I was a loyal friend and those friendships gave me caring and joy. I had a girlfriend down the street whose mom took me in. That was the first adult I met that told the truth—who was a real person. Another real person I met was a teacher. She loved me totally. She would take me in her arms and call me 'scrumptious.' She was alive and real. She knew about the world I used to live in and that I had come this far. Dad found out about this relationship and broke it off. I cried that something valuable was taken away from me."

What Jodie lost at home, she discovered on the streets of Los Angeles. Her childhood experiences had taught her to care deeply about society's victims, and she sought out ways to act on those feelings. While she was living in L.A., the Watts riots rocked the city in 1969. Jodie joined with labor unions marching in the streets. It was her first taste of protest action, and she savored it. When the older brother of one of her best friends became a Vietnam War casualty, Jodie and twenty-five companions staged an antiwar rally at a military recruiting station. "We cared that adults were sending their children to war. And none of the reasons we were in that war made sense. My stepfather did two tours in Vietnam, some as a fighter pilot. He was a gung ho, conservative military man, but he quit just before retirement. He gave it all up because he didn't like how the war was going. That was the first time I felt connected to him."

At age sixteen Jodie began working on Senator George McGovern's presidential campaign. At a meeting of campaign volunteers at a club in Beverly Hills she met actor Warren Beatty and a young maverick politician named Jerry Brown. "Jerry was the first person I had met that was against capital punishment," Jodie fondly recalls. "I had been looking for someone who thought my way. He became my hero. It was my first orientation to politics. I really liked political events and campaigning, the strategy meetings and teach-ins, making flyers and posting them, the one-on-one conversations. It was alive. It was rife with passion and intensity and caring. I walked the precincts, stuffed envelopes, answered phones, started going to avant-garde movies. I was hungry to learn."

In the summer of 1973, Jodie took a job as a purchasing agent at a 300-person insurance company, "making more money than I ever dreamed of." When Jerry Brown decided to run for governor of California, she became his chief fundraiser. "The year I worked on his campaign I didn't attend school much. We got a lot of things done fast. And when he became governor, I was at his inaugural. We were best friends. By the beginning of 1976, we were talking about his running for president. He called me one Wednesday night and, by

Sunday, we had created a fundraiser that brought in $150,000. I moved to his campaign office in Baltimore. I got to watch Congress the night they voted to pull out of Vietnam. I got to dance with Hubert Humphrey. I couldn't believe I was there."

After Brown lost his presidential bid, Jodie ran his victorious 1978 governor's campaign and later directed special environmental and community development projects in his office, before again working on a gallant but futile 1980 presidential run.

During this time, Jodie married a man she had met on the campaign trail "That part of my life was a Cinderella story. Before I worked officially as a maid, I played that role at home, cleaning house for my sisters and mean stepmother, and being abused all the while. Now, I had found romance and had literally 'danced at the ball.' It was like a fairy tale come true."

Jodie became pregnant the day the 1980 campaign began. "I rebelled against the traditional methods of childbirth, having the baby at home by midwife, then jumping out of bed to work on the campaign. We never even got a crib. We took the baby everywhere in a basket. I didn't take a day off. I got pregnant a second time during the campaign. I was talking to Jerry Brown while I was in labor. My husband followed me around with the kids. We lost the election by 50,000 votes to Pete Wilson. After that, I started a committee to elect majorities of democrats to the U.S. Senate working with Representative Nancy Pelosi among others. We would take retreats together to Mexico."

* * *

The day on the Mexican beach started like so many others had during the Democratic committee retreats, full of magical moments, summer spunk and warm relationships, with a brisk wind that whipped the ocean tides shoreward.

Jodie and her family were relaxing on a beach, collecting sea shells and watching the waves roll in from the ocean nearby. What they didn't realize was that a storm was brewing beneath the waves that would bring the fairy tale carriage to a crashing halt.

"A tsunami wave suddenly came at us and took me and my husband and daughter into the ocean. It washed us back on the beach, but the force broke my daughter's neck. Losing her changed my life forever. I went crazy for about a year. It was unbearable. I survived physically but not emotionally. When you're blown that wide open, your whole life is brought back, and you start all over again. A therapist saw the article about the incident in the *Los Angeles Times* and contacted me. I saw him regularly for a year. I envisioned running my car off a cliff virtually every day. My husband and I separated. I lost fifty pounds. Friends were worried about me.

"To get away for a while, I went to visit my best friend Arianna Huffington, and we went on a double date to the ballet. My date was a guy named Max. I thought I was Cinderella again, that I had found Prince Charming. He was smart, handsome and rich. He had created one of the first computer companies. He lived in what I thought was a museum. We lived in separate homes half an hour apart. For a while, it was wonderful to be married to a 'prince.' But in the end I didn't like having all that money. I wanted a simpler life back. I left the marriage after two and a half years.

"I also rebelled against my religion and went exploring. It took me on a most beautiful, very intense spiritual path. I've fallen in love with the work of the spiritual leaders. I've been a Buddhist; done Shamanic work, tasted the philosophy of Druid Non Dualism, where you live out of your experience; worked for the Dali Lama and with Thich Nhat Hahn. I meditate at a Zen Center, do yoga and live a peaceful, rich life. I've produced the World Festival of Sacred Music held every three years. I've been blessed to have many teachers in my life who taught me the right values and to have support and love from people. When I'm reminded of the hypocrisy of my childhood, I take the spiritual path and move on. It inspires me to action."

* * *

In Watts, the site of Jodie's first protest march years before, the streets had exploded with racial riots. Jodie made up her mind to do something to heal the wounds of that cultural war and prevent them from reopening again. She helped start a community self-determination institute that negotiated a peace treaty between warring gang members. She continues to work in Watts to this day, counseling and teaching life skills to troubled youth and lobbying for government assistance. "When people talk about war, they never mention that fact that many of the youth in Watts had fathers who served in Vietnam. It's a way the war comes home to us. The Watts war has been going on for twenty years with 10,000 casualties, more than the conflict in Ireland and the Middle East. It gets better there for a while, then it gets worse again. It's the culture they grew up in. Youth on the streets have nothing else to do, so they get addicted to drugs then go to jail and become worse criminals."

* * *

A month after the 9/11 attacks on New York City, Jodie was sitting with some girlfriends she had met at an environmental conference. "We were horrified about 9/11. We had hoped that it wouldn't lead to war. (Antiwar activist) Medea Benjamin had given a speech in which she said, 'We all have to be unreasonable women.' Initially, we formed an informal group we called The Unreasonable Women. It was environmentally driven, but we ended up discussing lots of issues. We decided to take action to stop the Indian government from committing war crimes in their country. Diane, one of our members, went on a hunger strike in Texas to bring attention to the situation in India. We joined her, and people around the world fasted with us.

"In the meantime, we heard rumblings of a preemptive strike in Iraq. We knew that Congress would be considering a war resolution. Medea (Benjamin) and (activist-author) Starhawk were already in Washington protesting against the World Trade Organization. I went to join them. At that point, we decided to form an official organization. We were going to call it Code Hot Pink, a response to the government's code alerts. That name was already taken. We ended up with Code Pink. We did press releases. We demonstrated outside the White House at 8 a.m. one morning and stayed until they made us leave. Diane climbed up a post and was arrested.

"Code Pink did a four-month peace vigil outside of the White House during the coldest winter in Washington in many years. They also organized massive rallies, sit-ins in Congressional offices, 'wake-up calls' at Congress members' homes, and lobbying of the UN Security Council. On one occasion, they draped forty-foot pink slips in the shape of women's lingerie off rooftops to call for the firing of what they called 'armchair warriors,' and presented pink badges of courage to lonely truth tellers who spoke out for peace."

In February of 2003, when the invasion of Iraq seemed a certainty, Code Pink organized a fifteen-person delegation to go to Iraq. It was the first of several visits that Jodie and other Code Pink members have made to that country, during which they have gotten a firsthand view of the battlefront. "We looked into the belly of the beast from a hotel in Baghdad. I fell in love with the Iraq people, with their generosity and authenticity. What happened to them is horrible. There was no food and little water. Buildings were bombed out, and nobody in this country seemed to care.

"I also went to Iran where there are drums of war. The people there can't imagine an attack happening. It's beyond their imagination. But the same thing happened with the people in Iraq." Code Pink has already begun to work on stopping the next war, including the publication of a book on the subject, which sent co-editors Jodie and Medea on a nationwide tour.

Meanwhile, Code Pink has grown into one of largest and most active antiwar organizations. There are some 100 chapters around the world, stretching as far away as Australia, Canada and Great Britain. They have worked on various progressive issues, but have focused on creating public awareness of the dangers and costs of war.

At the 2004 Republican National Convention, George W. Bush was about to give his acceptance speech to a cheering crowd. Barely noticeable amidst the packed partisans, a small group of unwelcome visitors dressed in pink had found their way to the floor. Jodie was one of them. "We had friends who gave us passes. We had been there for three days scoping it out. We wanted a place where we could be visible. Medea wanted to shout something. I chose not to say anything but to let my attire say it. I had on a pink slip with the words 'Bush: Bring the Troops Home' written on it. I was prepared to be arrested.

"Medea had recently been arrested for disrupting Condoleezza Rice's speech. Activists need to be disruptive, to break through the lies and bring more people into truth. We live in a different reality than some people who take in life through television. We don't trust the media. We tell the people on the fence the truth.

"About midway through Bush's speech, Medea blurted out an antiwar slogan and unfurled a Bring the Troops Home flag. Both Medea and I were literally dragged out of the convention by security guards.

"On another occasion, Bush was visiting Santa Monica on a campaign tour. Our mission was to follow him around town. The police apprehended us and took us to the Santa Monica airport in the pink slips we were wearing. Bush supporters coming in on buses got in our face, pushing us around. The cops had to separate us. I walked to where I was going to stand when Bush came in. I was surrounded by people screaming vicious things at me. I said, 'What have I done? What's the problem? Don't I have a right to be here?' I've had my life threatened a lot. It's frightening. But then I'm used to being abused. I've always been an outcast. I like being different. It has made me a champion of the underdog.

"I want to be out in the streets doing something not because there's an end in sight but to look into the belly of the beast. I believe in human nature. Some form of sanity will rise to the surface. I don't know how long it will take. But all things are possible."

Terrie Ten Eyck with her personal artichoke
(Photo courtesy of Terrie Ten Eyck)

A PERSONAL ARTICHOKE

By Burt Berlowe

Nowadays, Terrie Ten Eyck lives in the lap of luxury. Her spacious, two-story home and wine-colored garage overlooking a small lake is located in one of St. Paul's fastest growing suburbs. The house is actually quite modest on the outside compared to its elegant interior. Step inside and you feel like you've opened the cover of *Better Homes and Gardens*. On the main floor, several large rooms are meticulously graced with glistening, contemporary furnishings and decorations. Upstairs is Terrie's home office where she conducts business when she's not making one of her frequent trips as a corporate consultant, assisting organizations in creating healthy cultures.

Terrie seems quite comfortable living alone in these expansive quarters despite a recent life-changing event in her marriage that ultimately led to a divorce. As a means of healing, she has consciously worked to design a space of grace and comfort, so much so that you would never guess how far she has come to get there.

Amidst all of the fine décor throughout her home, Terrie's most prized possession is a small, seemingly inconspicuous item hanging from a plant on her porch. It is, of all things, a replica of an artichoke. While it is unusually decorative, it is not there just for show. It is the metaphor of Terrie's life.

Seated on her porch couch, Terrie reaches for the gold, glistening artichoke. Holding it in her hands, she explains what it means to her. "The outside of the ordinary and prickly leafed artichoke doesn't show the gift it holds inside," she explains. "But as you peel away the outer layer of leaves, you get to the heart of what really lies within. The metaphor for me is that it holds the story that we each have lived, and you realize that you can't judge a person by their cover. As you peel the raw leaf off"—she mimics the peeling motion with her hands—"you get to the core. You find out what's in the core of each of us. It's like the soul of a person—who we are, the judgments we make, the fact that we each have a story, and sometimes we let the story live us and we become victims. For me, I've learned over the years to look for the sacred beauty of the story—to take an experience I've had, no matter how painful, and seek to find the spiritual lesson. I've learned, using the artichoke as a metaphor, to look beyond the peel to the core of every human being."

Within minutes, the real meaning of Terrie's words becomes clear. Gradually, she peels away the layers of her life, revealing what really lies within her soul.

* * *

"I became pregnant at sixteen, gave birth at seventeen and was chasing behind a rambunctious, inquisitive one-year-old by eighteen. I didn't have a clue.

"I'm not sure that I learned much about parenting from my own parents. Part of the reason is that I was raised in an era when the primary answer I received to my questions of 'Why?' was, 'Because.' And the only answer to 'How?' was, 'You don't need to know that now,' which might be part of the reason behind my becoming pregnant at such a young age.

"Society didn't offer many alternatives for unwed mothers in 1972. I would not be allowed back to school in the fall to finish my senior year. I was ostracized from my loving church. The Catholic home for unwed mothers my parents took me to for an interview required my signature, promising I would give the baby up for adoption within three days of giving birth. I recall running out of the old brownstone convent immediately upon hearing the nun's matter-of-fact words, leaving my parents behind feeling shocked and disgraced by my action. I only knew one sure thing in my life at that time: I would not give up this child to some stranger. I had absolutely no idea how I was going to make it all happen, but failure was not an option.

"I took full responsibility for the care, support and upbringing of a child who looked to me as her fearless leader, the One Who Knew All. I imagined that she looked to me much like I did to my mother. I knew that responding to her with 'because' and 'you don't need to know that' with some measure of reproach was not the path I wanted to take, yet I wasn't sure which one was—or what paths even existed for that matter. All I really understood at that tender age was that I was in charge, and it was a lot of responsibility. And while I succeeded in many ways I'm proud of, I also failed that child to a degree as I modeled the parenting style I grew up with, a discipline that today would be considered abusive. Through it all, I learned about forgiveness.

* * *

When bruised once,
You turn Black.
It's hard to acknowledge that it could happen again.
Twice, you turn Blue.
Astonished.
Awestruck.
Ashamed at the ignorance.
But three times, four times,
An eternity of times
And you turn Yellow
With Fear.
Fear of Rejection.
Fear of Loneliness.
Fear that you've lost the Faith
that healed you before. *

"I remember the first time he hit me. I was seven months pregnant. It was my wedding night. As long as I refused to go to the home for unwed mothers, my parents had given me a choice: Get married or give up the baby. I got married.

"I did not expect to get married the day we did. The plan was for me and my boyfriend to go to the county seat with our parents to receive special dispensation from a judge to get married. The judge not only granted the dispensation, but kindly offered to marry us. I was not ready psychologically. I wanted to feel like a bride. Instead, I was wearing an ugly purple pantsuit and looked like a swelled grape. We didn't have our wedding rings with us, and it all seemed as surreal as the paper doll brides my sister played with when we were growing up. Yet at this point in life, I was still a child.

"That evening, he told me it was time for me to go to bed. It was 8:00 at night and our friends had only arrived for a make-shift wedding reception an hour earlier. 'What? Go to bed!? What are you talking about?' My hours-old husband believed that he now had the right to tell me to go to bed. When I protested, he firmly took me by the arm out of the room and away from our friends. His fist hit my chest like a bullet.

"'I told you to go to bed and that's the way this works. Now get out of here,' he growled. Stunned and afraid, I walked up the stairs to my childhood bedroom. I obeyed like the little girl I still was."

* * *

"The Air Force hospital where I would give birth was located in Aurora, Colorado, just outside of Denver. In the two months since we had been married, I had been punched and kicked several times. Days before the birth, I went flying into an armchair in our furnished apartment, the force breaking off three of the four stubby legs of the chair and causing the baby to move wildly within me. I blessed each moment of movement after each powerful blow. I feared for both of our lives—mine and the baby's.

"Twenty days later, on a cold, Colorado mountain morning, I was on my way to the hospital to give birth, seventeen years old, alone, a thousand miles away from anyone I knew and too pregnant to board a plane to go home. I was alone in a way words will never describe. Eighteen hours later, my daughter was born. As I lay in the recovery room shortly after midnight, her father came into my room. This man who called himself my husband tenderly came over to me with a soft 'hello.' I smiled back, surprised at his kindness. Then he leaned into my ear and whispered in a nasty tone, 'You blew it.' He wanted a boy. He walked out of the room, signed the birth certificate with a name different than the one I had chosen for a girl, and left the hospital. A taxi would bring baby Sheila and me back to the abuse a few days later.

"Restationed six months later to New Mexico, we were living in a two-bedroom trailer near Holloman Air Force Base. In the year we lived there, I only met one couple with a healthy relationship. They were like Steve and Billie Jo from Petticoat Junction, solid, good-looking farm kids as innocent as the state of Indiana they came from. Like me, the rest of the wives who lived in the park all dealt with alcohol, drug use, and/or violence in one form or another from their husbands. My husband was drinking, doing drugs and dropping me to my knees with a fist in the gut for forgetting to buy his V8 juice, or for not using the potato peeler the way he wanted me to, or for having the flu and puking through the night, or just because on the clearest blue sunny day he'd feel like it.

"I don't remember how I got to the hospital the last time I was there. What I remember most were the divorce papers delivered to me, which he filed on the grounds that I had deserted him by my being in the hospital with the injuries he caused.

"One week later in a courtroom scene made for the movies, we were legally divorced. I was eighteen years old. As I sat bruised and shaken on the witness stand, the judge asked me if the man standing in front of him—the one now stating he really didn't want the divorce after all, was the one who hurt me. I whispered, 'Yes.'

"With a force that caused me to jump, and then cry, the judge commanded 'divorce granted' with the smash of his gavel. I was helped down from the stand, hobbling from a cracked tail bone and unable to see through my tears of both relief and the reality that I was now eighteen years old, divorced and raising a child alone, 2,700 miles away from any family or friends."

* * *

Terrie clutched the wheel of the aging Impala Super Sport and steered it to a stop where the street came to an end in the city's high-rent district. She stepped out into the evening chill, walked around to the passenger side, opened the door and gently lifted out and cradled her small child wrapped in blankets. She pulled on the door to the back seat and crawled in. In a moment she was lying prone on the seat, her cramped head and legs pressing hard against its edges, her eighteen-month-old baby wrapped in her arms. There, once again, they would spend the night.

As part of the divorce settlement, Terrie was awarded a 1968 Impala Super Sport. Despite the legal ending of the relationship, her ex was still a threat to her physical safety. In an attempt to hide from him, she left the trailer she was living in. Her meager income as a waitress wouldn't support rent, so the Impala became her home.

"We lived in that car for months. We parked on a dead-end street that had two houses on it. The sheriff lived on the left side of the street. He would check me out now and then to ensure things were fine. He and his wife always left their outside light on at night, which made me feel like someone was watching. In the house on the right lived a waitress I worked with, her boyfriend and her baby girl. She told me I could use her bathroom and shower if I wanted; and, if her roommate was traveling, I could even use the third bedroom, despite the fact that it housed a family of mice who were happy with the bowl of moldy Kraft macaroni and cheese left under the bed.

"When I lived in a car, I was judged harshly by others. People said I didn't have aspirations. I learned about unfair judgment and how people with little stature aren't valued much in our culture. It felt that I was a lifetime away from the Catholic middle-class family I grew up with in a clean and manicured neighborhood in St. Paul. I worked daily to keep both my head and spirits up while I prayed for a better outcome.

"I drew strength from the moments when I dreamed of better things, even when reality eventually came home to roost. I distinctly recall the night I sat in the car, leaning against the steering wheel with my arms wrapped around it, staring up at the stars. In a moment of clarity that came from somewhere within, I felt the strongest sense of conviction I had ever experienced and can still feel today, 'Someday,' I said to myself, 'I am going to own a business and drive a Jaguar.'

"I always thought Jaguars were the most beautiful car on the road—sleek, sexy, sassy. And owning my business would afford me financial freedom. I was trying to save enough money to fly home and start my life over. But perspectives are different than reality when you're eighteen and living in a car with a restless baby."

When Terrie had to work at the restaurant, she would leave her daughter Sheila at a day care in a local woman's home. One night, she picked Sheila up after work. Her car wasn't working, so she got a ride from a friend. She was looking forward to that night as they would be sleeping inside the house and Sheila would have a rare night of sleep in a crib. Walking into the house, she went to lay Sheila down in the crib.

"As I unwrapped the blanket around her, the dim light of the hallway cast a weird shadow on her face. I looked closer and the shadow didn't fade as my head blocked the direct light. I lit the small lamp on the dresser and looked again. My heart raced with fear and panic.

"'Joe come here…Nancy!' I called to my friends.

"They hurried into the room.

"'Look!' I cried.

"As I frantically unbuttoned the front of Sheila's little yellow chick cotton pajamas, I began to weigh the injuries. Her nostrils were swollen shut, her little nose twice its normal size, and her eyes were bruised. She had a puncture wound that went completely through her earlobe. Her entire rib cage was black and blue, and I could make out large finger print bruises along her spine.

"I remember screaming, 'We've got to get her to a hospital.'

"Joe took us to the Alamogordo city hospital where a doctor examined Sheila. Then we were told to wait. Within fifteen minutes, two police officers walked into the room. They wanted information. Thank God for Joe. He explained the evening chronologically while I sat stunned and numb. They wanted police photographs to be taken at the station. The doctor informed me that Sheila would have to be treated at the Air Force base hospital, as she was still considered military. He assured me it would be all right to go to the police station first. Joe drove us again.

"I cried as I followed orders to remove all of Sheila's clothing and hold her, arms and legs apart, as the police photographer snapped numerous pictures from all angles. It was hideous and nauseating, the emotionless face of the photographer seemingly untouched by the fact that my baby girl was being posed naked, beaten and crying, while he might have been thinking about the ham sandwich he left on his desk. I felt the disgust well up inside of me, that I could only control through locking my jaw. A laser beam focus shot from my eyes to his face, my mind daring him to meet my glare so that the poison of it would pierce the center of his heart. I wanted him to look at me and say, 'I'm sorry,' or at a minimum to show some sign of human compassion. I left angry, not realizing that my misplaced rage toward him was intended for the daycare provider who, unbeknownst to me at the time, was being arrested as we left for the military hospital.

"Sheila would spend a week in the hospital recovering from her injuries. The base doctor said that there were definite signs of abuse and discredited the daycare provider's story that Sheila had fallen from a rocking chair. Three days after her arrest, the daycare provider went home, the prosecutor citing a lack of evidence. I was too stunned to be angry. For the first time in my eighteen years of life I began to recognize the feeling of numbness that had entered my emotional soul. I packed Sheila's bag to leave. I needed to 'get the hell out of Dodge.' As far as I was concerned, this place was teaching me lessons no one needs to learn. One of the most important of those was to find my own voice, lost somewhere in a lack of self-worth and self-respect."

* * *

"Oh, the world of my little town had changed in two years. I was finally graduating from high school with the little sisters and brothers of my friends, kids who smoked dope in their cars before school each morning, some of them high on LSD.

"I decided to walk on graduation day with the class of 1975, two years later than I would have graduated with my own class. I had been married, beaten, molested, divorced, homeless, and a mother of a two-year-old by the time I turned nineteen. Receiving this diploma was of particular significance for me.

"I had traveled a long way and through many difficult experiences. I was proud of having survived those two years. It took a lot of courage. For all of the times I was vulnerable, scared, wounded and hurt, I gave thanks for my life and the resiliency I found in each new day.

"Along the way, I made conscious choices. I wanted my diploma, not a GED. I wanted my own apartment so as not to live off family. I accepted a better paying, boring job over one that offered less pay but more fun. And I turned down countless opportunities to go out with friends over staying home at night with my child. I had purpose, and I was committed to it. I was able to get my life on track as I moved down the road to finding my inspirational ground and self-reliance, the next stop on my journey.

"About four months after I had settled in to an apartment in Minnesota, a knock came at the door. I opened the door to find my ex-husband standing there. Every drop of blood in my body dropped to my feet. He was in full dress uniform looking as handsome as ever. I found my voice, 'What are you doing here?' I was angry he was able to find me."

"I'm home on leave for a month."

"So, what do you want?"

"To talk..."

"About what?"

"Us...all three of us. Terrie, I made a mistake. I was young, stupid, immature. I didn't realize what I had and how much I'd miss you. I'm so sorry and I want to try to work things out. There's a lot at stake here with Sheila."

"There's a lot at stake here for my physical safety!"

"Terrie, I was wrong! I've changed. I've been to anger counseling and to the base chaplain several times to get help. I've stopped drinking."

"One year to the month after I moved back to Minnesota, I was on my way to New Mexico with him. For some unknown psychological reason, I missed him, I loved him, and I felt I owed it to Sheila to give it one more try. If it didn't work out, I'd be able to walk away knowing I did the best I could and I'd never look back and regret my choice.

"I arrived back in New Mexico to the two-bedroom adobe house we rented for $150, complete with tarantulas and 123 dead cockroaches spread across the yellow painted kitchen floor and in every box we had brought into the house.

"Within two months, I had a chipped shoulder bone and a broken nose. I was being held captive in our home, not allowed to leave during the day, make phone calls home or speak to anyone. Sheila's third birthday represented another milestone as it was the day we escaped, again, from the terror. An Air Force friend, Duckie, his wife and their seven foster kids, helped pack me up early one morning after my ex-husband left for work. They got me a plane ticket and shipped everything home via Greyhound. To this day, thirty years later, I often think about that time, and I continue to thank God for Duckie and his wife.

"When the plane made a stop in Albuquerque, four hours away by car, I called my ex-husband at work to say goodbye. He was shocked. How could I leave him on Sheila's birthday? How could I do this to him? He would kill himself! He would kill me! I would never be safe again!

"I hung up, this time feeling confident in my ability to pick up the pieces again. I had developed a sense of personal ownership for my choices and an unwavering courage to move forward, alone."

* * *

When Terrie got back home in the fall of 1976, she stayed with her sister and her husband for a month before finding another apartment. She went to work for an insurance company and earned degrees in human relations and psychology. She seemed to be back on the track towards self-reliance, but her problems with relationships were far from over.

In 1980, Terrie married again and had another child. "He was a nice guy and I knew he would never hit me, and he didn't. But I found out he had another problem. After work almost every day he would go to a bar nearby for his customary six-pack before coming home. Eventually, I gave him an ultimatum—alcohol treatment or the marriage. He worked hard and got sober. Thirteen years into the relationship, it was the lack of healing with his sobriety that kept us disconnected emotionally and spiritually. While there was still love and respect, there wasn't the spiritual partnership that develops when two people connect beyond the surface of daily working, eating, sleeping and watching television. One day I woke up and thought about my life, wondering how I would feel if this were my life when I turned fifty. The thought scared the hell out of me, as I was lonely and felt alone sleeping next to this man. I asked for change. He wasn't interested. His response was, 'I'm a lazy guy. If you don't like it, leave.'"

Years later, Terrie would find herself in yet another troubled relationship that ended in dissolution, leaving her to wonder what it was in her decision-making that created these unhealthy patterns. "I've never had a healthy male relationship. I had to take care of my ailing dad during his later years while I was young and pregnant. I went from caring for him to caring for every other adult male I chose for my life. I was unaware of the pattern I was in of being attracted to men with problems that I unconsciously wanted to nurse. One day, I came to realize that maybe if I could save a man in my life, it would make up for not being able to save my dad. It was then that I uncovered the powerlessness I felt and the futile attempts I made to help everyone else but myself. In a process of uncovering my truth, of peeling off the leaves of my life's artichoke, I realized I needed to focus on getting to me, to get to know who I was as an individual beyond that seventeen-year-old girl I'd left behind."

* * *

Alone in her home, with her children grown and on their own, Terrie took a sabbatical from work to spend time learning, receiving counseling, attending Al-Anon meetings, and developing a sense of her self from new perspectives. "I realized that I usually looked outside of myself for comfort and support. Learning to provide that for myself was not something I had ever learned. I was raised to be dependent on others. In junior high, my mother was still picking out what I would wear to school. Showing emotion, whether it was anger or even loud, joyful laughter was either prohibited or stifled. Showing how I really was inside wasn't something I had much experience with. Speaking my truth and being comfortable with me was new. I learned that what I was really interested in was giving beyond myself to a good cause without feeling like I had to fix the world."

The opportunity to turn that newfound interest into social change came unexpectedly as Terrie enjoyed material success in her professional life. She moved through corporate promotions swiftly, gaining leadership responsibilities and senior management positions where she earned six-figure salaries. And in the process, she says, "I discovered a world of corrupted egos and actions. I realized that I wanted to effect change with the leaders of organizations, to create healthy work environments where people could feel pride in, and appreciation for, their work."

Never forgetting the dream she once held while living in her car, Terrie started her own business, Intellectual Architects, in 1994. By 1997, her business flourishing, she signed a two-year lease on a 1998 Jaguar XJS convertible. During her master's program at St. Mary's University, she created a leadership product called Spirited Cultures (formerly Fearless Leadership). This leadership-learning process is a reflection of her own individual journey as a parent, a corporate leader and a human being. "Basically," she says, "it's where people gather to learn together and to explore how to be more fully effective human beings—physically, mentally, emotionally and spiritually. It's a process wherein we learn that life is not only about ourselves, but about each other and the greater whole. It's about how to be human together in a different paradigm. Today, my dream is about creating Spirited Cultures within the workplace, in families and communities, where everyone is included, respected and treated with dignity. It all comes from the tough lessons I turned into gifts. The life I've lived is bigger and better than the dreams that have come true.

"My life is evolving today, and I'm not sure what the next path will bring. But wherever I go in the future, I know it will involve thinking outwardly while taking care of my own self in more healthy ways. While it's been quite a journey and this story is but a microcosm of the whole, I'm still the same person I was living in that car. It came as a surprise to me that some of the same people who judged me negatively when I lived in the car were so proud of me when I had a six-figure income and a beautiful home. The value of what I own or where I live says nothing of the value of who I am as a person. The material world, while nice, is not what it's all about for me. What it is all about is what's at the center of the artichoke—ourselves as individual, spiritual beings, and each other, being there for one another in ways that serve a greater purpose of the heart. How we each get there is not for any of us to judge. For we each have our own unique stories, and this one is mine."

*Poem by Terrie Ten Eyck

Lama Shenpen
(Photo courtesy of Tony Simon)

A CHANGE OF HEART
By Tony Simon

Lama Shenpen Drolma is one of only a handful of North America women to be ordained as a Lama in the tradition of Tibetan Buddhism. The path that led her to Tibetan Buddhism is an exceptional story of tireless efforts to understand and respond to a landscape of suffering and injustice.

"I was fourteen when I first got involved in political activism," the Lama explains, "first in the civil rights movement, then in the peace movement, and finally in the feminist and battered women's movements. In the early '70s, I began working with the economic issues underlying wife beating. At the time, I felt that wife beating was rooted in a lack of economic independence that women who work twenty-four/seven as homemakers for no remuneration are socially and financially dependent on their husbands."

During her early years, the Lama-to-be was known by her real name—Lisa Leghorn. She was a pioneer in the feminist movement—organizing consciousness-raising groups, authoring analysis, establishing women's shelters, and raising public awareness about women's oppression. She lectured widely in hundreds of venues around the country, including many television and radio talk shows, wrote many articles, and co-authored numerous publications, the most extensive of which was a book called *Woman's Worth: Sexual Economics and the World of Women*, a cross-cultural analysis of women's unpaid labor. But after years of research, organizing and activism, Lisa became concerned that she wasn't getting to the root of the problem, and that her own limitations were compromising her effectiveness.

"I felt like all the things we were trying to do didn't change consciousness, only concepts, and only sometimes. Through our efforts in educating the public, there was some shift in people's ideas about women's role in the family and the world. The idea that it was okay to beat a woman evolved over the years, as did people's concepts about a woman's place being in the home. But wife beating continued, as did economic and political inequality. I started to think that something deeper needed to change. We can try to change outer conditions—legally, socially, politically, economically, but until we change the consciousness that gives rise to those outer institutions, our efforts will just produce another version of the same old thing. The more community organizing I did, the more I saw that any change we make is superficial unless we can change minds. The question became for me: how do we transform consciousness in order to truly uproot the causes of suffering?

"It also seemed more and more that my organizing had become too reactive, that everything I was doing to help battered women—legislative lobbying, training social workers, crisis hotlines, shelters—just wasn't enough. On one occasion, we went through a truly exhaustive process to try to protect a woman and her children from a man who could have killed all of us. It was a very dangerous situation and quite traumatic for everyone involved. We went to extraordinary lengths to protect her, and at the end of it all, she went back to him.

"That was a major turning point for me. This woman knew how violent he was, and she didn't have any illusions that he had changed—so why did she go back? I just couldn't understand it. At that point, I started to see that the causes of suffering were deeper than I had thought, that there was something else going on that I didn't understand.

"I also saw my own disappointment when she went back to him. The purpose of my work wasn't to break up families, so why was I so upset? It was partly because I cared about her and her children and wanted to offer them an alternative. But I also saw how invested I was in her going the way I thought she needed to go to be safe and how that was causing me to burn out. I needed to find a relationship to my work that allowed me to keep going. I realized that I had to go beyond simply reacting to suffering to developing a more creative, proactive response that included a vision of possible alternatives.

"What you need is faith."

Lisa's Christian friend looked straight at her, emphatically suggesting the solution to her struggle. The unexpected words jolted her momentarily, leaving her without a ready response. Later, she would ponder the comment within the context of her own belief system.

"I knew he was right. But I had to ask myself, 'Faith in what?' My faith had been placed in social change movements and ideologies, in things that were fallible and emphasized dichotomies like man/woman, black/white, have/have not and so forth. Slowly, I began to sense that the dichotomy itself was the problem—our tendency to treat one another as 'other.'"

Eventually, Lisa realized that her search for a deeper approach to problems had something to do with spirituality—that in order to move forward, she needed to find a spiritual path, although she had no idea where it would lead her.

For a while, the path meandered and Lisa walked with an open mind. She explored various spiritual traditions, trying to find what would suit her best. Then in 1987, she met a Tibetan Buddhist meditation master named H.E. Chagdud Tulku Rinpoche and began to study with him. She eventually became his interpreter and the administrator of his burgeoning North American activities. In 1996, he ordained her as Lama Shenpen Drolma.

"When I found Rinpoche and began to study Buddhism," Lama says, "I discovered a context for understanding my life's purpose, something I had always felt intuitively—the aspiration to do everything I could to help end the suffering that so many endure so much of their lives. Through Buddhist meditations, I began to see how experiences of warfare, dissension, conflict and disharmony really begin in the mind; that if we transform the mind that gives rise to duality, then there will be no framework with which to experience reality dualistically, whether racially, sexually, politically or economically, Buddhist teachings contain a profound and extensive understanding of duality, how we give rise to it, and how it leads to suffering.

"As I started to meditate, I witnessed the origins of duality in my own mind; the strong habit to separate a sense of myself as the perceiver from the objects of my perception, then to create judgments based on those perceptions. For example, the process of seeing someone we disagree with can move us to harsh judgments and to blurting out something hurtful. My experience of non-dual awareness, on the other hand, has been completely expansive, open and compassionate towards others—a genuinely equal regard for all living beings.

"Through teachings and direct experience, I finally got to the root of suffering. With the blessings of my teacher, I received methods I could use to resolve dualistic, self-centered habits of mind and help others to do the same."

At Lama's behest, Rinpoche created a nondenominational format for teaching transformative tools that people could use regardless of their spiritual tradition. He called it "Bodhisattva Peace Training," and authorized Lama to teach it. She has since offered the training to at-risk youth, youth workers, battered women's advocates, peace activists and a variety of others. She has compiled and edited the trainings into a book titled *Change of Heart: The Bodhisattva Peace Training of Chagdud Tulk*. At Iron Knot Ranch, a Buddhist retreat center in southern New Mexico, Lama is establishing an institute for training teachers with a goal of eventually making the course available throughout the world.

"For social change, or any kind of change to be effective," Lama muses, "we have to be able to envision and articulate a way forward that is intrinsically positive and based upon complete confidence in our capacity as human beings to be the best we can be. Our strategies must be grounded in a firm belief in what is inherently good in all of us and in effective means for actualizing that potential. If we don't act in this way or if we don't act at all, then we are just reacting to the negative in ourselves and others.

"Buddhism is not the only path that offers the means to make such transformation possible. The power of the work of Martin Luther King, of Mahatma Gandhi, and of many other great visionaries who led us through pivotal changes in history lies in the fact that they believed in, spoke to, and awakened the best in everyone. No matter which spiritual path we follow, as long as it offers methods for actualizing the sacred qualities inherent in each of us, it will offer those who rely on that path the means to help end suffering and bring about happiness for themselves and others.

"For peace to prevail, we must do more than change our ideas. We have to change our hearts. We must resolve our selfishness and negativity completely, so that we have an openness of heart from which to create something different. Until we give rise to a genuine compassion towards every human being equally, we can't create something truly peaceful. This change of heart is the purpose and promise of spiritual work."

Jane Evershed with her artwork showing a mother who had just given birth to genetically deformed baby caused by depleted uranium in the 1991 Gulf War. She is standing across from Alliant Techsystems, a manufacturer of military weapons in Minneapolis (Photo by Michael Bayly)

MY ART IS MY ACTIVISM
By Andrea J. Peterson

Ever since she was a little girl, Jane Evershed wanted to be an artist. Her talent blossomed at a very young age, aided by art materials from her Auntie Rannie. In school, she always won the art prize.

But something else was going on that would make Jane a special kind of artist. From the time of her childhood, she was acutely aware of the pain and suffering of others and the injustice that caused it.

Jane was born in Worthing, England. Her mother is a South African who met Jane's father during World War II when the British came to her country.

They moved to England until Jane was nine, when she returned with her mother to South Africa.

South Africa at that time was steeped in apartheid. Jane lived there until she was twenty-four and saw the effects of the racism firsthand. "The inspiration for me to do my art and poetry was sparked by growing up white in South Africa and seeing (racial) disparity right on my doorstep," she says. "When I became an adult, I naturally felt guilty about earning a living at the expense of the indigenous Africans who did not even have the right to vote in the country of their birth. I made up for it in my own way by doing political cartoons for the Confederation of South African Trade Unions Newspaper at no charge."

As a white woman, Jane realized how privileged she was to receive a good education. But she often wondered where the African kids were at school, especially the Zulus where her family lived. Her education soon became about much more than book learning. "Growing up in South Africa was almost like a school for learning about oppression because the injustice of the world was so obvious and blatant. And because I went there from England when I was nine years old, they weren't able to brainwash me successfully, like a lot of other children were, into believing they were superior just by virtue of being white."

The tension and turmoil in South Africa from apartheid continued to build, increasing fear among the white South Africans and casting doubt on how much longer they could safely live there. Jane remembers her father saying, "What do you think—we have another five years or another three years?"

"People knew that time was running out and they couldn't maintain it because there were twenty-three million African people in South Africa and only five million white people," Jane explains. "So it was impossible to maintain apartheid. It had to be maintained through the South African police and a lot of guns and curfews. It just became too huge to monitor."

The unfairness of apartheid crystallized for Jane one day at a traffic light when she saw an old Zulu man crossing the street. "I realized that he had basically been going into the bowels of the Earth to dig up gold and diamonds on behalf of the rich white elite of South Africa. This was a group to which I reluctantly belonged, yet from which I gained great privileges. I had been brought here as a child of nine from England to rack up the white side of the equation."

In addition to the cartoons she drew for the trade union paper, Jane also participated in anti-apartheid activities, which eventually landed her in jail. While in prison, she noticed how the jailers made African women sing for their supper. "It was so insidious. There was this beautiful singing, but they used it to humiliate them. They knew all the psychological tactics to keep people down and being shamed.

"I was only there for two days and a night, but it was long enough to make me realize that I could end up spending the rest of my life in jail if I stayed in South Africa. Because there wasn't freedom of speech in that country, I realized that I would be better off outside of the country, speaking out."

Jane was able to leave South Africa in 1984 and made her way to the United States. "I saw it as my responsibility upon arriving in America to use freedom of speech to promote awareness of apartheid. I sought to use my education to help dismantle the very system that had hoped to brainwash me."

Leaving South Africa broadened Jane's perspective, allowing her to see injustice as larger than apartheid. "It was when I left, after the fact, that I realized that women were oppressed on a far greater scale in South Africa than elsewhere. It was hard to see the context of that country because there is oppression of both men and women. But women are at the bottom of the rung, the most oppressed. There's still such male superiority. When I saw the oppression in South Africa, I also realized the oppression of women worldwide is a serious problem."

Jane's awareness of the universal oppression of women has grown and clarified to the point where she is completely committed to empowering women to have a greater role in governing the world. "What seems to be missing from our society, as far as global rule goes, is the unempowered women element," she says. "If I were out in space looking down on the Earth, I think I'd start right there with the fact that women are disenfranchised.

"And I don't say that lightly because people say, 'Oh, it's so simplistic to say that's a male/female problem.' It's not men against women against men. I'm not talking about that. I'm talking about the fact that there are thousands of cultures on the planet, but only two sexes. And there's been no feminine input. I know I'm starting to sound like I'm blaming men, but the system doesn't allow women to put their energy in so that we can have some balance.

"I think the thing is, these women are working, healing, taking care of children, taking care of the elderly, and it makes them missing from society. Through my cards and paintings, I feel I can reach a wide audience of women and inspire and empower them."

Jane's words are backed up by personal experience. She raised kids as a single mother, making a living from art. "It was a very challenging thing," she says. "But I did it."

One of Jane's passions is to get women into positions of power so that they can change the system. "Gender parity is underrated, but so essential. It would only take about thirty-three percent of women in government for policies to change away from protecting the military protectorate. More government funds would be allocated for domestic issues like education and housing if more women were in government."

Once she started pulling on the thread of oppression first encountered in the apartheid system of South Africa, and then connected to the worldwide oppression of women, Jane has found it tied to the arms race, nuclear proliferation and abuse of the Earth. She fears for our planet's survival.

"We women don't have our seat at the table of global consequence. Patriarchal systems pretend that God is supreme, yet it is evident that money is the real god of worship. Under patriarchal systems, you get the most money by buying and selling arms. So God is money, His son is the gun and all armaments combined, and the Holy Spirit then becomes profits retained therein. The trinity of Earth, Heaven and Spirit has been made pornographic by the raping of the Earth, which is legitimized by patriarchal law. Patriarchal standards refuse to integrate the laws of nature in their day-to-day dealings of profit over everything, hence the global devastation we witness today. This is the time of woman."

Talking with Jane, one hears both her fear and dismay over the current condition of the world, and also her belief that there is hope that the world can be saved and nurtured for future generations. One of her most exuberant paintings is called *Who Let the Girls Out.* "The most beautiful energy on planet Earth is little-girl energy," Jane says. "If you look at this painting, you've got all these people deciding our fate. If you look closely, it says, 'Hell is on our agenda.' What we need is an infusion of girl energy and love in reverence to the earth. And so, I've shown here a beautiful fish, butterflies, moths, flowers and wildlife. Patriarchal systems take the ingenuity of nature herself to create weapons, like the streamlining of the sand shark and the stingray, and usurp it to destroy the very Earth form where the ideas came from. It seems so ludicrous to me."

While Jane has been an artist throughout her life, she didn't start painting in earnest until she arrived in America. Her oil paintings began with her *Dream for South Africa* series, which she created to support herself financially and also to remember the natural beauty of South Africa while addressing apartheid. As she realized the worldwide extent of female oppression, she created the *Power of Women* series. She has gone on to create several more series, including *Realm of the Nurturing Man, The Sacred Scarred Earth, Revisiting Our Souls*, and *The New Millennium and Beyond.*

Jane paints because she has to. Her artwork is truly self-expression. And it keeps her alive in more ways than one. As she explains, "Being an artist saved my life many times because it's both therapy for me and I make a living from it. I also use it to convey a message."

A self-taught artist, Jane paints in several different styles, although all are united by a bold use of color as well as strong visual energy. Her *Dream of Africa* and *Power of Women* series, for example, are characteristic of much of her work with her vibrant, energetic use of color and shapes. These may be two-dimensional images, but the people inhabiting them fairly dance off the page.

Some of Jane's allegorical portraits have a quality reminiscent of Frida Kahlo's work. Jane is willing to consider the comparison since they're both women artists with a conscience working on human-size paintings. But after that, Jane says, "She is a far superior painter and a true master of her craft. My art is a vehicle to convey a message. I'm not concerned with the mastery of it."

Recently, Jane has been commemorating the actions of women activists, including Mary Kelly, an Irish woman who took an axe to a Boeing 747 that was ferrying munitions through Shannon Airport in Ireland. (The painting) *Nuns on a Higher Plane* pays homage to three nuns who smashed up an Air Force fighter jet. Jane has been inspired by these and other contemporary antiwar activists and has created their portraits "to bring light and inspiration to other women to see that there are many women doing incredible, brave things."

Jane has also produced several graphic paintings illustrating the horrible effects of depleted uranium in munitions in Iraq. One painting shows women running screaming from hospitals because they've given birth to children with horrific deformities, including some without spines. Another shows a child's face with a grotesque rearrangement of its features, with the nose above the eyes. At first glance, it appears Picasso-like, but Jane assures me it represents reality. "I try to bring awareness to what's really happening during war through my art."

In April of 2003, Jane was arrested along with twenty-seven other protestors outside of Alliant Tech in Edina, Minnesota for trying to give a letter to the CEO about the company's use of depleted uranium in its weapon systems. Jane explains: "We were called the Alliant twenty-eight. We all went on trial and were found not guilty under international human rights laws. That's about the most radical thing I've done lately."

Jane has joined the board of Women Against Military Madness (WAMM) and has spoken and taught at numerous high schools and colleges. Her artwork has been commissioned by various organizations, including the League of Women Voters for the seventy-fifth anniversary of women's suffrage. Her print commemorating that anniversary was presented to Hillary Rodham Clinton in Washington, D.C.

The house where Jane lives has been used both as a backdrop for her political beliefs (she has hung various antiwar signs there) and as her professional gallery for her own shows and for fundraising events for other causes. After years of living in a spacious, gracious home with an inspiring view of Lake of the Isles, she downsized to a smaller space after her children moved. She wanted to practice what she preached about living simply and about humans needing to live in harmony with nature. "As long as we're on Earth, we need to experience what it's like to be an earthling. We're living as earth-things. We go from our house to our cars to the mall, on roads, back to the house. I love looking to nature for answers. Everything's been ingeniously created. It makes human beings look dumb. Our biggest mistake has been to fiddle with nature, when it was already perfect to begin with."

Towards this purpose, Jane has purchased thirty-five acres of natural beauty near Hayward, Wisconsin, which she eventually plans to turn into an artist and writer retreat center. For now, a little A-frame is the only building on the property, but it represents more than simply shelter. It is the seed for the beginning of Jane's dream of providing a place where others can reconnect with nature and nurture their creativity.

"My dream of dreams, pipedream that it is, is that I would love to see the military turn into environmental protectors. Instead of being a destructive force, the military needs to be a protective force. The best thing they could ever do if the Earth is ever going to survive is to protect the Earth."

*Jane multiplies the reach of her message by reproducing her paintings on note cards, posters, bookmarks, gift bags and journals. Her cards and posters can be found in many gift stores. Her paintings are also reproduced in her annual calendar which is available through major booksellers. Her products are being sold in the United States, Canada, England and other countries. Her website is www.janeevershed.com.

Chapter Eight
Generation Next: The Future Makers

INTRODUCTION

And I particularly say this to young people of every faith in every country – you, more than anyone, have the ability to re-imagine the world, to remake this world.

—Barack Obama

With all of its history and references to current affairs, this book is really about a world still being born. Its primary target is what we call Generation Next, the young, budding compassionate rebels who are and will be shaping the future of society for many years to come.

How the world of future generations turns out depends on how well current leaders and activists pave the way. In telling the stories in this book, we have almost always begun with the experiences of formulative years. In every case, those experiences have set a pattern of behavior that carried through into adulthood. All children have the potential to be compassionate rebels and make positive change. Only some will be up to the challenge.

After a prolonged period of apathy, youth activism is popping up everywhere. Young people are protesting war and campus military recruiting, globalization, global warming, and other relevant issues while working for positive solutions to those problems. An exploding hip hop culture has empowered youth of color to influence elections and public policy and to take back the streets of urban America. And, most recently, youth played an instrumental role in the campaign and election of Barack Obama, events that have signaled a generational shift bubbling up in our country, bringing with it hope of a better world in years to come.

The following chapter is about that hope. It features stories of young people who have turned their anger and rebellion into a positive force for social transformation. They are the next generation of leaders, the makers of the future, the architects of the change that is coming to America.

Ben Grosscup testifying at NOFA public meeting
(Photo by Vince Connor)

STOKING THE FIRE
By Burt Berlowe

It seems like 1776 all over again. Inside the New England community hall, an American revolution is brewing. In a blatant exercise of direct democracy, local citizens have gathered in a town meeting to take governing into their own hands.

Standing in the center of the room speaking to the grassroots gathering is a young man born more than 200 years after the colonial town meeting became the staple of an emerging new country. Ben Grosscup, midway into his twenties, burning with youthful fire and veteran moxie, is leading the rebirth of a public process as old as the nation itself.

Ben is a complex combination of academic wisdom and street savvy, a former "boy wonder" of Twin Cities activism with a long list of social transformation accomplishments that belie his age. He can espouse organizing theory and discuss complicated genetics issues even as he is helping his family plan a neighborhood meeting to discuss protests against the Iraq War. He has walked the streets of Iraq, campaigned for presidential candidates, been involved in anti-globalization, anti-nuclear, antiwar and pro-environmental demonstrations, sometimes leading to arrest and jail time. He has written academic papers on biotechnology, social ecology, radical political thought and organizing theory, in addition to producing and marketing two music CDs. Most recently, he has led efforts to save America's food supply and preserve its democratic tradition. It's all part of an evolution that began when Ben was just coming into boyhood.

* * *

Ben shifts in his chair into a lotus yoga position, crossing his legs under each other as he scarfs down some yogurt and granola, gesturing with his free hand for emphasis.

Nearby, on the brightly lit sun porch in his Minneapolis home, a guitar case wearing an anti-globalization sticker lies on the floor, looking up at a copy of a CD of Ben's original protest songs. In a stack close to Ben are samples of material he has written—articles and booklets in progress on subjects like "Re-thinking radical politics in an era of advanced capitalism." It is all a clear indication of his ongoing political transformation.

"When I was in the third grade," Ben recalls, "I was writing letters to the president saying 'good job on the Gulf War.' I was captivated by the thought that it was great to be attacking Saddam. I was politically aware, but I was also very vulnerable to intense media exposure. My father had been involved with the Democratic Party. I went with him to various party conventions. In 1992 when I was in the fourth or fifth grade, (Bill) Clinton was running, and I was excited about the campaign. I convinced my dad to take me to the Democratic State Convention. I amassed an impressive ensemble of campaign buttons. I went on to volunteer on local campaigns the next two years. I was becoming totally politicized.

"The longer I worked on electoral campaigns, the more skeptical I became of a system based on militarism and violent coercion by the ruling class and by the lack of real democracy in our country—the belief that the only way to effect social change is to elect good people to office. I wanted to be part of a movement to reclaim political power through direct democracy. I was anti-capitalist from pretty early on, and have been railing against it for a long time. In high school, I became more indoctrinated into radical politics. A friend gave me some literature from the Socialist Labor Party that was written in the early 1900s. I ate it up and all of a sudden I gained an anti-capitalist vocabulary. But I learned that the words that animated the struggles of a century ago had less resonance with my contemporaries, including my parents, who were always most willing to entertain my fiery tirades against capitalism. That's when I became a social anarchist."

After reading a book his teacher gave him called *The Teenage Liberation Handbook*, Ben dropped out of high school and finished his course work through home schooling. He enrolled in a Catholic college in St. Paul in 2000 but cut classes several times to attend protests. He then volunteered at a Catholic Worker House for about six months. "I was searching for community then. The Worker House had a strong commitment to anti-militarism and social justice that I liked. For me, living at the Catholic Worker House was an experiment in intentional community. I learned so much about responsibility and serving others, but I also learned that I was an atheist."

While at the Catholic Worker's House, Ben took part in two anti-nuclear movement actions and connected with the anti-globalization and anti-bio-technology movements in April of 2000. He was influenced by *Bringing Democracy Home*, a pamphlet of essays handed out at an IMF (International Monetary Fund) demonstration that contained writings on social ecology and raised questions about direct democracy. "Reading that pamphlet was a 'reconstructive moment' for me," he says. "I realized the need to reconstruct the movement to get everyone involved."

* * *

"Didn't we shut it down? Didn't we shut it down?"

It is the last day of November, 1999. The victory chant is beginning to rise from the large, boisterous crowd of protestors marching down the noisy Seattle, Washington streets. The anti-globalization movement is in the process of shutting down a meeting of the World Trade Organization (WTO), while enunciating a new vision of direct democracy as an alternative to capitalism.

Teenager Ben Grosscup is huddled unprotected with a group of protesters in a human barricade that is designed to keep delegates out of the nearby convention center. Suddenly, tear gas from police canisters fills the air and breaks up the dissident gathering. Ben painfully recalls the panic reaction he felt as the gas stung his eyes and burned his face. But it did not dampen his spirit.

"We didn't think protest as usual was the appropriate response," he says, recalling the historic event. "We wanted to disrupt the conference. People saw the wrath of the state and realized that we could shut down its institutions. I saw huge groups of people fighting for the same things. The sense of solidarity I felt with strangers, including volunteer medics who washed out my inflamed eyes, transformed me.

"When we protest, often we're asking for changes that the institutions can't really provide. In capitalism, growth depends on helping the wealthy at the expense of everyone else. Its goal is not human welfare. It is market growth. Saying that that makes life better for everybody is patently untrue, and people around the globe are coming to realize that more and more."

A month after the historic WTO protest, at the ripe age of eighteen, Ben visited Iraq with a group of activists. The U.S. sanctions against Iraq were in effect and were causing extraordinary suffering among the populace of that country. Ben went to a forum on the sanctions and was so appalled by what he learned that he started attending demonstrations against the U.S. policy. "We wanted to build person-to-person connections and become more educated about the seriousness of the situation there," he recalls. "We showed Iraqis that we care about them."

While in Iraq, Ben interviewed a woman named Um Heider (mother of Heider). "Hers is a terrible story." he says. "She was going to buy candy. On the way to the store, one of her children was hit by shrapnel fire from a U.S. Tomahawk missile. When I met him, he still had shrapnel in him."

When Ben and his group returned from Iraq, they began doing talks across the country focusing on personal stories of human suffering taking place under U.S. sanctions. "There was tragic story after tragic story," he says. "Our policy on Iraq has been enormously devastating and morally reprehensible. Face-to-face connections can jolt people out of propaganda and make them realize that we're hitting civilians with our weapons. There have been hundreds of casualties from the bombings that are supposed to protect them. It's terribly unjust. To refer to the human lives lost as 'collateral damage' is ridiculous. The war is all for the purpose of establishing American military power. Iraq should demand reparations for war crimes the U.S. has perpetrated against them. We need to raise the stakes of the antiwar movement and raise social costs, creating a situation where the government would lose control of our country because of its war effort."

Ben's experiences in the anti-globalization and antiwar movements are reflected in his music. His CD project began with an anti-NAFTA protest in Quebec City. "I had an outstanding arrest, so they wouldn't let me into the demonstration. I was in jail for a day or so. During this time, I worked with the Independent Media Center, uploading songs on the Internet. I had played guitar in a Ska band but left because I wanted to compose politically charged music."

After his visit to Iraq, Ben wanted to record a CD of original antiwar songs. He e-mailed musicians he knew asking them to send songs they had written about Iraq. The result was a CD called *Stoking the Fire* produced by Voices in the Wilderness. In 2002, he made his own CD of original protest songs called

Ben Grosscup's Greatest Hits. He had found another way to speak his mind and build solidarity.

In 2001, Ben became a student at The Institute for Social Ecology (ISE) in Plainfield, Vermont, a combination college, think tank and activist organization, where he took courses in direct democracy, nurtured his interest in critiques of biotechnology and further formulated his thinking on major issues. "I was interested in how capitalism is threatening our lives in new kinds of ways, not only the destruction of the environment and evisceration of the working class, but how it turns everything into commodities to be bought and sold at an auction.

"Biotechnology is a product of society," he muses. "It's also the basis of the problems in society. I'm scared of what's happening and is proposed to happen. The only way to attack it is to change the social matrix within which technologies are produced. We should build technologies for human-scale society. What we have now doesn't do that. Our knowledge hasn't been applied in socially useful ways. A lot of people think they don't have a stake in a system whose logic is to grow and expand and reduce parts of the world to its own terms. I'm trying to fight that in many ways."

In January of 2006, Ben went to work for the Northeast Organic Farming Association (NOFA) organizing a campaign against genetic engineering of foods. He had become exposed to the idea of town meetings while at ISE in 2002-03 and was ready to direct the campaign in Massachusetts.

"I have put a lot of effort into town meetings because they are a vestigial form of direct democracy with roots that date back long before the American Revolution. There has been renewed interest since 2000 in bringing resolutions on political issues to town meetings in some parts of New England—especially Vermont and Massachusetts. These have included measures voicing opposition to agricultural genetic engineering, the Patriot Act, the military occupation of Iraq and federal inaction on the climate crisis.

"Town meetings are the supreme legislative body for the municipality politically empowering people with the capacity to discuss budget and zoning issues and adopt resolutions. We asked the question, 'Do we want to have corporations taking over our food?' We said, 'Let's organize communities so that we can do something about the quality of our food systems.' We trained citizens on strategies for approaching these meetings and to talk to their neighbors. The resolutions called for a moratorium on genetically modified products, labeling of those products, and liability reform. We had town meetings throughout Massachusetts and passed resolutions in several of them. In March of 2006, citizens of Montville, Maine voted to amend their town plan to prohibit the growing of genetically engineered crops.

"The resolutions were mainly symbolic and usually didn't get enacted into legislation. The Agriculture committee of the Massachusetts Senate and House held a hearing on legislation in 2004 that was introduced at the request of thirty different towns throughout the state. But the power of the biotech industry is entrenched, and we were not able to get to the point where we had champions willing to take a chance and challenge them. The resolutions were a way of educating people and getting them to push the issue further against the opposing food industry which claimed that genetically engineered products are safe.

"It was due in large part to the eighty-five towns in Vermont that passed resolutions against genetic engineering that the state enacted the first-in-the-nation law requiring clearer labeling of all genetically engineered (GE) seeds sold within its borders, and in 2006, legislation permitting farmers to sue GE crop developers under private nuisance law. When a state is dangerously unresponsive to popular demand, we are right to respond with the urgency of the causes we champion. It hearkens back to those moments in American history where town meetings played an important role in people's lives. Resolutions are an important way to bring power at the local level."

Ben's organizing of colonial-style grassroots gatherings across New England was part of an ongoing examination of democracy and power, the ways in which corporations exercise power over common citizens and how people can take back that power.

With that in mind, Ben left NOFA in April of 2007 to work at the Massachusetts headquarters of the Bill of Rights Defense Committee (BORDC), a national organization based in Northampton, Massachusetts that provides strategic support for activists around the country who have raised opposition to the U.S. Patriot Act and other erosions of civil liberties since 9/11. BORDC has helped citizens in over 400 municipalities across the country convince their city and county governments to enact resolutions opposing the Patriot Act for its violations of the Bill of Rights. It has also worked on such contemporary civil liberties issues as habeas corpus, torture and warrentless wiretapping.

At BORDC, Ben engineered a new people's campaign for the Constitution that included staging town meetings across New England. "The people's campaign is important at this moment in history in order to stave off a gruesome form of tyranny. We are facing a constitutional crisis where the government doesn't uphold the constitution. We need to restore constitutional rights that have been lost and reassert the government checks-and-balances system.

"After an initial surge following the enactment of the Patriot Act, some of the groups working on this issue fell apart. I am in the process of restarting this grassroots movement on civil liberties. We now have a perfect storm. The time is right to preserve our civil rights and our ecosystems by revitalizing ways to express dissent, to make this an historic moment.

"We are building a large coalition of groups interested in this subject. We are encouraging city councils and other local governments to enact resolutions, rather than depending on the federal government. The crucial goal of this stage of organizing is to open up a space in which the citizenry of a municipality can consider and openly debate specific measures that begin to address concrete problems facing their community, People must come to expect from their world that they have the right to self-govern."

* * *

Ben leans forward in his chair, handing me some copies of politically charged CDs he has recorded and materials he has written at college. He glances up over his recently acquired beard and looks to the future.

"We all share a general interest for a safer world where people are free to determine their own lives. We have to figure a way to move that discussion forward. That's critical for building solidarity in a global world, to create a situation where the political context would shift considerably towards the will of the people. For example, I thought, 'Wouldn't it be great to build community gardens connected to a broader political project in our cities?' This would be direct democracy and community economics. Every community would have a communal garden and have control of it." Ben has recently taken a part-time position with NOFA that will include working on this idea.

"Our society is broken. People feel disconnected. I believe that if we don't destroy capitalism, it will destroy us. It will transcend humanity as we know it into a kind of posthumanity. I ask myself, 'How can I help move the movement forward and create a new free society?' The key word is 'action,' always action. We need to raise our expectations and expand our vision to think beyond what is immediately possible rather than just adapting to the world as it is. Potentially, this could give us the kinds of structures to bring out voices that aren't being heard as much but who are striving for a radically different kind of society—one that is dependent on nurturing the natural world and humanity and that can get at the root causes of the social crisis. That is how I avowedly live.

"I believe in the revolutionary struggle. My hope is not optimism as much as sensibility that I bring into the world that which maintains my convictions and aspirations in a world that goes against them. I truly see a need for radical change in this society if we are to have a future."

Ben continues to use music as a way to promote the change he espouses. Since the release of *Stoking the Fire*, Ben has performed at various activist events as a singer and storyteller with the Pioneer Valley Folklore Society, representing a new generation of folk artists railing against oppression and for liberation. He has recently recorded a CD with a fellow musician Dan Inglis. The name of it, not surprisingly: *Shaking of the Ground*.

Gabriel Johnson Ortiz
(Photo courtesy of Gabriel Johnson Ortiz)

CHANGING TWO WORLDS
By Stacy Larsen Stafki

There are many degrees of separation between the lily-white, middle-class Minneapolis suburb of Anoka and the barrios and villages of Central America. It is a distance measured not just in actual miles or differences in language, climate and topography, but also in how people live their lives. The differences are vast and stark. It is difficult to imagine a resident of either place feeling at home in the other's community. But for Gabriel Johnson Ortiz, living in both of these contrasting worlds has become a matter of course; working to change them for the better has become a way of life.

Slightly built and only a quarter-of-a-century old, Gabriel has the soulful eyes of someone who has seen so much, yet his fire and passion continue to burn. He is a young multi-cultural revolutionary, knowledgeable beyond his years, who has dedicated his life to educating people about the actions of the United States military in Latin America, and what they can do about it—a quest that has only just begun.

* * *

The twelve-year U.S-funded civil war in El Salvador (1980-92), changed the lives of thousands of the country's residents. It also impacted the life of one small boy far far away. Gabriel was born in Minnesota to a Mexican mother and American father around the time the war began. He was raised in a politically and culturally active household, which helped him form his early beliefs. He was barely of school age when he learned about the U.S. government giving aid and weapons to Latin American countries to keep indigenous populations from organizing a governmental overthrow. Many of the soldiers using those weapons against citizens were trained at The School of the Americas (now called The Western Hemisphere Institute for Social Cooperation) located in Fort Benning, Georgia.

The escalation of the civil war and the assassination of Archbishop Oscar Romero piqued Gabriel's interest and he began to make the connections between the struggle for livelihood and military economic control. While most kids were learning to read or ride a bike, Gabriel was helping his parent's support a hunger strike in St. Paul organized by the Central American Center in Minneapolis to raise awareness of the slaying of six Jesuit priests in El Salvador. That effort was a turning point in his activism. "I had a need to tell people what our government was doing: training Latin American leaders in military tactics and then giving them arms to use against their own people," Gabriel says.

In 1990, when Gabriel was ten years old, his family moved to Guatemala, where his parents worked as coordinators for the Center for Global Education. He saw the country's struggles firsthand. "I realized the real problems people were facing, especially the indigenous people, and how the government was treating innocent people with the help of the U.S. government. There was a lot going on in Guatemala and Mexico, and I decided to help out any way I could."

The following year, Gabriel participated in the 500-year campaign against oppression in Guatemala, in indigenous peoples' rallies across Central America and in an effort to award the Nobel Peace Prize to Rigoberta Menchu, native of a small Guatemala village, who was trying to draw attention to the massacres happening there. Gabriel also began going to protests. "I went to a couple of encounters with indigenous people and saw what was happening to them. There was a lot of violence against the people at the hands of President Garcia—many thousands were massacred and thousands more were displaced from Guatemala and fled to Mexico. The government had total control of speech and unsponsored actions. It was like a military state where any opposition to the government was squelched. My father was in charge of a delegation that traveled back and forth between Guatemala and Mexico."

At midnight on the first day of 1994, the streets of Mexico erupted in chaos and violence. As the recently signed North American Free Trade Agreement (NAFTA) went into effect, thousands of citizens hit the streets of Chiapas, which borders Guatemala, with machetes, clubs and guns to declare war on the Mexican government. It was a short-lived uprising, but it proved to have widespread support around the countryside and in the cities.

The Johnson-Ortiz family saw this uprising as a great opportunity to teach the world about indigenous rights and the struggles of common people against the Mexican government. In 1995, they moved to the small highland village of San Cristobal de las Casas in Chiapas, Mexico, a southern province that borders Guatemala. When Gabriel's family moved in, they did not have jobs. What they did have was a burning desire to tell the world the stories of the Chiapas people.

Gabriel's dad began collecting the voices of the Mayans of Chiapas. Gabriel pitched in, helping his mother transcribe and collect women's stories that they would tell to the Americans and other people helping with the struggle. "We wanted to know what the Chiapas women thought of the racism and poverty the indigenous people were facing and what role citizens should have in the democratic process." Gabriel explains. Teresa Ortiz, Gabriel's mother, put the stories into a book called *Voices of Mayan Women in Chiapas.*

Meanwhile, Gabriel began to show up at citizen-sponsored marches and meetings supporting the indigenous people of Chiapas. In 1996, he went to the International Encounter for Humanity against Neo-Liberalism, sponsored by the Zapatistas. He listened to speakers like Noam Chomsky and Winona Laduke and learned more about indigenous people's struggle around the world, and how to educate others about it. He came away from that educational experience ready to make a real difference in the lives of the people of Chiapas.

* * *

It was called The Cloudforest Initiative. Started in 1997 by the Ortiz family, its mission was to support efforts for peace, justice and integral development of the Mayan communities in Chiapas by helping small, indigenous farmers sell their goods at a fair price. Gabriel played a major role in this ambitious project.

"My job was to seek a market for fair trade and organic coffee. I went around to different markets and measured their interest in carrying a special brand of coffee that ensured a fair price for the farmer while providing funding for a habitat for birds. We organized a few farmer co-ops who called themselves Mut Vitz (Big Mountain) and Yachil Xojobal Chulchan (New Light in the Sky) in San Cristobal." Cloudforest is now a thriving nonprofit that sells goods in retail shops and on the internet.

After Cloudforest was established, Gabriel helped start a Center for Indigenous Youth in San Cristobal and worked there as an organizer. "It was such an important place for youth to go because it gave them a place to live as they were trying to sell their products in the community," he says. "They were often forced to work for the land owner, and lots of them were living on the streets. We gave them a better, safer place to be with good role models."

Now living in Minneapolis, Gabriel continues to make social change in both of his home countries. In Central America, he recently went on a tour with a group showing a movie on the sale, trafficking and murders of hundreds of Mexican women. He has demonstrated with peasant farmers and organized several marches in Mexico calling for the recount of the allegedly stolen presidential elections of 2006 and to stop violence in Oaxaca and in San Salvador Aternco, where peasants won a battle to halt the construction of an international airport on their lands. He has made several trips to Chiapas to visit family members and help create murals in four different Zapatista communities. He has also organized local artists to participate in the first International Art of Resistance Encounter in Mexico City. Back home, Gabriel has been an organizer for Hotel and Restaurant Employees (HERE) Local 126 during a national campaign to unionize hotels. He has also worked with indigenous groups like the Minnesota Alliance for the Zapatistas and with the Minnesota Immigrant Rights Action Coalition, organizing immigrant rights marches "to improve the lives of thousands of immigrants who work crappy jobs but help our economy and the lives of the American people."

In virtually everything he does, Gabriel's feet remain firmly planted between two worlds. The imprint they are making is very large indeed.

Nathan Middlestadt at peace rally
(Photo by Michael Bayly)

THE BUTTON MAKER
By Burt Berlowe

FUCK WAR!

The bold black words seem to jump off the round, white, newborn buttons lying on the studio apartment floor. Staring up at me, they represent the brash, insurgent language of the new antiwar movement. They are a plea for attention, a cry of anger and an in-your-face call for action. They yearn to be stuck on lapels, collars and pockets, beneath bobbing signs and raised fists, and shouted from the parched lips of those thirsty for peace.

The creator of the button is seated nearby—youthful, clean-cut looking Nathan Middlestadt, a movement maker, the driving force behind student antiwar activity on the University of Minnesota campus. Nathan is a founder and leader of the Twin Cities chapter of Students Against War (SAW), one of the most active college peace organizations in the nation.

Nathan's cozy abode reflects his passion. Several of the buttons, profane and otherwise, lie around waiting to be sold as a fundraiser for SAW. Posters that say "A Place for Peace" and "A Place for Action" are stuck to his wood-paneled walls. A computer in a corner is his link to the world.

On the day of our interview, Nathan is in the process of completing a survey that will be administered to University of Minnesota students, gauging their attitudes towards a potential war with Iraq. A few weeks earlier, he had led a SAW meeting in a campus classroom that discussed, among other things, planning a student walkout that would occur immediately after the Iraq war began, as well as the hosting of an upcoming national student peace conference. Immediately after the meeting, the small group went to a candlelight antiwar vigil being held in the University commons.

Questioning and bucking the establishment is nothing new for Nathan. He's been doing it for most of his young life.

"I'm originally from a small suburban town called DePere, outside of Green Bay, Wisconsin," Nathan recalls. "In late middle school, I started listening to punk rock and reading Leftist literature, both of which had a big influence on me. I was initially interested in such things as government conspiracy theories, particularly about UFOs, but then moved on to human welfare and environmental issues. I didn't know too many other kids my age that were like that. That was partially due to the incredibly conservative political environment in Green Bay. The town revolved around paper mills that were polluting the river. There was a push to try to clean that up, but anyone working against the mills was seen as threatening the mill workers' jobs.

"I was always perceived to be the rebel in the family, the troublemaker. At times, it was hard to convince my nonactivist family that I was doing what I did because I believed in it. Initially, they looked at me as headed down the wrong path. They feared that I was going to end up in a really bad situation. We did a lot of arguing in my late teen years about lots of different issues. Eventually, I was able to change how they looked at the world.

"We went to a really conservative Lutheran church. Even now, I get irritated at my little brother reciting what he was taught by our pastor. When I went through confirmation, I watched a lot of right wing fundamentalism in videos. At the time, it seemed normal, like everybody thought that way. I had a really odd school situation. I was always outside the mainstream. I got into a lot of fights. I went against prevailing notions of fashion and political views. Sometimes, I dressed punk. One day a week, during my sophomore year, some friends and I would wear three-piece suits to school that we got in thrift shops for four bucks. It was just a prank. We had activity fairs. We organized booths where we discussed party politics. I had a friend who was a vegetarian who convinced me to stop eating meat."

Nathan originally wanted to be an aerospace engineer on the side of space exploration not military application. But he was afraid that anything that he could contribute could be used for military purposes. "In my junior and senior years, I had a major reconsideration of my life. I started reading more about activist issues and third-party politics. When I was ready to vote for the first time, I wasn't pleased with either major party."

The day Nathan registered for college classes, he began looking for ways to get involved. He saw a notice about a fundraising party for the Students for (Ralph) Nader (presidential) campaign and ended up working with them. "We were successful in creating debate on campus, and were able to get formal federal recognition of the Green Party in Minnesota," he says. "I was doing organizing I wouldn't have had any clue how to do in high school. It's been pretty constant since then."

Before long, Nathan was involved in starting a maverick campus organization called Students for a Democratic University (SDU). "That was a painful experience. We had a lot of trouble deciding what we wanted to do. We were able to organize some successful events, including a decent sized protest in 2000 against the biotech industry's involvement at the University during a biotech advocates meeting. We also occupied Morrill Hall (on campus) demanding a meeting with University President Mark Yudof on the biotech issue. We got the meeting. But they just paid us lip service.

"There was a big push for corporate contributions to the University. Corporate donations have a lot of strings attached that were hurting the academic learning environment and undermining the University's mission and commitment to students. Our group only had about ten people and we squabbled about what we wanted to do. We finally decided to become involved in a major drug company lawsuit against South Africa in an effort to stop them from purchasing generic prescriptions. We got the University to issue a statement supporting the release of a patent that would not allow generic drug makers to offer their products at reduced prices."

Internal conflicts, burnout and attrition eventually took its toll on SDU and it soon fizzled, leaving a gap that wasn't readily filled. "There wasn't much around to take SDU's place," Nathan says. "The Campus Greens hadn't got off the ground. There was MPIRG (The Minnesota Public Interest Research Group), but they were not an independent organization. It seemed that people didn't have the passion or guts to respond to issues."

On September 11, 2001, Nathan had just begun doing his laundry in his dorm and had run out of detergent. It was about 8 a.m. "I went to buy some detergent at a nearby co-op, and they had the radio on announcing that a plane had just hit the World Trade Center and then the Pentagon. I thought 'That's odd.' I thought it was fiction. I was puzzled and horrified. I went home and did what most people did, watched TV the rest of the day. The U cancelled classes at noon. A couple of days afterward, a graduate professional student association, the Minnesota Student Alliance Governing Board, organized a campus gathering with about 5,000 people that had a nationalist overtone to it. They announced that, 'We're going to get the people that did this,' even as they were playing 'We Shall Overcome.' They gave militaristic speeches. I understood that people felt pain and anguish about that day, but they didn't even know who did it. They just assumed it was Muslims.

"A couple of days later, I started Students Against War (SAW) with students from the Nader campaign. We began building an email list and found out that the activist community was not a whole lot of other people, that we all knew each other. We held our first meeting within a week after 9/11. We knew that rhetoric was flying and that we would be going to war. Afghanistan was pointed out as a definite target. We didn't believe going to war was going to solve anything. SAW advocated institution of a world court to bring international perpetrators to trial.

"Our group included pacifists, socialists, anarchists and others against war. There were political leanings all over the spectrum, including some (politically) moderate students. We created a framework that we could agree on, saying 'no' to war and racial scapegoating, and targeting of Arabs, and 'yes' to peaceful, diplomatic resolutions and civil liberties. Even if we don't care about what goes on somewhere else in the world we ought to worry about the consequences to ourselves if we give the government unchecked power.

"We held protests and teach-ins on campus. We had up to 250 people at a teach-in on the role of art and discourse in times of war. About one-hundred people came for a three-hour event about the role of academics and intellectuals during war that asked the question, 'Do we let ourselves be stifled? Do we tone down our political message, or do we move more resolutely?' There were also lots of events going on not that were not SAW-sponsored. Rallies downtown drew hundreds of people."

Nathan went with some friends to a rally in Washington, D.C., his first national protest. The march started at Freedom Plaza at 14th and Penn and ended at the Capitol. "Police tried to regulate the crowd and closed in. One officer went a little nuts and started pepper spraying everywhere, even getting some of the other officers. We argued with some counter-protesters for a half an hour. A counter-protester punched one of our members when he began burning an American flag. That was the picture that made the front of the *Washington Post*. We were primarily protesting against a planned bombing of Afghanistan. The bombing began a week later.

"I came back from D.C. feeling empowered, having never experienced anything of that scale. We didn't stop the bombing of Afghanistan, but we laid the groundwork for future actions. There's now massive opposition to war like has not been seen in decades. The demonstrations are the largest since the Vietnam War. There's a rebirth, a revitalization of that movement. I'm happy to see it despite the circumstances it's arriving under."

SAW subsequently organized citywide events and demonstrations, working closely with The Antiwar Committee and Friends for a Non-Violent World in the Twin Cities and developing national contacts. SAW groups formed in Duluth, Minnesota; Madison, Wisconsin; and other cities. There is even a Cambridge Students Against War in England.

Meanwhile, on its own campus, Nathan's SAW group had to tread carefully. "Some other student groups have gotten into trouble," Nathan explains. "SOAR (Students Organized for Animal Rights) was placed on probation by the University because it was linked to the ALF (Animal Liberation Front), which attacked laboratories that were experimenting on animals. The University is always looking over our shoulder. But that doesn't limit what we can do. They don't show up at large demonstrations. And we're not destroying property or busting heads or anything like that."

SAW continued to fly by the seat of its pants. "Our members didn't have official titles," Nathan says. "We used strange names like a Czar of Information and a Duchess of Peace. We needed to define people as leaders. We needed to get bigger if we wanted to stop this war. We had to take the focus off national demonstrations and bring them home. If we sent 1,500 people to D.C. from the Twin Cities and paid significant money to go there, we could get two or three times as many at local protests doing the unconventional that is harder to ignore, rather than just holding banners on highways. There is a possibility for real change on a broader scale. But instead of staying with the far left liberal, socialist or anarchist cliques, we need to appeal to a larger audience if we're going to be successful. We couldn't isolate ourselves within our narrowly defined boundaries. We had to grow and expand. We had attracted attention and brought issues to the forefront. But we needed improvement if we wanted to create a broader movement."

One of the ways that SAW expanded was by going beyond college campuses to organize younger students. Nationally, SAW chapters helped organize a Books not Bombs walkout at high schools around the country after the bombing of Iraq and advertised themselves as "a network of college and high school students and young workers." The Minnesota SAW opened a chapter at high schools in conservative Minneapolis suburbs. In 2002, SAW was listed by the Hennepin County Sheriff's office as a subversive organization because it promoted student walkouts and blocking of traffic. That was the same list that includes the Klu Klux Klan and the Animal Liberation Front, among others.

As he prepared to graduate from college, Nathan planned to pass the torch of SAW to forthcoming students. "My goal was to transfer what I know to other people so they can carry on. The biggest thing I wanted to happen when I left was for SAW to have an ongoing activist presence."

Unfortunately, that never happened. in March of '04, Nathan had to fold SAW due to lack of continuing support. "We disbanded following a last-ditch fundraiser attended by too few people. It was easy to get people to do one-time events but not to commit to longer involvement."

While finishing school, Nathan began life after SAW. He operated his own website called Bush Watch that monitored the president's activities, and continued to seek more ongoing opportunities to promote social change. "I would like to do what I do now full-time and get paid for it without worrying about being homeless," he says. "I also believe that teaching is really powerful. I am interested in the Teach for America program that is in twenty areas across the country, where you teach high school in lower-income areas in inner cities or rural areas. You can make a real difference teaching, helping people help themselves, creating something larger than yourself. I like the idea of helping people think critically and move beyond their own confines. Rather than pushing a point, I would prefer to address an issue and let the students find out on their own. I'm of the belief that if you think your argument is strongest, you will be able to prevail.

"I don't see myself leading a complete and full life if I'm not having an influence on the way things are being run. That has to extend to what I do in my personal life. I can't separate what I do in life from what I want my world to be. I can't see myself sitting idly by waiting for someone else to do it and be happy with that. In my utopian vision of the world, I want a more humane system of mutual respect and understanding. There should be a provision that everybody has adequate food, health care and housing. And that workplaces should be democratically organized. We can't just want to stop war. We have to address its roots."

Brandon Madsen
(Photo from YAWR file)

READING 'RITING AND RECRUITERS
By Burt Berlowe

Military recruiters must be confronted in every high school, every campus, every recruiting office on every street corner, in every town and city across America. The days of deceiving, manipulating and victimizing our young people must end.
— Ron Kovics, US Marine Sergeant Viet Nam war and Author of *Born on the Fourth of July*. Quote taken from the 2009 peace calendar of the Syracruse Cultural Workers.

It happened just like clockwork. On the first anniversary of George W. Bush's second presidential term, in four cities at different ends of the country, groups of high school students spontaneously stood up at their desks, turned towards the door and quietly marched out of class. Walking together in their respective gatherings, they headed for the streets, breaking the silence and order in an explosion of sound and fury. Signs popped up, banners unraveled, voices unleashed chants and screams.

In Seattle, Washington, over 1,000 students walked out of some fifty area schools and poured into Westlake Center across from Puget Sound. One of the protest leaders shouted out the name of each participating school, and students roared back an answer. With hip hop, spoken word and fervent speeches ringing in their ears, the crowd marched to the Capitol Hill Arts Center where some of them proceeded to sit back down—this time in the middle of the street.

Not far away, in the military town of Tacoma, a contingent of about 100 students staged the first organized antiwar protest in that city since the Vietnam War. They marched to the Tacoma Mall military recruitment station, then back to the strip mall, where their chants of "While you're shopping, bombs are dropping," and "1-2-3-4, We don't want your racist war," turned the heads of consumers away from store windows.

On the other end of the United States, students from over a dozen high schools and colleges joined a citywide protest against the war and military recruitment on Boston Common, walking to a military recruiting station across the street, then back to the State House. They came from the city and the suburbs and as far away as New Hampshire, many of them protesting and/or speaking before a crowd for the first time.

In the Upper Midwest city of Minneapolis, Minnesota, about 2,000 students from over forty high schools, middle schools, and colleges walked out of class and headed to the University of Minnesota for a large rally. They then marched through the campus, taking over streets. They ended up at a military recruitment station, blocking the nearby intersection for thirty minutes without a permit. In anticipation of the protest, the recruiting station had closed for the day.

Just a few blocks away from the Minneapolis recruiting station is the headquarters for this national youth protest movement. It is located in an inconspicuous residential duplex in a low-moderate-income neighborhood in south Minneapolis. The only sign identifying one of the units as an office is the small lettering below the front yard mail box that reads: YAWR. That stands for Youth Against War and Racism.

The first floor unit housing YAWR looks very much like many inner-city apartments. The living room and dining room are joined together, separated by a wall from a kitchen in the rear, and across shiny hardwood floors from a stairway leading upstairs. A small bookcase full of titles by the likes of Leon Trostsky and Noam Chomsky flanks a large table in the center of the dining room. The top of the table is littered with socialist newspapers, bread wrappers and jars of jam left over from a lunch just finished by a bespectacled young woman who had emerged from the kitchen. A stocky African man named Teddy is perched at a laptop computer.

Accompanying me into the apartment/office is twenty-year-old Brandon Madsen, looking sort of like a blonde Jesus, with long stringy hair careening down both sides of his youthful face and settling on the shoulders of his socialist T-shirt.

Brandon is one of the founders of YAWR, organizing it while he was a student at Kennedy High School in Bloomington, Minnesota. He has taken taking a year off from college in Madison, Wisconsin to help the organization grow. As America continues to be bogged down in yet another war abroad, YAWR is targeting the system that sustains warfare—military recruitment and the young people who are its victims. It is a challenge that Brandon welcomes as a significant step towards more extensive systemic change.

"My parents were never super-political," Brandon says. "But I was always curious about politics, asking questions like, 'What are terrorists?' or 'What are communists?' I also had a natural instinct to rebel against authority. In junior high school, I was always trying to shake things up things and do what was out of the ordinary. In high school, I got into politics after I read a book by Chomsky that I bought at a punk rock concert. It made me ask questions I'd never thought about before, such as, 'What was the history that led up to 9/11 and why did it happen?' I came to realize that 9/11 had dealt a crushing blow to the image of the U.S. as portrayed in society. It wasn't just about random terrorism, but about why do they hate America.

"I was in German class at Kennedy High when someone came into room and announced that the Twin Towers were being attacked. They cancelled all activities and classes for the day. To me, it seemed like the attack came out of nowhere. I had no conception of how or why that would happen."

Brandon attended his first peace rally in March of 2004 on the one-year anniversary of the Iraq invasion. The group rallied and marched to the state capitol. "The march was a great experience. It was good to have an expression other than arguing and to be with other people around me with the same sentiments."

At the march, Brandon met Ty Moore, an organizer with The Socialist Alternative. He was impressed by what he heard about that organization. "It all made sense and fit together like nothing I had ever heard before. A Chomsky book I read not only talked about how to deal a crushing blow to capitalism but also had a message of what to do, how to get from the society you have now to one of Socialism: worker-run with production and distribution from the bottom up and where elected officials are always accessible. I became a Trostskyite and member of Socialist Alternative, which has at least one organization on every continent with several in the U.S."

In 2004, employees of the Metropolitan Transit Commission (MTC—the bus company) went on strike, crippling the city's transportation system.

Brandon joined the workers on the picket line and at rallies. At the same time, he began talking with a couple of his fellow student activists about an idea he had to form a student organization to protest U.S. involvement in Iraq. By the beginning of his senior year, Brandon and two of his friends had formed an organization they originally called Students Against War (a different group than the one started by university student Nathan Middlestadt.) They later changed the name to Youth Against War and Racism.

The founders of YAWR decided to go beyond opposition to the Iraq War. They became pioneers of a movement aimed directly at military recruiters and their focus on poor, minority students in American high schools. They wanted to do something to help young people, especially the most vulnerable, have other choices than joining the military. "We wanted to use the money being spent on the military for jobs and education and to end the racist justifications of war," Brandon says.

In recent years across the nation, military recruiters, concerned about dwindling numbers of enlistees, have begun invading high schools, camping in hallways and aggressively approaching students. Kennedy High School was one of their favorite targets. "They would go so far as to follow students to class and harass them into giving out their phone number to call later," Brandon recalls. "They followed me a few times, but they especially went after minorities." A provision in the No Child Left Behind Act required schools to give recruiters information on students or face a withdrawal of government funds. A student can opt out of this provision but only before the time when the recruiters visit.

"You have to be able to beg, cheat or steal to be successful at military recruiting," Brandon continues. "They don't pitch it on the basis of fighting for your country, but rather that you'll be able to pay for college and you won't have to be selling drugs. A student with Military Families Speak Out was told he would spend his time in the service designing video games and compiling college credits. He ended up going to Iraq and beating down doors.

"Just to find out what it was like, I went to a recruiting station and pretended I was interested. They said, 'If you get in the Army, you can play guitar.' They wanted to sign me up right there. They said, 'Look at all the great things you can do. You may get sent to Iraq, but you won't have to fight. You can do other things. You'll get a massive amount of college money guaranteed.' Following my visit, the recruiters called me to make small talk and ask what I like to do. I said, 'I like to criticize and oppose recruiters coming into schools.' They still called back."

In the fall of 2004, a few months after they had adopted their new name, YAWR developed a counter-recruitment plan at Kennedy then sprung into action. They found a teacher advisor, made flyers to hand out and planned a teach-in during the first week of school to train students how to respond to the recruiters when they come. Initially, school administrators resisted the YAWR campaign, by setting up bureaucratic roadblocks—refusing to approve distribution of the flyers and telling the students they were violating school rules. Through constant pressure and negotiation, YAWR eventually got the school's permission to table and distribute flyers.

"The next time the recruiters were scheduled to come, we were ready to go," explains Brandon "Then the night before, I got a call from our teacher advisor saying that someone from The American Legion had gotten hold of one of our flyers and threatened to pull funding from the school if we set up our table. The school administration reversed its policy and told us we would not be allowed to table while the military was there. I called an emergency meeting on how do deal with this. We decided to go ahead with it anyway. We distributed a petition explaining to the students what we were doing and calling for a protest in the school lunchroom. By the next day, we had gathered a lot of signatures. When we set up the table in the school hallway, someone from the administration came up and questioned what we were doing. We said it had been approved. They said we had to take it down or be suspended."

Meanwhile, a sense of panic had overtaken the office of the Minneapolis Superintendent of Schools. For a day and a half, they had been flooded with hundreds of phone calls from students complaining about the Kennedy administration's resistance to counter-recruitment tabling. By the time Brandon and his YAWR cohorts walked into the district office, the superintendent was ready to give in. "He said it was all a misunderstanding and that we should go ahead with our tabling as long as we stayed within the guidelines. We set up our table during lunch hour directly across the all from the recruiters. They didn't react to us. They were frustrated that our table was more interesting and the students were going there. We had swarms of people. We were taking business away from them. After school, we had a victory celebration."

For the most part, Kennedy students were excited about the fact that their school was taking on the recruiters. It marked a dramatic change from the political apathy that had previously characterized the student body. "The success of building this campaign proved what can happen when young people get energized to get involved," says Brandon. "It doubled the size of our group."

Throughout that year, the recruiters' presence at Kennedy dwindled. By the time Brandon had gone away to college the following year, they had stopped visiting entirely. But recently they have begun to return, causing him to call for a policy to restrict school recruitment. "No Child Left Behind blackmails schools into letting recruiters in. I would be surprised if the money would actually be taken away from the school if they violated the policy. That would cause such a political backlash. I think we should call their bluff. Military recruiters should not be allowed to come in any more often than other job recruiters. They should be restricted to the school resource center and not just be able to roam the halls and harass the students. Because of their history of sexual misconduct, it's doubly important that they be supervised at all times. And they should have to schedule visits at least a week ahead of time so that we can build support for a counter action."

YAWR took a policy request to the St. Paul School Board. The night they came to testify, the line was long. Most of those waiting to speak were supporting YAWR's demands for counter-recruitment action. There were parents and students and representatives of Vets for Peace, Neighbors for Peace and Military Families Speak Out, among others. It was the second time YAWR had presented its case for reforms in school recruitment policies. The school board had not taken any action the first time. But this time they agreed to convene a special meeting to discuss the issue. In early 2008, YAWR successfully pushed the St. Paul School Board to pass a resolution substantially restricting military recruiters' access to schools and opening the door to a more substantial presence for the counter-recruitment movement in that city's schools. YAWR is currently pressing for similar action in Minneapolis.

"The only way to stop war and change recruiting practices," Brandon says, "is to continue to make trouble for the establishment. In the Vietnam War, it wasn't just the marches but the soldiers laying down their arms and refusing to fight that made a difference. Historically, war has always been an integral part of the system. We have to make it cost more to continue the war than to end it. That's a huge task ahead of us."

The school walkouts have become a chief weapon in YAWR's antiwar/anti-recruitment arsenal. Brandon recalls the event he organized during the national walkout day November 2, 2005.

"It was really successful. There were 2,000 Twin Cities students that walked out at several schools simultaneously with other cities and states. We organized a noon protest at the University of Minnesota. It was done around our main demands against war, against recruitment in schools and for money for education not war. It was the biggest thing we ever organized.

"We had a second walkout in April of '06. It wasn't as big as the first one. It rained that day and at some schools administrators falsely announced that the event was cancelled. I assume they made that up. There was a group of anarchists that spontaneously threw red paint on the recruiter's station then ran away. That was a big mistake tactically. It put some people in danger of police suppression that weren't expecting it. We took swift action to minimize it. Everyone sat down and made it clear they weren't responsible. Police waded into the crowd grabbing people that didn't do anything. Some with paint on their hands were arrested and released after the charges were dropped. Instead of focusing on the walkout, the media reported on the vandalizing."

On September 4, 2008, the final day of the Republican National Convention in St. Paul, and just the third day of classes, several hundred youth walked out of Twin Cities high schools in a YAWR-led antiwar protest. They marched from the State Capitol in St. Paul to Harriet Island along the Mississippi River on the outskirts of downtown, where they staged a theatrical mock trial of giant puppet caricatures of Dick Cheney and other "war criminals" from the Bush administration.

"I don't think the walkouts alone stop war," Brandon says. "But they have mobilized people and established a new organizational layer that has laid the basis for new chapters and new members." And, in fact, the core activist base of YAWR is continuing to grow, due in large part to a successful activist training camp organized in August of '08 in partnership with the Ruckus Society, Fellowship of Reconciliation, Socialist Alternative and the Headwaters Foundation for Justice. The camp produced a whole new group of youth leaders and laid the foundation for future young people's movements in the Twin Cities and beyond.

"What I like about the walkouts is that they point the way forward to the kind of tactics that are necessary," Brandon continues. "If we had a strike against the arms industry, that would end the war. If kids would refuse to go to enlist, there wouldn't be enough troops to make war politically viable. We have to take a really strong approach to undermine the whole basis for war. We need a working-class movement where those who make and transport weapons would refuse to do it. The only way to end the war is to end the system of imperialism as a whole. I have hope that it will happen once the nature of the system is exposed. It's important to win victories, to feel the power of ordinary people. Winning victories raises expectations of what we can do next.

"Throughout history, it has always been youth who have been at the forefront of every major movement for change. Now, once again, young people are paving the way forward. There is a growing radicalization movement among students. They are starting to gain hope that they can change things."

Brandon is already looking beyond his tenure as YAWR organizer, finding other students who will take over after he leaves. He is also pursuing a lifelong interest in foreign languages. He has taken classes in German, Russian, and Indonesian and wants to learn Spanish and Somali. He recently attended an international program summer school in Belgium with some 300 people from around the world. Eventually, he would like to teach English as a Second Language in elementary or high school. But he has no intention of giving up social change organizing. "One thing this experience has told me is that I want to continue doing political activism work. A job will pay the bills, but my heart and soul is in political organizing."

**Emilie Brill Duisberg (second from left) digs to save the Earth
(Photo courtesy of Emilie Brill Duisberg)**

SAVING PARADISE
By Burt Berlowe

*...They paved paradise
And put up a parking lot.*
—From the song "Big Yellow Taxi" by Joni Mitchell

Ever since she can remember, Emilie Brill Duisberg has loved the Southwest—not the legends and stories of cowboys and Indians that were part of her hometown's history, but the real thing: the wide open spaces and clear blue skies, the giant Saguaros, indigenous shrubbery, and multicolored rocks that cover sloping foothills and patches of inner-city land; the eerie stillness and calm of the desert that seem to insulate it from the outside world; the almost mystical power it has to absorb you into its free and natural place.

That is the way Emilie recalls her childhood days in the southwestern city of Tucson, Arizona, where she grew up, and in other parts of the state as well. "When I was about three, my parents bought a small tract of land in the Dragon Mountains in Cochise County and built a cabin that they made our getaway.

I spent most of my time there, wandering through the desert, getting lost, and finding my way again. We would also go on outings to the Coronado National Forest and Saguaro National Park, where we looked for rocks and geological formations. My mother would point out plants and birds, and my father would check out lizards. It was great being out in the fresh air, marveling at nature, at a plant growing out of a rock or a bright desert wildflower."

The West of Emilie's childhood in Tucson looks much different today. It is being rapidly replaced with a newer, slicker version. Miles of once-open desert land have been paved over and covered with sprawling shopping malls, tourist-beckoning hotels and traffic-clogged roads. Expensive housing communities cover the foothills all the way to the base of the mountains that surround one of America's fastest growing cities. Air and noise pollution and mercury readings are up, as are crime statistics. The natural ambience and enchantment of the desert Southwest remains ever-present but no longer dominant. This is the New West now.

Emilie knew from early childhood that the environment around her was undergoing significant change. "My parents had been there for thirty years. By the time I was six or seven years old in the early 1990s, they would make comments about how Tucson was rapidly developing from when it was nothing but desert. They looked at the growth as a spiral getting out of control. The urban heat island effect has made the temperature hotter. The amount of pavement and pollution just keep increasing, and commercial development that is not essential and not pretty or fun to visit spreads and spreads. Places I remember as being completely undeveloped are now paved over, some of them close to home."

* * *

On a typically hot summer day on a street corner near her home, seven-year-old Emilie is doing what many kids her age would do to make some money: running a lemonade stand. Only there is something noticeably different about her endeavor. At the end of the day, she turned her profits, about $15, over to her mother, who wrote a check to the Nature Conservancy. This is how Emilie first became a member of that organization. She credits her parents with having "a powerful influence" on her when she was young and setting her on a course she continues to follow to this day.

As Emilie began reading environmental literature from organizations like the Nature Conservatory and the Sierra Club, she would see descriptions of areas of stunning beauty in Arizona and New Mexico where she had been as a child. "That touched me on a personal level. When I read about dam and freeway building and their adverse environmental affects on those areas, I felt great anger. It made me angry that something valuable had been abused."

Emilie kept the anger on the back burner during her high school years, but in college she began to feel empowered enough to take action. After an unhappy year at Middlebury College in Vermont, too far away from her native desert and difficult for her to relate to, she returned home to enroll at the University of Arizona.

Within months, Emilie was embarking on an adventure that would transform her life. "An ecology professor at the U of A was taking students to Costa Rica for the summer. I met him randomly and he invited me to go with him. I spent over a month with twelve other students backpacking through the Costa Rican forest. Discovering old-growth rainforest was an exotic experience for someone used to the desert. We spent much of our time on the Osa peninsula on the Pacific coast of Costa Rica, in Corcovoda National Park. This area is extremely remote and difficult to get to. You can hike in, take your chances a four-seat Cesna air, or take a small, open motorboat and make a beach landing. We took boats into the park and hiked out when we left. As we traveled down the peninsula's coast, we looked out and saw waterfalls cascading into the sea and flocks of bright red macaws flying above the trees…it was pristine.

"We spent three weeks camping and exploring Corcovado, and saw rare and endangered wildlife every day. We saw four different kinds of monkeys (howler monkeys, spider monkeys, squirrel monkeys, and capuchins), and had several close encounters with Bair's tapirs. One of the most amazing was a tapir we came across on the beach, who walked to within twenty or thirty feet of us and stood downwind for several minutes, just smelling our scents. Most of the animals we saw were not shy; they had not been exposed to human violence and had not learned to fear us. We had any number of adventures during our three weeks, a couple brushes with danger (which is only to be expected in the wilderness), and happily immersed ourselves in the breathtaking beauty of the natural world."

Emilie explains that the national park was created by executive order of the president of Costa Rica in the 1970s. It contains a biological research station and parts of it had once been a cocoa plantation with pasture for livestock. Although the Costa Rican government has a robust history of conservation, almost all the entries in the park's guestbook were foreign tourists. It seems there was little interest on the part of the Costa Ricans themselves to visit their country's protected lands. In fact, there are many pressures on the park, including poaching of both plants and animals and gold mining. This fact was driven home when Emilie saw the park rangers go off on their patrols carrying machine guns, prepared for the confrontation with poachers or miners.

The people living immediately adjacent to the park boundaries are indigenous. They live in poverty and have minimal rights to the resources within the park. Conservation for conservation's sake seemed to be at odds with the unmet needs of the poverty-stricken populations living near the park, and highlighted an environmental conflict that recurs all over the world. Emilie's experience in Costa Rica educated her on issues of land use and human exploitation of natural resources. "The trip crystallized things that I had always felt about the connections between power structures, human relationships, and conservation, and the good and bad ways that can play out." She decided to apply that knowledge back home.

* * *

It was a scorcher of a day during one of the hottest summers in Arizona history, the kind of stifling heat that sends even Southwest natives scrambling for shade, air conditioning and backyard swimming pools, the kind that can quickly wilt the energy and willpower of even the most fit and hardy. On a row of sun-drenched city streets, Emilie pounded the burning pavement, trudging from one door to the next, asking for money. She was working for the Arizona Public Interest Research Group (AZPIRG) on its clean energy campaign that would require utilities to generate more energy from renewable sources. She was turned away more often that not and found little satisfaction in the methods used by AZPIRG.

"I was disappointed in AZPIRG. After learning more about how the campaign was being run, I felt the organization was being disingenuous, using the issue to build up their membership, thereby furthering their own survival as an institution, but not necessarily the cause itself. I wasn't impressed by their lobbying and their adversarial approach. And I wasn't comfortable asking for money and having to make a quota. But I got an interesting look at how environmental activism is often done. I wanted to learn how to make the movement more successful."

Back on the University of Arizona campus, Emilie worked with fellow students to create several rainwater-harvesting projects, and helped develop a course in rainwater harvesting, which subsequently became part of the University curriculum and a permanent course offering. Rainwater harvesting refers to the practice of capturing rainfall and either directing it to vegetation or storing it for later use, rather than encouraging it to run off and flow into the city's storm water system. Because it maximizes the use of rainwater, which is a water source that is almost always overlooked, rainwater harvesting is an extremely effective groundwater conservation technique. The student projects save and put to use hundreds of thousands of gallons of rainwater that are previously being lost, and the student group Emilie helped found is still working with University staff to make the campus more sustainable. For Emilie, this was the beginning of bigger things to come.

* * *

In the late fall of 2006, working from a two-room storefront in Burlington Vermont, using primarily word of mouth, blogs and e-mail messages, a small group of Middlebury College students, led by activist/author Bill McKibben, created the Step It Up 2007 campaign. With no money and no official organization, they set out on an unbelievably fast track to plan a National Day of Climate Action on global warming for Earth Day of 2007. They began with a target of 100 events nationwide. That number was quickly left in the dust.

On April 14, 2007, Step It Up became the largest day of citizen action focusing on global warming in the nation's history, with some 1,400 events held in all fifty states, united around a common message to Congress: cut carbon emissions by eighty percent by the year 2050.

Three months earlier, Emilie was reading an online magazine called *Grist* when she saw an announcement of the upcoming Step It Up day of action. She scanned the list of states where citizens were planning activities for the event. Arizona was not on it. She set out to change that.

For a few months, Emilie had been playing with the idea of putting on a solar powered concert in her hometown. "My little brothers are musicians in bands, so it was perfect because I could promote solar power and get them an awesome gig at the same time. We held a 100 percent solar-powered concert on April 14th in the neighborhood park where my brothers and I used to play when we were little. Part of the concept of the first Step It Up was that people should gather in places that are significant to them, so we chose our childhood park. Six or seven bands played, all powered with photovoltaic panels attached to a demonstration trailer belonging to a local solar power company. Their amplifiers actually ran on solar electricity, rather than plugging into the city's grid. Over 2,000 people attended the event, which in addition to the musicians, invited local nonprofits, companies, and government agencies involved in environmental and sustainability efforts to display booths and activities for concert-goers. The event also featured several speakers, including congressional and state representatives, the dean of the University of Arizona College of Science, and other scientists from the University, discussing global climate change science and specifically, its effects on the Southwest.

"We've been hit hard," Emily says. "Temperatures have been rising significantly. The summer of 2005 was the warmest on record. Drought and very dry conditions have been increasing. Some climate models show that the Southwest could begin looking like the Dust Bowl of 1930s. Weather patterns may become increasingly unpredictable and violent.

"These kind of extreme weather events underscore our vulnerability. We have a lot of hubris. We go around acting like we've conquered nature. But we forget that we're part of nature. If we alter its balance on too large a scale, we will be unable to escape the consequences. I believe that we have a responsibility towards nature, that it is not ours to exploit it as we wish, and that we should show more respect for its complexity, which we do not fully understand. The Earth has warmed and cooled before, and we have little control over those cycles. However, where we do have control, we must take responsibility. Step It Up is asking for an eighty percent reduction in carbon emission by 2050. That's not an arbitrary number. Many of the consequences of climactic warning are positive feedback loops. Take, for example, the melting of the polar icecaps. Once the ice begins melting, it won't melt at a constant, linear rate. It will start melting faster, and then faster, and then even faster. So the key is to cut emissions to a level where we think we can prevent global climate from reaching a tipping point.

"Today, some of the biggest environmental issues facing the city of Tucson are traffic congestion and accompanying air pollution, and an unsustainable, insufficient water supply. Both of these are exacerbated by the explosive, ever-accelerating growth the city has been undergoing over the past few decades."

Emilie is resigned to the fact that she will never again see her hometown the same way it was when she was a little girl. The New West has advanced too far to be driven back. Although the archetype of the Old West remains an integral part of Southwestern history and folklore, it has largely been relegated to dusty archives, old movies and personal memories by unremitting metropolitan development. Emilie pledges to continue working to preserve what is left of the natural beauty and open space of the desert.

While Step It up doesn't yet have an official chapter in Arizona, Emilie is certain that the work done by that organization will continue there. Step It Up has an ambitious agenda of next steps as part of what it calls the National Climate Movement, focusing on legislative action and organizing events and projects across the nation. Furthermore, Solar Rock was held again in the spring of 2008 and is planned for 2009. It is becoming a local tradition that will continue to bring Tucsonans together annually to discover and generate alternate forms of energy generation.

Emilie is no longer officially part of Step It Up efforts in Arizona. She has graduated from the University of Arizona and joined the Teach for America program in New Mexico for two years, where she is an instructor in a low-performing school district. She isn't sure about her plans after her teaching stint. She may return home. But wherever she lives, she will remain active in environmental action, environmental justice and in human-environment relationships.

"We need to wake up and notice what is happening to our planet," Emilie says. "We need to reassess our daily decisions and think about what it would take to live more sustainably—even simple things like drying our clothes on a line or a rack, instead of in a dryer. Incidentally, dryers are the household appliance with the highest energy consumption, and they're totally unnecessary. We're not doing enough as a society about the problem. There are too many people on the planet, and we don't know that we can ever find a way to make them all live sustainably. But there are nevertheless things that individuals can do to decrease their impacts. I will continue to work on that issue. I hope to have some impact on global climate change and environmental issues whatever I end up doing in the future."

James Everett on the streets of north Minneapolis
(Photo courtesy of James Everett)

THE GOVERNOR OF HIP HOP
By Burt Berlowe

On a brilliant summer day in the center of a north Minneapolis park, across a vast expanse of sand and grass, hundreds of people—mostly black—young and old, are enjoying the annual Fathers' Festival, an event promoting the importance of family and offering a welcome respite from the daily turmoil in the city's most violent neighborhood.

The first few hours of the event have been relatively subdued—the patter of playground sounds and family conversation mingling with the chatter at display tables as the bandshell sat idly waiting for its chance to shine.

Then, suddenly and forcefully, the mood of the day begins to change. Piped-in hip hop music blasts from speakers. A bevy of young African American girls parades to a section of grass below the bandshell and begins bouncing and shaking to the music, drawing the scattered crowd toward them. Then, just as quickly, the music stops. One by one, a series of young black men hop up on the portable stage and rap into a hand-held mike, reciting emotionally charged rhymes and telling stories of how they had been rescued from desperate lives by something called the Sub-Zero Collective.

A stocky twenty-seven-year-old black man named James Everett paces the grounds nearby, a slight smile emerging between the edges of his small black beard as he watches the powerful evidence of the movement he had helped create. He is in familiar territory—the park, the neighborhood, the music and culture that had always been so integral to his life. But something is quite different now. He can walk the turf of north Minneapolis knowing he is no longer on fragile ground.

* * *

Chaos was reigning supreme inside the elementary school bus traveling through a rugged area of north Minneapolis. Swear words and paper balls were flying about, taunts and threats running amuck—much of it aimed at fourth-grade pariah James Everett.

Like the bus that day, James' world was frequently a noisy, chaotic place. His restless mind often struggled to track and process information seemingly coming from many directions at once. His wandering attention dashed quickly from side to side or up and down. Viewed as odd by many of his classmates, James often was a ready target of their anger.

As the bus slowed to a stop on a residential street corner, the tumult on board descended on James. Suddenly, he was being chased down the block by twenty other students. Frantically, he outran them all the way home.

Unfortunately, the place called home had never offered James much solace. He grew up in a dysfunctional family and community in Houston, Texas. "I never experienced poverty but was around others who did," he recalls. "In our yard, we had raspberry bushes and pomegranate, banana and fig trees across the front and a 250-year-old pecan tree over my swing set. I was the only kid in the ward with a swing set and a gated yard. I didn't realize how deprived and rough the area around us was. People would lose their homes if it rained too hard.

"There was abuse in my family. My father couldn't keep his hands off my mother. After they separated, I moved in with my mother. We lived in a modest house amidst rundown apartment buildings. Sometimes I stayed at a great uncle's house and went to daycare at a church up the street. I felt safe with my uncle. He would walk down the street and cars moved for him. He was like a grandfather to me.

"Eventually, we moved to an apartment in the suburbs. Mom was working as a head accountant for Tenneco Oil. Everyday, she would drive across town to pick me up at school and take me home. Because of racist policies, she had to do five white people's jobs. She always said that God would provide for her. We were doing pretty well until the oil company closed and she was laid off.

"Although it caused us economic hardship, the layoff may have enhanced Mom's ability to be a parent since she had more time to spend with me. Eventually, she remarried and I had a new stepfather."

It didn't take long for James to realize the kind of man his new stepfather was. "One day, I was outside playing when I discovered that my favorite wagon had been stolen. I wanted to go get it back. Mother said, 'Don't go there. It's not safe. You don't know what those white boys will do to you. Don't get far away from home.' Then my new dad came in and changed the tone. 'Someone stole my boy's wagon, and I'm going to get it back. C'mon, boy,' he said, and pushed me out the door.

"My stepdad checked every wagon in town. Eventually, we found a white woman with a wagon that looked a little like mine. He approached the woman and asked 'Does that wagon have my boy's name on it?' The woman went crazy. My mother came down to find out what was going on. 'What are you doin?' she hollered, then took me home while Dad walked off into the night. At 2:30 a.m., he returned with my wagon. It almost brought tears to my eyes. I thought that wagon was gone. He went two miles to get that wagon for me. That was my first taste of masculinity and a lesson that I should stand up for myself regardless of the odds against me.

"When I would come home after getting in a fight at school, Mom would let it slide. But Dad would say, 'Did you win? Did you whup his ass?' He was a tough guy but also very sensitive and passionate. He was also addicted to crack cocaine, and soon things started missing around the house. I learned firsthand how devastating that drug was to the black community. Eventually, Mom left my dad and started a culturally mixed daycare on the other side of town. I wandered away from home several times.

"Conflict started happening inside of me between who I was biologically and who I wanted to be. I had gone from being in a third grade gifted-and-talented program in Texas to 'James can't sit still or stay focused, maybe he needs to go to a special school.' I was learning how to deal with what they now call Attention Deficit Hyperactivity Disorder (ADHD). After we moved to Minnesota, my school career went downhill. They even put up barriers around my desk and slipped my homework underneath. I was always talking in class. My schoolwork was suffering, and I had to have a tutor. I always passed the tests somehow, but I had problems with homework. They considered sending me to an institution to break my spirit.

"The problem with ADHD children is that they never get the program. They can't figure out that Christopher Columbus discovered America because they're thinking of something else he did. They are already taking it to the next level. They're not very linear. The Information Age is linear. It requires us to absorb large amounts of information. There's like a train station always going through my head. I can be sitting at a table and sense someone in back of me sharpening a pencil. I realized that somehow I had to take control of my condition.

"I started getting into fights with people because my temperament was different. I'd always been a good talker but not a good fighter. Now I learned to be both. I fought on the same street corners where my biological father fought twenty years ago. I had lots of fights with kids on the bus. I remember one time when the oldest kids were throwing paper balls and hit me on the head. Others said to me, 'Don't turn around, they'll beat us up.' But I always had fire in me. If I got hit, something would boil up in and my knees would get weak and I didn't want to get hit again. I turned around to fight back and they came after me. I knew I was going to get chased home. I had warned my mom: 'Leave the door unlocked, I'm comin.' I jumped off the bus with about twenty kids chasing me. I flipped open the gate and ran in the house."

The school bus conflicts were only a small symptom of a growing crime problem in north Minneapolis during the 1980s. The neighborhood's internal conflicts were exacerbated by the integration of gangs from Chicago. James recalls that "there were fourth-graders stealing cars." He soon found himself caught up in spiraling violence.

"I was shot at many times. I once had a gun put to my head. The only reason the gunman didn't pull the trigger was that he found out he was my cousin. I've jumped out of cars at eighty miles an hour during high-speed chases with police on our tail. When I was in junior high, I sold dope with my friends to make money, and when we didn't have it we cooked up fake stuff. When I was fourteen, my mother kicked me out. I moved in with my uncle who was a drug addict. I thought I was a hustler, with pills always in my pocket.

"I watched a lot of things from my window—the real underbelly of the city: police chasing people and grinding their face into the alley because of the lifestyle they were living, not because they were living below the law. I watched guys talk about how a girl would make a good prostitute right in front of her and people smoking away their lives or being taken advantage of sexually because of crack cocaine addiction. I watched rich, big-time dope dealers drive by in their fancy cars, throwing people fifty and 100 dollars worth of dope for twenty dollars into big paper bags. Some crack head would come up and the dealer would shout, 'Come on, get what you want.' I saw firsthand the pain and dismantling of the African American."

During his teenage years, James had difficulty separating himself from his tattered environment. In an effort to fit in with the crowd, he called himself a "big baller," strutting the mean streets of the near North Side with a chip on his shoulder. One day, he went to a girl friend's house toting a pistol, a bag full of dope and some cash, expecting to make a big hit with her. But when he began to brag about the dough in his pocket, she surprised him with her retort:

"What you got, that's illegal money."
"What's the difference, it's money."
"It's illegal. It isn't going to last."

"It was the first time I was blasted like that by a young girl," James says. "It really got me thinking about what I was doing. Soon after that, my mother made me move back with her and all that (bad) stuff stopped."

As James began reassessing his life, he detached himself from the world for an entire week. He went into a cocoon and shut down, reflecting on his past, clashing and arguing with himself; his conscious and subconscious debating out loud. The turmoil manifested itself in an odd nightmare experience that shook James to the core.

I was roaming two streets in the underbelly of North Minneapolis robbing people in broad daylight. I ran up to someone's car, intent on making them my next victim. It was my cousin. He looked at me and said 'James, what you doin?' Then it was like God pulled me up by my belt loop out of the way and began talking to me. He said He had a plan for me, a way to go in life that was bigger than the things I was doing.

"After that, everything began to come together. In my insanity, I hadn't realized that there were shackles on me until I moved to get them off. I did a Muslim ceremony that is the equivalent of a baptism, during which I asked God to send me a signal that I was doing the right thing. I enrolled in an alternative school, studying offbeat religions.

"Because of my full life experiences, because I had three fathers, I had found out what it was like to be a full-fledged man. Because my mother was able to leave those bad situations, I had learned not to be subservient but to restore my connection with people and the system."

James began organizing neighborhood crime-prevention block clubs, started a nonprofit group that worked with kids who were trying to get money to buy drugs, and became a youth organizer for the Initiative For Violence-Free Families "My main purpose was to help people build new relationships with each other," he says.

In the meantime, he continued to be tormented by the effects of ADHD. He discovered that the prescription Ritalin he was taking was doing more damage than good. He got into an argument and ended up in a mental institution where "I met real crazies and found out how sane I was, also how people get strung out on different drugs and what it does to them. When I left there, I thought I was going to cry."

Eventually, James found a way to use his excessively active mind to his advantage, channeling that energy into a positive force for change. The train was still running through his head, but he found that he could process large amounts of information in a small amount of time.

Before long, James had become a professional youth-program organizer and was running six different companies, while being a full-time father. Most recently, he has found unique ways to combine music with political activism as a way to assist and inspire the next generation. He began as a deejay, taking the name Ray Freeze, spinning disks at clubs and other venues, as well as producing and filming youth-oriented events and performances, such as the award-winning cable TV show called "Don't Believe the Hype." Eventually, the deejay service became the Sub-Zero Collective. "With Sub-Zero entertainment, we're using deejaying as a device to launch a political movement.

"I'm the hip hop governor. I'm an official voice of black music. Hip hop is the vehicle, the instrument of the movement. There's a lot we don't allow, like no negative lyrics. We allow true expression through hip hop and rap. We make our money on speaking engagements and clothing sales. We can rebuild people into respected citizens. We have twenty different businesses under us. Sub-Zero is the lightning rod that fuels everything. We're the only organic hip hop political organization. Yo The Movement was started a few years ago in Minnesota. It exchanges resources with the Sub-Zero Collective, and, best of all we've got each other's back to the end, Brother."

* * *

On most any weather-friendly day, James likes to take his cart for a spin around the neighborhood. This is not your ordinary kind of cart but rather a specially constructed device that lugs around some powerful baggage. It contains a speaker system that James uses to broadcast his message of peace and hope, along with hip hop music, to anyone who will listen. It may also be a symbol of strange spiritual circumstances that have dramatically impacted his life.

"One day, I was riding down a north Minneapolis street near my home on a bike my mom had given me, attached to the cart with a speaker on board to play music and talk to passers-by. I had previously been reading about the Ark of the Covenant in Second Samuel in the Bible. In chapter six verse three, it talks about bringing the covenant of the ark down the hillside where there was rejoicing with joyous harps and flutes. My friends Don (a Minneapolis city councilman) and Sondra Samuels live on a hillside. And my wagon plays music. The Bible I looked at is the King James version with my name engraved on it. I live at 2353 James. Those numbers add up to thirteen. That is the number of transition—Jesus and his twelve disciples, a baker's dozen. A roofer who previously lived in the house engraved the word 'Jesus' on my roof. James was Jesus' half-brother and one of his disciples and played a significant role in his life.

"I believe all of this is more than coincidence. In playing your part of the movie of life you may be intertwined in your own density and the destiny of others more than you realize. Numbers don't lie. And I think these numbers are a message. I didn't go looking for this message. It just happened that way. It's a sacred blessing."

James became a Muslim in a special ceremony in 2001. It was a big step for him. Born and raised a Christian, his mom is one of the biggest gospel ministers in the Twin Cities. He says he felt a "calling" to be a Muslim. "It helped me to bring some reference to my life."

In 2007, James moved to Green Valley Ranch, Colorado in order to set up an office there of the Sub-Zero Collective. He has continued to maintain an official residence in north Minneapolis. He travels back and forth between the two communities, continuing his work on behalf of youth and the underprivileged.

In Minneapolis, he is leading efforts to build a Twin Cities Center for Arts and Technology that would create some 400 jobs. A $4 million project sponsored by the Sub-Zero Collective, the proposed center is modeled after the Manchester Craftsman's Guild in Pittsburgh. According to James, the center will be collectively owned and will serve everyone from welfare moms to youth. It would house facilities for the culinary arts, pottery, graphic design, pharmaceutical training and a recording studio. James calls it "the biggest thing to happen in north Minneapolis in years."

The main thoroughfare that separates north Minneapolis from communities to the south is called Olson Memorial Highway. It is named after former Minnesota governor Floyd B. Olson. In a 1936 speech, Olson emphasized his believe in social entrepreneurship, the radical idea that corporations should give money back to the community. To honor Olson and his message, the Sub-Zero Collective is involved in developing the Floyd B. Olson social entrepreneurship center to be built on the frontage road at James and Olson Highway. James is also assisting with the creation of a Hall of Fame for alumni of North High School, his alma mater. These projects are a partnership between the Collective and major area corporations.

In all of his work, James sees himself as a bridge between generations and a catalyst for mediation among dueling members of various age brackets. "There is a battle between the Baby Boomers and the Generation X (my generation). Power is never based on fairness. I am fighting the wrongful effort to destroy our whole generation thirty-five and under. The Baby Boomers are trying to destroy us with psychotropic drugs. We're being sent to Iraq. There is an attack on teen pregnancy, enslavement of women barely younger than ten for thousands of years. Pornography and exploitation of young girls runs rampant for the amusement of Baby Boomers. There are teenage girls dancing at night clubs. We're the toys. They have to get rid of twenty-eight to thirty-three-year-olds (like me) because we could bring about a revolution.

"I went from 'Damn,' to 'What the hell is wrong with me?' to 'I got it.' God allowed me to step through the cracks. I understand the struggles of those who went before me. Those who were the oppressed are now becoming the oppressor. It's time for Baby Boomers to be honest about the assassination of a whole generation. Like when the fish swims under the shark and gets the leftovers. What has happened is we're carrying the damn shark. He's eating off us."

James' response to this conflict is to continue to build the hip hop movement, creating marketing and distribution opportunities for artists in that field, while infusing the music with grassroots politics." The hip hop movement is stagnating as the Baby Boomers move on in transition," he says. "[At the same time], more people are rapping for freedom. And hip hop is the strongest in Minnesota than anywhere in the nation.

"The Collective is a fully democratic organization that is learning how to counter capitalism. We're the ones that can stop a capitalist dictatorship and build alternatives to capitalism though social entrepreneurship. We're developing a new kind of currency that compliments American dollars and creates a sustainable society without banks in control. As part of the movement from dollars to gold coins (Amero currency) that will emerge from the North American Union, we are introducing the idea of gold coins with famous people of color on them. Our organization is a living organism that emphasizes the solid difference between corporations and an American dollar society without bank control.

"This movement is a mix between mercenaries, entrepreneurs and freedom fighters. We're the Black Panthers without a communist spin. Wherever freedom has been promised to us, we're pursuing it. Our long-range goal is a global political party comparable to the United Nations. We have this model. We have a business plan. I want my views to live on forever. I believe they are the views of the people. My thoughts are that free men should be heard."

* * *

One of the reasons James moved to Colorado was to be there for the 2008 Democratic National Convention. He cut a deal with Glenwood Inglewood to be their official spokesman for the convention. In return, they agreed to give the Collective a percentage of their sales.

"Our ultimate goal is developing a generation of eclectic leadership that will result in the formation of a new political party. The political wild card in this country is the kids seventeen to twenty-six years of age. Many of the youth in the Collective come from alternative schools and tough family situations. We give them a chance to lead. The Collective is tied together by people understanding that we need change, by people of all colors and backgrounds saying 'enough is enough' and wanting to do something about it."

James is currently in the process of his own power transition. He is turning over the ownership of the Sub-Zero Collective to its membership. He will still be supporting Sub-Zero but will focus on the Internet, where he will become a virtual politician and activist. "I will have a website and a Blackberry wired to the country, so people can ask questions of politicians. It will be a way to bring Big Brother out in the open with live broadcasts and getting out the vote on the streets. It will be nonpartisan, supporting candidates but not parties.

"A hip hop-infused cultural movement is ramming down the throat of the capitalist dictatorship and getting resources back to people. We are the sexy alternative to capitalism. Until recently, the hip hop movement didn't have a leader. We're the ones to lead it. We're the helping hand that can turn into a fist. If we put our mind to it we can get anybody kicked off the city council. We can shut down faxes and flood City Hall with 500 calls in twenty minutes. We campaigned in the 2004 presidential election and our canvassing area had an eighty-percent voter turnout, the highest in Minnesota. No one can argue with our political success. Our political power and influence are not even a debate anywhere in the city. We've got raw, fresh energy and people waiting to speak. Pressure bursts pipes. It also turns coal into diamonds. We want to walk lines that other people can't walk, without losing our integrity. We have to be able to pass the torch to the next generation. It's a whole 'nother world we're going to be in. People just need the first stone to be thrown, and they will get the raw energy to speak and harness that energy to create a revolution."

Chapter Nine
The Reformers

INTRODUCTION
TAKING BACK OUR DEMOCRACY

Reform is the ultimate goal of any significant social movement. The dictionary defines the word "reform" as "making better by correcting faults or evils and introducing better procedures." Reform is a part of the process of social change but is distinguished by the extent to which that change takes place. It is the most dramatic, deep-seated and lasting form of system transformation.

In this closing section of the book, we examine three of the most significant reform movements happening in the U.S. around relevant areas of our culture: our election system, our media and corporate America. All of these insurgencies were brought about by extensive citizen dissatisfaction with the status quo and subsequent, massive organizing efforts. Beyond these individual issues, there is something much larger at stake in these reform movements—the status of American democracy.

In recent years, our democracy has been seriously eroded in many alarming ways. Election fraud and disenfranchisement have diminished the right of the people to make decisions about who governs them. Media consolidation has taken the airwaves away from the people and placed it in the hands of giant corporations and has begun to threaten the most democratic form of communication—the Internet. Government-sanctioned prying into the data and lives of average Americans and a strategy of empire building in this country and around the world have centralized power among the elite and taken it away from the people.

From our opening story of Californian Benjamin Sher and his Democracy Caravan to succeeding sections on electoral, media and corporate reform, there is an underlying theme that runs through this chapter: Americans are fed up with losing their democracy and are rising up to take it back.

Ben Sher with Howard Dean and the Democracy Caravan
(Photo courtesy of Ben Sher)

DEMOCRACY ON WHEELS

By Burt Berlowe

Benjamin Sher eases his thirty-six foot fifth-wheel trailer onto the northern California freeway on his way through America. His scheduled stops read like a Greyhound Bus trip: Placerville… Los Angeles… Phoenix… Albuquerque… Austin… Lawrence…Des Moines …. It is early October 2004, and the whiff of presidential politics is in the air. Across the country, candidates are scouring for votes, and Ben and his co-organizers are on their heels. Their target is not elective office but the very core of our political system. They are out to reclaim our democracy.

Ben's once-ordinary recreational vehicle has been meticulously converted into the first national Democracy Caravan. It is loaded with all the trappings of a grassroots political campaign—an on-board café, satellite Internet hookup, film facilities, stacks of flyers and a theme sign on the door that reads: "Got Democracy?" The first leg of his journey, made with fellow traveler David Schwenk, will take about 120 days and cover some 6,000 miles, visiting mostly small towns in California, Arizona, New Mexico, Texas, Oklahoma, Kansas, Missouri, Iowa and Florida, focusing on presidential candidate caucus activity, peppering the candidates on key issues related to democracy reform such as campaign finance, giant corporations' lobbying, and registering voters.

"Our objective is to plant more deeply in the mind of average Americans that we have lost our democracy and to work with them to take it back," Ben explains in a pre-trip interview. "We want to appeal to ordinary people, asking them about the state of the union and how it affects them. It's a populist campaign. Although I don't like that word. I prefer pro-democracy. We plan to use our caravan tour to build a new pro-democracy movement."

At first glance, the forty-four-year-old Palo Alto, California native doesn't seem like the type to embark on a rugged cross-country journey to build a national social change movement. Raised in a privileged household, weaned on mainstream politics, and a graduate of an exclusive college, Ben now leads a settled suburban life as a mortgage payer, small business owner and father of two boys.

Ben's decision to become a progressive activist has often put him at odds with the capitalist system he benefits from as an owner of small rental properties, as well as with the values of neighbors he lives with everyday. Nevertheless, he has made the difficult choice to use his education and social network to promote deep cultural change. The origins of that decision go back to his childhood.

* * *

Once upon a time, Benjamin Sher believed in American democracy. When he was in fourth grade, he helped his father campaign successfully for city council and later for the state legislature, discovering the upside of traditional electoral politics. But at the same time, he says, "I witnessed the decline and fall of American democracy through the lens of political campaigns. I watched the rise of the pollsters and the consultants, who are now becoming very rich in the process. That has caused me to lose faith in democracy. Some of these people are still my friends, but I find it awkward to be around them. I knew them when they were just getting their start and lived out of old Volvo station wagons. Now they have expensive homes and lifestyles and season tickets. Worse, those that made it to the top of their field have become media pundits and celebrities in their own right, part of a media-celebrity system in a constellation of corruption that has degraded our democracy to the breaking point."

Ben's commitment to make our planet a better place arose out of an incident in a high school class. "We were exposed to images of Earth from space and environmental groups featuring that image and books like *The Population Bomb*. It all added up to a sense of the fragility of the planet and the need to work on saving it. This led me to environmental activism both globally and locally. I remember working with The Committee for Green Foothills to save the Bay Area from development."

While attending Amherst College, Ben began reading books about corporations and their negative impacts on society. He became increasingly concerned about the excessive power of giant corporations, as well as "the rise of a new class of super wealthy in whose interest the country seems to be increasingly run. Again and again, he opines, "I have observed the public kneeling before a tyranny of the super-rich and self-proclaimed experts and giving up their rights.

"Power has even shifted away from our elected officials to places they have little power to effect—giant corporations, the super wealthy and large institutions. The time I felt most powerless was during protests at the Nevada test site against nuclear weapons.

"During those protests, I did feel the weight of just how difficult it would be to turn this ship of state around, away from a politics of greed and one based upon a love of money towards a politics of generosity founded upon a love of life. It made me mad. I began to think it was time to organize."

During the 1980s, Ben participated in anti-nuke rallies and was arrested and jailed several times. In the '90s, he became an early member of the Alliance for Democracy and learned much from the small think tank, POCLAD, the Program on Corporations, Law and Democracy. He worked on the corporate power campaign of the Women's International League for Peace and Freedom, taking periodic trips back East to meetings, retreats, conventions and so forth, as well as to anti-globalization protests in D.C., Quebec City, and the legendary "battle of Seattle," where demonstrators shut down an international meeting of the World Trade Organization.

"In Quebec City," Ben recalls, "I participated in the protest against the foreign ministerial. I got arrested while sitting peaceably on the street as the riot police rushed forth to clear the area. I refused to move and got hit with a baton on my thigh, which produced a huge bruise, and I spent twenty-four hours in a Quebec City jail. I had been arrested previously as an anti-nuclear activist in the '80s. But it was more profound getting arrested in a foreign country at a major international demonstration where tear gas, rubber bullets and pepper spray were the order of the day. Experiencing such violence firsthand has made me more militant overall."

Ben decided not to follow in his father's footsteps. "I'm fairly independent and would not have liked 'going along to get along' inside of a political party. I doubted that as a politician I could have gotten much done. Ultimately, movements have more power to affect reform than politicians do, who finally get the message only when the movement gets strong enough. That, to me, is the lesson of how reform gets done in American history."

* * *

As things got steadily worse in this country, especially after 9/11, Ben came up with the idea of the Democracy Caravan. The main inspiration for it came from his reading of the book *The Populist Moment*. It is about how tens of thousands of farmers came together by horse carts in the 1870s and 1880s. Farms were laid out in grids and meeting points were at the four corners of four farms. Farmer's alliances would gather at southern crossroads of the farms from the Gulf to the Ohio River with detailed plans for state charters, county organizations and sub-alliances, along with aggressive anti-monopoly oratory.

"That's my vision—to sweep people up as we move across the country, bidding people from all walks of life to 'join us at the crossroads,' where we will rally and organize to take back our country. We call ourselves Patriots of the American Street. Our crossroads will be shopping malls and Wal-Mart parking lots, art shows and neighborhood festivals, wherever the public congregates. We will attempt to get local supporters to meet us outside of town and escort us into Los Angeles, or we'll ask local organizers to meet us at the top of the pass and help us create a spectacle as we drive into L.A.

"We'll register voters, examine voting systems; hand out literature, do interviews, film people we meet; provide free books, articles, and Internet access from our on-board democracy café; and invite people to our evening gatherings for more in-depth discussions and entertainment. We'll help start democracy clubs and circles and partner with other organizations. We are seeking potential movement people who can rally their communities to pledge to restore democracy, and who will build and maintain a network. We want to communicate with small businesses, homemakers, steelworkers, families, artists, activists, educators, veterans, the unemployed average folks, to listen to what they have to say about the state of our union. Then we'll confront political candidates on democracy issues.

"We're nonpartisan. The idea is to build a movement, not support any particular candidate, but to encourage political debate on pressing issues such as electoral reform. That is the first order of business, the act of defining the current state of affairs in the U.S and then questioning all of the presidential candidates about our pro-democracy platform as they pass through their states in search of votes. One of our major activities will be doing video interviews of average Americans, asking them about 'the state of their household' and showing the film during our alternative state of the union address in D.C."

The purpose of the caravan is to build support and momentum as it goes. Ben has a core group of travelers committed to finishing the journey; others will be on board for portions of the trip, including researchers, musicians, organizers, fundraisers, and what he calls "road crews and local yokels," all of whom will contribute to the costs of the journey, making sure that the caravan pays its own way.

"The Democracy Caravan strives to change how we speak about politics in America." Ben explains. "The American people don't get a seat at the table. We get political spin fed to us through a complicit media run by the very corporations buying off our leaders. The caravan also has its origin in my view of democracy in an age of mass media since corporate television and radio are the primary shapers of public opinion both with respect to candidates and issues. I want the caravan to be a form of alternative media. In the absence of owning and operating our own television and radio networks, we must devise alternative methods. The Democracy Caravan will become a moving billboard that thousands of Americans will see as we drive across the country."

With all of its excitement and promise, Ben's caravan journey is fraught with risk and personal sacrifice. He expects to encounter traffic and police problems; harassment from those who don't agree with his mission; the unpredictable elements of overnight campouts; and stretches of loneliness, isolation, and uncertainty about what lies ahead. He is financing the entire venture despite being without steady income, living on savings and revenue from some rental property he owns.

But his most serious challenge could be dealing with the burden that the expedition is placing on his personal life. "The caravan has already put a strain on my family life. Just as a soldier in Iraq is taken away from his family, I will be away from my kids and wife about seventy-five percent of the time in the first year. They aren't exactly jumping for joy about it. My spouse doesn't understand or support my plan. My kids will probably have some problems because of my absence. I do hope to take them on some part of the journey later on. Being an activist is generally a hazard to family life. I hated to do it. But I feel so committed to the cause.

"I also will suffer a loss of social identity. Unless you have a regular job in the workaday world, you are more or less adrift around the great majority of folks whose identities stabilize around their job title. As a doctor, lawyer or businessman inside a firm, aside from job security and a big salary, you also get a whole social fabric. Activists get a constant nagging feeling of not really having grown up since they decline to act and dress the conventional adult role.

"We are faced with a daunting task," Ben says. "Many Americans feel too over-worked to pay attention to what is happening to our democracy. Many say it's a losing battle. We disagree. Dozens of organizations and thousands of people are working to rebuild a grassroots movement to take back our democracy. I believe the movement will take some thirty years to succeed. I have to look at this project in the long term. This is the beginning of a new era in society that will change the system. The Caravan will be an ongoing project that won't end until its objectives are fulfilled.

"Its time for us, the general populace, to recover the rich history of our nation's struggles, to extend democratic rights to more and more people. It's time to speak out with one harmonious voice. The Democracy Caravan is part of an effort to build a long-term, profound movement capable of restoring hope, equality and democracy in America. We believe the survival of democracy depends on cooperative efforts to maintain the liberty of self-government. We seek to educate, activate and mobilize average citizens to help build a pro-democracy movement capable of protecting the basic rights and freedoms of all Americans. The Democracy Caravan will be on the horizon as a traveling testimony to democracy in motion."

Following the successful completion of the caravan's journey, Ben has remained active in the movement to take back democracy. Recently, he has helped organize a response protesting the U.S. Supreme Court decision in the Citizens United case that expands the power of corporations to fund political elections.

THE ELECTION REFORM/VOTERS RIGHTS MOVEMENT

The election fiasco of 2000 and the questionable results of the 2004 presidential battle have generated a citizen movement in the United States to make the electoral process more democratic. In January of 2005, author/journalist John Nichols wrote in *The Nation* magazine, "At the grassroots level, there appears to be growing support for a count-every-vote, eliminate-every-opportunity-for-fraud standard that would radically alter the way in which the United States runs elections."

Electoral reform projects can include measures that change election laws, redefine citizen eligibility to vote, change the way candidates or political parties gain ballot access, and alter the definitions of electoral constituencies and district boundaries; design or implement new ballot systems or voting equipment; tighten scrutiny of elections to ensure safe, honest voting; limit the influence of bribes, coercion, and conflicts of interest; regulate campaign financing; encourage participation; and provide alternative vote-counting procedures and rules by which winners are determined.

Current electoral reform/rights efforts have been largely directed at ensuring secure, accurate, and transparent elections in response to concerns about the reliability and vulnerability of new voting machines, and addressing issues of voter disenfranchisement and the influence of big money in political campaigns. This includes such revolutionary proposals as Instant Runoff Voting, a national popular vote that would eliminate the electoral college, and public financing of elections. The main pretext of the movement is that the American election system is broken and badly needs fixing.

We have picked out a few stories that illustrate the breadth and depth of this movement and the individuals and organizations that are making it work.

David Cobb
(Photo from Internet)

TURNING GREEN
By Burt Berlowe

The new voting rights movement has a special meaning for David Cobb. Its underlying message of equality cuts deep to the core of his very being. His passion for the cause is born out of a personal struggle with oppression and the impact it has had on his life.

David grew up in poverty in a rural Texas ghetto. "My family was considered poor white trash," he recalls. "We were probably the only home in my generation without a flush toilet. My father was a 'junk man.' From the time I was seven years old, I would go with my dad and brother to the dump to collect waste. By sixth grade, I was working odd jobs to earn money and get out of the rural ghetto. Still, into high school, I was patriotic. I thought America was the best country in the world."

The experience of growing up poor did have an upside for David. "I began to understand oppression, race and class. I wanted white privilege. Nobody wanted to be seen as white trash. Because I was white, I was able to get out of poverty and make it to college. I also realized that I had been lied to, that America wasn't this great country after all. That was white-people propaganda.

I was being told a creation myth, the white slant on how great the U.S. is. Our country was not living up to its promises, and I wanted it to."

By the time he was in college at the University of Houston, David had begun to do his part to fulfill his promise, working on an anti-apartheid campaign that discouraged institutions from doing business with South Africa.

When the Reverend Jesse Jackson decided to run for president of the United States in 1984, David jumped on board and repeated the effort in subsequent elections for Jackson and Governor Jerry Brown. "I learned what it was like for whites to be working under black men and under women. I also learned that the election primary process in our country has, in essence, killed the democratic process. Our campaigns were full of great ideas but we didn't have money. Thus, the truth gave in to corporate power. In Houston, I was part of a campaign to raise the minimum wage. We had seventy-five to eighty percent support at the beginning, but then the opposition poured in over a million dollars and we narrowly lost."

In 1996, David Cobb turned Green. He had become disenchanted with some of the Democratic Party's policies and began seeking an alternative. "I found out about the Green Party. It was in a fledgling stage then, just a few chapters. It had begun putting up local candidates, building the party from the ground up. The system doesn't make it easy to be a third party. Organizers of alternative political organizations are considered as much out of the box as can be. In reality, there are two types of people who are generally out of the box: visionaries and kooks. The Green Party has both."

While practicing law in Texas, David worked on Ralph Nader's presidential campaign. He soon dropped out of law work to become a full-time organizer. In 1992, he ran a losing campaign for attorney general on a campaign to revoke the charter of corporations that violate the law and cause harm.

The 2000 election results stuck in David's craw. "I knew that (George) Bush had stolen the election, not just on election day or in the Supreme Court. Six months ahead of the election (Florida Governor) Jeb Bush and (Florida Secretary of State) Katherine Harris systematically purged black voters from the voter rolls. Then (Vice-President) Gore let them get away with it by not contesting the results and then presiding over the silencing of the black caucus that was protesting the outcome. I saw that there was more to elections than how the votes are cast and counted—that the voting system was encouraging people to vote against who they hate the most rather than voting for who they like."

In 2004, David took up Nader's mantle, running as the Green Party candidate for president. He garnered a small percentage of the vote but used the campaign as a launching pad that skyrocketed him into the midst of an exploding voting rights movement.

Further impetus for that movement came out of the 2004 election. "There were voting irregularities in Ohio, Florida, New Mexico and elsewhere," David says angrily. "(Senator John) Kerry pledged that every vote would be counted but then didn't challenge the outcome or ask for an investigation. The Greens initiated actions that led to a recount in Ohio and also filed a lawsuit challenging the election results." The lawsuit was eventually dismissed in court. David has continued to advocate for electoral reform through the Liberty Tree Foundation and other organizations focused on the issue.

"We've finally got a movement going for election reform in this country. We're working toward a new generation of a voting rights movement," he says, the enthusiasm growing in his voice. "It's a new movement for democracy. It includes electoral reform—i.e., voter-verified paper trails, Instant Runoff Voting, abolition of the electoral college, campaign financing—issues that get at the way elections are conducted. It is about making sure that everyone has an equal opportunity to vote and that their votes are counted.

"Elections are the infrastructure of democracy. We build physical infrastructure. We should build an infrastructure of democracy. We need to completely overhaul our election system. We have lost democracy in our elections. We need to democratize them. The election rights movement transcends electoral reform in moving us towards a more democratic society. I predict that within ten to twenty years Instant Runoff Voting will be used in every election and most cities will have public-funded elections."

David has never forgotten where he came from. His childhood battle to overcome poverty and racism has fueled his life's work. "I have a special interest in voting rights and in the larger issues of racial discrimination and the discrepancy between the wealthy and the poor," he says. "That is my identity in politics. I have an absolute commitment to creating democracy from the bottom up, to getting ordinary people in power, and in the process, transforming our society. That includes going away from a winner-take-all election system to having better ballot access for minorities.

"I want a society where everyone has their basic needs met. Martin Luther King spoke of 'the beloved community.' I want to help create a beloved community. It should be our birthright to be loving towards each other, to be our brothers' keeper. We all need to be part of that change. My mission is to make it so nobody has to live like I did when I was growing up."

Kirk Lund performing at showing of the film *Uncounted*
(Photo courtesy of Kirk Lund)

NEVER-ENDING TOUR
By Burt Berlowe

If our votes don't count, how can we call this a democracy?
—Bill Funk, a Utah town clerk and voting reform advocate in the film
Uncounted

In the small rural Ohio county the vote count had just begun. For all intents and purposes, the election seemed to be over, with George Bush re-anointed for a second term after a close, hard-fought presidential election that culminated with the results in this battleground state. Yet, in this and similar outposts around Ohio, polling officials were still pouring over the returns with a fine-toothed-comb.

Kirk Lund stood nearby, his lean frame bending forward, his piercing green eyes riveted on each ballot. He had driven up from Minneapolis as an observer called into action by demands for a recount of Ohio's votes that could affect the election outcome. What Kirk saw during that visit would further shake what little faith he had left in our electoral system and make its reform an integral part of his life.

* * *

Kirk tossed and turned in his cot, shaking with fright every time he heard another bomb go off nearby or saw the Army helicopters buzzing over his head. It was 1987, and there was a war going on nearby between U.S-backed soldiers and the Salvadoran guerillas. Fifteen-year-old Kirk and his mother, stepfather and sister were spending the night in a rural village where a young girl had been killed by mortar shells a week earlier.

It had all begun innocently enough. Kirk's mother was a Latin American educator and worked at the Center for Global Education at Augsburg College in Minneapolis. She organized travel seminars to El Salvador, among other places, and lived there for a year and a half with Kirk's stepdad, a missionary in San Salvador for five years. Kirk and his sisters spent much of their summers there, continuing that practice even as civil war raged nearby.

"My stepfather got out of the country in November of 1999," Kirk says. "I learned years later that he had fled his home when the Salvadoran military base was in our backyard and he was attacked and pursued by the Salvadoran military who wanted to kill him. As I studied more about the conflict in El Salvador and role the U.S. had there, the ideals of the communist rebels made a lasting impression on me. That was the beginning of my wanting to work for a more just foreign policy."

In 1984, when he was just eleven years old, Kirk marched in protest against the war in Central America. "It was during (President Ronald) Reagan's term. I still remember the chants we did: 'Ronald Reagan he's no good. Send him back to Hollywood.'

"I traveled to El Salvador and saw the war firsthand and as part of the group from the Center for Global Education. When I was fifteen years old, I traveled with Mom's group for four or five days. We had meetings with people from a wide range of sectors of Salvadoran society. We met with campesinos (peasant farmers), legislators from the Christian Democrat party and members of the Salvadoran military. As part of a college study-abroad program, we went to a cooperative farm in Nicaragua. That was all part of planting the seed.

"When I was in the ninth grade, I wrote a research paper about American foreign policy in El Salvador. That paper was the beginning of a journey that led to my going to law school at the City University of New York (CUNY) with a plan to pursue a career in international human rights law. The story that

I used in my application essay was about staying in the Salvadoran countryside listening to the bombing."

It was a scorching hot, steamy day. My mother and I were playing catch with a baseball out in the street, and I didn't quite understand why she felt uncomfortable about doing so. I was fifteen years old— not quite old enough to drive. The street wasn't paved. There was an ox cart parked off to the side of the road. We were in a small, rural village in El Salvador where the people knew poverty and civil war on a daily basis. The year was 1987, and this was first time I had witnessed poverty and war with my own eyes. With hindsight, my mother's discomfort about playing catch with her son in this setting is much clearer to me. We were using a real baseball and expensive gloves in a community where local children had only a rocky soccer field and a tattered ball with which to play.

That night, we stayed in the home of a Salvadoran family in that rural community. We slept on cots, all together in the same room. We could hear the family's pigs and chickens making noise just outside the door all night, but this is not what kept us awake. It was a far fainter but much more threatening noise that worried us, the sound of the Salvadoran military bombing the slopes of a nearby volcano. My mother continually reassured us that we were safe, but I was truly frightened. Only that day we had been told that a week before a young girl in the community had been killed by a stray mortar shell. This was the Salvadoran civil war up close. The seed that was planted in me during this experience has been watered and nurtured many times over. My journey to law school began with this trip to El Salvador.

While in law school, Kirk founded the Lawyers Artist Alliance and participated in a three-day hunger strike protesting denial of tenure to one of the professors. In 1994, he made his initial foray into electoral politics as part of a Citizen's Election Observer mission to El Salvador.

"My most recent and most rewarding trip to El Salvador came in 1994 as a member of the United States Citizens Elections Observer Mission. With new hope, after the ravages of a dozen years of civil war, the people began lining up before dawn to cast their ballots for every elective office in the country. I had the opportunity to help ensure that these elections were free and fair and not marred by violence like so many past elections in El Salvador. While we were waiting in line to receive our Election Observer credentials from the Salvadoran government, I met a law student from the U.S. who had traveled to El Salvador on his own and intended to seek Election Observer credentials. This was the first connection I made between a legal education and my interest in a career working for peace and justice."

* * *

How sad is the sound of the raindrops
On the roofs made of cardboard
How sadly live my people
In the houses of cardboard... *

Kirk saw the cardboard houses when he was in Central America—the peasant families struggling to survive in substandard living conditions. Ever since he was a child playing with his dad's tools in their Minneapolis home, Kirk had loved to build and repair things. When he found out about opportunities to build housing for the poor people of Latin America, it seemed like the ideal opportunity for him to combine his interest in construction with his compassion for the residents of the cardboard houses.

"In the summer of 1996, I quit my job (at an Applebee's restaurant in St. Paul), packed up my apartment and moved to northern Mexico to spend the summer building houses in a border town. I was privileged to work with twenty-one Mexican families in need to provide them with decent housing."

During the summers of 1996 and '97, Kirk made five trips to Latin America, building houses and supervising work crews with a nonprofit organization called Constructores Para Cristo (Builders for Christ) in the Mexico border town of Piedras Negras. It was long days from 5 a.m. to 10 p.m., often in 100-degree heat, doing something you have to believe in for the people who had been living in shacks made of cardboard and scrap wood and metal. We gave leftover construction materials to other neighborhood people for patch up work." Kirk also worked a stint as a site supervisor for Habitat for Humanity, renovating houses for poor people in Minneapolis and St. Paul, Minnesota, including the renovation of an 1890s row house on State Street.

During the summer of his first year of law school, Kirk took a trip to Cuba to study law at the University of Havana. He also served an internship with Texas Rural Legal Aid working on immigrant farm worker cases. "There were conflicts between the migrant workers and land owners. The owners had hired immigrant workers and refused to pay them what they had coming, as well as mistreating them in many other ways. It was a trial run for what I hoped would be a career in human rights law."

The spring day in 1997 began with a lot of promise for Kirk. He was working at Applebee's restaurant in St. Paul preparing to move to Mexico to for the summer construction stint with Builders for Christ. Then the strange feelings that had haunted him off and on for years flared up—the hypochondriac-like fears about his health, the urge to check and re-check locked doors and stove settings, the difficulty in focusing on the task at hand. He calls it "a watershed day" in his battle with obsessive-compulsive disorder (OCD)—a time when he finally was able to face his demons head-on. "I did what I thought was the mentally healthy thing to do. I talked to my dad. He referred me to a counselor who put me on Prozac.

"I can trace my OCD symptoms back to elementary school, but I had no idea what it was," Kirk says. "When I went to Mexico, I continued to struggle with it, constantly worrying that I had some debilitating disease. I was always worried about my health. I had to seek constant reassurance. I have often gone to the doctor for things I didn't have to go for.

"One psychiatrist I saw didn't want to add cognitive therapy and just kept changing my medication to try to find the 'magic bullet.' I was on several different medications under his care, some of which had bad side effects. One gave me dry mouth and I couldn't get enough water. Another side effect was weight gain. I put on fifty pounds.

"After I initially went on Prozac, I moved to Mexico for the summer to build the houses, traveled to Guatemala to attend Spanish Language school, then moved to Boston for a few months. While I was in Boston, I ran out of Prozac and wasn't seeing a psychiatrist at the time. The OCD symptoms had mostly gone away, so I quit taking the medication.

"When I moved from Boston back to Minnesota, I returned to my former job at Applebee's and worked at the Twin Cities affiliate of Habitat for Humanity, while applying for entrance to several law schools. I failed the New York bar exam the first time. I started a law firm with some friends then began to prepare for another try at the bar exam. But when I was studying for it, I had a full relapse of OCD along with severe depression. When I took the test, I could only get through fifty-four of the 100 questions. I was so demoralized, I didn't go back in to take the second half of the test. That was probably the worst shape I had been in.

"I'm continuing to have counseling and am now taking Zoloft, which helps alleviate the symptoms." Despite any stigmas that may be attached to it, Kirk is more than willing to talk about his OCD saga. "I'm not ashamed of my OCD," he says. "It is part of my life experience."

The year 1997 was significant for Kirk in another life-changing way. Even as he hit an emotional roadblock, he found a path to a new, fulfilling journey on and below the streets of urban America.

Kirk's interest in music began early. He started playing the viola in the fifth grade and has performed with it in community orchestras ever since. But it was the gift of a guitar in high school that was the precursor to his unorthodox music career. As a child, his parents took him to hear local Minnesota folk singers at a place called the Homestead Pickin' Parlor, where he later would take guitar lessons. During his senior year at St. Olaf College in Northfield, Minnesota, he wrote an honors thesis on the role of music in revolutions. His first public guitar performance came in the fall of 1997 during an open mike night at a club in Guatemala. He was in Guatemala to attend a Spanish language school where he learned to translate Spanish folk songs into English.

That same year, Kirk took his music career literally underground. While in Boston, he had seen street musicians playing in the subway. One day, he lugged his guitar to the Park Street Station and sat down and played. He continued to perform on the streets and in the subways in Boston, Washington, D.C, New York City, Chicago, and finally in Minneapolis. He vividly remembers his first subterranean gig in the Big Apple.

"The first time that I performed in the subway in New York City after I moved there to start law school—it was Friday the 13th— and I was headed back to the 14th Street/Union Square Station on the four-five-six line where I'd played at least once before while I was in town staying with a cousin. But on my way there, I had to change trains at the 59th Street Station because that's where the R train first stops in Manhattan. My new apartment (was) in Queens, just two blocks off the E,F,G,N and R lines, so I was riding the R train into Manhattan for the first time.

"Well anyway, this was the first time I'd been in the 59th Street Station and it looked like a good place to play. I decided to cross under the tracks to the uptown side of the platform. I thought it would be neat to get somebody to take a picture of me underneath the 59th Street sign, you know because of the Simon and Garfunkel song, ("The 59th Street Bridge Song/Feelin' Groovy"). So I set up to play. It was about 7 or 8 o'clock then. I sold two tapes that night." The first tape he sold was to a Spanish woman he met. They ended up in a love relationship that lasted several months.

Kirk says he's "been kicked out of lots of places who didn't want street musicians and ticketed in the New York subway for using amplification. I act like I don't know the rules even though I do." As he plays, he puts out an open guitar case for donations. "I once made $150 playing for seven hours to crowds going to a Minnesota Twins game. I've probably made ten to fifteen thousand dollars at it in the last ten years. But if you do it just for money, you'll be in trouble. The beauty of it is I'm doing something I like to do. And I meet lots of interesting people and hear their stories."

Kirk's first gig with a band was during a folk rock performance at a Methodist church in Boston in the fall of '97. "I was walking to the subway and stopped on College Avenue at a United Methodist Church and ended up joining the band. Several of the songs we played were written by the pastor. I played with them for several months. I also played in a bar about a mile away from my school called Hollywood's and at school parties. Many of songs were political. There's a great song called "Who Are the Terrorists?" that I sang in Manhattan right after 9/11. My street singing is an outgrowth of what I wrote about in my senior history honors thesis in college.

Kirk calls his musical troubadoring "The Never-Ending World Tour." When he performs, he uses Carlos as part of his name. "I chose it in eighth grade. Spanish kids have trouble saying Kirk so they call me Carlos, and I kept it as a nickname."

* * *

Politics have long been a part of Kirk's life. "In 1980, when I was nine or ten and in the fourth grade, we had a parade in the gym, and we made signs for (President Jimmy) Carter. I watched on a black-and-white TV when Mondale got slaughtered in the election. In 1993, I did an internship at (Senator Paul) Wellstone's office, working on immigration and refugee issues by writing letters to consulates and embassies to get families here together and out of refugee groups." In 2004, Kirk volunteered on the John Kerry campaign through MoveOn.Org and the League of Conservation Voters. Like many Kerry supporters, he was disappointed that the senator conceded so early after the returns came in rather than asking for a recount. But he had no idea what to do about it.

That all changed on a serendipitous day following the election. "I ran into Mark Halvorson and his wife Lisa. I had known Mark during the '80s when he worked at Augsburg with my mother. Mark asked me if I wanted to go to Ohio. I said, 'Sure, what are we doing there?' He said, 'Recounting the presidential election votes.' That's how I got involved with election reform."

At that time, Halvorson was the leader of fledgling group of progressive activists concerned about election integrity called CASEMN (Citizens Alliance for Secure Elections Minnesota) modeled after a similar effort in Ohio. CASEMN later changed its name to Citizens for Election Integrity Minnesota (CEIMN).

One of CEI's first tasks was working with David Cobb, the 2004 Green Party presidential candidate, who had demanded a recount of the votes in Ohio. Cobb had called for the recount after raising doubts about the results of the presidential election—a suspicion shared by members of CEI and that Kirk still holds to this day.

"I question the results (of the '04 presidential election) on a number of different bases. There were efforts to suppress the Democratic vote by distributing the machines in such a way that the inner-city, low-income and student areas likely to vote Democratic got too few machines. Largely Democratic precincts had extremely long lines of up to twelve hours resulting from not bringing enough machines out of storage or distributing them in such a way that resulted in shortages.

"There were also blatant examples of purging people from the rolls and hired guns challenging people's right to cast their ballot. Tens of thousands of provisional ballots were not counted. Big turnout usually benefits Democrats, so suppressing the vote largely benefited Republicans. Who knows how many people had to leave the lines to get back to work or pick up their kids or go on with their lives. It made for an extreme burden for people trying to exercise the right to vote."

Based on this information and using his authority as a third-party candidate in the presidential race, Cobb, along with the Libertarian presidential candidate, called for and was granted a recount of ballots in Ohio. Kirk was one of several CEI's activists to make the trip to the Buckeye State.

"We went to three rural counties within an hour and a half of Columbus. Bush had won Ohio by about 118,000 votes. Kerry had $50 million in the bank and could have challenged the count. He was involved just enough to say he was doing something but he really didn't do anything. All he had to do was clear his throat from the back of the courtroom and the judge would have started a recount the next day. Instead, the judge refused to expedite the recount because neither of the candidates calling for it stood to gain any electoral votes. Since Kerry didn't show up, we were on our own.

"Harden County in rural Ohio was the first county I observed. The recount was conducted in a county courthouse meeting room. The County Board of Elections met around a conference table. Ohio law says that each county board of elections must randomly select whole precincts totaling at least three percent of the vote in that county and recount them by hand. They didn't follow the law in Hardin County. They handpicked the precincts they wanted, not apparently maliciously, but against the law nonetheless. When we mentioned it they said, 'Don't tell us how to do our job.'

"They had seven optical scan vote-counting machines. Had they found any discrepancies—if the hand recount didn't match the machine total—they would have been required by law to count the other ninety-seven percent by hand. When I attempted to step behind the table to get a closer look, I was told that I couldn't stand there. I responded that there were no restrictions on where we could stand. I wanted to do a hand tally for one batch of ballots and compare it to the machine tally. But some guy said, 'You can't go back there' and was ordering people around. Turns out he was the Diebold representative, the company that made the machines. They finally did allow us to do a hand tally from one of the machines, but not from one that they did not test and calibrate before the recount.

"In one of the rural counties, I discovered that the person they had running the show was not an elected official but was hired by the county board to do elections. It was a worthless observation. There were thousands of ballots pushed furiously through the machines. There was no way to verify if the machine was counting what was on the ballot. And frankly, I don't trust the machines. The man running the count was of the mentality that an election is a failure if one person who was not entitled to vote is allowed to vote. I say an election is a failure if one person who should have been able to vote is denied that right. The vote counting could have been significant if he had hand-counted all the ballots. Instead the law was not being followed. The count didn't matter. There were many problems in that election. We were shocked that there were so many violations.

"There were seven counties in Ohio that used paperless touch-screen voting machines. They are the most populous counties. In Cuyahoga County, the recount that was done was completely meaningless. It was really a joke of a recount."

What he saw in Ohio only confirmed Kirk's thoughts about the outcome of the presidential election. "The exit polls had Kerry winning in Ohio. But at some point overnight it all flipped. I think Republicans and their supporters used a program in order to change the electronic vote total. The CEO of Deibold is from Ohio and was committed to Bush. Deibold was in charge of counting a large number of votes in that state. And their software was not available for public inspection. According to statisticians, there is a one in 10,000 chance that the polls were wrong in Ohio. I have no doubt that Kerry won the election." Most recently, Kirk was an observer of the audit CEIMN conducted during the '08 election and the recount of Minnesota's U.S. Senate race between Norm Coleman and Al Franken.

The various paths that have comprised Kirk Lund's "Never-Ending World Tour" in the context of his life journey have been steadily coming together. His early experiences in Central America engendered a sense of global social justice that led him to build houses for the poor, to defend immigrant rights, and to become involved in election reform. He continues to do housing construction and rehab while working towards a goal of becoming an international human rights and environmental lawyer in what he calls the "two-thirds world."

Kirk's musical interests became intertwined with his commitment to social justice in college when he wrote the honors thesis about the use of music in revolutions, and the connection has continued.

He recently brought together his passion for music and election reform when he performed live at a CEIMN-sponsored showing of *Uncounted*, a controversial documentary about voting irregularities in the 2000 and 2004 presidential elections and the real possibility that they could happen again. The message of the film resonates with Kirk.

"Election reform is the reform that makes all other reforms possible," he says. "It is the foundation for being able to make other necessary changes. It's akin to the environmental issue and global change. If you care about this or that issue, we better make sure there is a planet. Governments would look a lot different if elections were fair and not run by special interests.

"There are several things we can do to improve our elections. Electronic voting machines have opened the door to widespread election fraud. We should abolish them. Counting election results on paper ballots by hand is the best system." CEI has been a leader in this area, working with state officials to make Minnesota one of the few states to initiate a statewide audit of its election results.

"We need Instant Runoff Voting (IRV) so people can vote their conscience and not feel they are wasting their vote. With IRV, if your candidate doesn't win, your vote continues to count. IRV ensures that your vote counts toward the result of the election and that the winner has majority support. It also discourages negative campaigning and mudslinging because it is in each candidate's interest that their opponents' supporters rank them second on the ballot. It is an absolute necessity to give meaningful status to third-party candidates. And we need a system of proportional representation rather than the winner-take-all system we have for congressional elections.

"We should abolish the electoral college. It is an outdated system with the potential to subvert the popular vote. Some people argue that the electoral college is needed to protect small states. But as it is now, the candidates only go to battleground states. And lastly, we need public financing of election campaigns.

"These are the major things we need to reform our elections. You have to have a fair and level playing field for electing public officials.

"There has been a lot of work done in the last four years in election reform and a lot of victories. But they have been localized in counties and states. We have not succeeded in passing federal legislation to address election reform issues. There is still much work to do to make sure that what happened in Florida and Ohio doesn't happen again.

"What can people do? It has to start with contacting your elected officials. Let them know that this is an important issue. If you care about this country and where it is going, participate and get involved. Don't just stand on the sideline and complain."

*From the song "Cardboard Houses" ("Casas de Carton"), written by Venezuelan musician Ali Privera, translated to English by Kirk Lund.

Home-recorded tapes and sheet music of Kirk's songs and ordering information are available on his web site at www:http://people.freesitenow.com/ Never-Ending World Tour.

CHECKING IT TWICE

By Mark Halvorson,
Director Citizens for Election Integrity Minnesota

The 2006 election saw the nation's first citizen observation of a statewide election audit. This process was repeated during the '08 election. The audit was spearheaded by our nonpartisan group, Citizens for Election Integrity Minnesota (CEIMN). We believe that Minnesota's system of paper ballots with a post-election audit, accompanied by citizen observation, provides a compelling model for other states as we work towards restoring voting integrity nationwide.

CEIMN was formed by a small group of concerned Minnesotans in the wake of disturbing national reports of widespread voting irregularities and disenfranchisement in the 2004 election. CEIMN's first move was to recruit nine volunteers to observe the 2004 Ohio recount. The recount exposed dramatic flaws in Ohio's voting system and taught our group the critical importance of having a paper voting record, valid audits and the involvement of citizen observers in a transparent vote-counting process.

After the Ohio recount, CEIMN focused on lobbying for accurate and verifiable elections within Minnesota and on a national level. In the summer of 2005, we participated in a national gathering of state election officials in St. Paul. Two of our national partners in election reform, Vote Trust USA and Verified Voting, also participated. We were all struck by the brazen corporate influence on the voting process as election-equipment vendors such as Diebold and ES&S spared no expense in hosting lavish boat and train trips, dances and receptions.

In the fall of 2005, CEIMN learned about a new Minnesota law, the Post-Election Review of Voting Systems, authored by Minnesota State Representative Bill Hilty. Minnesota uses only optical scanners to count our votes—a paper-based system that allows for independent audits. Hilty's review law requires a number of precincts statewide to be randomly selected for a hand recount. This new law included trigger mechanisms that would require further reviews in counties where errors were found above a certain threshold (0.5 percent). However, some election officials were concerned that parts of the review law could make the law unduly cumbersome to administer. CEIMN brought these concerns to State Rep. Hilty. This led to a revised bill that passed with overwhelming support.

Recalling the importance of transparency learned in Ohio, CEIMN embarked upon a major effort to recruit teams of citizens to observe the post-election review, to provide an independent verification of the process. Minnesota's optical scan voting machines have a reputation for being accurate, based on numerous recounts, which led some to conclude the law was unnecessary. However, since such an assessment had never been undertaken, no one could say with authority how accurate the tallies by optical scan machines are. Furthermore, widespread national evidence of the vulnerability of voting systems has convinced us of the ongoing need for independent verification of voting machines.

CEIMN's Observing Project had four stages: forming an advisory board, recruiting volunteers, training and implementation. We achieved an advisory board that was politically balanced with experienced and respected individuals, including two former secretaries of state: Republican and Democratic. The League of Women Voters Minnesota then joined us as a co-sponsor, further enhancing the legitimacy and credibility of the project. In June, our volunteer-driven group hired our first part-time employee, whose job included recruiting, training, and overseeing the logistics of our volunteer base.

CEIMN's first major recruitment efforts took place at the statewide conventions for the Democratic, Republican, Green and Independence parties. We also tapped retired educators and League of Women Voters members for help. Training was conducted primarily via toll-free conference calls. Each volunteer signed a Code of Conduct based on the standards of international election observers, the Organization for Security and Co-operation in Europe.

In the end, CEIMN had observer teams present in seventy of Minnesota's eighty-seven counties. Based on our observer reports, we were impressed by the accuracy of the optical scanners. Statewide, the post-election review validated the accuracy of the voting machines tested. Only two counties found discrepancies sufficient to trigger second-level reviews, and even in those cases, our interpretation of the law indicated those reviews were probably unnecessary since the errors found were not relevant to machine performance.

CEIMN's next goal in Minnesota is to strengthen the review law by proposing an increase in the number of precincts audited. This project is a first step as part of or our long term vision to democratize the election process. At a national level, the next challenge will be to pass federal legislation requiring a paper ballot and random audits—two indispensable ingredients to restoring integrity to the voting process. Accurate and verifiable vote counts in the United States are essential to restoring voter confidence in our elections.

THE MEDIA REFORM MOVEMENT

This (the media reform movement) is one of the most significant movements to emerge in this century.

—Bill Moyers

What media policy needs is to be bathed in democracy. The coalition we envision will have its similarities to the civil rights movement or the women's movement since access to information ought to be a fundamental human right. It will stand outside political parties and encourage all of them to take up the mantle of democratic media reform.

—John Nichols
"The making of a movement" *The Nation* magazine

Few things impact all of our daily lives more than the media. Radio, television, newspapers, and, most recently and profoundly, the Internet, are deeply embedded in our culture as sources of news, entertainment, communication and the shaping of public opinion. In an ideal world, the media would be a paragon of democracy—literally belonging to everyone who uses it. In fact, that privilege has belonged more and more to corporate America. A few major companies have taken ownership of our media out of the hands of the people, regulating its content and outreach to suit their needs.

But once again, the people have fought back. A grassroots movement to reform and take back the media has been sweeping the country. It has had two main components: reform of the existing mainstream media, and a burst of what has come to be called "citizen journalism," or the creation of alternative sources of mass communication. There are some amazing success stories in the file of this fledgling movement. We have selected two: one features the nation's largest media reform coalition; the other profiles a small, locally based organization that has publicly challenged mainstream media; both told as personal stories of compassionate rebels making democracy happen.

**Josh Silver speaking at 2008 media reform conference
(Photo courtesy of Free Press)**

THE MEDIA BELONGS TO US
By Burt Berlowe

Josh Silver, glowing handsome and proud under the stage lights, stands at
the podium facing the energized crowd filling the shiny new auditorium of
the Minneapolis Convention Center. He speaks forcefully, passion poured into
every word.

> *We are at a crossroads. We need to break the corporate stranglehold
> on our democracy, to argue that truth is power....It is one of the most
> profound fights of our lives.*

It is the opening day of the third annual National Media Reform
Conference, and Josh is setting the tone for what is yet to come—two days
of celebrity speakers, workshops and networking designed to build a more
diverse and democratic media. Josh has a particular stake in what is unfolding
that weekend. He helped give birth to Free Press, sponsors of the conference
and a growing force in the media reform movement. He has watched the conference double in size in three years—now up to some 3,000 attendees from

around the U.S. and Canada. He tells the audience the story of this grassroots movement and urges them to get on board.

Everyone of us has the potential to be a powerful part of change....The future of the media belongs to us...

The luminaries—Bill Moyers, Amy Goodman, Naomi Klein, Arianna Huffington, Dan Rather, Phil Donahue—would come later. But for now, this is Josh Silver's moment to shine—one that he has been moving towards since he was barely old enough to walk.

* * *

From the time he learned to toddle across the stretch of rural New England land, Josh Silver learned the value of community and the meaning of democracy. He was a part of four families who lived communally, sharing property, goods and decision-making, along with an active lifestyle typical of the 1960s. His grandfather, mother, and stepfather were peace and justice advocates, and Josh followed close behind.

By the ripe age of fifteen, Josh had read Howard Zinn's *People's History of the United States*. "It had an impact on me," he recalls. "I became aware of the oppression of certain types of people. I had a profound paradigm shift. That same year, I was arrested for protesting guided-missile production at a GTE plant. I began to decide that war is not right and that we need to work for a more peaceful world."

When the first invasion of Iraq came under George H.W. Bush, Josh was again on the streets and in the paddy wagon, defending the need to promote social change. "I met a woman named Frances Crow, a legendary activist of the time in Massachusetts. I was going to go overseas and work at a refugee camp. She said, 'We need you here.' I decided to stay."

During the 1990s, Josh became a "reformer." At first, he was drawn to election reform, primarily campaign financing and how to get money out of politics. He led Arizona's successful clean election campaign in 1997 and '98, which gives political candidates access to public funds.

"After the 2000 election, I began to wonder how someone like (George W.) Bush could have been elected. I began to realize that the [mainstream] media reporting on elections didn't tell the real story. I also found out that seventy percent of people get their news from the commercial media that is shaping our public policy without informed consent. Yet, as of the turn of century, there was no national organization working on media reform. I wanted to change that."

One day in 2001, Josh placed a call to professor and author Bob McChesney. "I told him I thought we needed comprehensive organizing to penetrate the corporate media and create universal human values not just political ones. He said 'I've have been waiting for you to call for years.'" Within a year, the two, along with journalist John Nichols, started an organization called Free Press.

Free Press began with a staff of six people. It now has thirty-seven, along with over 9,000 paid members and 500,000 online activists. It is a national nonpartisan coalition working with some 800 organizations to increase informed public participation in crucial media policy debates and to generate policies that will produce a more competitive and public-interest-oriented media system. It is funded by some forty foundations and has an annual budget of about $2 million dollars. Its collaborators range from liberal groups like Move On.Org, Common Cause, The League of Women Voters, the American Civil Liberties Union and Sojourners, to the more conservative Christian Coalition, Parents Television Council and National Rifle Association, to name a few.

Free Press participates in a wide array of media policy issues that are part of a growing reform movement. These include media ownership, independent media, democratic governance, global communication and Internet access. It has sponsored three national conferences on media reform, with attendance growing each time. The 2008 conference held in Minneapolis drew over 3,000 energized attendees from the U.S. and Canada.

The Free Press Action Network, a group of dedicated citizens who want to move beyond online actions and get involved with media reform policy activism at the local, state, and national level, has been working within various communities on public education and research, letter writing, grassroots organizing, and lobbying. The Free Press Action Fund is their lobbying arm: a social welfare organization advocating for changes in public policy that will lead to a more diverse and public-service-oriented media system.

In 2003, Free Press was one of the leading groups running the campaign against media consolidation that turned out to be an impressive citizen victory. The Federal Communications Commission (FCC), with three Republicans outvoting its two Democrats, had approved a plan that would have allowed large corporate entities to increase their consolidation capabilities and own more media outlets. Free Press led a mass citizen uprising that included some two million signatures on a petition that helped push Congress to overturn the original FCC decision, and a federal court to later throw away the rules. More recently, it has launched initiatives like Save the Internet.com to preserve

Internet freedom and neutrality that is being threatened by proposed government action. As this is being written, a bipartisan net neutrality bill that would prevent Internet service providers from discriminating online is about to be introduced in Congress

In addition to Free Press, organizations like FAIR (Fairness and Accuracy in the Media), The Institute for Public Accuracy, Media Matters, the Media Alliance, and the Media Education Foundation have emerged in recent years as increasingly effective mainstream media watchdogs and policy advocates, sharing the same objective: that any democratic reform in the U.S. must include media reform.

FAIR has been working on a legislative agenda that includes anti-monopoly laws that restrict corporate ownership of radio stations, investigate media ownership regulations, establish more low-power noncommercial radio and TV stations and invest in public broadcasting.

Lawsuits challenging the excesses of media monopoly have been filed by groups like Rocky Mountain Media Watch and the National Consortium of Civic Organizations. Media groups in Honolulu and San Francisco have joined with labor unions and community groups to prevent the closing of newspapers that provide competition in those cities.

The Youth Media Council (YMC) is an organization that builds communications power and defends communication rights of youth, communities of color, and other groups working for racial and economic justice. Led by the council, young people and people of color have been working to take on the immense Clear Channel Corporation. Clear Channel owns twelve stations in the area, 1,200 nationally, including the right wing and hip hop stations. YMC worked with the community to increase air time for local artists on hip hop radio and to hold right wing radio stations accountable for balance and bias.

This latter action is indicative of one significant aspect of the grassroots media movement—citizen journalism. From Amy Goodman's *Democracy Now* to smaller radio outlets and alternative periodicals, reform activists are not just battling corporate media, they are creating their own outlets of personal expression.

One of the best recent examples of citizen journalism can be found in Minneapolis where an online newspaper called *The Daily Planet* features articles by local citizens lifted from community-based publications. *The Planet* was originated by a group called the Twin Cities Media Alliance, a unique diverse collaboration of mainstream and alternative media activists.

Free Press Co-founder McChesney has written, "There is a journalism crisis in this country as commercial interests, corporate interests and big media owners have said that journalism doesn't make sense to their bottom line. Working journalists across the country are alarmed at this; they're saying we've got to do something…and they're in the front ranks of the movement."

The media reform movement is more than organized groups. It is increasingly populist in nature with thousands of individual citizens participating at the grassroots level. "There is a big shift going on that is growing in size and scope and will continue to do that," Josh says. "We know of over 500,000 people across the country who are actively involved."

In looking to the future of the movement, Josh borrows from his somewhat distant past. The idea of democratic community that played such a key role in his upbringing remains foremost in his thinking.

"I am obsessed with the idea that media is moving towards digital and eventually all media will be that. My goal is that every home in America will have ready access to broadband connection as a God-given right. Every website can be connected to a larger network, breaking the commercial bottleneck on access and distribution of media content. The outcome of today's media reform debates will shape the media and, with it, the viability of our fragile democracy for generations."

John Slade on the air
(Photo courtesy of John Slade)

MEDIA ON TRIAL
By John Slade

For much of the winter, Peavey Plaza had lay frozen and dormant, waiting for the warmth that would bring it alive, turning on its bubbling fountain, blaring concerts and rallies, and the chatter of downtown workers lunching on the steps that lead just below the surface of Minneapolis's famous Nicollet Mall.

But as February of 2003 was born, Peavey awoke to find itself thrust into a provocative new role. It became an outdoor courtroom. Huddled together in an early afternoon chill on a makeshift stage raised above patches of snow, a gathering of activists rendered judgment against a mighty big foe. They put the media on trial.

Just across the street from one of the defendants—CBS TV news affiliate WCCO—a group known as the Counter Propaganda Coalition (CPC) railed against the sins of corporate media. Flanked by a sign that read "Pro-War Mass Media Surrender to the People," several "expert" witnesses read a list of thirteen charges and gave testimony. Then, a jury of some 110 people carefully deliberated. As the charges were read again, the jury members shouted out "Guilty" for each one. The verdict was unanimous.

On December 2, 1999, I was at my computer. My luggage was still unpacked, and my coat still smelled faintly of tear gas. I had at my side the *Seattle Post Intelligencer*, where as-yet unresigned Police Chief Paul Schell was claming that the WTO (World Trade Organization) protests had been handled with minimal force, and the police had not shot rubber bullets at protesters. On the screen in front of me was the Indymedia Center webpage, where a young man was holding up a rubber bullet and lifting his shirt to show the bruise it made when he was hit.

How did a small-town Republican boy end up on the streets at the WTO protest? I blame Ronald Reagan and Norm Coleman (the Republican Senator from Minnesota). It's their fault. Ronnie had gone and turned me away from the Republicans by being so darn anti-choice and by funding secret wars against democratically elected governments in Nicaragua. Being at Macalester College also helped since activist students on campus had been breaking the corporate media barrier and getting the word out about the Contras. It was just too much.

After graduating, I worked a bunch of phone jobs. Then I went back to school to get a master's in linguistics, and found a phone job with flexible hours that didn't involve sales—I was a tele-relay operator for the hearing impaired. Norm was mayor of St. Paul at the time. You see, Norm, who had been a pot-smoking unwashed hippie protester, was on his power-seeking trajectory from Woodstock roadie to Administration lackey. At that time, he was messing with the unions—and since we'd formed a union at the Relay (the place I worked), Norm had no problem letting the jobs leave town when a powerful telecom decided it wanted the state's Relay contract.

This left me a union activist without a union job, and that led to the Industrial Workers of the World. A former Relay co-worker of mine had been getting involved with the Highway 55 protest, which had occupied houses and trees in an attempt to stop an urban highway expansion. That protest, backed by the local American Indian Movement and Earth First was a center of radical activity. So to carry a union card again, I became a Wobbly (an IWW member). When some of the Wobs decided to join the protest in Seattle, I said, What the heck!

The night of November 30, we had left the streets and were watching coverage of the protests on local news. The whole thing was eerie—cops were still rioting, pushing a group up to a local neighborhood out of downtown. The news was full of violence and lies—the police were being restrained, protesters were looting, etc.

This is why the Indymedia network was so important at the beginning of the century. As the global justice movement continued to protest, in Quebec

City, Washington, D.C., and Miami; as the Bush administration started using more and more anti-democratic means—protest pits, exclusion zones, infiltration and spying—to control protest, and as the corporate media was becoming more concentrated (AOL-Time Warner) and more propagandistic (Fox News), local Indymedia Centers (IMCs) sprang up across the country and across the world. When the Italian police shot and killed a protester in Genoa, the Italian Indymedia covered it and got raided. Mayday protests, animal rights, immigrant rights—all got covered by IMCs. The first big use of the Internet as an end-run around corporate-controlled media was the IMC network.

While the infrastructure of the IMC was and is important, we wanted to do more. The opportunity to directly confront media bias (and the beginning of the Counter-Propaganda Coalition) came hard on the heels of a major peace demonstration in St. Paul in October of 2002, following the untimely loss of Senator Paul Wellstone. Over 10,000 people turned up. The dominant local paper, the *Star Tribune*, covered the demonstration—kind of. On page twenty-three, the largest peace demo in town since Vietnam got one-half of a story. The St. Paul demo was part of a national day of protest; the story covered both the local and national marches. There was one picture, of the D.C. protest. The police were quoted on crowd size, and the story said it was nothing more than a Wellstone memorial. It was a tribute to Wellstone, to be sure—but for his antiwar position.

On two days notice, a group of us mobilized sixty people to protest the *Star Tribune*. We entered the lobby, chanting and singing. This was the birth of the Counter Propaganda Coalition (CPC).

There are two trends in media activism—media reform and media revolution, to use an over-broad generalization: Do we try to make the mainstream media more responsive, or decry it as a corporate sham and build a replacement? CPC's mission statement highlights our main concerns: to counter corporate media bias, to promote and produce alternative media, to educate in real media literacy, and to use tactics ranging from satire to non-violent civil disobedience. We have become a presence in the Twin Cities activist community. We have made media a part of the agenda for some groups, and encouraged local media organizing.

In February of 2003, we put the corporate media on trial with a demonstration outside WCCO radio in downtown Minneapolis. The assembled crowd found them guilty of bias. We have held or co-sponsored a number of independent media fairs, where we spread the word about alternatives. At one of them we awarded the Golden Vacuum Award because the corporate media "sucks." We have worked with groups like the Free Media Greens, the Twin Cities Media Alliance, and numerous peace and social justice groups. We worked with Free Press to help turn out more than 600 people to an FCC fact-finding hearing, where over 200 testified, all of whom said that our corporate media system is failing us. We've marched in a media-themed group in the (Minneapolis) May Day parade, with a corporate media vampire, the club of patriotism and the golden microphone.

The highest-fun activity, however, is our Counter-Propaganda Caroling. As the winter winds blow, every year since 2002, we've been going out into the world writing and singing silly songs, most of which are based on Christmas carols. "Buy Me the World," "Wal-Mart the Corporate Monster" and "The Twelve Lies of the Media" (For the first time this morning, the media lied to me…) are three favorites. To give you a flavor, here's the first verse to "Little Hummer Boy," sung to the tune of "Little Drummer Boy."

I use lots of gas / In my SUV
And on the road I pass / In my SUV
You must look out for me / And my SUV
Because I must drive free / In my SUV, my SUV, my SUV…

These songs have been sung in malls, at antiwar demonstrations, on the (light rail transit) commuter train, and at the downtown Minneapolis glitz-and-shopping parade, Holidazzle. Recent songs include "War Hawk," to the tune of Elvis's "Hound Dog," "God Rest Ye Stupid, NASCAR Dad," and "Oh Little Town of New Orleans."

O little town of New Orleans, where does the water lie?
Above thy deeply flooded streets, see Air Force One fly by.
Yet in thy dark streets shineth a Halliburton light.
As all environmental rules are waived for them tonight.
The chaos born of Katrina showed FEMA at its worst
While help poured forth from normal folks,
Their lies were well-rehearsed.
We didn't see it coming; we had no way to know.
When bad things happen to poor folks –
We never watch that show.

*In addition to being a founder of the Counter-Propaganda Coalition, John Slade has run a local Indymedia website and co-hosted a cable TV show about media-related issues.

THE CORPORATE REFORM MOVEMENT

The economic recession that is plaguing America as this book is being written is largely a product of corporate domination. The powerful engine of capitalism that has traditionally steered our economy so efficiently has recently driven it into the ground. There are many reasons—greed, arrogance, mismanagement, to name a few, all steeped in a system that rewards wealthy bosses over the workers that are literally and figuratively beneath them.

In recent months, government's main response to failing corporations has been to bail them out financially and/or to demand that they make administrative changes—efforts that have thus far met with mixed results. What is missing from this equation has been a real discussion of true corporate reform —the type that requires companies to have a social conscience and to direct their efforts towards creating meaningful societal change.

While the words "corporate reform" are not heard very often in the halls of Congress nowadays, they are repeated frequently among groups of ordinary citizens who are building a movement around the issue primarily at the local level.

There are numerous grassroots organizations working diligently on the issue of corporate reform—some of whom are mentioned in our resource section. We have chosen to highlight one of those efforts in Minneapolis.

Like their counterparts in the election and media reform movements, activists pushing for corporate change have had to linger in relative obscurity overshadowed by issues of war and peace, national security and economic stability. They have had to wait for the appropriate time to bring the issue to national attention. That time may have finally come.

John Karvel at home
(Photo by Michael Bayly)

BUILDING DEMOCRACY
By Burt Berlowe

John Karvel guides me into the room that begins to tell the story of his life. The compact, square space in the back of his modest St. Paul home doubles as a study and a sort of museum and gallery, displaying the wares and heritage of a self-made handyman. John has personally built many of the objects in the room. But he is proudest of the old roll top-style desk sitting idly against one wall. "My dad made that for me," he says. "He was a furniture maker. He was a big influence on me. He was always self-employed, had an office at home. Now this room is where I do my work."

Actually, John doesn't spend a lot of time in his office. You are more likely to find him in a neighbor's yard, hammering away at a large nail and the foibles of corporate America, building a wall, a relationship and a movement all at the same time.

John is seated at a table in his living room, his profile highlighted by gray light seeping through the front window. He is alone in the house as is often the case since his recent divorce, and as seems to befit his life's journey.

"I grew up with the comfort of independence," he recalls. "Rochester (Minnesota), where I was born, was a very comfortable middle-class town with a big ego. I thought it was the center of the world. People came from all over the world to go to the Mayo Clinic. But it was not a worldly town. I was very isolated from a world view. I didn't have much exposure to other cultures and income levels.

"In high school, I was active in sports—wrestling and baseball—and on the student council and National Honor Society. I was a model student. At the same time, there was an underlying current of existential anxiety in the midst of this comfortable life. It didn't feel meaningful. My mother had encouraged me to think for myself. But I became a rebellious teenager and didn't always fit into my family. I didn't feel comfortable in church, not identifying with any particular religion. Basically, I was rebelling against all authority."

John's adolescent years came in the midst of the counterculture 1960s. His alienation from mainstream America placed him amidst a culture of like-minded youth who were turning their defiance into political action. Without realizing it, he became part of a growing student movement that was taking over college campuses across the country. He ran for student council on a platform of change, proposing to alter the school dress code to allow the wearing of blue jeans. "I wanted student power that would be equal to that of the administration. I just picked the idea out of the air and began organizing around it." John lost his bid for student council by one vote to the captain of the football team. But the student council adopted his dress code proposal and convinced the administration to lift the ban on blue jeans.

Once he had learned how to make change, John probed deeper. "I wanted to pursue meanings and connections in relation to social action. In college, I majored in philosophy, existentialism and phenomenology (the study of how you know what you know and how your experience affects you). But I lost interest when I realized how little I knew about the world. I concentrated instead on studying and getting a classic liberal education."

In 1969, John ventured precariously into the "real world," struggling against his better instincts to make a go of it in corporate America. His first job out of college was as a computer programmer at the Honeywell Corporation in Minneapolis. It only lasted a few months. "I couldn't stand the restrictions of a corporate environment," he explains. "I would arrive ten minutes late for work some days and would make it up by staying past my scheduled work time. After a few weeks, I got hauled into the supervisor's office. He read me the riot act telling me that I had to arrive at exactly at 8 o'clock every morning. My independent rebellious childhood popped up and I responded, 'I'm not cheating you if I work over time to make it up.' He said that wasn't adequate, that I had to be there exactly on time. I tried to comply but found it too hard. It became like a cultural prison with martini lunches and the whole thing. I wasn't comfortable with that. So I quit.

"A similar thing happened when I drove cab for a while. I had hair growing down to my collar. When I found out that was against their dress code, I left."

John was delighted when his parents decided to buy a farm in rural Minnesota. "I had always wanted to live in the country," he says. "We were one of the few organic farms in the area. We had little support from the community. We grew grain and sold it to a nearby mill. Later, we built our own mill."

John's farming experience ultimately changed his life. He met his future wife on the farm. She tried to convince him to get out of the organic business. "She used to say, 'Why are you doing this? You could make more money doing regular farming.' At the same time, I was breaking new ground by running an organic farm. I realized that if we want a good living planet, we're going to have to work together. I was learning to be an activist. Unfortunately, my wife-to-be was right. We had financial problems from the outset. We had to borrow money to pay for the mill and had trouble repaying it. We tried refinancing, but that didn't work. When we had a crop failure, we couldn't recover and had to sell. I went back to the city and started over again."

In an attempt to make a clean break with his past, John left behind the disappointing days in Rochester and the rural countryside for a crack at metropolitan Minneapolis. But he carried with him much of what he had learned in his past: a penchant for rebellion and self-reliance, and a handyman's desire to fix a broken American system.

He built a business—River Town Contracting Company—from the bottom-up, teaching himself by reading handyman magazines and watching episodes of the TV show, "This Old House." He attracted a steady clientele of customers, many from his immediate surrounding community. Following a divorce from his wife of twenty years, he spent much of his time co-parenting his daughter and volunteering at her school, while shoving aside a larger goal. He says of that dilemma: "When you're trying to raise a daughter, how can you possibly try to change the world?"

As his daughter grew up, John began to rekindle his desire to make social change, but he wasn't sure how to direct it. Then one evening in 2003, he was watching a Bill Moyers show on the subject of NAFTA (The North American

Free Trade Agreement) which, among other things discussed how a corporation can sue a national government. As an example, in California, a company made a chemical that contaminated groundwater. California wanted to get rid of it. The company sued for $900 million.

"Watching that show made me realize how out of control corporations are in this country. I went to bed thinking about it. Then I had this idea in the middle of the night that we should change the law to create a model for what corporations can do. I began to discuss it with people I knew but dropped it because nobody else grabbed it.

"But a few months later, I was reading an article on the Web by Robert Hinckley who had a similar idea in Maine. I went to Marjorie Kelley, one of my (construction) clients and a university economics professor to discuss my concerns. She offered to help and gave me a copy a book she had written on that subject." The two later went together to a conference that addressed how to bring about institutional change. The result was John's proudest venture: The formation in 2002 of the Council for Corporate Redesign (C4CR).

C4CR held a series of startup meetings with about a dozen in the organizing group, mainly college professors and activists, and developed a consensus model and mission statement. They pulled no punches in their criticism of corporations. Partnering with a similar group, they co-sponsored showings and discussions of the provocative movie *The Corporation*. Their main achievement has been the introduction of a revolutionary bill in the Minnesota State Legislature calling for a Code of Corporate Responsibility for the state. The legislation would substantially reform corporations by making them more accountable to their shareholders and customers. It says, in summary, that "directors shall manage the corporation in a manner that does not cause damage to the environment, violate human rights, adversely affect the public health or safety, damage the welfare of communities in which the corporation operates or violate the dignity of the corporation's employees."

"The bill we support makes corporations more socially responsible," John says. "It's about changing the paradigm of corporations to a partnership model rather than a hierarchy model. It would increase corporate accountability but not at the expense of human rights. It has a 'do no harm' clause that says that corporations can make a profit but must not do harm to citizens The corporation can have all the say in how it makes its products, but it must consider environment issues for the larger community, not just the workplace.

"We want to redefine directors' duties in a corporation. Current corporate regulations just put a Band-aid on a system that is not serving its industry and America well. Under current law, directors only have to be accountable to stockholders. We want the shareholders to have control over the corporations so that it will affect all of our lives. That could even mean shareholders serving on corporate boards of directors. Studies show that socially responsible businesses are more profitable for their shareholders over the long haul. Our proposed model makes the most money for the shareholders."

The C4CR bill has been picking up support in the Minnesota Legislature even as it has been facing the opposition of powerful corporations resistant to change. In response to opponents, C4CR set up its own lobbying arm and brought in a think tank.

But the movement to enact the Code is not just happening in Minnesota. It has been endorsed or is being considered by various labor, environmental, and peace and justice organizations in locales ranging from California to Great Britain. John's goal is to have it become law in all fifty states.

"Our mission is to envision a society in which corporations always work for a more peaceful world. We want corporations to rejoin the natural community. We don't say to anyone, 'You're wrong and we're right.' We just tell them that we need to change the existing paradigm to meet changing needs. And we want it to come from the bottom up."

* * *

John Karvel isn't your run-of-the-mill handyman. He is a one-man company who can fix just about anything. He also builds close relationships with his customers, using his work as a tool to open doors to activism, networking and finally, institutional change.

"My work is a service. It's doing whatever needs to be done. What happens when I work for someone is that we become friends. Before you know it, we're talking about what's going on in the world and how we can make it better. Some people are interested in corporations, some in a more sectarian society, some in other issues. But they all realize the need for change. One customer said he was not going to let me on his roof anymore because my work for corporate change is so important he didn't want me to fall off. He's not kidding. When he has a job on the roof, he's going to hire someone else."

Since his divorce, John has maintained a close relationship with his daughter Leteisha, whose custody he shares with his ex-wife. He has volunteered at her school in various capacities, from organizing events to promoting the teaching of peacemaking skills. They have both learned the Marshall Rosenberg model of nonviolent communication and have been teaching it in elementary schools and elsewhere. John gives an example: "We teach second-and-third graders that if someone says something bad about your appearance, you just say back, 'Well it's your opinion, and it doesn't agree with mine.' You hold your own perspective and don't take it personally."

Leteisha is clearly following her father's path but laying out her own journey as well. Dissatisfied with the lack of interest in conflict resolution at her school, she sought out another learning environment that was progressive and "not within the system." In the meantime, she is holding her dad's feet to the fire. One day, the two of them went to a restorative justice fundraiser. John struck up a conversation with someone about societal problems. Disagreement turned into verbal confrontation. Afterwards, John was scolded by his daughter for not using nonviolent communication skills—that instead of confronting his adversary, he should have asked him what his needs were.

But not everything in this father-daughter relationship is serious. "Since the divorce, we're having a different kind of fun," says John. "I built a trampoline and a climbing wall for her in the back yard. We also indulge in a sport called flat surfing. That involves surfing behind anything on the water, such as speed boats or kayaks. We like to go down to the river and flat surf whenever we can."

John's bond with his daughter is an example of a larger objective. His work in corporate accountability, in teaching peacemaking to kids, in recruiting customers to help build social change is all ultimately aimed at improving the world for the next generation.

Turning towards the shaft of light coming through his living room window, John recalls a question he came across years ago that sums up the purpose of his work and his life. His soft voice rises a module or two as he says it.

"How do we love all the children of all people for all time?"

AFTERWORD
WELCOME TO THE REVOLUTION

... Years from now, you may remember it as the moment when your own story and the American story converged, when they came together, and we met the challenges of a new century.

—Barack Obama at a 2009 Earth Day tree
planting ceremony with Student Conservation Corps members.

It all begun with a story.

Late on election day 2000 near a Palm Beach County, Florida polling place, a handful of area residents were discussing the vote they had just cast in the race for president of the United States. Everything seemed normal until one of them began to tell a story about his experiences. He had gone into the booth expecting to find the usual, simple kind of voting apparatus. Instead, he told his friends, he had been confused by the layout of the butterfly-shaped ballot and wasn't sure he had voted for the right candidate. The story sparked similar tales by friends, and soon hundreds of citizens realized their mistake and the storytelling spread. Hundreds of people came forth with shocking tales of their election travails which were eventually told at rallies, press conferences, and in front of a commission investing election irregularities. As one form of democracy had been diminished, another had risen in full force.

As their ranks grew, this small group of ordinary people banded together to sound off about the ballot and demand a revote. These were not your run-of-the-mill, stereotypical protestors. They were little old ladies, middle-aged working people, fresh-faced students, and busloads of African-American children who stayed all night in a church to show their support. Later, they would be joined by scores of minority, labor and women activists in large demonstrations that made the words "count every vote" a household mantra.

What started as a few words between friends soon became a massive exercise in democracy, climaxed by a large protest rally during the presidential inauguration as the pomp and circumstance of this most regal and revered American tradition came under siege. The signs and the shouting were everywhere -- along the parade route, near the podium where the president-elect was to speak, amidst the crowd of onlookers stretched for miles across the Washington, D.C. Mall. Thousands of ordinary citizens from around the country came together in a forceful demonstration that would reverberate through the nation's capitol and the rest of the country for years to come. This massive effort to disrupt the coronation of our 43rd president was not merely a spontaneous and isolated act of dissidence. It was a massive effort to take back democracy, what one protest leader called "A second American revolution."

And it all began with a story.

The culture of storytelling permeates our society: from books, TV, music and movies to church sermons, political campaigns and family get-togethers. Stories entertain and inform us, preserve and share history, bring people closer together and call us to action.

There is no doubt that stories can change the world. Virtually every significant movement or action in our history has started with someone telling a story – whether to one friend or relative, or to a large audience, whether in a brief anecdote or a longer narrative.

It is out of these individual stories and actions that active communities and larger movements are made and that the fabric of a caring, democratic culture is woven out of the strands of whole cloth. In the process, each personal narrative, like those in this book, becomes an integral part of the American story.

Despite its many highly visible and effective efforts, much of the work of the compassionate rebel revolution has remained "under the radar," substantially ignored or marginalized by mainstream media and, therefore, largely hidden from a public view. Instead we are inundated with negative and sensational stories and "establishment" points of view that don't do justice to what is really happening on the streets and in the backyards and living rooms of grassroots America.

Everywhere I go, I find people who feel that their voices are not being heard, that their opinions and feelings don't matter, that there is no use in bucking the system. To overcome that, we need to listen to, tell and promote stories like those in this book that give us cause for hope and move people to action.

It's been said that "whoever tells the stories defines the culture." If we want to change the culture, we have to change the stories that are defining it and provide venues for those stories to be told. That is the way the compassionate rebel revolution is built — one action, one story at a time.

In our first compassionate rebel book the authors referred to themselves as "story carriers." That meant that we were committed to carrying the stories we heard into the public realm so that they could get the exposure they deserved and serve as inspiration to those who would read them.

In the process, we have learned firsthand about the power of storytelling. The intimate and compelling experiences of our compassionate rebels have moved and shaken us. We have come to believe that everyone—yes EVERYONE has a compassionate rebel story to tell and, given the right circumstances, a desire to share it.

This is where YOU come in. If you think about your own life, you will undoubtedly find times when you have been a compassionate rebel. It may have been through individual acts of kindness, generosity, charity or public service within your family or community, or as part of group actions designed to change the world. You may have rebelled against a perceived injustice or the status quo, or perhaps even against your own past. Somewhere deep inside of you there is a compassionate rebel story yearning to be told and the desire to act upon its outcome. Just by reading this book and immersing yourself in the lives of its characters, you have begun to become part of something much bigger than yourself. The next step is up to you.

We will be continuing to collect compassionate rebel stories to put on our website or in future publications. If you would like, send us your story. Tell us about your "rebel moment," that sudden epiphany of chance or opportunity when you moved from innocent bystander to committed activist, or about what you eventually did to change your corner of the world. You never can tell. You just might make history.

Welcome to the revolution!

COMPASSIONATE REBEL RESOURCES
TOOLS FOR BUILDING A REVOLUTION

Chapter One: Ground Zero Heroes

Organizations/Websites

William Rodriguez: 9/11keymaster.com, william9/11.com.

9/11 Truth Seekers: 9/11truthseekers.org.

The 9/11 Truth Movement: 9/11truth.org.

Scholars for 9/11 Truth and Justice: stj9/11.org.

Minnesota 9/11Truth: mn9/11truth.org.

Patriotsquestion9/11 Truth: patriotsquestion 9/11truth.com.

Architects and Engineers for 9/11 Truth: ae9/11truth.org.

9/11 Research: 9/11researchwtc7.net.

NewYork9/11Truth: ny 9/11Truth.org (New York city group seeking to put a referendum on the ballot to open their own new 9/11 investigation).

9/11 Truth Europe: 9/11trutheu/en (one of many international 9/11 truth groups).

We Are Change: wearechange.org.

Muslim-Jewish-Christian Alliance for 9/11 Truth: mujca.com.

Families for Peaceful Tomorrows: peacefultomorrows.org.

The Beyond September 11 Project, University of Minnesota Human Rights Center, beyondseptember11.org.

Books by David Ray Griffin

9/11 Contradictions: an Open Letter to Congress and the Press. Olive Branch Press, 2008.

The New Pearl Harbor Revisited: The Cover Up and The Expose. Olive Branch Press, *2008.*

Debunking 9/11 Debunking: An Answer to Popular Mechanics and Other Defenders of the Official Conspiracy Theory. Olive Branch Press, 2007.

9/11 and the American Empire: Intellectuals Speak Out. Edited by David Ray Griffin and Peter Dale Scott,Olive Branch Press, 2006.

The New Pearl Harbor: Disturbing Questions about the Bush Administration and 9/11. Olive Branch Press, 2004.

The 9/11 Commission Report: Omissions and Distortions. Olive Branch Press, *2004.*

Other Books

Truth Jihad: My Epic Struggle Against the 9-11 Big Lie. Kevin Barrett, Progressive Press, 2007.

9/11: The Greatest Crime of All Time: The Best of Global Outlook. Ian Woods, *Global Outlook* magazine, *2006.*

Towers of Deception: The Media Cover up of 9/11. Barry Zwicker, New Society Publishers, 2006.

Beyond 9/11: Media Literacy in a post 9/11 world. University of Minnesota Center for Human Rights, *hrusa.org/september/activities/medialiteracya.htm.* Published as part of the center's Beyond September 11 project.

September 11th Families for Peaceful Tomorrows: Turning Our Grief into Action for Peace. David Portorti, RDV Books/Akashic Books, 2003.

Radio Shows

Truth Jihad Radio and *No Lies News.* Host Kevin Barrett: noliesradio.org.

Videos

9/11 Truth Rising: infowars.com/truthrising.

9/11 Press For Truth: 911pressfortruth.com.

Zero: An Investigation into 9/11; zero9/11movie.com.

Loose Change: loosechange9/11.com.

Rethinking 9/11: Why truth and reconciliation are better strategies than global war: Ground Zero Minnesota, gzmn.org.

9/11 Mysteries: 9/11mysteries.com.

9/11 Blueprint for Truth: The Architecture of Destruction: ae9/11truth.org.

Zeitgeist: zeitgeistmovie.com.

Beyond Retribution DVD: peacefultomorrows.org.

Chapter Two: Peace Messengers

Organizations and Websites

Veterans for Peace: veteransforpeaceorg.

Iraq Veterans Against the War: ivaw.org.

Iraqi & American Reconciliation Project/Muslim Peacemaker Teams: mpt-Iraq.org.

Voices for Creative Nonviolence: vcnv.org.

Citizen Soldier: citizensoldier.org (for information on Camilo Mejia).

The Committee for Conscientious Objectors: objectors.org.

The Nonviolent Peace Force: nonviolentpeaceforce.org.

The PeaceAlliance: thepeacealliance.org (lobbying for a Department of Peace).

Minnesota Alliance of Peacemakers: <u>mapm.org</u>.

Women Against Military Madness: <u>worldwidewamm.org</u>.

Friends for a Non-Violent World: <u>fnvw.org</u>.

The HumanRightsandPeaceStore: <u>humanrightsandpeacestore.org</u>.

Books

Moment of Truth In Iraq. Michael Yon. Richard Vigilante Books, 2008.

War is a Force That Gives Us Meaning. Chris Hedges, Random House, 2007.

War and Peace in the Gulf: Testimonies of the Gulf Peace Team. Edited by Bela Bhatia, Jean Dreze and Kathy Kelly, book design by <u>studioonthenet.com</u>.

Road From Ar Ramadi: The Private Rebellion of Staff Sergeant Mejia. Camilo Mejia, The New Press, 2007.

Making Peace: Healing A Violent World. Carolyn McConnell and Sarah Ruth Van Gelder. From *YES! A Journal of Positive Futures,* 2006.

People Power: Unarmed Resistance and Global Solidarity. Howard Clark, Pluto Press, 2000.

The Umbrella of U.S. Power: The Universal Declaration of Human Rights and the Contradiction of U.S. Policy. Noam Chomsky, Seven Stories Press, 1999.

The Causes of War. Michael Andregg, Ground Zero Minnesota, 1997.

Vietnam: Our Story One on One. Gary D. Gullickson, VV Publishing, 1991.

Chapters Three and Four: Freedom Riders and Freedom Fighters

Organizations/Websites

The National Immigration Solidarity Network: <u>immigrationsolidarity.org</u>.

Interfaith Coalition for Immigrant Rights: <u>icir.igc.org</u>.

National Network for Immigrant and Refugee Rights: <u>nnirr.org</u>.

The Farm Labor Organizing Committee, AFL-CIO: <u>noacentral.org</u>.

Center for Victims of Torture: <u>cvt.org</u>.

Books

You Can't Do That: Marv Davidov, Nonviolent Revolutionary. Carol Masters and Marv Davidov, Nodin Press, 2009.

A Window to the World. Oliver Chin, Frog Books, 2003.

Bridge: Building a Race and Immigration Dialogue in the Global Economy. Eunice Hyunhye, National Network for Immigrant and Refugee Rights, 2004.

Uprooted: Refugees of the Global Economy. David M. Donahue, Hunter House Publishers, 2002.

Activists Beyond Borders: Margaret E. Keck, Cornell University Press, 1998.
Endless War: How We Got Involved in Central America and What Can Be Done, James Chace, Vintage Books, 1984.

Chapter Five: Community Builders

<u>Organizations/Websites</u>
Neighbors for Peace: <u>neighborsforpeace.net</u>.
Minnesota Neighbors for Peace: <u>mnneighborsforpeace.net</u>.
Fellowship for Intentional Community and communities bookstore: <u>ic.org</u>.
The National Co-op Directory: <u>nationalco-opdirectory.com</u>.
Organic Consumers: <u>organicconsumers.org</u>.
The Organic Valley Co-Op: <u>organicvalleycoop</u>.
Anathoth community farm: <u>anathothcommunityfarm.org</u>.
Wages Cooperative: <u>wagescooperative.org</u>.
Attraction Retreat: <u>attractionretreat.org/ECO/bell</u>.
(St. Paul) East Side Neighborhood Development Company, Inc.: <u>esndc.org</u>.
Latino Economic Development Center: <u>ledc-mn.org</u>.
Resource Center of the Americas: <u>americas.org</u>.
This is My Home: A Minnesota Human Rights Education Experience: <u>thisismyhome.org</u>.

<u>Books</u>
For lists of publications on building community and intentional communities, see the Fellowship for Intentional Community bookstore listed above and the previously mentioned <u>humanrightsandpeacestore.org</u>.

Chapter Six: Care Givers

<u>Organizations/Web Sites</u>
Mission from Minnesota: <u>missionfromminnesota.org</u>.
Give us Wings: <u>giveuwings.org</u>.
Humanitarian Services for the Children of Vietnam: <u>hscv.org</u>.
Network of Spiritual Progressives: <u>spiritualprogressives.org</u>.

<u>Books</u>
The Left Hand of God: Taking Back Our Country From The Religious Right. Rabbi Michael Lerner, Harper and Row, San Francisco, 2006.
For the Love of Children: Daily Affirmations. Jean and Mary Steiner Whalen, Redleaf Press, 1995.
Spiritual Politics: Changing The World From The Inside Out. Corrine McLaughlin and Gordon Davidson, Random House, 1994.

Lifting the Spirit: Human Rights and the Freedom of Religion or Beliefs. umn.edu/
humanrgs/edumat/hreduseries/TBS/lifting.html.

Chapter Seven: Speak Out Sisters
Organizations/Websites
Windustry: windustry.org./samantha-smart.
Code Pink: codepink4peace.org.
The Million Moms March: millionmommarch.org.
Ironknot Ranch: ironknot.org.
Jane Evershed: evershed.com.
Sisterhood Is Global Institute. sigi.org.
The Feminist Majority Foundation: feminist.org.
The National Organization of Women: now.org.

Books
Local Action, Global Change. Julie A. Mertus, 2008, Paradigm Publishers.
Stop The Next War Now: Effective Responses to Violence and Terrorism. Media
Benjamin and Jodie Evans, Inner-Ocean Publishing, 2005.
Change of Heart: The Bodhisattva Peace Training of Chagdud Tulku. Lama Shenpen
Drolma, Padma Publishing, 2003.
Becoming Human: The Origins and Development of Women's Human Rights. q.umn.
edu/humanrts/edumat/becominghuman/indes.html.
In Our Own Words: A Guide for Human Rights Education Facilitators. Nancy
Lowers, Sisterhood is Global Institute, 1999.
Women Activists: Challenging the Abuse of Power. Anne Witte Garland, The
Feminist Press, 1988.

Chapter Eight: Generation Next: The Future Makers
Organizations/Websites
National Organic Farming Association: nofa.org.
Bill of Rights Defense Committee: bordc.org.
Students Against War: geocities.com.
National Youth and Student Peace Coalition: nyspc.org.
Campus Antiwar Network: campusantiwar.net.
Youth Against War and Racism: yawr.org.
Step It Up: stepitup2007.org.
The Hip Hop Caucus: hiphopcaucus.org.
Yo The Movement: yothemovementblogspot.com.
Subzerocollective: decidio.com.

<u>Books</u>

Fight Global Warming Now: The Handbook for Taking Action in Your Community. Bill McKibben, Step It Up, 2008.

Beyond Heroes and Holidays: A Practical Guide to k-12 Anti-Racist Multicultural Education and Staff Development. Enid Lee, Teaching for Change, 2006.

Never Again a World Without Us: Voices of Mayan Women in Chiapas. Teresa Ortiz, Epica Task Force, *2001.*

Global Uprising: Confronting the Tyrannies of the 21st Century: Stories from a New Generation of Activists. Neva Welton and Linda Wolf, New Society Publishers, 2001.

Sustainable Economics Curriculum for High School Economics Courses. 1.umn.edu/humanrts/edumat/sustecon/toc.html.

Chapter Nine: The Reformers
Election Reform
<u>Organizations/Web Sites</u>
Liberty Tree Foundation: libertytreefdr.org.
Citizens for Election Integrity Minnesota: ceimn.org.
America Votes: americavotes.org.
Fair Vote: fairvote.org.
Immigrant Voting: immigrantvoting.org.
Rock The Vote: rockthevote.org.
Verified Voting: verifiedvoting.org.
Common Cause: commoncause.org.
National Popular Vote: nationalpopularvote.com.

<u>Books</u>

What Went Wrong In Ohio: The Conyers Report on the 2004 Presidential Election. Rep. John Conyers, Academy Chicago Publishers, 2005.

Witness To A Crime: A Citizens' Audit of an American Election. Richard Hayes Phillips, Canterbury Press, 2008.

Fooled Again: How the Right Stole the 2004 Election and Why They'll Steal The Next One Too (Unless We Stop Them). Mark Crispin Miller, Basic Books, 2005.

<u>Videos</u>

Invisible Ballots: A Temptation For Electronic Vote Fraud, New America Media, 2004. www.invisible ballots.com.

Uncounted: The New Math of Federal Elections, a film by David Earnhardt. uncountedthemovie.com.

Stealing America: Vote by Vote, stealingamerica.org.

Media Reform
<u>Organizations/Web Sites</u>
Free Press: freepress.net.
Independent Media Center: indymedia.org.

<u>Books</u>
Be the Media: How to Create and Accelerate Your Message Your Way. David Mathison, natural E creative group, LLC, 2009.
The Communication Revolution. Robert McChesney. The New Press, 2007.
The Exception to the Rulers: Exposing Politicians, War Profiteers and the Media That Love Them. Amy Goodman, Hyperion Books, 2004.
Embedded: Weapons of Mass Deception: How the Media Failed To Cover The War In Iraq. Danny Schechter, Prometheus Books, 2003.
Our Media, Not Theirs: The Democratic Struggle Against The Corporate Media. Robert McChesney and Josh Silver, Seven Stories Press, 2002.
The More You Watch, The Less You Know. Danny Schechter, Seven Stories Press, 1997.

Corporate Reform
<u>Organizations/Web Sites</u>
Citizens For Corporate Redesign: C4CR.org.
Citizen Works: citizenworks.org.
The Center for Corporate Policy: corporatepolicy.org.
Council For Corporate Responsibility: uscorporaterespnsbility.org.
The Ecumenical Council For Corporate Responsibility: eccr.org.
Responsible Minnesota Business. aboutrnb.org.

<u>Books</u>
The Best Democracy Money Can Buy. Greg Palast, Penguin Books, 2003.
Pigs at the Trough: How Corporate Greed and Political Corruption are Undermining America. Arianna Huffington, Three Rivers Press, 2003.
Unequal Protection: The .Rise Of Corporate Dominance And The Theft Of Human Rights. Thom Hartmann, Rodale Press, 2002.
Compassionate Capitalism: People Helping People Help Themselves. Rich DeVos, Penguin Books, 1993.

CPSIA information can be obtained at www.ICGtesting.com
Printed in the USA
BVOW071249011012

301739BV00005B/2/P